# The
# BEGGAR
## and the
# PROFESSOR

# The BEGGAR and the PROFESSOR

## A Sixteenth-Century Family Saga

EMMANUEL LE ROY LADURIE

TRANSLATED BY
Arthur Goldhammer

THE

UNIVERSITY

OF CHICAGO PRESS

·

CHICAGO & LONDON

EMMANUEL LE ROY LADURIE is professor at the College de France and a member of the Academie des Sciences Morales et Politiques. He is author of *Montaillou: The Promised Land of Error, Times of Feast, Times of Famine: A History of Climate since the Year 1000, The Territory of the Historian,* and *The Mind and Method of the Historian.*

The University of Chicago Press, Chicago 60637
The University of Chicago Press, Ltd., London
© 1997 by The University of Chicago
All rights reserved. Published 1997
Printed in the United States of America
06  05  04  03  02  01  00  99  98  97    5  4  3  2  1
ISBN (cloth): 0-226-47323-6

Originally published as *Le siècle des Platter, 1499–1628. Tome premier: Le mendiant et le professeur,* © Librairie Arthème Fayard, 1995.

Library of Congress Cataloging-in-Publication Data

Le Roy Ladurie, Emmanuel.
    [Mendiant et le professeur. English]
    The beggar and the professor : a sixteenth-century family saga /
Emmanuel Le Roy Ladurie ; translated by Arthur Goldhammer.
        p.    cm.
    Includes bibliographical references and index.
    ISBN 0-226-47323-6 (alk. paper)
    1. Platter family.   2. Platter, Thomas, 1499–1582.   3. Platter,
Felix, 1536–1614.   4. Platter, Thomas, 1574–1628.   5. Protestants—
Switzerland—Basel-Stadt—Biography.   6. Physicians—Switzerland—
Basel-Stadt—Biography.   7. Authors, Swiss—16th century—
Biography.   8. Basel-Stadt (Switzerland)—Genealogy.
I. Goldhammer, Arthur.   II. Title.
DQ398.54.P53L413   1997
949.4'3203'0922—dc20
[B]                                                          96-23340

♾ The paper used in this publication meets the minimum requirements of the American National Standard for Information Sciences—Permanence of Paper for Printed Library Materials, ANSI Z39.48-1984.

# CONTENTS

# AUTHOR'S NOTE

Many of the notes, including both endnotes and (in the majority of cases) notes incorporated into the body of the text, use references of the following type: (T 54) or (F 21) or (T2 383). These refer, respectively, to pages 54, 121, and 383 of the 1944 German-Swiss edition of the *Lebenbeschreibung* by Thomas Platter Sr. (T); the 1976 edition of the *Tagebuch* by Felix Platter (F), edited by Valentin Lötscher; and the 1968 edition of the *Beschreibung der Reisen* by Thomas Platter Jr. (T2), edited by Rut Reiser. (Full references to these works can be found in the bibliography.)

In quotations from the works of the Platters, which were written in a "Basel dialect" of German, I have followed the authors' practice of not capitalizing nouns (in contrast to contemporary High German usage).

In the text, moreover, the reader will find a few rare quotations of actual dialogue among the personages. Although invented dialogue is an accepted practice in certain literary histories that aim to achieve verisimilitude, as well as in historical fiction, this book, as a purely historical work, belongs to a very different genre, and I have refrained from inventing any dialogue here. Dialogue fragments were included verbatim in the texts of the Platters themselves, particularly those of Thomas Sr. and Felix, and I have simply quoted them as I found them.

Finally, all dates prior to 1582 are cited according to the "old style" of the Julian Calendar. In that year the Gregorian Calendar was instituted, and subsequent dates refer to it.

# Platter Family Tree

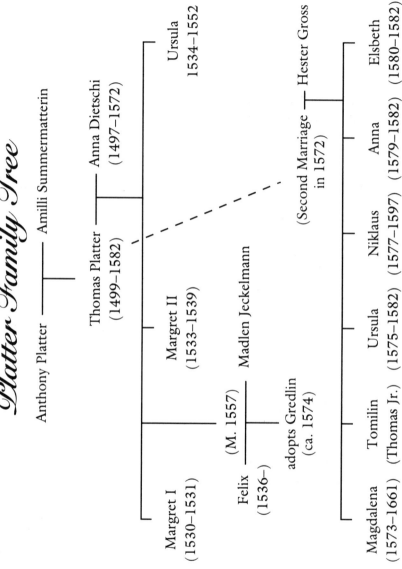

Anthony Platter —— Amilli Summermatterin

Thomas Platter —— Anna Dietschi
(1499–1582)        (1497–1572)

Margret I
(1530–1531)

Felix
(1536–)
(M. 1557) Madlen Jeckelmann
adopts Gredlin
(ca. 1574)

Margret II
(1533–1539)

Ursula
1534–1552

(Second Marriage —— Hester Gross
in 1572)

Magdalena    Tomilin       Ursula        Niklaus       Anna          Elsbeth
(1573–1661)  (Thomas Jr.)  (1575–1582)   (1577–1597)   (1579–1582)   (1580–1582)
             (1574–)

PART ONE

# Father and Son: Thomas and Felix Platter

## CHAPTER ONE

# Pilgrimage to the Valais

In 1563, in the final weeks of spring (F 401), Thomas Platter, an erstwhile highland shepherd and vagabond who had gone on to become first a printer and later a boarding-school teacher and headmaster in Basel, decided, at the age of sixty-four, to leave Basel on a pilgrimage of reminiscence to the land of his birth: the German-speaking Upper Valais, situated downstream from the Rhone glacier and upstream from Lausanne and Geneva, the heartland of francophone Switzerland. Linked to the Helvetic Confederation since the fifteenth century, the Valais region had long been divided between the Francophile party of Georg Supersaxo and the "minions" of the Milanese state, to which a powerful personage, Cardinal Matthaeus Schiner (1465–1522) had thrown his support, only to end up as one of the biggest losers at Marignano in 1515.* Since the 1550s, the Valais, whose bishopric and central town had long been Sion (or Sitten), had been (relatively) hospitable to "heresy." The silent majority remained Catholic, but the nobles, including several of Thomas Platter's former boarders, inclined toward Protestantism. The area remained basically rural and pastoral, if only because of its mountainous terrain.

On June 1, 1563, in Basel, Thomas sat down to a meal, probably the evening repast. To this feast he had issued a neighborly invitation to his son Felix Platter, a fashionable young doctor and graduate of the University of Montpellier, who had already begun to attract a considerable clientele among the aristocracy or at the very least the bourgeoisie of Basel and its environs, drawing patients from even as far away as southern Alsace, Wurtemberg, and the Black Forest. Felix lived a short distance from Thomas in a house on Freie Strasse, or "free street," near the city walls and the so-called Gate of Ashes (Innere Aeschentor). He came to dinner with his shy, pretty young wife, Madlen. Although married for more than five years, the couple still had no children. They were joined by Madlen's father, Franz Jeckelmann, a surgeon. Anna Dietschi, the elder Platter's

---

*The battle in which King Francis I of France defeated the Swiss allied with the Duke of Milan.—TRANS.

wife, probably served the diners, but her presence (on this occasion at least) is not mentioned in our sources. No surprise about that.

During dinner Thomas brought up an idea he had been mulling over for some time: "Madlen," he told his daughter-in-law, "you should make the journey with me and take the baths in the Valais. You have no child, and as you know, the Valaisian waters are effective against sterility."[1] Madlen had only to nod her assent. In this house the old man's words were generally taken as orders, and in any case the young woman was not averse to the journey he proposed. Surgeon Jeckelmann, who on this occasion was in uncharacteristically good spirits (*lustig*), immediately chimed in: "I'm coming too." He owned his own horse, which solved one transportation problem. Felix, who also owned a horse, quickly made up his mind to join the group as well. Thomas, who was fond of asinine creatures, had brought back a mule from a previous trip to the Valais: just the animal for Madlen to ride. The headmaster himself was an indefatigable walker: he had not forgotten his youth as a mountain climber and hiker. Hence he would travel on foot. Anna, his wife, would stay home and keep an eye on the house on Freie Strasse. Preparations for the trip were quickly completed.

In fact, the group set out the very next day, on the afternoon of Wednesday, June 2, 1563. The four travelers were joined by Pierre Bonet of Porrentruy, Felix's French-speaking servant. From his long sojourns among the "Welches,"[2] the young doctor had retained a fondness for the French language, even if he used it only in conversation with his servants. A pharmacist from Sion, the principal town of the Valais, accompanied the spa-bound tourists; his first name was Hans (we cannot be sure of his last name). Hans and Thomas, the two Valaisians, both traveled on foot yet always reached the inn ahead of their companions on horseback. Because Madlen was a delicate, nervous city girl, whenever the group came to a difficult ford, one of the men took hold of her mule's bridle to make sure that nothing would go awry.

On June 3, in an arduous stretch of the Jura not far from the craggy rim of the "Wasserfall," Pierre Bonet stepped on a nail. His foot became so infected that he could not go on. Felix, a surgeon as well as a physician, took charge of the case. Knife in hand, he dug out the wound and cleaned away the mud and pus. In pain and frightened, the injured man fainted and then, overwhelmed by his ordeal, defecated on Madlen's apron as she tried to nurse him. By the time the others had finished their picnic dinner, however, Pierre had regained consciousness and seemed to have recovered his strength. The caravan was able to proceed.

From June 4 to June 6, the travelers worked their way southward, staying with friends or friends of friends from Basel, people with connections to various city officials and Protestant clergymen. In Erlenbach (F 404), they ate for the first time a sort of cracker made from dried bread and stacked up by the dozen on long needles.

On June 8, near Saanen, Jeckelmann, accompanied by a pastor who was the son of a monk, drank his first Valais wine and gave signs of being quite pleased with it, indeed slightly inebriated. His joy was not to last: after losing one of his gloves, he vented his wrath on the rocky trail and declared the Valais a place fit for devils. This was the first of what would prove to be a series of angry outbursts. The day's journey ended in Gsteig (altitude 1,200 meters), at an inn where there was no one to greet the travelers but the wife of the innkeeper, who was away. The woman had just given birth. She had, she said, neither money nor food. Madlen was obliged to improvise a meal from eggs and milk. Apparently there was no shortage of protein.

On June 9, Thomas and his family (F 404) climbed to the peak of Sanetsch (2,243 meters). The peasants were cutting hay. It was hot and dry. Pink willow-herb flowered amid the grass and boulders. The horses stumbled. The travelers passed wine merchants headed north, their pack-horses laden with tall kegs of wine for the people of the highlands. Jeckelmann shamelessly quaffed several glassfuls straight from the keg and ate cheese provided by Hans, the apothecary. As if by miracle, the surgeon's foul mood vanished: he even forgot about the glove he had lost. Meanwhile, the travelers admired an astonishing irrigation system built by the local peasants, not unlike the irrigation systems that exist today on the lower slopes of the Himalayas. The water came from a glacier and flowed directly by gravity into a series of larchwood conduits, which directed the irrigating flow into gardens and pastures. As they drew near a bridge, Felix was astonished to see a woman astride a packhorse. She carried a keg of wine on her back while spinning yarn with a distaff under her arm as easily as another woman might knit. Meanwhile, the horse, with scarcely any prodding from its rider, fearlessly crossed a bridge so narrow and dangerous that Felix himself scarcely dared set foot on it. The plainsman was terrified to go where the mountain woman moved easily. (This equestrian spinner calls to mind the Giantesses of Provence, mythical creatures about whom Thomas Platter Jr. would learn, much later, while traveling in the south of France. These Giantesses could supposedly spin or weave while at the same time carrying heavy stones on their heads—stones to be used for the construction of a great Roman monument.)

Felix tossed a stone over the side of the bridge, counting to eighteen before observing its splash in the rapids below. Characters in Shakespeare's *Hamlet* also counted to measure time; in Catholic countries, people used to use the time it took to say an *Ave Maria* or a *Pater Noster* for the same purpose. Given the height of the bridge that we can deduce from this scientific observation, it is easy to understand why the young doctor from Basel was so impressed by the courage of the woman on the horse.

A short while later, Felix, overcome by dizziness and heat, fainted. His wife thought he was dead. She shouted at her father and father-in-law to turn back. But the young doctor came to and—always the professional—asked for a blanket or cloak. This was to make him sweat, which would then lower his body temperature. He was soon back on his feet. At four in the afternoon, the group reached Savièse (F 405), in a region of irrigated fields and isolated farms with fine views of the Alps. The recovered patient drank a healthy draft, a *trunck,* which fully restored his strength. After climbing a steep, arduous path strewn with loose pebbles, the three urban riders (Felix, Jeckelmann, and Madlen) and the two highland hikers (Thomas and Hans) at last arrived at Sitten, alias Sion, toward the end of the afternoon.

Sion was different. Relaxed men in shirtsleeves strode about with bare swords at their sides; scabbards were not used. Such liberties were permissible in the highlands. Captain Marc Wolff, formerly one of Thomas's boarders and a local "castellan,"[3] was the secret (?) lover of the wife of a local scholar, a pharmacist by trade. He proposed to put the travelers up. Thomas, always somewhat puritanical, refused. The group stayed instead at the inn of Franz Gröli, another graduate of the Platter boarding school. Thomas had former students everywhere. Gröli was the castellan's son and married to a noblewoman; he was the father of a medical student soon to become a doctor. In other words, this was the high society of Sion. On their very first night in town, the visitors from Basel drank canteens of wine by the dozen. They were in high spirits. Felix and his wife slept on the first floor, near the "noble room," which could be heated in winter. The stove, unlike stoves in Basel, was covered with stone rather than ceramic tile. The two fathers, Jeckelmann and Thomas, shared a room on the second floor.

The whole week was amusing and pleasant. The saffron and pomegranate were in bloom in the countryside. The four visitors from Basel received countless invitations, especially from Captain Wolff, who harbored no ill will toward Thomas for his haughty attitude. Always the lady's man, the captain offered Madlen some lovely items of clothing as a gift. Captain Heinrich in Albon, who belonged to a family, soon to become Protestant, that had distinguished itself in war, notarial practice, and humanism, also spared no effort. His wife, a woman with a yen for wine and men, did everything she could to get Felix into bed, but the great physician politely declined (she would repeat the offense a few weeks later at the baths in Leuk, where the promiscuity of bathing gave her new opportunities but with no greater success than before). All this reveling was highly ecumenical: religious differences were forgotten around the massive silver mugs made by the great silversmith Exuperantius. The Catholic bishop invited the visitors to dine with him and offered to stable their horses. What sweet revenge for Thomas, the former shepherd of the Valais, who had been so poor in his childhood! The canons invited the surgeon Jeckelmann to dinner. Of course one of them, a future bishop, had also been a boarder at Thomas's school. An easygoing Catholicism, a papistry of good cheer, reigned in this small highland town, which in this respect differed from the surrounding flatland, from the rather stiff climate of Basel and Zurich.

Eventually, however, the visitors had to move on. From Sion they headed northeast along the Rhone. An escort accompanied them, as was customary for travelers of some importance. They stopped in Saint-Leonhard at the home of Alexander Jossen, an episcopal treasurer and an old friend of the Platters, as well as the bishop's grandson by the left hand: they were delighted by the gorgeous woodwork in his home, paid for perhaps by the money of the faithful. Across slopes and vineyards they made their way toward the baths at Leuk. They stopped at the home of a veteran of the battle of Marignano, a man wounded in the thigh in 1515 and still paralyzed. This gentleman, Petermann Hengart of Platea (F 410), had accumulated any number of blessings, civil as well as military. He was both sheriff and ensign as well as the bishop's nephew and the son-in-law of the great Supersaxo. The visitors were received sumptuously. After another, similar stop at the home of yet another gentleman, Peter Allet, the Platter-Jeckelmann quartet, father, son, daughter-in-law, and father-in-law, finally reached Leuk (known as Loèche in Romansch). At the inn the four travelers shared a room with three beds. It would be pretentious to call Leuk a "spa," but there were numerous hotels in the town. The baths at Leuk had regained some of their importance as a tourist spot and a locale for real-estate investment as the Renaissance economy flourished in the second half of the fifteenth century. Said to be good for gout and skin diseases, Leuk's waters also attracted infertile women, as was mentioned earlier. An unpleasant joke had it that the promiscuity of the bathers at Leuk had something to do with the observed increase in *post festum* natality. In any case, Jeckelmann and his daughter arranged to stay at the Hotel Ours for three crowns each for four weeks, including room and baths. Felix and Thomas continued on to the highlands of Upper Valais. Old Thomas planned to visit the house in which he had been born, or at any rate the old family homestead. The two men proceeded on foot; Pierre Bonet, Felix's servant, having recovered from his foot infection, took his master's horse from Leuk back to Sion, to the providential stables of the bishop, where the animal would be kept until its owner returned. For this pilgrimage to his mountain roots, Felix had literally disguised himself: he wore a red silk doublet, red pantaloons, and a fuzzy velvet hat. One can only assume that he wished to dazzle his highland kinsmen with the sumptuousness of his attire (this was not the most attractive side of his personality). Thomas, who knew and liked the highland natives from childhood and experience, dressed more soberly.

On the first stretch of this final stage of their journey, Felix and Thomas planned to stop at Visp (also known as Viège), on a tributary south of the upper Rhone. Felix wrote that Viège was "a pretty place," but in saying this his intention was primarily to disparage what came afterward. A first delegation of the Platter family, or that portion of the family that had not emigrated from its native region, came to greet the two visitors at the inn. One imagines the country folk doffing their hats before these "successful" cousins from another world. Early in the morning of June 19, the two visitors proceeded upstream along the Visp river valley. They crossed bridges of wood and stone, some of them quite recent and high enough so that Felix had to count to sixty before the stone splashed in the water below. The most noteworthy of these was the stone bridge of the Matter Visp, built in 1544 by the architect Ulrich Ruffiner, whose upper arch stood 65 meters above the rapids (F 416). Here is evidence of the architectural vitality of the sixteenth century, a time when even the remotest of valleys showed signs of the increased pace of commerce and trade. Although the trail narrowed as it climbed, it was still wide enough for caravans of pack animals to pass. To Felix, who lacked experience, it seemed at times little more than a footpath cut into the rock. His right hand hugged the cliff, his left hand hovered over the abyss. At times his courage amazed him. Meanwhile, riding a horse down this same narrow path, a cousin came down from Grächen to meet the two visitors. His name was Hans in der Bünde, and he belonged to one of the better-off peasant families of Grächen, the birthplace of the original Platters.[4] To be sure, at this altitude (Grächen stood at 1,610 meters), the wealthier families were hardly any better off than other people. Cousin Hans was dressed in the old style. He wore trousers and a jacket and seemed disconcerted by Felix's provocative scarlet outfit. He greeted the elder Platter (F 411), whom he knew by hearsay, with a question: "Welcome by God, Cousin Thomas. Is that your son?"

Hans used the familiar form of the second-person pronoun as a matter of course. He then jumped off his horse, which he rode practically bareback and guided with just a plain rope, eschewing bit and reins. Always helpful, the skilled horseman offered to ride double with Felix, who strenuously declined for fear that he might fall off and plummet to his death. The two Platters proceeded on foot to Grächen, accompanied by Hans, who continued to ride. Along the way, Thomas showed Felix the spot where his grandfather Summermatter, also named Hans (and, if we are to believe him, 126 years old at the time), had answered little Thomas's question in 1504 or 1505: "Grandfather, do you want to die?" "Yes, little one, if only I knew what kind of food they would cook for me up there" (F 412).

As they drew near their destination, the route, wending its way among the larches, grew arduous. Felix had to agree to mount his cousin's horse. To have maintained his refusal would have seemed impolite. Once the doctor was in place, Hans jumped on behind him, holding him by the waist while Felix, frozen with terror, shut his eyes. His cousin, riding behind, guided the horse with his strange rig. The travelers next crossed a relatively flat field and a dark pine forest that served as a lair for the bears still numerous in the region. Snowy peaks loomed in the distance. And then came the first human contact with Grächen: a blind centenarian (?) and his grown, white-haired children, all living in the same house as an extended family, watched as the three men passed. The elderly man served up the old story of the Platters' ancestor, Thomas's grandfather, more than a hundred years old, who was supposed to have lived this way in Grächen with ten other old men in 1505. Thomas had known this story by heart since childhood and even believed it. Then a female cousin of the Platters, a "Platterin," wearing a gray skirt and with her hair down, served a milk soup in a house occupied by very elderly peasants, a hut with larch beams. Milk and cheese dishes were the staple of the highlands. Tired, Felix collapsed in this old-folks' hut and briefly lay down on a straw mattress. Hans in der Bünde's house was located a short distance away from the home of the woman in the gray skirt. He invited his cousins over for another meal. Thomas Platter asked after a beautiful girl who had tended geese and with whom he had spent part of his childhood, and someone showed him the way to her house. Now very ugly, she was busy smashing pine cones. The reunion, after more than fifty years of separation, came as something of a disappointment. Nevertheless, the former goose-tender was a good-hearted woman: she clasped Felix to her bosom and called him "dear cousin" (*laube vetter* rather than *liebe vetter*). This dialectal dissonance caused the not very charitable physician to burst out laughing. After this sentimental interlude, Thomas and Felix returned to the home of Hans in der Bünde, the fearless horseman. Was Hans's wife perhaps put out that Felix had fallen asleep in the midst of the earlier family reunion? In any case she was unfriendly to the two men from the city and even to her own husband: "You've brought me guests, eh? Well, then, you take care of them, in the devil's name!"

Once again she served them milk, but this time generously sprinkled with pepper. Felix's throat burned. He cooled it down with excellent Val d'Aosta wines, which Hans had in his cellar. So the village was not as autarchic as it might have seemed, nor was Hans's house as wretched as it appeared. Pepper and wine were semiluxury or luxury items imported from Liguria and the Piedmont, carried up from Aosta and Genoa on the backs of pack animals in direct or indirect exchange for local products such as wood, livestock, and cheese. The bedding was rustic, however. After the evening meal, straw was spread on the floor close to the fire (nights were cool at this altitude), and the guests were invited to lie down.

Although old Thomas's highland simplicity had survived four decades of urban life, he could not stop himself from discreetly letting his son know how disappointed he felt at this treatment: "As you see, Felix, they make quite a fuss over me."

A further surprise awaited Felix the following morning. A crowd of little girls from the various hamlets of Grächen milled about the house where the two men from Basel had spent the night. Each of the girls was carrying a chamber pot full of urine. They wanted the great doctor from Basel to inspect the liquid—in other words, to provide them with a free consultation. Felix, who ordinarily preferred to treat nobles or wealthy clients, obligingly complied. More moving was the visit to the home of the brother of the late Simon Steiner, an old friend and probably a cousin of Thomas's. When Felix looked back on the occasion in his memoirs, however, he mainly recalled the wretchedness of the surroundings: the tourist clad in red silk liked to see himself as a civilized emissary among the barbarians of the forests and mountains. With antiquarian pedantry he referred, for instance, to Simon Steiner as Lithonius.[5] Steiner had been born in Grächen into a poor peasant family. Like Thomas, he had scored a "success" in town: in Strasbourg he had been the *famulus* (assistant) of the great local reformer Martin Bucer and later a teacher in Johannes Sturm's Latin school. To honor his memory, Thomas and Felix called on his brother, who had remained in the country on a plot of land that belonged to the family. Unlike Simon, the brother had never known success in the city. Thomas offered him his affection. Felix offered him alms of ten shillings.

The high point of this "homecoming" was the pilgrimage to the Platter family home, which Thomas had left in the first decade of the sixteenth century. Like many other dwellings in the area, it was a stout, simple cabin of larch logs, comfortable enough in its distinctive style. Wood was plentiful in these high Alpine valleys. The construction was old, probably dating back to the thirteenth century. The cabin stood close to a high crag or plateau (*platte*), a circumstance that may have been the origin of the name Platter: in these parts, the family was named after the house rather than the house after the family (F 415). In his memoirs Felix described this august dwelling as the birthplace of his father Thomas—but he was mistaken: Antony Platter, Thomas's father, mired in debt, was forced to flee his creditors shortly before 1499. He moved into a house some distance away but still within the limits of Grächen, a witch's house known as *Auf den Graben* (By the Grave). It was there that Thomas Platter was born. But Thomas and Felix ignored this episode, important as it was, and focused their attention exclusively on the fifteenth-century family homestead at the place known as *An der Platte*. The visit took place on the beautiful day of June 18, 1563. Taking advantage of the sun, the two men, accompanied by acquintances and kin from the village, cousin Hans among them, took the noon meal at the house and washed down their food with a good deal of drink. Then they moved on from the cabin to the nearby *Platte,* whose dominating view made Felix dizzy. There they drank some more: afternoon and evening flagons, *trunck* and *abendtrunck*. Felix dug into his purse for another crown, this one for a local artisan whose name was not recorded, to carve his (newly acquired) coat of arms into the rock. Felix's blazon consisted of a white rock in relief with a white dove taking off from the rock against a background of blue sky. Rock on rock: of course there was no thought of coloring the bas-relief carved on stone in the open air. But the symbols spoke for themselves: the flat rock was Thomas, faithful to his roots; the dove was Felix, who, being fond of doves anyway, used one to symbolize how high he had already climbed in the world and how much higher he still dreamed of going. The physician never knew for sure whether the work of art he had commissioned was completed. To tell the truth, the ground he walked on scorched his feet. He was eager to leave this mountain eyrie, to which he never returned. Once the last goblet of wine was downed, the young doctor hastened that very evening down the mountain to Saint-Niclaus below. From there he returned as quickly as possible to the company of his wife, who was waiting at Leuk with her father. Thomas, who accompanied his son on this return journey, was preoccupied with very different thoughts. This brief excursion home had given him a new lease on life; it was his last contact, for he was now an old man, with a childhood for which he remained nostalgic despite its frequent misery, a childhood that had begun some sixty years before in this remote, not to say God-forsaken, parish of Grächen, where "little Thomas" had indeed been born into extreme poverty in 1499.

# PART TWO

# Childhoods and Undertakings
## (1499–1551)

## CHAPTER TWO

# The Platter Childhoods: Thomas

Tomilin (little Thomas) was born in the ninety-ninth year of the fifteenth century. The boy's father, Antony Platter, still lived in his native Grächen. His mother, Amilli Summermatterin, was the daughter of Hans Summermatter, an elderly man said to have celebrated his one hundred and twenty-sixth birthday in the year of Thomas's birth. At one hundred he had married a woman of thirty, who had borne him a son, or so the story went. That is more or less all Thomas has to say about his maternal grandfather.

Amilli could not breast-feed her child. Did Thomas truly survive the first years of his life on nothing but cow's milk sucked from a pierced horn?[1] The boy must have had an iron constitution not to have succumbed, in the absence of breast milk from his mother or a wet nurse, to the raging infant mortality of the time. Death was commonplace: Antony, Thomas's father, died of plague in Thun, near Bern, where he had gone, as the men of the Valais customarily did, to obtain wool for his wife to spin and weave. After Antony's death, Amilli Summermatterin remarried and had several more children. Two of Thomas's elder sisters also died, one of them of the plague. Amilli personally buried two other children cut down by the same disease. And two brothers died in battle, as Swiss mercenaries. "From pestilence, war, and famine, preserve us, O Lord!" Hunger was never very far from the Platter household, which was on occasion victimized by usurers. Yet the extreme mortality in the Platter family was not a consequence of poverty alone: even after Thomas became a well-to-do burgher, he lost nearly all his children to the pestilential conditions common at the time in the cities of Germanic Switzerland.

Not knowing what to do with the surviving children of at least two marriages, Amilli sent little Thomas to board with his father's two sisters. Essentially his mother abandoned him (abandonment being fairly common at the time). While living with his aunts, Thomas had a frightening experience. One night, after the grownups had gone out for an evening with neighbors, the boy, who had been left sleeping on a tabletop bed of straw, ventured out alone. He lost his way in the snow, and for a time no one could find hide nor hair of him. When they did find him, it took some doing to warm his nearly frozen body. (Other rural memoir-writers looking back on their earliest memories mention similar experiences.)

Shortly after his third birthday, Thomas was presented to Bishop (soon to be Cardinal) Schiner, himself the son of a goatherd and a man of some considerable importance in the politics of the Valais.[2] An inveterate enemy of the French, Schiner was a prelate who wore the boots and helmet of a soldier, a bishop who rode into battle as readily as other bishops bestowed benedictions. (Schiner, by the way, was of great help to the future "heretic" Ulrich Zwingli in the early stages of Zwingli's brilliant career. But let us not get ahead of ourselves.) Did the bishop, seated on an armchair in the parish church of Grächen in 1502, really predict that Thomas had a future as a priest? The belief that such a prediction had been made was one reason why people in the village encouraged the boy to consider acquiring an ecclesiastical education, this being a traditional (though by no means easy) avenue of advancement for peasant lads who showed precocious intellectual ability. Thomas's family, though impoverished, had a number of prominent kin in the region, and his relatives were pious. Hence the boy's ecclesiastical vocation was encouraged if not foreordained: if joining the clergy (or becoming a printer, teacher, or doctor) was what it took to climb back up the social ladder, then so be it.

At age seven or eight, Thomas tended goats for one of his aunts. Like many a malnourished country boy, he was a small child, and his goats, no more than a few dozen in number, could easily knock him down when they came bounding out of his aunt's barn before dawn. One time he lost his shoes in the muddy snow. Often he went barefoot. In embarking on the hard life of the goatherd or shepherd, which in those days was the common fate of the pauper's child, he came to know older shepherds, some of whom treated him kindly. Once, when some of his companions mistakenly surmised that he had fallen from a mountain trail and vanished, their tender concern for his safety touched him. Between playing quoits on the slopes and enjoying snacks of rye bread and cheese, Thomas discovered the perversity of goats: they climbed so high up the steep terrain in their search for greenery that the goatherd could barely keep up. One day, Tomilin had a terrifying experience: after a fall, he found himself lying flat on a rock, clinging to a few tufts of grass as his feet flailed above a yawning abyss. Too young for pants, he wore only a short tunic, which he kept with him throughout his extensive later travels in Germany. He owed his life to an "older" friend, also named Thomas and already an experienced rock climber, who somehow managed to make his way down to the treacherous rock and grab the younger boy by the fingers. In later life the rescuer came to claim his reward, but Thomas, by then grown up, insisted that if he had survived, the Almighty deserved all the credit: it was sometimes easier to repay debts with prayers of thanksgiving than with cash. "God preserved me," Thomas wrote (other peasant scribblers used virtually the same words).[3] Divine protection was useful: vultures and crows scoured the slopes, to say nothing of bears, which were everywhere in Thomas's nightmares.

Tomilin at some point moved to the home of another peasant, a safe enough place as far as he could tell. There he played with the farmer's daughter, who was socially a cut above him because her father owned a herd of goats. The games they played were typical of rural children's games: they rode wooden horses and built mock irrigation systems like those found throughout Europe (and not just in the south). *Claudite jam ripas pueri, sat prata biberunt.* While working for his new master, Thomas again came to know the perils of the mountains, which were as deadly for the shepherds and goatherds of the past as they are for mountain climbers today.[4] Once, he spent a whole day searching for a lost herd of goats. Another time he spent an entire night clad only in a tunic, without hat or shoes, clinging to the roots of a larch tree: he had fallen again, and it was not until morning that he realized how deep was the chasm into which he had nearly plunged. While holding on for dear life, he had also had to fend off bears, real or imagined, and a goat antelope that he mistook for a stray buck. The life of the goatherd, he decided, was not for him. So he made another change: he found work tending cows, which was safer since these animals, unlike goats, preferred the lower, gentler slopes. Yet pleasant memories from his goat-tending years stayed with him: one day he lay on his back and dreamt of soaring above the mountain peaks until the sight of a huge hawk overhead brought him back to earth. He also hunted for "crystals," a sometimes lucrative pastime for young highlanders in the sixteenth century and later. And of course he participated in games: throwing stones, blowing shepherds' horns, and pole vaulting. Close calls were commonplace: falling rocks passed just inches above the climber's head. Thirst was harder to bear than hunger: shepherds were known to drink their own urine, and the baskets of food they carried on their backs were often almost empty. The straw pads they carried for sleeping (in wintertime) were infested with lice and bugs. One got used to these pests, but the louse, which carried typhus, had its role in history too.

Thomas's work tending cows on the lower slopes soon came to an end. The boy was not stupid, as his family was quick to realize. No one had forgotten Bishop Schiner's prediction. Aunt Fansy, the benefactress who had already employed the boy in several capacities, now took him to her elderly cousin Antony Platter, a priest who happened to have the same name as Thomas's late father. Thomas thus gave up tending cows after a brief stint, only to find himself treated like an animal: Antony, a pitiless teacher of the old school, boxed him on the ears and made him cry out, as Thomas described it, "like a stuck goat." Tomilin became even more depressed than he had been while risking his miserable neck on steep mountainsides. By now he was ten or eleven years old. In the home of this uncle, who may have run a small school, Thomas learned very little. All he could remember was learning to sing the *Salve Regina:*

Salve Regina, mater misericordiae,
Vita, dulcedo et spes nostra, salve.

(Hail, Queen [Mary], mother of mercy
Our life, sweetness, and hope, hail.)

Whatever schooling Tomilin may have received from his uncle, it did not last long. The elderly priest gave the boy a gold piece and sent him on his way, essentially casting him out into the world on his own. As we know from the work of distinguished scholars, West European attitudes toward childhood have changed considerably since the sixteenth century. In other parts of the world, such as Brazil (where more than six million children live on their own) and the Andes, things may not be so different today from what they were in Europe in the sixteenth century. In any event, Thomas set off to beg for his bread, but also to study. With his older cousin Paulus, also a grandson of the allegedly centenarian grandfather—the stalwart trunk of the Platter family tree (and still a source of strength, pride, and virility some fifty years later)—Thomas headed for Germany. His mother's brother, Simon zu den Summermatten, advised him that this was the best thing for him, even if it meant permanent exile.

The child therefore left his native Valais and discovered, on the other side of the Grimsel pass, still in mountainous country but at a lower altitude, civilization, or at any rate what passed for civilization in this part of Switzerland: tile roofs, ceramic stoves (which Montaigne, two generations later, so admired during his travels in this region), and geese, which the child had never encountered in the highlands. The little highlander, now on his way to Germany, at first found these geese almost as diabolical as a boy named Carl, who beat him cruelly after giving him a small coin, then demanding it back almost before Thomas had had time to put it in his pocket. After several days on the road, Thomas also discovered the rules of chess, a game he had never before seen played. In order to eat, Thomas had to beg: his Upper Valaisian dialect, extremely rare in these parts, made the boy popular with potential benefactors. Begging proved marginally profitable. Paulus, who was living off the fruits of his little cousin's labors and did not hesitate to beat him if he found the proceeds insufficient, was delighted.

But to get back to the geese: the journey from Grimsel (via Lucerne and Zurich) to Breslau survived in Thomas's (selective) memory as one long confrontation with these birds. Having left his "savage" fellow citizens of Upper Valais behind, the boy perceived the goose as the symbol of a culture, or, rather, of a sophisticated agriculture: a discovery. Soon, however, they became living targets, to be killed or stolen. This prey supplemented the meager rations of a group of young travelers led at times by a young, vigorous, and incontestable leader, Antony Schallbetter, a stout fellow capable of dissuading any would-be marauders that might turn up on German highways. Schallbetter somehow managed to obtain candles and a tinder-box. Did he steal them from a church? In any case, he was the only member of the group with the means to provide light at night. At his beck and call he had five or six older boys, close to twenty years old, known as "graduates," along with three younger lads, referred to as "schoolboys" (although they attended no school), who ranged in age from eleven to thirteen, Platter among them. Intermediate in age between the schoolboys and the scamps was Cousin Paulus: he disciplined the younger boys by pinching their calves and behinds and continued thrashing Thomas as before. The younger Platter, with his highlander's skill at tossing quoits and rings, specialized in chasing ducks and geese whenever the gang came upon a village. To believe Thomas, such bird-hunting was tolerated provided one took care not to get caught: that, at any rate, was the case in free Silesia, where age-old communal customs were still in force. Before reaching that province, however, the gang of boys first had to make their away across most of Germany. Along the way they feasted on geese, which they either stoned (a sport at which Thomas's son Felix would also excel) or liberated from the sheds in which farmers fattened the birds to serve as dowry for their daughters. No sooner was a goose pinched than it was plucked and made ready, its head, feet, and innards destined for the stew pot and the remainder for the spit, to be broiled along with turnips. The meal might be rounded out with fish snatched from the bottom of a freshly drained pond and boiled in beer obtained from an obliging farmer in exchange for a share of the looted fish. Thomas also hunted geese with a sort of boomerang and shared his take with his friends and with a "schoolmaster" who joined the group for a while and apparently had no scruples about partaking of filched fowl. Indeed, it was the *magister* himself who encouraged the boys to go after the indispensable birds, though he knew that what they were doing was illegal.

Generally speaking, the diet of our little wanderers seems to have been variable rather than uniformly miserable, though on many days it was deplorably unhealthy.[5] During certain stretches of the journey, between Dresden and Breslau, for example, Paulus and Thomas subsisted mainly on what they could gather: true, they ate onions, both raw and salted, but they also survived on grilled nuts, crab apples, and the like. At other times, within the walls of Breslau, for instance, they dined royally: it was probably a year of abundant harvest and low grain prices. In any case, Breslau (today Wroclaw in Poland) was well supplied because it was the center of a farming region, a market town for the lands bordering on the southern Baltic. Better yet, the ready availability of grain in the city meant that beer was plentiful, and the Polish peasants amused themselves by getting Tomilin and his companions drunk. In his memoirs, written much later, Thomas never alludes to the fact that Silesia was partially Polish except when he describes these drinking bouts: the German traveler, availing himself of a common expression, says that on feast days he got "drunk as a Pole." By the time Thomas wrote, of course, the Slavic nation had already come under military pressure from the Russians. Meanwhile, in Frauenburg (Frombork), Copernicus was beginning to work out his heliocentric cosmology. Modernity—the "Age of Copernicus"—was about to dawn.[6] But Platter had other things on his mind.

\*     \*     \*

Food and drink varied, but the vermin were ever-present. In Dresden, bedrooms were full of lice: one could hear swarms of them moving in the straw. In Breslau, the lice in the bedding were so thick that Tomilin preferred to sleep on the floor. Every now and then he deloused his cloak, washed his tunic in the Oder, and threw the crushed lice into a hole dug for the purpose. Whether out of piety or for a joke, he covered the insects with earth and planted a small cross on the mound. The slaughter of the bugs was Christianized: these lice died a sanctified death.

Crime was another scourge. Although Silesia was by no means a hotbed of vice, at this level of society and among this mobile population, criminality was commonplace. Thomas himself engaged in petty thievery in rural areas, where minor stealing was tolerated but thieves were punished if caught. Once he was spotted with the feet of a goose sticking out from underneath his tunic; a group of hatchet-wielding peasants bent on recovering their property chased him in vain. Itinerant children were vulnerable to all the perils of the road, which sometimes claimed the lives of travelers.

Thomas mentions two brushes with danger. One time, at an inn near Nuremberg, he and his friends crossed paths with a self-professed murderer. The other incident took place near Naumburg,[7] when the young itinerants ran into eight shady characters armed with crossbows (petty criminals like these could not afford firearms). In both instances the youngsters escaped with nothing more than a fright. There were other frightening moments as well: in the forests of Thuringia and Silesia, for example. Europe in the early sixteenth century was still thinly populated, although the population was rapidly returning to the level it had attained before the Black Plague; much of Germany still resembled a vast, often dangerous forest interspersed with ample clearings. In trading the mountains for the forest, Thomas did not always come out ahead. Between Nuremberg and Breslau, however, he no longer had to worry about his old mountain enemy, the bear: here, *batzen* (bear) was simply the name of a coin, equivalent to one-fifteenth of a florin, just about the price of a duck or goose.

At first Thomas's ideas about geography were vague and imprecise. As if in a dream, the boy traveled from Zurich to Nuremberg and from Nuremberg to Naumburg, Dresden, and Breslau, not without side trips that we have no way of tallying up. All this hiking may have taken several months or several seasons or several years—it is hard to know just how long he was on the road. In the course of his travels he visited, or at any rate passed through, eastern Switzerland, Bavaria, Franconia, Prussia, Saxony, Silesia, and perhaps Hungary: at the time he had other things on his mind than mastering geography. We cannot even be sure of the chronological order in which the narrator visited the "eastern" provinces. How different are the travelogues of Thomas's two sons, Felix and Thomas Jr., whose "higher" social and cultural status ensured that from early youth they would share the geographical concerns of other Renaissance humanists: their accounts detail their routes village by village. Of course they kept running logs of their journeys, which was not the case with Thomas Sr., who at this time was still almost illiterate. In any case he did not carry a notebook suitable for keeping records of his travels.

What about school in all these travels? In the case of our Valaisian vagabond, it was intermittent at best. In Naumburg, Thomas begged while his companions sang. The local schoolteacher, accompanied by a group of poor children, tried to force the young Helvetians to sign up for his courses (for which they would have had to pay). The young nomads proved recalcitrant: they ambushed the teacher and assailed him with stones. Then they beat a hasty retreat, but not before making off with some geese. In Halle (Saxony) another attempt was made to get the boys into school. But the older boys treated Thomas and his cousin Paulus miserably, and the two fled to another school in Dresden, which proved so lousy in both the literal and figurative senses that they ran off a second time, to Breslau, pursued by dogs and accompanied by hunger. In the capital of Silesia, where food was plentiful, the visitors from the west took courses at a school connected with St. Elizabeth's Church, where the Swiss influence was strong. Each of the city's seven parishes had its own school. The classroom was heated, and pupils sang and took dictation. The schoolmasters no more had printed books than the "primitive" bandits encountered on the road months earlier had had firearms. Only one of the dozen teachers in the school possessed a text of Terence, one of the classics of the day. The older boys had notebooks and could thus take better advantage of the teaching than younger children like the Platters. Did the ex-goatherd from Grächen have any means of taking notes? Apparently not. Did he know how to write? In any case, he seems to have spent much of his time in Breslau begging. He also met various distinguished individuals, including, if we believe his account, one of the Fuggers (the famous banking family). Thomas proved rather successful as a beggar, benefitting from the popularity of the unfortunate Swiss, thousands of whom had been massacred at Marignano by the troops of Francis I: Germans felt an instinctive sympathy for them. By the time of that crucial battle (1515), Thomas had lived a full fifteen years. He must have spent several years roaming Germany from west to east. Soon he would travel the same routes in the opposite direction. To be sure, sixteenth-century hikers were a hearty lot, and for them covering a vast territory was not an unthinkable feat.

The culmination of Thomas's fitful schooling came in Munich (somehow the boy had continued on, or returned, to Bavaria). To gain access to this heavily fortified and guarded city, one had to show proof (genuine or counterfeit) of having a relative, friend, or place to stay inside the walls. Thomas, who arrived from Dresden, became an assistant to a soapmaker, who was married to a pleasant enough woman and happened to be an anticlerical (which was a problem in this ultra-Catholic region). The young Helvetian helped his master boil the mixture from which soap was made. In the course of his work he purchased ashes in the countryside, which prevented him from completing elementary school, or so he claimed. School also served as a pretext: as a "student," Thomas was able to persuade the local authorities, who were strict in such matters, to grant him the right to sing in the streets, which helped in his begging (the boy's voice had already changed, and he made progress in his singing). Apparently soapmaking didn't provide enough to feed him, and in any case Paulus's insatiable appetites had to be looked after, for this disagreeable cousin was still living off Thomas's earnings. The reformer Luther had also been a singing beggar in his youth. Did he meet with similar misadventures?[8]

From Munich, Thomas moved on to a place that was even worse: Ulm. He traveled there with Hildebrand Kalbermatter, the illegitimate young son of a Valaisian priest. The two boys remained—voluntarily or involuntarily—under the thumb of Paulus and an older boy, Achacius of Mainz. Evidently non-Swiss youths were allowed to join the gang. But Thomas and Hildebrand did not stay in Ulm for long. They returned briefly to the Valais and then went back to Munich. During this phase of Thomas's travels, schooling was out of the question. The former "schoolboys" had grown up. By now Thomas must have been sixteen, and despite repeated efforts he still did not know how to read. Still working for the indefatigable Paulus, he spent his time displaying a piece of cloth to passersby and offering to make them a vest in exchange for a cash payment. This dodge worked well enough until the swindlers were fingered. Thomas seems to have been particularly miserable during his stays in Munich subsequent to his initial stint with the soapmaker (who had treated him well). The two older boys went on (or back to) forcing the younger ones to beg. Paulus and Achacius even made Hildebrand spit into a bowl to prove that he had not consumed any of the food he had begged on behalf of his tormentors. Thomas was forced to snatch bones from dogs in the street just to survive. Like a servant, he picked crumbs out of cracks in the floor—but to eat. As luck would have it, his picaresque adventures led him to a room in the home of a kindly widow, a saddle-maker by trade. Widowhood and the trades were the only avenues to emancipation available to the women of the time. The sympathetic hostess gave the young man a bowl of soup and wrapped his feet in furs that had been hung beside the stove to warm (another advantage of these German stoves compared to decrepit French fireplaces).

*   *   *

By now Thomas was sixteen and eager to be rid of Paulus. He was nearly grown, and his bitterness toward his older companion had built up over the years. Paulus, meanwhile, was bent on exploring new territory of his own: he had begun to chase girls, in particular the soapmaker's servant, and the soapmaker showed him the door when he found out. In Munich Thomas slept on grain sacks in the market. He met a butcher's wife, a former barmaid and convinced Helvetophile, who judged him to be a bright lad and gave him a room. She often sent him out to buy beer and to deliver hides and meat. After a beating from Paulus, who was still trying to hang on to his erstwhile "slave," Thomas made up his mind to leave Munich. With a heavy heart, he left the kindly butcher's wife: once again his desire for schooling was his excuse for moving on. After bidding (a discreet) farewell to the great Bavarian city, Thomas decided to head for Salzburg, despite the absence of any festival at the time (as a professional nomad, his geographic knowledge was by this time considerable, though not at all systematic). So after Switzerland, Bavaria, Saxony, Prussia, and Poland, it was on to Austria—or so Thomas thought. To hasten his journey, he attempted to hitch a ride, as we would say nowadays, in the wagon of a drunken peasant. The ground was covered with heavy frost, and Thomas had no shoes, only torn stockings. In Passau, the sentinels on duty at the city gates turned him back. He then decided to head for Switzerland by way of Freising. There he was warned that Paulus was looking for him, halberd in hand. Thomas was ready to do anything to avoid falling once again under the sway of the older boys. For years his begging had kept them alive. So he set out at once for Ulm, dozens of miles away, and covered the whole distance without stopping. There he tended turnips for a widow who had taken him in before. He worked in a garden not far from the city walls, where the widow grew turnips, cabbages, and other vegetables. Of course Paulus soon turned up, and Thomas fled again, this time toward Konstanz, in the direction of home. Along the way he had a scare: he thought he was going to be attacked by a stonecutter, who turned out to be a practical joker. The man liked to scare people but was not a real threat. Finally, Thomas reached Konstanz and was delighted to see Swiss country children in their white blouses. With his conventional (though not indelible) Catholic upbringing, Thomas thought he had died and gone to heaven. From there he went to Zurich, a city in the grip of the plague, and once again it was the same old cycle: beg first and then, in the hope of picking up a bit more learning, feed the "graduates," who were perpetually ready to "haze" would-be scholars starved for wisdom. Once again he had to endure threats from Paulus, who tried to lure Thomas back by sending Hildebrand, the priest's bastard, as his emissary. But enough of this.

\* \* \*

Thomas returned to the Valais two or three times in these difficult years: he stayed either with an aunt or cousin ("extended family" was not just a word) and visited his mother. She was a sturdy woman, on her third marriage after being twice widowed, who survived by taking farm jobs such as haymaking and threshing—jobs normally reserved for men. She had a blunt manner: when her son ate unripe grapes that made his hair stand on end and gave him colic, she said, "Eat them if you like, and die for all I care." Another time she asked if the devil had brought him. But everyone agreed that she was honest, upright, and pious. What mother hasn't lost her temper when her son ate too much green fruit? Thomas tasted the milk of human kindness while staying with aunts or among good German burghers but not at home with his own mother.

\*   \*   \*

One thing is missing in all these accounts of Thomas's travels: death. It is unthinkable that there were no deaths among the adolescents and children, the "graduates" and "schoolboys," who roamed Switzerland and the still more dangerous Germany in the company of young Platter. Thomas, who during hard Silesian winters had been obliged to discover the discomforts of the hospital, does not mention losing any of his comrades. Was this a taboo subject? A blind spot in Thomas's memory? Or a matter of indifference? In any case, Thomas was a sensitive boy, and at times even tender.

If death is absent from Thomas's memoirs, childhood is perforce amply represented. Peter Laslett, the author of the widely read *World We Have Lost,* lamented that few documents from before 1800 deal with childhood as such. Platter's memoirs would have served him well. They are among our three or four most important sources concerning the lives of peasant children in early modern Europe. The others are the hard-hitting texts of Jamerai Duval and the future Captain Coignet, both of whom begged as boys, and Rétif de La Bretonne's *Monsieur Nicolas,* which deals with peasants in somewhat easier circumstances.

\*   \*   \*

In Zurich, though, Thomas was unable to make much intellectual progress. His new friend Antonius Venetz invited him to head back north, to Strasbourg. Alsace in this period was experiencing an intellectual and religious transformation along with substantial economic and demographic growth.[9] Thomas has nothing to say about any of this: his interests did not extend that far. About Strasbourg, the Alsatian metropolis, he is laconic: "Many poor schoolchildren, wretched school." From Strasbourg, the two boys moved on to Sélestat. There, they received valuable instruction in the local school, but there was too much competition for food among the large number of impoverished pupils. Platter reached Sélestat in September 1520. Shortly before, he had suffered another attack of colic after eating unripe walnuts that had fallen to the ground: always short of money and good food, Thomas was perpetually ready to swallow anything. He was then twenty-one (and not, as he claimed, eighteen, for he had somehow miscounted the years). He left Sélestat around Pentecost of 1521—the year, as he expressly notes, of the Diet of Worms. This was when Luther, summoned to appear before the imperial diet, declared to Charles V: "Here I stand, I can do no other." Clearly Thomas was beginning to take an interest in the Reformation. That he was aware of such an event was not unusual: Sélestat was in a German-speaking region, and Thomas was a poor youth who, though not yet an intellectual, hoped to become one. Openness to reform was fairly widely shared. A few years later, in a different social setting, it found a rather different issue in the Peasants' War, whose causes were at once evangelical and "communalist."

In any case, the school at Sélestat was good for Thomas Platter. It was there that he really learned to read—in Latin, of course, and none too soon. The school was run by Johannes Sapidus (whose real name was Witz). A competent Hellenist, Sapidus was hostile to obscenities and barbarisms, which offended his sense of propriety. He favored methods that some people nowadays consider old-fashioned: his students were required to learn texts by heart and study grammar diligently. He was a fervent teacher of "the Donatus," a grammar dating from Late Antiquity that was still quite popular in medieval and Renaissance schools. It was the work of the fourth-century writer Aelius Donatus, who also taught Saint Jerome and wrote a commentary on Terence. Sapidus was an adept of the Rhenish strand of humanism, which was greatly influenced by the *devotio moderna,* a form of piety that flourished in Flanders and the Rhineland between 1300 and 1500. Christocentric, the *devotio moderna* emphasized the inward, subjective, emotional aspects of religion: enthusiasm, meditation, virtue, asceticism. It frowned upon interminable prayer, hierarchy, formalistic charity and ritual, the apostolic succession, and proselytism.[10] *The Imitation of Christ* made its tenets familiar to a broad audience. Adepts of the *devotio moderna* were deathly afraid of any rift with Catholicism, however, in contrast to Thomas, who did ultimately break with the Church. Sapidus was more cautious. To be sure, he detested the corruption of the clergy, but he rejected any radical reform of religion along Lutheran or other Protestant lines that might have challenged the dogma or temporal structure of the Church.

The Alsatian teacher's methods were simple, if stringent: "In my school, if you work, everything is free. If you are lazy, you will pay through the nose." In a school full of children, Platter and Venetz were already grown men. Both were mangy, especially Venetz, whose clothes Thomas peeled off in the morning as if skinning a goat. A former goatherd who had been beaten like a kid and who now skinned men as if they were goats—was Thomas's destiny set out in advance? In front of the other schoolchildren Sapidus described in gruesome detail the physical disgrace that had befallen Antonius and Thomas on account of a tiny mite (the cause of mange). Yet Thomas retained fond memories of the Sélestat schoolmaster, whom he would later describe as his "dear *Praeceptor.*" In this small Alsatian town, whose sixteenth-century cultural splendor is often evoked by humanist scholars even now,[11] Thomas learned, if not to write, at least to read tolerably well—and even to stumble his way through the inevitable Donatus, which, over a period of a thousand years, initiated some thirty generations of schoolchildren into the arcana of Latin. Eventually Thomas learned the Donatian *Ars major* by heart, even though he could not yet write: it was not for nothing that the sixteenth century cultivated the arts of memory. By the time he felt ready to leave Sélestat, Platter possessed a good basic knowledge of spoken Latin: according to the methods then in use, writing and reading were distinct objects of study. This distinction would persist among the literate well into the eighteenth or even nineteenth century.[12] In Thomas's day, to be a decent reader at age twenty-one was no mean feat. What extraordinary lengths he had gone to—over more than a decade—to attain a level of education that even the indifferent student achieves today without much difficulty.

Eventually Thomas had to leave Sélestat because begging, that source of most "scholarships" in the waning Middle Ages, had ceased to pay. Some 900 schoolchildren, many of them beggars, had strained the generosity of the town's fairly small population. By attracting several hundred students to his school, Sapidus had precipitated a crash in the "alms market." Some of his "graduates" would later carry on his work, going on to become excellent teachers in what is today the French *département* of the Haut-Rhin.

By Pentecost of 1521 Thomas had returned to Switzerland. He went first to Soleure, where there was a good school and the food was decent but he wasted many hours in interminable religious services. Lutheranization was just beginning to make inroads. Growing restless, Thomas decided to revisit his Valaisian roots. While staying with two aunts, he had clear proof that now, in his early twenties, and having overcome many obstacles, he was at last well on the way to literacy: in twenty-four hours (by his own account), he taught a young cousin his *abc*'s. The lad, Simon

Steiner by name, clearly had the right stuff. Following in the footsteps of his modest master, he grew up to become a teacher in Strasbourg and a friend of Bucer. Obviously, a child did not have to attend school to acquire the rudiments of an education. A friend or relative could teach anyone eager enough to learn.

Thomas soon learned how to write as well. His progress was unstoppable: a Valaisian priest taught him "a little" about writing, and he quickly made rapid strides in the art of inscribing marks on vellum and paper, if not in the actual composition of texts. The following spring (1522?), our young man once again quit the high valleys of southern Switzerland, but not before bidding his mother a tearful farewell: perhaps she was not quite so hard-hearted as he makes her out to be elsewhere in his book. "May God have mercy on me," she cried. "I have had to watch three sons leave home for lives of poverty!" At that moment the other children she had lost to plague and war were surely on her mind as well. For all its gruff exterior, the Platter family preserved a discreet fund of affection for its "needy" members. But standards of family feeling in those days were very different from what they are now and even more different from what they were in our parents' and grandparents' day. Certain stereotypes should be banished from our minds. In an interesting recent book, the sociologist Michel Fize writes: "From ancient Rome to 1945, the model of family authority governing relations between parents and adolescents changed little. The father reigned as head of the family."[13] This may be an overstatement. In fact, Thomas, like many of his contemporaries, scarcely knew his father. And while his mother did not abandon him entirely, she did leave him with aunts and cousins. Authority, though, generally came from the male side. While still very young, Thomas worked for a living or at any rate helped to support his various patrons. He earned an income, unlike children in the late twentieth century, who cost their parents money. The Platter clan, with its flexible, interlocking networks, treated him harshly but also accorded him a measure of affection and care without which he could not have survived. And when he left the Valais yet again in 1522 or 1523, he did so in the company of two of his brothers (he had a whole slew of them, of whom several had survived childhood). The journey nearly proved disastrous, for Thomas came close to dying one sparklingly clear, bitter-cold night on a snowy slope that he tried to descend too quickly. Perhaps in his horizontal peregrinations around the Holy Roman Empire he had lost some of his mountaineering skills, unlike his brothers, who retained the surefootedness that went with the highland lifestyle. But Thomas quickly regained his footing.

Leaving his two brothers in Entlebuch, where they found modest employment, Thomas once again settled in Zurich. There, in a plague year, he stayed with a woman named Gwalther and tended her baby, Rudolf. Little Rudolf would grow up to become the learned pastor of Saint Peter's Church in Zurich. Apart from his part-time chores as baby-sitter, Thomas sampled the teaching of several masters, among them a certain Knöwell, who had studied in Paris, where he acquired a taste for pretty girls. Platter's favorite teacher was Myconius, whose real name was Oswald Geisshüssler, from Lucerne. Myconius was an original: a very learned man whose motto was not "study or pay" [T 60] but "work (intellectually) or die." He did not beat his students (some of whom were twenty years old or more, after all), but he did require them, and Thomas in particular, to go beyond what they had memorized from Donatus. They were obliged to learn Latin declensions and conjugations and to check their knowledge against the texts of Terence, a playwright for whom Thomas's appetite had been whetted at Saint Elizabeth's school in Breslau. Myconius proved to be a vigilant but not abusive teacher: a cuff on the ears and a backhand slap on the cheek were the only blows that Thomas received. He did sweat, though: by dint of hard work, he eventually learned to distinguish the nominative from the genitive and the third declension from the first.

Above all, Myconius became a kind of friend for Thomas, though his affection could be gruff and condescending. The young man, often malnourished, found a way to pay his master for meals by recounting tales of his wanderings in Germany, at that time still fresh in his mind. In addition, the two men together became acquainted with the early stages of the Protestant Reformation (Myconius being only slightly ahead of his pupil in this regard). The light of the Gospel had begun to shine; the struggle against "false idols" was under way. Myconius, a cantor (though not a priest), was obliged to take part regularly in masses, matins, and vespers at the Church of Our Lady. He, too, sang for his dinner! Such jobs were a mainstay of young clerics of the period.

Myconius much preferred teaching to officiating in the Roman style, which he disliked. He accordingly delegated some of his responsibilities to Thomas, who took his place as cantor or sacristan and "bellowed" (*sic*) requiems in his master's stead. Bellowing was no longer what was wanted, however: the urgent task of the hour was to explain the Gospel text in the new manner of the Lutherans and, before long, the Zwinglians. Myconius thus played an important role in Thomas's career, because he was also a friend of Zwingli's and aided him in the early stages of his work. Zwingli (who shared Myconius's dislike of certain hymns) was at times more extreme than the German reformers. He had nevertheless forged ties with Luther on the basis of their passionate mutual interest in such subjects as grace and free will, the psalms, and Saint Augustine.[14]

To believe Platter, moreover, Myconius was quite different from the hordes of would-be priests who went to ordination with little in their heads beyond a few notions about how to sing hymns. Such men knew nothing of Latin grammar and had never meditated on sacred texts. To Myconius these men of counterfeit learning were worse than ignorant.

\*   \*   \*

In 1522, some five or six years after Luther's emergence into the public arena, Thomas Platter experienced a religious crisis. Thomas explicitly describes himself as a follower of Luther, although he knew little at the time about Luther's ideas, with which Zwingli, the spiritual and political leader of Zurich reformers, was far from being in total agreement. Until this sudden turn in Thomas's religious beliefs, brought on in part by the general spiritual ferment in Switzerland's large cities, he had been a good boy, respectful of traditional religious notions that are sometimes described as naive. He had aspired to become a priest, and that ambition had led him to roam Europe, from Switzerland to Germany to Poland and back again, in order to learn how to read and write—abilities that long eluded him for want of competent, devoted teachers. Then, suddenly, during his stay in Sélestat, basic literacy came to him like a bolt out of the blue, suffusing his whole being and transforming him through and through. His original religious vocation had not lacked sincerity, yet all it took was a thunderous sermon by Zwingli, who flayed Christendom's corrupt shepherds for losing so many of Christ's lambs, for Thomas to become a wholehearted partisan of the Reformation.

As a child, however, Thomas had dreamed of serving zealously at a handsomely decorated altar. He had invoked the Virgin along with Saints Catherine, Barbara, and Peter, the patrons, respectively, of childhood, education, a pious death, and the entry into the hereafter. Here was a full program, an itinerary, for life and death. The ecclesiastical calling, which had been drilled into the Valaisian goatherd's soul from a tender age, was also linked very early to a desire for social advancement and even social revenge. Thomas and his mother were very poor, and all the boy wanted was a chance to bounce back. He came of good stock: there were people of substance among his forebears and collateral kin. The Platters on his father's side and the Summermatters on his mother's owned homes and farms on the rocky plateaus. One of Thomas's cousins, old Antony Platter, was a priest. More than that, the boy's uncle (his mother's brother) was a castellan in the Visp district (being a castellan meant, as we saw earlier, not that he was a nobleman but rather an official responsible for law and order in a handful of villages, something between a steward of the castle and a local chieftain). Modest clerical ambitions such as Thomas's were traditional and perfectly legitimate in this milieu of substantial peasants and minor officials. But now, all at once, the New Testament and even the Old Testament had struck the young man like a thunderbolt, descending out of the blue like the eagles and bears that snatched young goats from the highland herds.

Now that Thomas could read, he kept a copy of the New Testament, which for some seasons now the printers had made widely available, in his knapsack. He took it out and brandished it frequently. And he learned it by heart, as he had once swallowed the Donatus: from Latin grammar to the grammar of the heavens. Platter also took counsel from Myconius and the sermons of Zwingli. He felt sufficiently well educated to refute the cult of the saints, starting with Saint Peter (Saint John came later). Thomas joined a large group of recent "heretics," who attacked doctrines that had been professed in Latin Christendom for a millennium. Catholics had joined heaven to the fallen world below through the mediation of the host on the altar; through the real presence of God in the sanctuary; through the sovereign pontiff; and through saints whose relics were piously preserved. Together, these things gave celestial sanctity a *point of contact* with the terrestrial life of mankind, an incarnation here below.[15] Unfortunately, perhaps, the Lutherans, Zwinglians, and men like Thomas Platter confused this Roman suture, this Catholic structure, with the cult of Baal and other idols condemned by the Bible, which their cumbrous Germanic intelligences assimilated all too rapidly. And so the clear Latin unities, the harmonious fusions of Heaven and Earth, were replaced by a dramatic German dichotomy between the old Teutonic folklore of forests and elves and the pure light of the Gospel. During one stay in the Valais, for example, Platter decided to consign a statue of Saint John to the oven; the paint on the heavy wooden figurine sputtered horribly before the object was totally consumed.[16] The statue must have been one of those handsome Rhenish Swiss icons of the late Middle Ages that are nowadays so highly prized by art lovers and dealers.[17] At the age of twenty-two Thomas thus underwent a cultural transformation: to learn to read and write, to enter the world of letters, manuscripts, and printed editions, meant nothing less.

Having passed through the looking-glass, the Helvetian was ready to turn on "wicked priests" he had known, like the one in Silesia who, be-

cause Thomas had eaten cheese one morning, refused to grant him abso-
lution, which barred him from taking communion and thus in good logic
kept him from partaking of the substantial postcommunion meal.
Thomas thus joined the flock of the Good Shepherd who "giveth his life
for the sheep" (John 10:11). He traded his rural "ignorance" (which in fact
hid a considerable fund of knowledge of pastoral agriculture) for new
ideas from the city. After his sacrilegious sojourn in the Valais, Thomas
returned to Zurich (around 1525).[18] The journey was a pious pilgrimage
to Zwingli's new Jerusalem and a farewell (though not a permanent one)
to the Valaisians. Good-bye to all those country bumpkins, intellectually
vacuous people good for nothing but milking cows, as Zwingli, himself
of rural background, derogatorily observed. It was so tempting for
Thomas to "spit in the soup" that had tasted so good back in the days
when he was a young boy romping with his goats in green mountain pastures. Zurich with its bracing spiritual climate drew Thomas as a light
draws a moth. In the city he met new people, but soon he was off again on
a month-long excursion to Lake Uri. He traveled by boat as well as on
foot. Along the way he found time for a monumental "bender," made
possible by the generosity of a wine merchant. The journey was also
marked by a storm on Lake Uri that nearly sank the frail bark carrying
Platter and all his worldly possessions. We are reminded that the existence of memoirs from the past is a matter of chance: the writer has to be
lucky in both life and death. Following this excursion, Thomas returned
to Zurich. There he lived chastely in a friend's room in the house of an old
woman, the hospitable and shrewd Adelaide, who seems to have had the
manners of a madam in a brothel. The two youths were famished. At
times they were compelled to stave off starvation by eating what they
could scrape off the bottoms of pots. So Thomas was not out of the
woods yet: he still had no real home. One could hardly treat one's body
worse than Thomas treated his, but then the body is but a wretched carcass, a miserable tabernacle that the immortal soul makes its temporary
abode. And who was to blame for Thomas's plight? Street-singing was
scorned as a priestly custom hence no longer serviceable as a way of begging alms. Soon the people of Zurich would take up a general collection
to provide for the poor now that individual begging was looked upon as
an outdated practice, a relic of the past.

Thomas eked out a living by working the land outside the city walls,
hauling logs for food and wages, and performing the duties of a sacristan.
These activities brought in just enough to pay old Adelaide the rent on
his half of the tiny room he shared with his friend. Platter meanwhile
risked his neck carrying letters from Zwingli, Myconius, and other Protestant leaders to their heretical disciples in the Five Cantons. This mes-

senger work became even riskier at the time of the Baden conference (1526). The Catholics, still very powerful in the Empire and even in the Confederation, sought to silence the rapidly growing Helvetian and Zwinglian heterodoxy. French agents were numerous in Zurich, as were francophiles generally. It was in Zurich, in fact, that Thomas first encountered the powerful influence of the great kingdom that loomed so large on the western horizon of his new homeland. The "Welch" factions would not have been unhappy to see Zwingli consigned to the flames without trial. Of course the great man was well aware of the danger. He never left Zurich, where he was protected by supporters and bodyguards from would-be assassins who, riding horses with padded shoes, prowled the city by night in search of the heretic leader. Zwingli was present at the Baden conference, however, if not in body then at least in spirit, for he was represented by his friend Œcolampadius, who received his instructions and acted as his spokesman.

Communication between Zurich and Baden was maintained by messengers, who were at times literally runners. Volunteers, including Platter and other young men and even boys, ran the roads between the two cities and arrived, as was only fitting, covered with dust and sweat. Thus reports from the Baden conference reached Zurich, and Zwingli's reactions were then carried back to Œcolampadius. Sometimes Thomas or one of the other messengers drove a hay wagon or accompanied a shipment of chickens as cover on the dangerous journey. There were nevertheless many close calls; Thomas himself had quite a few. As always in underground resistance operations, children were less likely to be suspected than adults. It was a little boy, for example, who carried one batch of urgent letters from Zwingli to Baden. Arriving at his destination in the evening, he found the gates of the city closed and promptly climbed into a hay wagon and fell asleep. At dawn, the carter, unaware of his sleeping passenger, drove his wagon into the city. Meanwhile, the messenger boy, slumbering soundly on his soft bed of hay, did not awaken until the wagon had come to rest right in the middle of town. Rubbing the sleep from his eyes, he slid down the hay stack into the street, quickly scouted out the scene, and set off to deliver his message—all under the noses of the soldiers charged with arresting and locking up Protestant emissaries No one was any the wiser.

*   *   *

Thomas's sudden change of religion was followed by a period of intense intellectual and, more precisely, linguistic fermentation. Platter was typical of a certain kind of self-made man: instead of amassing a quick fortune, he discovered culture, rose in society, and fathered a family of distinguished children. There were many such men in early modern France: think of the ancestors of Louvois, Colbert, Villeroy, and others like them. In Thomas's case, however, we have the unique good fortune of being able to examine the beginnings of such a saga of social ascent in the story of an ex-goatherd. So many families have, out of misplaced pride, obliterated all traces of the humble but ingenious ancestor who started them on their way up the social ladder. Disdainful of such snobbery, Felix Platter instead asked his aging father to dictate his memoirs, for which we owe him a debt of gratitude.

\* \* \*

But the year is still 1526. Thomas, his appetite whetted by his perilous exploits as a secret agent, set out to master three languages simultaneously: Latin, Greek, and Hebrew. (Learning classical German, or *Hochdeutsch,* with which young Thomas was certainly familiar—he quotes the Lutheran Bible—was the least of his concerns. Virtually all of his writing is in the Basel dialect. It was not given to everyone to become a Luther, the man who made the German tongue anew.) When it came to the three ancient languages, Thomas, always short of time to study, spared no effort. At night he chewed on raw turnips and even sand and drank cold water to keep himself awake in order to spend more time with his eyes open and his nose in a book. (Graduate students might find these tips worth noticing.) Platter even bought a Hebrew Bible from Venice with the modest inheritance he received from his mother. This experience with the Bible was among his first completely private and personal relationships with a book—with The Book. Thomas was fed, housed, and kept warm at first by Myconius and later by others in Zurich and nearby towns in return for teaching them the language of the Old Testament.[19] He taught them what he had learned the day before. During the Renaissance, culture was transmitted at a prodigious rate. It spread from person to person by contagion, like the plague.

Hebrew, however, did not suffice to keep this teacher alive—though merely to call him a teacher shows the extraordinary strides made by this former illiterate, now a humanist and scholar of sorts. Other things interested him as well: Thomas was susceptible to the "workerist" propaganda put out by Zwingli and other reformers who believed in the eminent dignity of manual labor (Adam hoed, Eve sewed, and Jesus was a carpenter). They also worried, as Richelieu, Colbert, and Voltaire would do after them, about the possible overproduction of priests and Latinists—in a word, intellectuals. Earn thy bread in the sweat of thy brow! Had such ideas been taken seriously, sixteenth-century universities might well have found themselves without students. And in a sense they were taken seriously. Anticlericalism, which was rampant between 1525 and 1529, did not bother to distinguish between students, or readers generally, and those who were studying specifically to become priests: all were derided as "priestlings." After spending some time as a teacher of Hebrew, an experience, as we shall see, that would have its importance later on, Thomas embarked on a new phase of his life in which he sought to apprentice himself to a master craftsman while also continuing his studies, "pounding the books" and working with his hands at the same time.

*   *   *

As it happens, Platter chose to take up the art of ropemaking, a choice dictated by a chance encounter with a young master ropemaker. The ex-Valaisian used part of his inheritance to purchase a quintal of hemp (and it is because of this that we learn of his mother's death, which must have occurred some time in 1525 or 1526 and apparently had little emotional impact on her son). Thomas began training with his new "master." Hemp in hand, he braided rope. His young master, though elegantly dressed, must have been close to broke, because he was unable to provide his new employee with raw material. Or perhaps it was just one of those old guild rules according to which a newly hired apprentice has to add some capital to the business, in this case a quantity of hemp. This investment was supposed to cover the cost of training the neophyte.[20] Platter worked at a frightening pace: when the master slept (Thomas had rooms in his employer's house), the apprentice read and took notes on Homer and Pindar at breakneck speed. The former goatherd thus emulated, on a more modest scale, Rabelais's Gargantua, improving himself both intellectually and manually.

When he finally learned, more or less, how to make rope (and he was never to become very good at it), Thomas decided it was time to leave the shop owner's employ, just as he had earlier left the "protection" of his older cousin Paul. He hastened to the disreputable house of his former landlady, the affable Adelaide. But Platter had no intention of wooing the bevies of young women who presumably worked for the elderly madam. He simply took lodging in the bordello: in that oasis of carnal indulgence, he merely rented a room where he could read Euripides. His copy of the playwright's works is filled with notes made during six weeks of non-stop reading, during which no one knew where he was. One won-

ders if the puritanical Zwingli knew similar pleasures. If our neophyte
ropemaker also indulged in fornication while reading in the brothel, he
kept no record of it. At the end of his stay with Adelaide, he made up his
mind to take to the road once again, this time heading for Basel. Did he
fear the wrath of the employer he had left in the lurch? In any case, he
decided to make himself ready for such an important departure by
bathing his entire body, something he surely had not done in quite some
time. His contacts in the world of prostitution may have been useful, because the bawdy houses now controlled the baths. In a bathhouse run by
a woman, Thomas took a hot dip, which made him sick, and injured himself in a fall, topping it all off with a nocturnal mudbath. Was it unwise to
scour away all at once the filth of months if not years? Having thus
warmed, cooled, and deodorized himself (if the final mud bath did not
restore some of the odor that the scouring had removed), Thomas picked
up his bundle of clothes and set out for Basel, which he reached in two
days. There he decided to pitch his tent and ply his new trades, teaching
and ropemaking.

At first things were difficult in Basel. Thomas found work with Master
Hans Stähelin, the Swabian ropemaker whose shop was located near the
cattle market. Stähelin, a violent man always ready with an insult, was not
popular among workers. Here we find one of the rare allusions in
Thomas's prose if not to class struggle then at least to the bitterness of
relations between different social groups. Later, his son Felix would not
be much more loquacious on this subject. In any case, Master Stähelin
was unpopular. Thomas had no difficulty finding a job in his shop: there
was little competition for the spot. The "red ropemaker," as Stähelin was
known, now employed an apprentice and two workmen, one of whom
was Thomas, who with some exaggeration claimed to have completed an
apprenticeship in ropemaking in Zurich. Stähelin treated his workers
very badly, giving them rotten cheese which his wife hastened to throw
out the window the moment her husband's back was turned. Because
there was virtually no heat, the winters were hard. The boss's young apprentice called Thomas, whose ropemaking skills were minimal, a "cow's
mouth" (T 80). The master was, as one might imagine, hardly more in-
gratiating: he disliked the fact that the new man from Zurich spent his
Sundays and holidays, nights, and even working hours reading Plautus in
the original. Plautus, Platter: Thomas unstitched his edition of the Latin
comic writer and cleverly stashed its pages in bundles of hemp until
Stähelin discovered his secret, which provoked a stream of frightful invective.[21] "Priestling" was the supreme insult in those days, and Thomas
heard it on this occasion. Obviously Zwinglian propaganda had had an

impact here too: clerical work, and indeed intellectual work generally, enjoyed no better reputation in Basel than it did in Zurich. Eventually, however, the ropemaker grew used to Thomas. He was the only man in the shop who could read and write and therefore keep the books, recording inflows and outflows of raw materials, finished goods, wages, and the like.

\* \* \*

Stähelin even allowed Thomas time off to teach Hebrew, though he may have reduced his wages accordingly. In any case, Thomas taught for an hour every Monday at the school connected with Saint Leonhard's Church. He had eighteen pupils, who in the beginning giggled at the filthy workman's attire in which their new teacher was obliged to appear before them. Most likely the students paid for their lessons. Valaisians counted their pennies, and the young "teacher" gave nothing away for free. His dress may have been odd, but he was more than competent. Thomas for the first time enjoyed the status, and stature, of an intellectual: he was part of the small but luminous circle of Basel humanists. Among them was one Cratander, alias Andreas Hartmann of Strasbourg, a printer, bookseller, and publisher of Plautus. There were close ties at the time between Basel Protestants and religious dissidents in Strasbourg, all of whom had the German language in common. By contrast, French-speaking Geneva was less closely connected with Basel than were German-speaking cities on the banks of the Rhine. But things would soon change: Calvin was coming—Calvin, that slender but sturdy Picardian bridge between "heretical" Germans and Gauls. Thomas also saw a great deal of that prodigious scholar Beatus Rhenanus, who worked with Amerbach, another important local printer. Beatus would soon become one of the scientific luminaries of Sélestat and Upper Alsace.[22]

Thomas Platter also had close ties to another resident of Basel, Oporinus (Johann Herbster), who would later produce an admirable edition of Vesalius's treatise on anatomy. Johann was first a teacher and later a printer. In his teaching Thomas used a Hebrew grammar published in 1524 by Sebastian Münster, a linguist and cosmographer. Münster did not actually set up in Basel as a professor of Hebrew until the summer of 1529. Hence we may assume that Thomas's career as a teacher in Basel must have ended by 1528 at the latest, at which time the erstwhile ropemaker was at most twenty-nine. The chronology I am proposing here can easily be checked against the established facts: Thomas states that he never knew Münster except through his celebrated grammar, from which he had taught students without having met the author. On one occasion Thomas even crossed paths with Erasmus, who lived in Basel for a time. The great humanist offered the former goatherd a few words of encouragement. Erasmus left Basel (where he had been since November 1521) in April 1529, a date compatible with my proposed chronology. Platter also met a young man who came to him to study Hebrew and who had something of a propensity to tell tall tales. Subsequently this man traveled for almost a decade, making the rounds of Jewish rabbis in Crete, Asia, and Arabia, or so he claimed after returning to the bosom of his Swiss family.

During his lectures on Hebrew, which brought him into contact with so many people, Platter liked to comment on the Book of Jonah, the prophet who spent three days in the belly of a whale or sea monster before being cast upon a shore. In Zwinglian propaganda this monster was often equated with the Anti-Christ or the Church of Rome, as the occasion required. Topical or not, the allusion was colorful and pleased Thomas, who passed it on to his audience.

Following his mystical phases in the Valais and in Zurich, Thomas became a confirmed teacher in Basel and would remain so until the end of his life. He no longer gave private lessons in Hebrew to a few pupils from the city's outlying districts. Now he delivered full-blown lectures to twenty-odd fledgling Hebrew scholars who met in Saint Leonhard's Church. The timing could not have been better for a convinced anti-papist like Thomas, for Basel, under the leadership of Œcolampadius, was just experiencing its Protestant revolution, which would culminate, to the detriment of local "papism," in February 1529.[23]

*   *   *

Thomas's first experience as a teacher was cut short by the brief little war that Basel Protestants and their allies from Zurich and elsewhere waged against five Catholic cantons (Lucerne, Uri, Schwyz, Unterwalden, and Zug) in the late spring of 1529. Platter, not quite thirty, was active in the tiny Protestant army. He wore his employer's breastplate, hauled wine for combatants and merchants, and carried messages to captains in the field. At Kappel in midsummer a cease-fire was declared. Catholics and Protestants shared a huge pot of milk soup, symbolizing the end of hostilities. The conflict, though relatively insignificant, nevertheless left a legacy of rancor and hatred. The Basel forces insisted on a ceremonial burning of the treacherous anti-heretic treaty that the papist cantons had signed with the "king of the Romans," Ferdinand of Hapsburg. The treasonous

document was reduced to ash as Thomas looked on. A few moderates in
the Protestant camp wanted to examine the accursed treaty before it was
incinerated, but anti-Catholic extremists threatened violence if the offending parchments were not burned immediately. Zwingli, a maximal-
ist, denounced the Treaty of Kappel as a hasty mistake, an "appeasement"
that would only sow the seeds of another war (in which, when it came in
1531, he was to meet his death). Although the spirit of moderation did not
prevail in 1529, it did eventually take hold in Switzerland, where Protestants and Catholics found it possible to coexist in peace. Thus despite a
brief resurgence of religious combat in 1531, the Confederation managed
to avoid the fanaticism and horror of the religious warfare that would
devastate its neighbor France some thirty or forty years later.

*   *   *

The clatter of arms and the impassioned rhetoric of Zwingli gave way to a
period of greater calm in Thomas's life. These were relatively idyllic years,
although Thomas still lived quite modestly. He returned to Zurich and
Hut Macherin's inn of ill repute, where he shared a room with Simon
Steiner, the cousin to whom he had taught his *abc*'s. The two men remained close even after Steiner went off to teach in Strasbourg. When
they were rooming together in Zurich in the late summer of 1529, Simon
was living on free food that was handed out to the poor in a deconsecrated Dominican monastery. Had Thomas tired of the old life? In any
case, he took a significant step: he married Anna Dietschi, the servant of
his master Myconius. Born in 1497, Anna was two or three years older
than her husband. She came from a family that included, in Zurich alone,
burghers, goldsmiths, and nobles, whose coat of arms bore a gold crown.
But the pedigree is misleading: Anna married without dowry and
brought few resources into the marriage. She belonged to a penniless
rustic branch of the prestigious Dietschi clan. Her parents had lived in
the country, and her brother earned a living making baskets, seats, and
brooms in Lucerne.

Left an orphan, young Anna soon found work as a maid. She worked
hard as a servant and spinner and helped her employer, Myconius, by
processing hemp; meanwhile, she filled her trousseau with tunics she
made herself out of coarse fabric. She was no pauper: until her marriage
she had never slept on straw (but later would share a bed of straw on occasion with Thomas, a man quite familiar with rude accommodations in
three countries). A shy woman, Anna was as pious as her husband. The
newlyweds, though well past adolescence, observed a postnuptial custom

that was widespread in Christian Europe: they went two months without sleeping together. Housing problems may have been the reason for their abstinence: the couple continued to live separately, Anna with Myconius, Thomas at Macherin's "inn." Whether out of choice or necessity, therefore, they continued to abstain longer than was strictly required (if indeed abstinence was required at all). They finally decided to take the plunge only after being egged on by Myconius in his characteristic friendly, good-natured way: "Wen wil tu by dim Anni ligen?" (When will you lie with Anna? [T 86]). After some weeks they made up their minds, not least because they were afraid of seeming ridiculous in the eyes of a priest to whom Thomas had once taught Hebrew and who now offered them a place where they could spend nights together. Much later, when Thomas was an old man thinking back on Anna's past, he remarked how wages had risen over the course of the sixteenth century: at the time of the couple's marriage in 1529, servants earned roughly two-thirds of what they were paid in 1572, when Thomas came to write his memoirs. But Platter's reckoning failed to take account of inflation: rising prices would probably have more than offset these increased wages, leaving domestic servants worse off than before.

More prosaically, Thomas and Anna's life together was punctuated by quarrels over money and debts. In the long run, however, these fights only made their marriage stronger. I would not go as far, however, as those who say that marital squabbling is "an excellent form of therapy, an antidote against divorce and a kind of nuptial life insurance policy"[24]—though it is true that Thomas and his wife would remain together without serious rift until Anna's death. After several weeks in Zurich, the couple decided to head south, to Platter's native Valais, where they hoped to find work in the teaching and ropemaking trades. As ropemakers they were a team: Anna worked with the distaff and spinning wheel, while Thomas braided rope. One of their first stops was in Sarnen, a canton of Unterwalden, which, to believe the possibly exaggerated Swiss folktales of the period, was a region full of inveterate drunkards. The local innkeeper, a lutist, and his wife, both completely drunk, could barely manage to make up a bed for the young couple; the two hosts then spent the night sprawled on benches in the tavern. At the break of dawn, the innkeeper, recovered from his monumental binge, managed to present our student of ancient languages with a bill (possibly a little stained with wine). With some annoyance Thomas paid what he owed.

The journey from Unterwalden to Visp (in the Valais), across the Alps and through the Grimsel pass, was made in two stages. The traveling was unpleasant at first. Thomas and his wife were not accustomed to stale bread, and at high altitudes they ran into snow. Snowflakes adhered to their clothes and skin. They also met with hostility from the still-Catholic natives of the Upper Valais, who were not overly fond of Zurich or Zwinglians. Nevertheless, on the descent into Visp (also known as Viège), they met good people (T 88). At the baths in Brigg, reputed to be good for injured limbs, nasal fluxes, the shakes, deafness, and cramps, they met a friendly barber, who also kept an inn and was in charge of the baths, and his mistress, who helped him in his various capacities. After giving birth to a child in Zurich, this woman had fled her father's wrath. (The father, incidentally, became a national hero in the next outbreak of religious war: he died for Switzerland, presumably but which Switzerland?) A little farther on, and at a somewhat higher altitude, Thomas was reunited with one of his sisters, Christine, who was accompanied by her husband, nine children, and two of her husband's elderly aunts, each said to be over one hundred years old. Christine gave Thomas what she could spare from their mother's modest legacy: some linen and an ass. The animal allowed Thomas and Anna to continue their journey in comfort, carrying their baggage the rest of the way to Visp.

*   *   *

In Visp Thomas knew true prosperity for perhaps the first time in his young life (the date was approximately 1530). He worked as a ropemaker and schoolteacher and earned additional money selling wine and apples to his students (the money to buy apples came from a loan from his uncle, Antony Summermatter). In rural and mountainous areas in those days, schoolteaching was a prestigious profession: a teacher commanded respect and often received gifts in kind from his pupils' parents. Thomas and Anna lived in a fine house that had been set aside for the local schoolteacher, a house with glass windows and a borrowed bed supplied free of charge. The parents of Thomas's students (of whom there were some thirty during the summer but only six during the winter) paid him a cash fee supplmented by gifts of milk, vegetables, and quarters of mutton. Platter's many unmarried female cousins (of whom there were at least seventy two in the region) kept him supplied with butter, cheese, and eggs. The schoolmaster even found it possible to put some money aside. When Thomas left Visp after a relatively brief stay, he took with him thirteen pieces of gold. For the time being his debts were no more than a bad memory. At the time, learning was hard to come by in such plebeian surroundings, but it could help to pull the person who did manage to acquire it out of poverty.

Thus Thomas enjoyed a newfound prosperity, but he was hardly a hedonistic materialist. People in town also had certain expectations of him. Ever since he was a child, they had believed that he would become a priest: this reputation had spread far and wide, to villages well beyond his birthplace and among his seventy-two still virginal female cousins (T 90). It was expected that he would celebrate a memorable first mass in a parish in the Valais, at which time dozens of young ladies taking part in the traditional procession would heap him with gifts. While Thomas was still off acquiring an education, this wonderfully exciting event had often been discussed in anticipation by the women of the highland hamlets when they gathered in the evening around the fire. So one can easily imagine the disappointment these Catholics still in awe of their clerics must have felt when Thomas returned home with a wife who helped him sell apples to schoolchildren, a woman who had to be something of a *huren* (whore, T 50). The word shocked poor Thomas, whose wife was in fact absolutely virtuous, like her husband. What is more, in this bigoted, backwater community, Thomas would have been expected to attend mass and even chant prayers: in those days attendance at mass was a duty incumbent upon any schoolmaster worthy of the name. But he found the Catholic mass a burdensome and vexing chore. He did not like to violate what he called his "conscience" by faking conventional piety, insisting instead on freedom of expression, though he himself had left precious little liberty to poor Saint John, whose effigy he had consigned to the oven's flames.

At some point Thomas could no longer bear the pressure. He returned to Zurich to consult his spiritual master, Myconius, who was also a kind of father-in-law, for he had given Platter his own servant as a wife (and as a matter of fact still owed Anna a considerable sum in unpaid back wages, which he never did pay: it was possible to be learned and pious and still be dishonest—or broke). Myconius recommended that Thomas pitch his tent somewhere else, outside a Valais that still worshiped idols. Perhaps he ought to return to Basel, where there were opportunities to be found. So much for the good life in the Valais: no more quarters of mutton, no more butter or cheese. Thomas had tasted plenty, but not for long.

In looking back on this period before heading north to stay, Thomas reflected on life in the highlands, and indeed in Switzerland and Europe generally, in light of his experiences. His account is not simply another version of the usual sixteenth century triptych: famine, pestilence, war. For him the things that stood out were cold (or, more precisely, snow), pestilence (to be sure), and, more surprisingly, childbirth (which all too often spelled death). Snow was an affliction of high altitudes: on his return to the Valais from Zurich after seeking Myconius's advice concerning his troubled conscience, Thomas, accompanied by one of his students, had a bitter journey through the Grimsel pass. The two travelers almost froze to death in deep snow (T 91). Like modern mountain climbers, they fended off disaster by moving all the time, continuing to walk in order to avoid freezing. This episode probably took place in early August 1530.

Platter recounts another bout with cold at high altitude in which he came close to "giving up the ghost." Buried in snow, he experienced an almost pleasant sensation as the heat drained from his heart to warm his extremities (such, at any rate, was the "physiological" explanation he gave after the fact). A man appeared to him as if in a dream and earnestly admonished him as in the Gospel, "Rise and walk." He did so, and thus managed to avoid the fate of one *Hibernatus,* who lost his life in the Tyrolean Alps some four thousand years ago.[25]

And then there was pestilence. Earlier in his memoirs Thomas remarked on the broad swathe that the epidemics of the early sixteenth century had cut through his family, claiming his father and several sisters among others. In 1530, the curé of the parish in the Valais where Thomas and Anna were living died of plague: when the disease struck, everyone shunned the man except for one young boy. Anna, already a good Protestant and afraid for her own life, rejoiced at this death, because the priest was unfriendly and widely disliked. In recalling this story, Thomas mentions two other serious outbreaks of plague that he witnessed in Zurich.[26] (Incidentally, he always introduces passages of remembrance with the same turn of phrase: "Speaking of boots," "speaking of plagues.") The two plague epidemics filled a pair of common graves with some 1,600 bodies. On the first occasion, Thomas himself seems to have been infected: a boil or bubo appeared on his thigh. One of his aunts healed him with God's help and a dressing of cabbage leaves. To reach the home of this merciful and skillful relative, he had been obliged to hike for miles. Walking was difficult because of his abscess, and he was so weak that he fell asleep eighteen times in half a day, although he was ordinarily a man who could hike all day without tiring. During the second episode of plague, Thomas had no bed of his own; he slept between two young women, both of whom soon showed symptoms of the disease. They died, he says, yet he emerged unscathed. A tall if tragic tale? There is perhaps a grain of truth to the story: Platter might have developed an immunity to plague after his earlier bubo responded to the cabbage-leaf cure.

The birth of Anna's first child, probably in the fall of 1530,[27] also proved dramatic for both the mother and her husband. As was customary in the

Valais in the Middle Ages and Renaissance, the mother was assisted by an aristocratic midwife who engaged in this kind of work "for joy" (*freid*) and who offered her services for free, for it would have been a sin to receive payment for bringing a new soul into the world (T 93). This was an old-fashioned attitude: in the more modern Basel, midwives were paid for their services. But not even old-fashioned good will could insure against infant mortality. The noble midwife was assisted by several other "distinguished" women, proof that Thomas had risen several notches in the social hierarchy of the Valais. While Anna was in labor, Thomas sweated profusely, to the point where his shirt became soaked: Henri IV was in a similar state when little Louis XIII was born. Thomas actually witnessed the birth, although the women, bent over Anna, kept him from seeing what was going on. Religious conflict continued around the birthing bed: the midwives, all of whom carried wooden rosaries, prayed to Saint Margaret and urged Anna to sponsor a mass in the hope that she might be favored with a relatively painless birth. To these entreaties she simply responded: "I am faithful to my devoted God!" Neither Thomas nor Anna approved of the worship of "idols." Her time with the very Zwinglian Myconius had clearly had its impact on her. The baptism was inevitably Catholic, of course, and the baby, a little girl, was named Margretlin ("little Margaret" [T 94]), reflecting the hagiographic tastes of the respectable midwives. Yet while the baptism was Catholic, the godfather (flanked by the same "distinguished" godmothers who had assisted at the birth) was Protestant, a "friend of the truth." Thomas once again scandalized the "conformists" of Visp by publicly announcing to anyone who wished to listen that, should he be widowed, he would sooner become an executioner or "carcass butcher" than a "priestling" (*sic*). The anticlericalism that would become such a prominent feature of French politics in the late nineteenth and early twentieth century clearly had deep roots.

Ultimately, Thomas was unable to appreciate the priest-ridden Upper Valais for its scenic beauty. His wife, though a "heretic," was physically comfortable there but unwilling to remain for long. Toward the end of 1530 or the beginning of 1531, Thomas packed his bags and moved on. The locals did all they could to encourage him to stay. The bishop, a man named von Riedmatten, even sent a cousin with flattering offers of advancement that would have launched Platter on his way to some of the better-paid posts in the diocese. Thomas's reply was full of modesty: "I am too young and ignorant." Of course it is difficult to take this reply seriously, since Thomas, a teacher of thirty-two and a man risen from the common lot and determined not to fall back into it, already knew Hebrew, Greek, and Latin. The bishop guessed that Thomas was hiding something and saw his refusal as a sign that he harbored dark (heretical) intentions. Yet Thomas remained on good terms with the bishop's family, and some of the prelate's nephews, including a future bishop, became boarders in the school that Thomas founded fifteen or twenty years later—in Basel, however, not in the Valais. The local bishop was not the only one to regret Thomas's departure: the ex-Valaisian's sister was also unhappy and blamed Anna Dietschi-Platter for orchestrating the move. To be sure, relations between the two sisters-in-law, one a city girl from Zurich, the other a country girl from the Valais, were not always good. But in this case Thomas's sister was wrong: it was Thomas who wore the pants in the family and made all the plans. Thomas was no homebody, and he was restless. The only people happy to see the Platters go were the local curés: there was a whiff of heresy about this family, and the priests were glad to see them leave.

\*    \*    \*

So Thomas set out once more, carrying his clothing and his baby on his back in an improvised wooden carrier. He led his wife, also on foot, by a rope, as a peasant might lead a cow. This expedient was necessary because Anna had only recently given birth and, being a city girl, was not sure-footed on mountain paths. In effect, husband and wife were tied together as two mountain climbers might tie themselves together today. As a fare-well gift, one of the respectable godmothers had given the Platters' child, Margretlin, two ducats. Catholic, German-speaking Upper Valais had not done badly by Thomas: he left with thirteen pieces of gold, which he had managed to save out of his earnings as a teacher and merchant. This time the destination was Basel, but the family stopped for a brief visit with Myconius in Zurich. They stayed just long enough to take advantage of the good master's hospitality, for Myconius was as generous a host as he was tightfisted as an employer. Of course he owed Anna back wages from her time as a servant, and putting up the itinerant couple was also a way for the "elderly" scholar to discharge his debt.

\*    \*    \*

From Zurich the Platters moved on to Basel. Thomas again carried the baby, who at six months was bigger now than when they left the Valais. Anna, assisted by a schoolboy, caried the family's belongings, except for the things that Thomas arranged to have carted from Visp to Basel by way of Bern. The man who agreed to carry those things was a friend by the name of Thomas Roten, who also came from a prominent family in the Valais—apparently these family contacts among people from the same area were quite important. In Basel, Platter was no longer the lonely, shivering schoolboy he had been when he first visited the city. By this time he had many contacts and substantial support. "Pious people," local supporters of Œcolampadius, strongly recommended him for a position as tutor (*provisor*) with his old friend and protector Oporinus, who had settled in Basel without difficulty. Thomas thus became a sort of assistant schoolmaster in the school run by Oporinus. Now, Oporinus, who had adopted a Greek pseudonym in place of his real name, Johannes Herbster, was involved in a campaign to rebaptize as many individuals as possible in this fashion: in Basel, the "renaissance of Latin and Greek" meant just that.

In 1526, Thomas had made the acquaintance of Oporinus, who was then teaching at Saint Leonhard's school in Basel. Besides being associated with the first-rate Hebrew scholar and cosmographer Sebastian Münster (T 163), Oporinus was also a secretary to Paracelsus, the "Doctor Faustus" of sixteenth-century Swiss medicine. His career began brilliantly. By 1538 Oporinus had become a professor at the University of Basel. Then, in 1542, he embarked on a new career as a printer. In 1543 he produced a typographic masterpiece: the admirable treatise on anatomy by the eminent Renaissance anatomist, Vesalius—"seven books on the construction of the human body"—in a superb folio edition of 700 pages with a woodcut title page.[28] After a long history of indebtedness and poverty, the printer-professor at last achieved a comfortable position by marrying a third and then a fourth wife—both women with substantial dowries. His career as teacher, printer, and paramedic served as a model for Thomas Platter, who, when his wander-years were over, became first a teacher, then a printer, and then again a teacher. Platter also exhibited a constant interest in medicine, as we shall see, and his two sons would later follow medical careers: medicine was a means of social advancement.

In 1530–31 Platter was still on the best of terms with the Basel elite. His mentor Oporinus lived in an imposing house near the bishop's residence, a location that afforded him a kind of preeminence. The new arrival in Basel also enjoyed the friendship of Heinrich Billing, the son of an innkeeper whose fine voice had earned him a position as a member of Saint Leonhard's chorus. By his mother's second marriage, he was also the stepson of the Bürgermeister of Basel, Jacob Meyer zum Hirzen, one of the lay leaders of the Reformation in the city. Billing had helped Thomas Platter land his first "stable" teaching job in the city. Of course the word "stable" has to be taken with a grain of salt, for Thomas's roaming days were not yet over, and who knew what tomorrow might bring? One day

Billing offered a gift to his "excellent friend" Thomas and his wife Anna: a glass shaped like a boot and as big as a bottle. With this misshapen goblet the Platters could conveniently tap the keg of wine that was the principal ornament of their cellar (*keller*). Husband and wife both drank, and the ritual at the keg was at times comical: "Drink," Thomas commanded his wife, "because you are breastfeeding" (Margretlin was well past six months at the time). "No, you drink," Anna replied, "because you're studying and no one can say that you're frittering your time away."

Indeed, the couple, though not wealthy by any means, had at last risen from poverty: never again did the Platter table want for wine or bread. In the early modern period, the consumption of wine marked a person's ascent into the lower middle class, as the case of Vauban (who rose to become Marshal of France in the seventeenth century) would corroborate. The Platters liked to drink after bathing in the public baths. In their present situation they washed more frequently than Thomas had done ten years earlier. The teacher earned a good salary: forty livres a year. The city was not stingy with teachers of Thomas's caliber. But he had to pay a quarter of that as rent on his small home at the sign of the Lion's Head (near Oporinus's house and the bishop's residence).

If the Platters ate reasonably well and were lodged decently, their furniture, picked up second-hand, was rudimentary at best, apart from a chair and a good bed ( purchased for five livres not far from Heinrich Billing's house). As for the kettle and cistern, Thomas had retrieved these items, both with holes in them, from the scrapheap at the city hospital.

This rather happy existence was not to last, however: Thomas had problems with his health, and he had not yet rid himself of the wanderlust of the eternal student. As a scholar he burned the candle at both ends. A glutton for work, he survived on just a few hours' sleep. To have gone from complete illiteracy to a post as teacher of Hebrew, Latin, and Greek had obviously required an effort that might have ruined the health of many a man. Thomas suffered from dizzy spells. Occasionally he stumbled about the classroom, supporting himself on a bench or wall. Neither bloodletting nor powders of ginger, nutmeg, and sugar, Galenists nor Hippocratics, brought him much relief.

Seeking advice about these troublesome but not life-threatening spells, Thomas went to see the "celebrated" Doctor Johannes Epiphanius (who, despite his supposed celebrity, has vanished from the historical record except for the incident I am about to recount). Epiphanius was a Venetian who had lived for a long time in Munich, where he had married a pretty woman. Later he was obliged to flee the Bavarian capital with his wife in order to escape persecution and possible decapitation at the hands of Duke Wilhelm IV von Wittelsbach, who suspected the physicians of his duchy of harboring Lutheran ideas and of eating meat during Lent. Although not initially hostile to the "heretics," the duke soon changed his mind when it dawned on him that the reformers might well be political as well as religious dissidents. In 1522 he banned anything having the remotest connection with Lutheranism. In 1524 he sought and received from Pope Clement VII special powers to maintain surveillance over abbeys and bishoprics. In 1541 he invited the Jesuits into his territory. Under such a ruler, anyone who wished to deviate from sound doctrine was well advised to tread carefully or take to the road. Epiphanius chose the latter course.

In Basel, where everyone knew everyone else, the members of the small but illustrious intellectual elite were of course aware of one another. Thomas Platter, who was fascinated by medicine (it was one of his "hobbies"), soon struck up a friendship with the Italian-Bavarian émigré Epiphanius (whose Latinate name had more to do with the influence of the Renaissance and the Reformation than with his Venetian roots, which had long since been forgotten or severed). Thomas described his dizzy spells to the illustrious physician, who was certain he could cure them. The two men immediately struck a bargain. Anna and Thomas Platter agreed to serve as maid and valet in the doctor's new home in the still-Catholic town of Porrentruy, where Epiphanius had become the personal physician of the bishop (T 98). The prelate in question was none other than the dashing and corpulent Philip von Gundelsheim, an ecclesiastic in his forties who had begun his career in the cathedral at Basel. Epiphanius was also a hearty, vigorous fellow: with the bishop's permission, he had taken to selecting bottles from the cellar of the episcopal residence and then having them transported to his home, where he liked to remain in his garden until midnight, clad only in a nightshirt while drinking his wine uncut and consuming quantities of food. Hence this episode must have taken place in the warm season of 1531, for winters in the Jura were cold and hardly conducive to semi-clad nocturnal revels. By day, Epiphanius found time to take an interest in the dizzy spells of his valet-patient, who also became his student, for he undertook to teach Thomas the rudiments of medicine, which the student was all the more eager to learn because he knew that medical knowledge was even more apt to lead to social advancement than knowledge of Hebrew or Greek. (Later, his son Felix would share this utilitarian attitude toward learning. Neither the father nor the son was any less solicitous or charitable toward the sick because of this, but their concern for the health of others was only an incidental consequence of their interest in the art of medicine, which they saw primarily as a way of getting rich.)

In any case, Thomas's health problems were the immediate reason for his decision to leave Basel for Porrentruy. Once again he took his wife by the hand and hoisted his daughter onto his back: it was the child's third "journey by backpack," after her earlier trips from Visp to Zurich and Zurich to Basel. The people who had gone to so much trouble to find Thomas a teaching post in Basel were most unhappy about his departure. Their protégé was more erratic than they had realized. But after the move Thomas saw them only rarely, on his visits to Basel to purchase drugs for his new master. Epiphanius's treatments did wonders for the health of his new servant, but his methods proved less effective in his own case: Physician, heal thyself! The cure for Thomas's dizziness was simple: Epiphanius eschewed both bloodletting and potions in favor of natural medicine. "Go to bed early with your wife, who will be your doctor." Broadly speaking, this was the Venetian doctor's prescription. "Remain in bed in the morning as long as you please, until someone knocks, and when you wake up have your Anna serve you a nice big bowl of soup." *Natura sanat, medicus curat:* medicine treats, nature heals. The care of women was preferable to bloodletting, enemas, and apothecaries' preparations. The Epiphanian "pharmacopoeia" appears to have been effective: Thomas's dizzy spells disappeared, never to return, except when he stayed up too late at night. Thomas later taught the same proven methods of treating dizziness to his friends in Basel, who apparently had gotten over their anger about his departure. Among them were the *bürgermeister* zum Hirzen, the father of Thomas's friend Heinrich Billing; dear old Myconius; and, some years later, one Cellarius, also known as Martin Borrhaus, a client and colleague of Thomas's (F 92).[29] Born in Stuttgart, Borrhaus was a curious fellow who had started out as the protégé of an important family. He spent time in Tübingen and Cracow as an itinerant student, befriended Melanchthon, quarreled with Luther, and married three times. After arriving in Basel in 1536, he worked as a glassmaker, alchemist, and professor. His efforts to decompose complex compounds into simpler constituents made him one of the (many) precursors of modern chemistry.

Comedy (the Molièresque doctors confounded by the gentle remedies of natural medicine) turned into tragedy: the plague returned in the summer of 1531. The hot months were the season of epidemics. The Platters had been in Porrentruy for almost three months. The first victim to be claimed by the lurking germs was Margretlin Platter. The little girl had just celebrated her first birthday (and was just beginning to walk).[30] She died after much suffering. Her parents were in tears: they proved to be more affectionate and understanding than Thomas's mother had been in similar circumstances: Amilli Summermatter had suffered too much in her own wretched life to be deeply affected by the tribulations of her children; when all is said and done, she was a woman not much moved by the woes of her offspring, or even by their deaths. Margretlin was buried by a colleague of Thomas's, a schoolmaster in Porrentruy. Anna, though overwhelmed by her daughter's death, found the strength to make a wreath of flowers for her, but the joy had gone out of her life and for a time she lost all interest in the singing that her husband loved so much. Her sadness (which was typical, according to Thomas, of families stricken or threatened by plague) bothered the normally jovial Epiphanius: "Your wife is sad," he told Thomas in substance. "This probably means that she will soon come down with the plague, or else that my wife will. So do what you must to get her out of my house." Thomas had no choice but to follow the orders of Herr Doktor (as Epiphanius was called). He took Anna to Zurich, probably to Myconius, her former employer. Epiphanius's fears proved to be well-founded. Margretlin had contaminated the doctor's entire household, except for Thomas, who may have acquired immunity to the plague when the (supposed) bubo on his thigh was successfully treated some years earlier. The doctor's wife, who also developed a bubo on her thigh, was the first adult to take to her bed (on the second floor). The great doctor himself, terrified by his wife's affliction and well aware of what that lay in store, began a drinking bout that lasted for days.

On his return from Zurich one Sunday night, Platter found his master sitting in front of a bottle with his face down on the table; he was "choking on wine." Between hiccups, Epiphanius lashed out at Thomas for having obeyed his orders, as if, through some mysterious alchemy, Anna's departure had caused the dubious doctor's wife to become ill. Epiphanius's own fatal odyssey began the next morning: the doctor awoke with the plague. He fled the afflicted town and his sick wife without a word, hastening after his bishop, who had taken refuge some time earlier at his summer residence in Delémont, close to forests and plains in which the prelate liked to hunt. Outbreaks of plague were opportunities for heroism, and more than one bishop rose to the occasion: witness the case of Archbishop de Belzunce in Marseilles in 1720. Philip von Gundelsheim, however, was a coward who turned tail and ran at the first sign of danger, despite his exalted position among the Jurassians of Helvetia.

Did Epiphanius, accompanied as was only fitting by his servant Thomas Platter, really hasten after the bishop? It was certainly his intention to do so, but in the event he was unable. The sick physician could barely walk. In a day he managed to cover only a mile after leaving Porrentruy, a community that now found itself without a doctor for body or soul. That night Epiphanius could not keep food down. The second day of his calvary, Tuesday, was even worse. After renting a horse—not a charger but a litter-bearer—the two men continued on to Delémont only to be turned back at the town's gates. In time of plague, communities barricaded themselves behind walls—the only protection to be had.

Epiphanius, so delirious from the sickness and the summer heat that he fell from his horse several times, was not in great shape. The bishop, safe in his residence inside the walls, was informed that his doctor was at the gates, however, and ordered the townspeople, or at any rate the guards who enforced the townspeople's wishes, to admit the ailing physician, whom he invited to dine with him that evening. His guest's pallor, so different from his usual ruddy complexion, worried him. Epiphanius explained that he was suffering from sunstroke and from the aftereffects of his drinking bout. Evidently Gundelsheim, who knew the Venetian's capacity for wine, found this explanation convincing. The bishop and the doctor, who had occasionally hunted together, ceremoniously addressed each other as Herr and Herr Doktor. As men of distinction, members, respectively, of the clerical and medical orders, they used the formal second-person pronoun with each other but addressed Thomas with the informal pronoun. Epiphanius grew worse during the night: he soiled his bed. Platter, always the devoted servant, slept in the same room as his master, on an adjoining mattress. At dawn he obligingly washed the sick man's sheets so that "people would not see right away" (*das man nit glich sähe*). The two men were afraid that someone would realize that Epiphanius was sick with the plague. The next morning, the bishop, who had gone out early to hunt, jumped from his horse the moment he returned and immediately began to "grill" Thomas: "Does your master have the plague?" Someone had told His Eminence (*gnädiger Herr*) that Thomas's daughter had died of the plague and that Epiphanius's wife still lay agonizing in Porrentruy with a bubonic infection. The news did not travel from Porrentruy to Delémont, it flew.

Confronted directly by the bishop, Thomas hemmed and hawed. He spoke vaguely of a malady brought on by a sudden chill when the doctor drank a large quantity of cold water during the torrid journey, but no one was fooled. The bishop summarily threw Master Epiphanius and his valet Thomas out of his house. In search of a room, the two men made the rounds of the village, but nobody would take them in. In the end, however, they found shelter at the White Cross Inn and a bed befitting the station of a "lord" of Epiphanius's rank. The innkeeper, a woman, was sympathetic to their plight: throughout this episode, certain women proved more merciful than any man, but not everyone of the female gender proved kind. The desperate physician's thoughts turned, a bit late, to the wife he had left behind in Porrentruy. Thomas, to whom he spoke from time to time in Latin, was sent to fetch the ailing "Epiphania" and bring her to Delémont, dead or alive. Understandably, the lady (who apparently had recovered from her illness, her bubo having disappeared) sent the messenger packing and denounced her husband as a scoundrel, indeed a *welche,* that is, a Latin (whether she meant French or Venetian hardly matters)—a supreme insult in the mouth of a Bavarian woman. The age-old antagonism between Germans and Latins often came out in dramatic moments. Epiphanius could die, for all she cared. She washed her hands of him. Let God deal with him.

Platter, however, would not be deterred. In his usual reasonable style, he reminded the lady from Munich of the realities: "Woman, I think he is going to die" (*Frow, ich gloub, er werde sterben*). He then reminded her that she—or at any rate she and her husband—had debts in Basel. Their creditors, such as the apothecary, a certain elderly gentleman, and the fornicating host of the Swan Inn might well insist on immediate payment. Epiphanius was a political—or, if you prefer, religious—refugee in Basel, where he had arrived from Munich with nothing to his name but his medical skills. He had not had time to attract a clientele, let alone amass a fortune. After being recalled to her senses by Platter, "Frau Epiphanius" had no choice but to see the situation as it was, namely, unpleasant. When she calmed down, she gave Thomas, whom she trusted (not altogether justifiably, as we shall see), a small consignment of things to sell in Basel in order to prevent her creditors from seizing her property: the consignment included fine linen and a small quantity of silver. Thomas, whose feet were firmly planted on the ground, also "borrowed" his master's medical formulae (*experiment buch*), which he planned to copy in his spare time for his own use. He had not given up the hope of one day becoming a physician, if not actually a doctor of medicine. In that way he hoped to avoid ending his days as a schoolmaster, as with good reason he suspected he might.

With "cargo" in tow, Thomas returned to his stricken master's side on Friday evening. The bishop, still afraid of the contagion, had meanwhile ordered that the doctor be placed on a horse and led by a servant to Münster, also known as Moutier, a short distance from Delémont (T 167). This village, succumbing to reformist currents emanating from Basel and to an impetuous French evangelist named Guillaume Farel, had gone over to the Protestants. Thomas, though a Zwinglian, knew when to softpedal his religious preferences: in Porrentruy he had managed to coexist with a "papist" bishop and the prelate's personal physician, a Lutheran. In Moutier, however, the only religious decision that was likely to arise was that of choosing last rites: Epiphanius hovered near death. Despite being accompanied by a servant, he had fallen from his horse on the short ride from Delémont.

A night passed, and then a day. Saturday night was terrible. The innkeeper in Moutier, totally in the dark about what was going on, agreed to take in the corpulent, sickly gentleman who arrived on horseback from Delémont. When he finally understood that plague was involved, he flew into a rage, attacking among other people his wife, who had registered the sick guest. The bedrooms being on the second floor, the innkeeper threatened to throw Platter and his master down the stairs (*die Stägen ab werffen* [T 102]). Answering in similarly heated terms, Thomas refused to budge. So there he was, with Epiphanius and a reform pastor who had come to Moutier to celebrate the Sunday service. More Christian than the bishop, this minister of God tried to console the dying Venetian and exhort him to die a good death. He had less success with the parishioners of Moutier: none would offer the dying man so much as a stable or pigsty (*süwstellin*) in which to die in peace. The only person Thomas could find to do his master this one last favor was, once again, a woman. Originally from Basel, this lady was pregnant and close to giving birth. She lived a stone's throw from the inn where Epiphanius lay dying. The fact that all three—the charitable lady, the dying physician, and the Valaisian servant—had all lived recently in Basel obviously had something to do with her generous gesture. She was friendly to Platter, to whom she referred as "my good neighbor" (*gsell*); with the more eminent physician she was more formal. In any case, her patent good will contrasts sharply with the disagreeable attitude of the natives.

Another woman (this one paid by Platter) helped transport the doctor to the pregnant woman's nearby home. In tears, this Good Samaritan kissed the dying Epiphanius twice on the lips—a moving gesture that involved real risk. She seated her stricken guest on a comfortable chair and later had him placed on a carefully prepared bed, worthy of a man of Epiphanius's social station and medical reputation. She even coaxed him to eat two bowls of soup. While transporting the dying man from the inn to the home of the good woman from Basel, Platter had heaped abundant insults on the local peasants, who lined both sides of the main street. He castigated them for having cast God out of their hearts, a charge to which it seems they listened without reacting.

Thomas was now torn between contradictory imperatives. His devoted friendship for Epiphanius, of which he had given ample proof (though, to be sure, he was also performing his duties as a valet), demanded that he remain at the dying man's side to the end, but his own interests had become pressing. Eventually the latter won out. In a choking voice, speaking in a pidgin that was half Latin and half dialect, Epiphanius himself urged Thomas to return to Basel. He gave his valet a gold toothpick that he removed from a neck chain as well as several rings, which he hoped would provide enough money to keep "Epiphania" alive for a while. About to succumb to the plague, the alcoholic old doctor's brain was clouded: had love for his wife really been rekindled? The question did not occur to Platter. With a few kind words he bade his benefactress farewell. Although the woman's baby arrived on the very day of Epiphanius's death, she nevertheless saw to it that the old man received the first-class burial appropriate to his status "as a doctor" (*wie ein doctor*). Meanwhile, Platter made sure to pack Epiphanius's medical notes, which he still planned to copy, and went straight to Oporinus's house in Basel.

After Epiphanius died, the good woman reimbursed herself for her expenses and kindnesses by selling the sumptuous garments he left behind. She had no trouble at all converting the doctor's wardrobe into hard cash. Epiphanius, who died like a pauper, without surgeon or pharmacopoeia (*weder schärer noch artnzy*), was laid out on a bier like a rich man but as naked as the day he was born. His cast-off finery could be seen on the backs of the village worthies, who took what blessings fortune brought their way (much as coastal dwellers appropriated the cargo of ships driven onto the reefs by a storm). Platter came away from the experience with something like a medical apprenticeship under his belt. This was worth more than the few florins in wages of which the plague had deprived him. But Thomas's medical education was to proceed no farther; later, his two sons would easily surpass him.

Now came two weeks of legal wrangling in the courts of Basel, an ordeal that Platter claims to have survived with honor intact. But we have only his version of the facts, which is all to his advantage. The dead man's creditors (the apothecary, the innkeeper, and perhaps others) hoped to settle Epiphanius's debts by seizing his worldly belongings, including the gold toothpick and the thick book of medical secrets. Oporinus and Platter did what they could to delay the proceedings and meanwhile duplicated the disputed book, each copying half its pages. Later, each made a second copy of the half originally copied by the other. In the end, the original of this much-coveted formulary wound up in the collection of one of the creditors, probably the apothecary, while the modest "libraries" of Thomas and Oporinus were both enriched by the addition of handsome handwritten reproductions: the golden age of the manuscript was not yet over. The dispute over the disposition of Epiphanius's property apparently left no rancor. Twenty years later, Thomas's son Felix became the godfather of the illegitimate son of Klingenberg, the innkeeper who was among the doctor's creditors. The child was the product of the hosteler's fling with the servant of the man who had been Thomas's attorney in the case and who had since then become a friend of Klingenberg's.

Throughout this legal wrangling Epiphanius's young widow was all but forgotten. She had survived the horrible plague of 1531 but was ruined nonetheless.[31] All her property had been seized (*alle ding iren genummen werin* [T 105]). Much later she paid a call on Thomas: she wanted her husband's formula for a purgative made from dried grapes (*purgatz mit den rosinlinen* [T 105]), which he had recorded in his book. Did she plan to sell it? She hadn't a penny to her name. Thomas sent her on her way with a twinge of regret: she was pretty (*sy was hüpsch*). He never heard of her again. All she got out of this short and brutish tale was the scar on her thigh left by the bubo.

These few plague-ridden weeks, and particularly the week of Epiphanius's death, occupy a disproportionate place in Thomas's narrative, roughly 7 percent of the total number of pages. As he explicitly states, he always regretted not having followed the medical calling. The best he could do now was to pass his interest in medicine on to his sons.

*   *   *

For Thomas Platter, the summer of 1531 was a time of plague. The following fall was a time of war, a conflict that Thomas managed to squeak through more or less unscathed. In early October, the five "papist" or "forest" cantons—Lucerne, Uri, Schwyz, Unterwalden, and Zug— spurred on from Vienna by the Hapsburgs, decided that they had had enough of Zwingli's aggressively imperialistic theocracy. Over the years Zwingli had established a dictatorship of virtue in Zurich. He had withdrawn from the city's Catholics the toleration that he rightly claimed for his fellow Protestants living under the authority of the Roman Church. The five cantons had mustered a small but well-trained army. Attacking from the south, these troops marched on the territory over which Zurich claimed authority. Things went badly for the Protestants (*es übell erging*). The Zurich troops, badly organized, politically divided, and militarily ineffective despite the presence of courageous Zwinglians in the ranks, were defeated at Kappel on October 11, 1531. Zwingli himself, wearing a helmet and armed with sword, axe, and mace, fought like a wild man but lost his life in the battle. In the nineteenth century the prophet's smashed helmet and weaponry found their way into the Swiss national museum.

Kappel awakened Swiss Protestants to the limits of their power. They reined in their expansionist impulses and resigned themselves to coexistence with the "papists." (The peace would endure, largely without friction, until the so-called War of the Sonderbund in 1847. This shifted the balance of power in favor of the Protestants without giving them a political and religious monopoly that might have undermined the subtle equilibrium on which the stability of the Swiss Confederation depended.) On the night of October 11, 1531, just as lamps were being lit in the early evening, news of the disaster of Kappel reached Zurich. The alarm was sounded. On that day Platter happened to be in the city visiting Myconius. Was this just a friendly call, or did Thomas want to be on the scene at a moment when the fate of religious reform in German-speaking Switzerland hung in the balance? As news of the defeat spread, many men of fighting age took up positions on the bridge. Obviously some number of men capable of bearing arms had remained in the city. Was their failure to join the army one of the reasons for the defeat? In any case, Thomas was among those who now took up defensive positions. His conscience was easy, for he was not a citizen of Zurich. The defenders occupied the bridge and its approaches and before long fanned out along the river bank as well. They were on the lookout for enemy marauders: emboldened by victory, the enemy might try to attack and occupy the city. But no marauders appeared. The Catholic cantons had no interest in exploiting their victory. Their aim had been to restrain the imperialism of the reformers, not to annihilate them—a goal that would have been beyond their means in any case.

The night was cold. The defenders lit huge fires, and those with shoes, including Thomas Platter, removed them to warm their feet: no longer was Thomas one of those poor wretches obliged to go barefoot in summer or to wear clogs in winter. In the early morning hours the wounded could be seen in the torchlight, limping home. It was a horrifying sight: one man had lost a hand, another supported his wounded head unsteadily with his hands, and a third held his own guts, which were spilling out of his body. Even small wars are tragic, be they between Greek city-states or Swiss burgs. Meanwhile, the halberd Thomas had borrowed from Myconius was nearly stolen. Platter remained confident, however. The few captains (*houptlüt*) who had survived the rout of the Zurich "army" straggled home, some having lost their way in the fields, others accused of treason or at any rate of cowardice in the face of the papist enemy. Although Thomas's stomach was growling, no one offered him food, since he was not a member of any of the city's regular militias. With the courage of a philosopher, he decided to return to the city, which meant crossing a bridge guarded by sentinels armed to the teeth. They kept a close eye on everyone entering the city: not only were the authorities afraid of a "Trojan horse" tactic on the part of the enemy, they also feared the arrival of useless mouths to feed and of wounded outsiders in need of care. Thomas had a hard time making his way back to Myconius's residence.

Such stunning reverses were common in the 1530s. A few years later, French Protestants had their turn: in 1534, after the Affaire des Placards, Francis I abandoned his relatively benevolent policy toward the Protestants and moved toward a more discriminatory position. In German-speaking Switzerland, the situation was less grave, yet the expansion of Protestantism had clearly been stopped. The treaty that was signed shortly after the Battle of Kappel had the effect of freezing the boundaries between the rival religions for a long time to come. Hopes of a new surge of reformist sentiment on one side and of a total Catholic victory on the other proved unfounded. The peace, quickly established *de facto* and soon ratified *de jure,* did not immediately put an end to every alarm. In late November 1531 the Catholic peasants of Schwyz who had been among the victors at Kappel began their homeward march. Choosing the shortest path between two points, their army passed close to the walls of Zurich.

For the defeated but still inviolate city (no enemy had ever breached its walls), this was a humiliating affront and a terrifying provocation. Zurich was afraid. Rumors of treachery and impending slaughter swept the city. A month earlier Zurich had lost a battle. This time it might lose its "virginity" (it was in such terms that people spoke of the honor of a city not yet polluted by the invasion of an assailant).[32] The fear proved salutary, because it gave rise to a defensive reaction: citizens poured into the streets. Myconius issued an order to his faithful disciple: "Thomas, you will lie by my side tonight" (*Thoma, lig du hinacht by mier*). Thomas did as he was told. In their shared bed, both men lay with one eye open. Each kept a halberd by his side. In the morning the "Schwyzians" abandoned their bivouacs outside the city and moved out in the direction of home. The alert, though very real, was now over.

Even though Zwingli was now gone, many people in Zurich still smelled the flames of inquisition. The ground burned their feet. Take, for instance, Georg Göldli, one of the leaders of the Protestant "army." He had led his troops badly enough to hasten defeat and was in fact accused of treason by his men, since, as it happened, his brother was serving in the Catholic ranks. Charges were brought against Captain Göldli in 1532, a year after the battle, but he managed to fend off his accusers. No sooner was he released from prison than he moved to Constance, where he died in 1536. He had found it wise to put as much distance as possible between himself and Zurich (T 168).

Myconius would soon leave Zurich as well, but for different reasons: there was nothing left for him to do in that threatened and dangerous city. Unemployment, a scourge less dire than plague but serious nonetheless, loomed. In addition, the death of Master Ulrich (Zwingli) had deeply upset Myconius the teacher: he and Zwingli had long been close, and Myconius had always respected the slain Protestant leader as a man of superior intellect and spirituality. Platter claimed to have strenuously encouraged Myconius to leave for Basel and to have used his contacts with the Billing family to try to get his former teacher a position as (reformed) preacher at Saint Alban's that had been left vacant by the death of Hieronymus Bothanus, also known as Bothan, at Kappel.

Platter may well have embellished his role in this case and made himself out to be more important than he actually was, but it is indeed true that the "bald preacher," as Myconius was known, left Zurich at the time Thomas mentions. We find him in Basel in December 1531, where he had become acting pastor. His career as teacher and minister had thus taken him from Basel (where he had been earlier) to Zurich to Lucerne, back to Zurich and then once more to Basel. There, from 1531 until his death of plague in 1552, Oswald Geisshüssler, known as Myconius, would achieve all that a Protestant could hope to achieve in both his ecclesiastic and teaching careers. The two friends, Oswald and Thomas, were still young by our standards (one was in his forties, the other in his thirties), and their journey from Zurich to Basel in the fall of 1531 did not lack for suspense or excitement. In the village of Mumpf they encountered a party of four rather disreputable-looking noblemen on horseback. One of these stout fellows, the Junker Hans Egloff Offenburg, was "one of the most ornery rascals and drunkards recorded in the fighting annals of that time" (T 110, 169). And Myconius was not wrong to have been somewhat suspicious of these men. A few weeks earlier the quartet had attended the solemn funeral for Zwingli and others who had fallen at Kappel and elsewhere in the holy war against papism—not to mourn but secretly to celebrate the deaths of these "heretics." Apparently, Offenburg and his three friends had entered into a pact with the pro-papist opposition in Zurich, an opposition that was only too glad to be rid of the pious dictator.

The four noblemen were even more suspect in the eyes of a loyal Protestant like Thomas because at least one of them had family ties to the Catholic bishops of the region. Platter was therefore glad he had seen through the thin disguises of these papists, who were in any case rarely sober. In the inn at Mumpf the Junker "squadron" drained flagon upon flagon and raised a dreadful ruckus. One of the younger nobles tried to force Myconius to have a drink with him, drawing an indignant protest from the "elderly" professor (the geriatric epithet was applied to the forty-year-old professor by the the jolly topers) (T 110).

"That will do, my friend," Myconius retorted. "I already knew how to drink before you knew how to do your business on the wood shavings." (Were wood shavings used in outhouses for the same purpose as sawdust or leaves?) Late that night, as a final round was being drunk, one of the revelers had the audacity to put his elbows on the table, a gesture that incurred the wrath of his father, Wolfgang Daniel von Landenberg, who was even drunker than his son. Drunkenness was one thing, but putting one's elbows on the table—why, the very idea! Platter and his companion, mute witnesses to these proceedings, quaked with stifled laughter. A commoner, Myconius had little respect for the nobility, or at any rate for certain crude, pretentious, uncouth gentlemen who wore swords at their sides, for whom he had almost as much disdain as for Catholic priests.

In Basel, Myconius found lodging with Oporinus (*by dem Oporino*, as Thomas put it in his mixture of German and Latin). Oporinus had been a benefactor of many a "right-thinking" visitor from Zurich. Soon thereafter, toward the end of 1531, Myconius was named minister and schoolmaster of Saint Alban's. Platter rather indiscreetly lets drop that he occasionally assisted the new preacher by "ghostwriting" sermons on particularly delicate topics such as "why God got us all into this mess" (the mess in question being the defeat and death of Zwingli). Whether Thomas had anything to do with it or not, Myconius's sermons drew crowds and pleased men of learning, including those whose predilection was the Greeks as well as those whose specialty was theology.

So successful was Myconius that in the summer of 1532 he succeeded Œcolampadius as the spiritual if not political leader of Basel. Œcolampadius had died at almost the same time as Zwingli, in the fall of 1531, but of nonviolent causes. A replacement was needed, and Platter's friends took advantage of the situation. In general, the movement of religious reform drew much of its leadership and support from the middle to lower strata of society: there were sons of the middle class (such as Luther and Calvin), of the relatively well-to-do peasantry (Zwingli), and even the poorer peasantry (Platter). The rise of Protestantism among Saxons and Anglo-Saxons, Alemannis and Welches, was more than just a change in spiritual behavior. It was also quite simply a social upheaval affecting class status and marriage (the successive marriages of King Henry VIII of England are a case in point, to say nothing of the marriages of nuns and clerics) and provoking violent rebellion (such as the Peasants' War in Germany).

At a more modest level, Thomas clearly wanted to persuade his readers that he was responsible for Myconius's brilliant career. It was through his "contacts," he says, that Myconius obtained his ministry. He had accompanied his teacher from Zurich to Basel and even financed the journey (which had not cost very much). And he claims to have provided Myconius with the subjects (and even texts) of some of his sermons. We are not obliged to take Thomas at his word: he sometimes wrote to impress any members of his family who might read his memoirs. In all this story about Myconius's departure from Zurich, we almost fail to notice another "permanent" move to Basel: that of Thomas himself. (To be sure, he did not altogether forgo the pleasures of the road, but Basel henceforth became his home.) By the end of 1531, Zurich held no further prospects for Thomas, civilian or military. He judged that he would be better off returning to Basel to study and earn his living. Anna would rejoin her husband later. It was far easier for her to move now after the unfortunate death of little Margretlin, for the baby, though much loved, had greatly complicated the couple's travels.

Thomas thus continued his education in Basel. Truth to tell, he found his studies more amusing than the company of his rather ill-tempered wife, who for the time being was providentially separated from her husband. Thomas enrolled in the Untern Collegium am Rheinsprung, which for centuries remained the central institution of the University of Basel. His "good master" at the time, in whose course he enrolled officially in the summer of 1534 (later than he implies, but he may have attended lectures as early as 1531–32), was Phrygio, whose real name was Konstantin Sydenstricker. Born in Sélestat in the 1480s, Phrygio grew up in the humanist ambiance created in this Athens or Florence of the north by the scholar Beatus Rhenanus, a friend of Erasmus, enlightened lover of the ancient classics and writings of the Church Fathers, connoisseur of ancient and Germanic geography, and editor, coeditor, or annotator of the works of Pliny, Seneca, Tacitus, Velleius Paterculus, Livy, Augustine, Jerome, Chrysostom, Tertullian, Thomas Aquinas, and Erasmus. With this background Phrygio became first a curate in Basel and later, in 1532, a professor at the university, from which he moved to Tübingen in 1535, but before that it fell to him to transmit to Thomas the lessons of the Renaissance.

The Valaisian not only attended lectures at the university but also seems to have been provided by his *alma mater* with a small room or at any rate a bed. He slept at the university as other men sleep in barracks. Without a wife to cook for him (Anna having stayed behind in Zurich), Thomas ate for three denarii at the Pilger Stab (Pilgrim's Staff), an execrable student restaurant that left diners feeling almost as hungry when they came out as when they went in. But his teacher Phrygio often invited Platter to his table along with another teacher, Christian Herbort, who was considerably older. To Thomas, Herbort was a parasite (a specialist in *schmorotzen* [T 115]) as well as a turncoat, with his "butt firmly between two stools," as Platter put it, half-Catholic and half-Protestant and always ready to turn with the prevailing winds: a Protestant in Basel and a Catholic in Freiburg or the Valais. When Montaigne visited Basel in 1580, he was still struck by the number of such "flexible" spirits in Switzerland.

In the early years of this latest residence in Basel, Thomas met with circumstances that contributed to his success. The university had been profoundly disrupted by the triumph of the Reformation in the city in 1529. Normal academic activities did not resume until 1532 or so, and then only slowly and of course under new masters professing new beliefs. Times had changed, and Platter had come a long way since his revolutionary phase, when he had supported iconoclasm (burning the statue of Saint John) and embraced working-class populism (choosing ropemaking as his trade). He had matured: at age thirty-five, in the summer of 1534, he ceased to be an eternal student, an advanced though impecunious disciple, and accepted a teaching position, which he would thereafter hold, with brief interruptions, to the end of his life. He of course had the requisite professional experience: he had taught at many levels, from familiarizing his cousin with the *abc*'s to giving lessons in the Hebrew language. But Thomas's promotion was not solely the result of his personal merits. He also benefited from the fact that many Catholic professors had abandoned their posts in disgust at the triumph of "heresy" in the city. In addition, many people, including members of the intellectual elite, had been cut down by the plague, and this also improved Thomas's chances.

In 1534, then, Thomas became almost a full-fledged teacher, a sort of lecturer or senior lecturer holding a post superior in status to that of a secondary (or elementary) schoolteacher but below that of a full university professor. He taught what we would now describe as first-year undergraduate courses in Greek (a language that he knew well, along with Latin and Hebrew). In his teaching he used the *Dialogues* of Lucian, a writer impatient of human ambitions and celestial deities. Did continual study of such texts make Thomas a skeptic, or at any rate less of a mystic than he had been ten or fifteen years earlier? For Greek grammar he relied on the work of Ceporinus (Jacob Wiesendanger). A native of the Winterthur region and former teacher at the monastery school in Basel, Ceporinus had published his grammar in that city in 1522. The work went through numerous editions and proved to be a lasting success, at least in Switzerland. Its style was modern, Cartesian *avant la lettre,* with "its long chains of simple, easy arguments." Grammar was explored in all its dimensions: nouns, accents, declensions, adjectives, adverbs, prepositions, and so on. Thomas, having left the mountains and their traditional culture behind, now discovered, and filled his students' heads with, subtle classifications. When necessary he concentrated the minds of his students with a smart box on the ears. Such methods were common at the time (everywhere but in Montaigne's château, apparently).

At this point, however, Thomas embarked on yet another temporary but important excursion: he learned the art of printing. The plague, still lurking about, claimed the life of one Jacob Ruber (or Ruberus in pedantic Latin), a close friend of Thomas and Oporinus. Ruber had been a proofreader in the print shop of Johannes Herwagen (or Hervagius), a native of Austria who in 1527 had married Gertrud, the widow of the illustrious printer Johannes Frobenius. For some years Herwagen had been in partnership with other members of the Frobenius family, renowned among typographers, but since 1531 he had been on his own, employing helpers but doing business without partners. After losing Ruber, Herwagen managed to replace him for a short time with a local student (or intellectual) of remarkable intelligence, Simon Sulter or Sulzer. It was but a short step in those days from scholar to proofreader, because scholarship alone was not enough to keep the pot boiling. But Sulzer may have had other sources of income, or perhaps he was simply enamored of pure research and culture, regardless of the cost (F 170). Typesetting was not compatible with his real interests. He therefore passed his job as printer's assistant on to Thomas Platter.

Though reluctant at first to accept the job, Thomas allowed himself to be talked into it, "giving in to the warm urgings of my friend." It may be worth mentioning that even so illustrious a scholar as Oporinus was not loath to earn extra money from time to time as a proofreader. For four long years, from 1536 to 1539, Thomas thus worked as both a teacher and a proofreader. Out of toil and woe came a new calling for Thomas: that of fully qualified printer and indeed publisher. This was Basel, after all, a center of German printing, much as Lyons became the center of French printing in the sixteenth century. Before long Platter was filling in for his employer: when Herwagen traveled to Frankfurt for the book fair, it was

Thomas, back in Basel, who supervised the shop in the master's absence. Thomas had certainly acquired an impressive variety of skills in his first thirty-six years: he had been a shepherd, goatherd, cowherd, mountaineer, schoolboy, beggar, nomad, student, singer, professor of three ancient languages, ropemaker, typographer, and proofreader, and he was not yet done: he would end his life as a school headmaster and real-estate entrepreneur. He was a Renaissance man in the full sense of the term. Yet like many of his contemporaries he had little use for the calendar: rarely does he give precise dates for any of the important events in his life, except his birth (for which the date 1499 may have been approximate)—and of course we know the exact date of his death thanks to his son Felix, who took the trouble to record it in the manuscript.

For the time being, however, Thomas was still very much alive: indeed, he was making children. After a more or less obligatory period of separation, he resumed married life with Anna. His first daughter, Margretlin, born in the Valais in 1530, had died of plague in 1531, as we have seen. His second daughter, Margretlin II, was born in 1533 (F 50 and T 144). Thomas, having taken the cure at the baths in Brig, was working for Herwagen as a proofreader and living with his wife in the schoolmaster's house attached to Saint Peter's Church. At the time the schoolmaster was a man named Antony Wild, a defrocked Franciscan, who would soon move to the Collegium, where his distinguished career was cut short by the plague in 1541. Little Margetlin II preceded him to the grave, also succumbing to a rather nasty if brief resurgence of the disease in 1539 after the major outbreak of 1538.[33] A third daughter, Ursula, was born in 1534, after the Platters, having come up in the world, had moved once more. In fact, Ursula's story reveals just how far they had come: the new house, which adjoined Wild's, had a window, and the little girl (*kindlin*) was about to fall out of it one day when a certain Marc Wolff, who boarded with Thomas, saved her by grabbing her tiny feet (*fiesslinen* [T 119]).

Thus it may have been as early as 1535 or 1536 that Platter began his lucrative business of taking in boarders: students who paid to sleep under his roof, eat his food, and take his lessons. Thomas became a surrogate father (and when necessary a stern father) to the growing number of boys and youths who lived with him in a series of houses. Anna played a major role: who else (apart from any servants they could afford to hire) was to make the beds, do the laundry, and prepare meals for this host of noisy young men who had other things on their minds besides rhetoric? Platter of course taught. Glutton for work that he was, he also began printing under his own name in 1536. These years thus marked a clear advance for the family both socially and professionally. Long gone were the days when little Thomas, the mangy schoolboy, had begged for his supper on country roads and city streets, though his memories of those days remained vivid. In 1536 he became the father of a fourth child: it was on October of that year that his son Felix—aptly named, for this was the "happy" child—was born (F 52). Felix would outlive his three sisters: Ursula, too, died of plague in 1551, exactly like her two elder siblings. And he would carry the memoir-writing tradition inaugurated by his father into the second half of the century.

Paternity, of course, has religious significance. God—the "devoted God" of the Protestants—bestowed his blessings on it. Yet Thomas did not blame God for the deaths of his three daughters. "Margretlin also died of plague," he wrote (*Margretli starb mir ouch an der pesetelentz* [T 144]). Thomas extolled the supernatural force that overwhlemed him. He felt no need to offer even a pious explanation for the judgment of heaven that had decreed the deaths of so many of his relatives and children. He was in this respect closer to the "enlightened" and often optimistic theology of Zwingli than to the neurasthenic ideas of Luther, imbued as those ideas were with fatalistic notions of predestination to disease or death on express orders of the Creator.

## CHAPTER THREE

# The Platter Childhoods: Felix

Felix Platter, the only son of Thomas and Anna, was thus born in Basel in October 1536, shortly before the city's annual fair. Indeed, the traditional "gifts from the fair" were placed on the new mother's bed. As for the father, Felix himself was his mother's gift to her husband. And what a present he turned out to be! Over the next half century, the boy would bring his father all the honor and happiness a man could wish for. The year of Felix's birth, 1536, was also the year in which Thomas printed with his own hands the first Latin edition of Calvin's *Institutes of the Christian Religion*. But, as everyone knows, once a child is born, its parents love it more and more, whereas a person who makes a book (whether author or printer) is concerned with it only as long as it takes to produce it: once the book is out in the world, it consumes less of one's thought. If Felix was aware that his birth coincided, as if by Calvinist predestination, with his father's edition of Calvin's work, it surely would have encouraged him in his decision to describe his coming into the world as a sign of God's grace.

Felix provides certain interesting details concerning his mother and father. Thomas, he says, was the owner of a print shop, the scion of a "large and respectable family" from the Valais. Anna, we are told, came from an "old and honorable family, several of whose members were ennobled" (*dorunter ettlicher geadlet worden* [F 50]). Technically, these assertions are not false. Thomas, as we have seen, did indeed come from a line of substantial Valaisian peasants with some distinguished relatives. And Anna's family, the Dietschis, did include nobles, goldsmiths, and other burghers from Zurich and the surrounding region. Yet a few lines later Felix concedes that before her marriage his mother was illiterate and employed as a servant by Myconius, who had suggested that he be named "Felix," a forecast of the happiness he would later enjoy in considerable measure. He also tells us that Thomas, in the prime of life, often thrashed his apprentice, Balthasar Lazius (also known as Ruch).

Little Felix was baptized by Benedikt Wydmann, the pastor's vicar. Felix's godfathers were Simon Grynaeus, a native of Sigmaringen in Germany and distinguished professor of theology and Greek, and Johann

Walder, a printer. Here we see both the division and the unity of labor: Grynaeus edited the Greek classics, Walder printed them. The boy's godmother was Ottilia Nachpur, the wife of a wealthy cloth merchant (F 52–53). Thus the university, the printing trade, and commerce were all represented: these were the spheres of society that Thomas moved in or aspired to enter. By contrast, when his second wife brought him additional children some forty years later, nearly all the godparents were drawn from outside the economic sphere, from the world of judges, ecclesiastics, intellectuals, and municipal government. Slowly but surely, Thomas had made his way up the social ladder.

Felix's birth was a great joy for Thomas's cousin Simon Steiner, known as Lithonius, who, like Thomas, sprang from a peasant background in the Valais. He had assisted the reformer Bucer in Strasbourg and gone on to become a professor of Greek at the Gymnasium in the Alsatian capital. Married but without children, Lithonius, with Thomas's blessing, intended to treat Felix *de facto* as his own adoptive son, but his premature death in 1545 put an end to this dream. Felix did, however, inherit his cousin's fine library, the books from which were marked with a cloverleaf. It is remarkable to observe how illiterate peasant children like Simon and Thomas grew up to be astonishing bibliophiles.

Unusually for the time, Felix, in recounting his childhood, set out to be a conscientious historian. He drew a distinction between his own authentic memories (from his later years, obviously) and things that he had learned from others about himself (mostly having to do with his early years, of which he had no personal recollection: as he put it, "'36, '37, '38, up to 1539"). Many of these memories concern either pranks or injuries or both. In 1539, for example, in a time of plague (the first of many epidemics mentioned by Felix), some practical jokers interrupted his mother as she sat spinning thread with a distaff and showed her a skull stolen from a nearby cemetery with a candle inserted in one of its eye sockets. Frightened, Anna leapt up and knocked over Felix's cradle, resulting in an injury that left a scar on his nose. Another time, while slicing bread, Anna slipped and cut the tip of the middle finger of little Felix's right hand, leaving him with another scar for life. As a result, the little boy was frightened by the sight of wounds and bruises. A little later he had a nanny with a mutilated finger, and his refusal to eat porridge served by a hand thus truncated led to the woman's dismissal. For years Felix continued to exhibit an obsessive dislike of people with mutilated limbs or broken bones.

Looking back, decades later, on his first three years, Felix recalled one authentic personal memory as if it had happened the day before: his elder sister Margret was carried into the house unconscious after being accidentally struck with a pickax by a servant digging in the yard. The grownups gathered in a panic around the senseless child. She sooned regained consciousness, however, and before long was running around the table in her nightshirt. A few months later, however, she died of the plague. Perhaps the superimposition of these two "snapshots" (the first, of Margret unconscious, masking the second, of her actual death) accounts for the vividness of this image in Felix's mind. In 1539, an amazed Felix looked on as the artist Matthäus Han, age twenty-six, from a family of master glaziers, decorated the facades of the house that Thomas Platter had purchased the year before, which bore the resonant name *Zum Gejägd* (To the Hunt) (F 55–56). Han drew an outline of a stag with its horns, then of a hunter with his dog (*hundt und jeger*). On the facade of the house across the street, the same artist drew a scene depicting a number of Moors. The Moors figured frequently in the folklore of the time, owing to their important role in the wars of the early sixteenth century: they almost captured Vienna in 1529. The king of France became their ally in 1532.[1] In one of the heated rooms of the Platter home, moreover, there was a small birdcage made of iron wire painted all the colors of the rainbow. Much later, Felix would have his own home painted in the gaudy French style.

The summer of 1540 was very hot, hot enough to advance the date of the grape harvest by two weeks and to melt glaciers and snow fields in the mountains. This sweltering summer left Felix with other memories as well: a woman invited to Sunday dinner at the Platters' gave him a handful of pretzels, and a friendly carpenter took him by the hand and bought him white bread for a few pennies (the daily bread in Switzerland and adjacent regions of Germany was usually black). Another memory also involved eating—and indigestion: little Felix ate too many cherries in celebration of his first pair of pants, which were as red as the cherries themselves; his new trousers paid the price for his overindulgence. Until then Felix's regular costume had been a tunic, which he wore much longer than his father had worn his. Felix's childhood had little in common with Thomas's rude beginnings some thirty to thirty-five years earlier. One thing remained the same, however: little Felix became fascinated very early with horses and horsemen.[2] One of Thomas's brothers, a soldier, had given him a toy horse in the early years of the sixteenth century. A soldier named Meltinger, about whom we know nothing except that he lived in a house in the middle of the block the Platters lived in (at what would later be 92, Obere Freie Strasse), had a horse that he kept in a stable rented from Thomas, and Felix always looked on with great pleasure whenever the steed was led in or out.

Distractions also stuck in Felix's mind. He remembered his father's workmen playing skittles; a wooden doll, purchased at the fair, which was flexible enough to use in fencing games; and riding perched on the shoulders of his father's boarders, students from the leading families of the Valais, who lifted him high enough to touch the ceiling. Grownups sometimes bantered with the boy: every snowflake, they said, was an old woman, falling, falling, falling. On Christmas Eve, Saint Nicholas came riding on an ass and handed out gifts to all the laughing children, Felix among them. Here, then, is evidence of a long-standing opposition between Christmas customs in the north and south, dating back to at least the sixteenth century: in German-speaking countries, good Saint Nick was the focus of attention, whereas in Provence and Romansch-speaking areas, the "yule-log" was the centerpiece of the winter celebration. Thomas Platter Jr., Felix's younger brother, would discover this for himself while traveling in the south of France during the winter season a half-century later.

Another miracle was Felix's discovery of eggs on the straw bed occupied by Canis, the dog belonging to Herr Grauwenstein, a vintner and Latinist who lived across the street. Grauwenstein and his wife liked to invite Felix for dinner and serve him eggs, which they of course claimed had been laid by Canis. The story shows that the Platters continued to frequent common folk—craftsmen and vine growers—even though Thomas, with his grand ideas, would have preferred to give the impression that he hobnobbed exclusively with distinguished clergymen and professors. Unfortunately we have no access to the vast wealth of folktales that little Felix must have heard from the grandmothers of other children (his own grandparents were long since dead). The Platters' only son delighted in the ghost stories that these old women told, which terrified him. He was afraid to sleep alone (night terrors are of course common among children), and was obsessed with thoughts of screech owls, which were said to peck at people's heads (to steal their souls, perhaps?). He also worried about the black cow that provided milk to a nearby hospital, because he was afraid it might swallow him whole. In the end Felix was allowed to sleep in Thomas's bed to put an end to his nocturnal frights.

Felix's earliest memory of a political or religious kind is precisely dated (and partially reconstructed from the testimony of others): it concerned his one and only meeting with Calvin in 1541. The Picardian theologian was on his way from Strasbourg to Geneva. In 1541 his path crossed that of Thomas Platter, who, with his boy in tow, was escorting his old friend Hans Rust to the new house Rust had just bought at Kalchmatt in Simmental. The three travelers from Basel met the future dictator of Geneva in Liestal (F 93). Thomas Platter and Calvin spoke at length (their conversation had to have been in Latin). They discussed the *Institutes of the*

*Christian Religion,* which Thomas had of course printed in 1536. Felix's account of the meeting is partially reconstructed from the later testimony of Rust and his father, but the young narrator also remembers having drunk several glasses of sugared or sweet wine served to him by Jacob Murer, the son of Liestal's innkeeper, in whose establishment the meeting took place. Jacob, who was a student in Basel, returned to the city with Felix and Thomas, while Rust continued on to his new home.

This episode from Felix's childhood is actually the culmination of a long digression involving Hans Rust. Using fragmentary personal memories fleshed out with family stories, Felix brings Rust's saga to life. Hans Rust was the son of a former abbot, Thüring Rust, who quit the monastery, became a Protestant pastor, and took a wife. His boy Hans later became a court clerk, alchemist, and poet. In the 1520s, when people around Bern were destroying "papist idols," he developed a technique that thrust him into the front ranks of iconoclasts. The religious idols that the reformers wished to destroy had of course been gilded and regilded many times over. Rust invented a special powder which, when burned, gave off fumes that could be used to remove the gold from statues slated for destruction. He was thus able to recover the precious metal without having to scrape each object by hand, as Protestant goldsmiths had been doing previously. Once scraped bare of all its gold, the pious object could be consigned to the flames.

Moreover, Rust, a master alchemist, kept his furnaces running full blast, transforming mercury into silver—or so the sometimes credulous Felix Platter believed.[3] The profits from this activity had supposedly made him a wealthy man, and, being wealthy, Rust lent to the poor in order to avoid the sin of avarice, which would have damned him otherwise. He even laid out a handsome sum to buy the buildings (*gebäulichkeiten*) of the old Trub monastery where his father had been abbot before taking off his habit (F 92). Certain forms of privilege carried over, apparently, from Catholicism to Protestantism; in any case, the abbatial infrastructure remained in the family. Hans Rust's marriage to Sara Rimlenen, a seamstress employed by the Platters, was quite a raucous occasion. Thomas's boarders, dressed as clowns, were such a riot that Myconius, the grave pastor who succeeded Œcolampadius as the Protestant spiritual leader of Basel, nearly peed in his pants. Rust had a number of children with biblical names like Sarah and Rebecca who threw snowballs with Felix, as well as a son Hermes, whose name recalled the divine magic of Antiquity. Rust also had two other sons, one of whom, a student in Paris, died young and penniless; the other, despite being a student in Catholic Bologna, was destined to become a Protestant pastor. Hans Rust was friendly with Martin Borrhaus, an associate of Thomas Platter's (F 92). An alchemist who also liked to travel,

Borrhaus claimed to be able to decompose compounds into simpler elements. Felix, the future physician, would remember what he had learned from Borrhaus when he later became interested in medicinal formulas while studying at the University of Montpellier.

*   *   *

Plague and death, meanwhile, continued their macabre dance. Plague struck in the middle of the annual Basel crossbow contest in 1541. Archers from the city and throughout the Confederation competed on Petersplatz.[4] They tried to hit moving targets shaped like men and painted black and white. Little Felix actually believed they were men (F 57). Masked revelers mingled with the fife-and-drum corps and flailed at young spectators with slapsticks, hurting some, including Felix, badly enough to send them to the hospital. In the middle of the competition, one well-known archer, Hans Knüttel, a member of the Saffron Guild, collapsed: he had been stricken with the plague and died a short while later. The crowd fled in panic, and the festival ended abruptly. Another victim of plague that year was Simon Grynaeus, the Hellenist and theologian in whose home Felix remembered having cavorted in his tunic when he was four or five years old. Platter's cousin Simon Steiner returned to Basel from Strasbourg, where he was teaching, for a brief visit. Felix recalled this visit as in a dream: it was among his earliest memories, he says. He paints a picture of Simon in lederhosen emerging from the washroom on the second floor of Zum Gejägd. Steiner, too, would die of plague a few years later, in 1545.

*   *   *

Felix felt a particular loathing for a washtub in the middle bedroom of Zum Gejägd. The bottom of the tub still showed traces of blood where a baby, the son of the previous owner or tenant, had fallen into it. The child had been left unattended in its cradle and had somehow toppled into the tub, whose cover had then fallen on the tiny victim. For several days it was feared that the child had been kidnapped, until his body was found lying on its stomach in the washtub. The child's nurse had been negligent (many Basel burghers, including the Platters, employed nannies). Felix never entered this "accursed" room without feeling a shiver down his spine.

*   *   *

As the elderly gentleman looked back in 1612 on the child he had been between 1540 and 1545, fear sometimes gave way to nostalgia. He remembered, for instance, the little green writing case that had been kept on a dresser seventy years before. As a child he had stood on tiptoe trying to reach it, but he was always told that he could not have it, despite his tears.

\*　　\*　　\*

Memories often ran together and were sometimes misdated. A "Welch" (that is, French- or Romansch-speaking) vintner by the name of Mumelin, who lived close to the Platter's house, a married man and a father, used a pickax to murder another neighbor who had mocked his mediocre German, his incomplete mastery of the local dialect—an incident of Renaissance racism. In punishment for this killing, Mumelin was beheaded. On another occasion, in 1549, a person named Vetterlin, who lived across the street from Zum Gejägd, committed a robbery. He, too, lost his head. Two capital crimes committed by two residents of Felix Platter's street make one wonder if the crime rate at the time was particularly high, or if beheadings were particularly common. The latter seems more likely, because houses in Basel were not always locked.

\*　　\*　　\*

Felix also remembered having been dandled on the knees of some of Switzerland's, and indeed Europe's, leading intellectuals and physicians. We have already encountered Professor Steiner of Strasbourg. In 1543 the boy met Vesalius, the great anatomist, whose assistant, Franz Jeckelmann, a surgeon, would fifteen years later become Felix's father-in-law. And then there was Hieronymus Gschmus, also known as Gemuseus, the son of an Alsatian merchant, who had roamed Switzerland, France, and the Piedmont in pursuit of an education before becoming a physician, professor, philosopher, naturalist, editor, and son-in-law of the renowned bookseller Cratander; his brother became the Protestant reformer of Mulhouse. In short, Gemuseus was a typical Renaissance man, whose obscurity today is undeserved (F 61).

\*　　\*　　\*

Felix often played with toys that Thomas's boarders bought for him at the town fair. He was particularly fond of a puppet swordsman that Heinrich Billing the bürgermeister's son and a close friend of Thomas's, had brought from Strasbourg. When Felix remembered pulling this puppet's strings, he was truly revisiting his early childhood, because Heinrich Billing died in 1541, before the boy's sixth birthday (F 62).

\* \* \*

This remembrance of the toy soldier leads here, as so often when military memories are evoked, to an image of paternal glory: Felix remembers Thomas as a robust man of forty, armed with a lance or halberd and buckled into his uniform. The printer-professor marched in step with other burghers of the municipal guard on holidays and in drills just outside the city walls. His friend Heinrich Petri, a master typographer, was also fond of sticking his chest out. Petri, the son of a Basel printer, had been a student in Luther's Germany. It will come as no surprise, then, that he was married to a widowed former nun. He later remarried, taking the widow of the bookbinder Hieronymus Frobenius as his second wife. He was thus a part of the group of printers and typographers that included Frobenius, Hervagius, and Episcopius—the very milieu in which Thomas Platter launched his brief career as a printer. By the 1540s, Thomas, having shed his crude highland ways, enjoyed the full confidence of his fellow citizens, as evidenced by his admission to the Bear Guild, of which he and Petri were both members. Recognized by all as an honest man, Platter was entrusted with the guild's silver, two basketfuls of which were kept in his home (T 62). (In English universities, whose colleges of fellows are the direct descendants of medieval communities, one can find similar corporate hoards of silver today.)

\* \* \*

Felix also has many detailed things to say about the plague, though his chronology is rarely precise. Many of his memories date from the fourth to ninth years of his life; some are later. At least two women in the neighborhood died of plague. One, whose last name was Wettenspiessen, died sometime between 1539 and 1542 (T 62). The other, Christelin von Ougstall, had married into a family of vintners on Freie Strasse and was the mother of a girl named Pascasia (from the Latin *pascha,* Passover, hence Easter) because she was born on Easter Sunday in 1542, shortly before her mother's tragic death.

In 1539, the first year of the great epidemic that cost little Margret Platter her life,[5] Thomas and Anna for obvious reasons sent Felix to live in a house some distance away with a printer named Görg, about whom little is known (F 62). Felix mingles personal memories with stories he heard from others. He was not frightened by the infection, he tells us, but was afraid of the sun. The sun's rays entered through a slit in the windowshade, revealing motes of dust in the air that made the little boy anxious. His elder sister Ursula, who shared his exile from home, apparently put ideas into his head: the two children imagined that the dust could turn into a monster that liked to snap off people's heads and eat them. Was it now that Felix first became interested in saws and planes for making wooden toys and even musical instruments such as lutes? Most likely memories of different periods ran together in Felix's mind; it seems doubtful that he learned woodworking in 1539, when he was only three or four years old.

In any case, the child who so disliked mythical monsters returned from Görg's as a budding carpenter with his miniature adze and plane. Though forbidden to do so by his father, Felix, three or four years old at the time, surreptitiously entered the front room of the house which contained the body of his sister Margret, who had died a few hours earlier. (Despite what some historians have argued, apparently not all children in this period were expected to acquire firsthand knowledge of the dead.) Pears were piled on a bench in the death chamber. Felix filched a few, then hid behind the oven and ate them: love of fruit was a constant of his childhood. Like many children, Felix believed that people could easily return from the dead: lift a piece of slate from the roof and his sister would fall from heaven into his arms. The same image would occur to him in a dream thirty-five years later, when he was thinking of "adopting" a baby.[6]

\*   \*   \*

At a very tender age Felix showed signs of an artistic sensibility; his father, as a poor mountain lad, had not had an opportunity to develop any of his artistic talents except for singing. Felix took an interest in the lute and the violin. He secretly liked to leaf through illuminated parchment prayerbooks, whose colorful pages were pleasing to the eye. Among them perhaps, was a Fouquet or a Bourdichon, destined for destruction by Thomas Platter, who used the vellum for bindings. Today, any antiquarian bookseller would be horrified at the thought that such masterpieces, any one of which would easily fetch millions at Christie's or Sotheby's, were so casually destroyed. Little Felix apparently had good taste, as did the princes and patrons who had commissioned the beautiful works that the boy's father recycled without a second thought.

Many plague deaths (including perhaps that of the Wettenspiessen woman and certainly that of Christelin von Ougstall) occurred in 1542, most likely in the summer. The following February, the young nobleman (*junker*) Gedeon von Ostheim rented a room in Thomas's house (F 64). The name Gedeon (or Gideon) comes from the Book of Judges: Gideon is the hero who smashes the altars of Baal and other idols despised by the ancient Hebrews (see Judges 6). Such a name identified him as a second-generation Protestant, born in the 1520s, when his parents were smashing idols and defying the papists. The scion of an Alsatian noble family that had distinguished itself in the wave of Helvetic iconoclasm in 1529, Gedeon later participated in the Reformation "reconstruction" of Basel: in 1566 he began building a town house for himself, a fine dwelling in which Prince Henri de Condé, a leader of the French Huguenots, stayed in 1575 while traveling between Strasbourg, Basel, and Bern in search of allies (F 64).[7]

Felix's contacts with Gedeon von Ostheim in 1543–44, when the young nobleman took his meals at Thomas Platter's table, were on a rather less lavish scale than Ostheim's relations with the Prince de Condé. Essentially all that Felix remembered was that his father's noble boarder had given him a velvet hood or cape (*sammat schlepplin*) that proved quite durable.

Felix received another gift in 1544 from Captain Georg Summermatter. As the name suggests, the captain was a relative of Thomas's mother, but their destinies could not have been more different. Amilli Summermatterin had slipped, through her own or her family's misfortune, into the ranks of the impoverished peasantry. Captain Georg, however, came from a more prosperous branch of this increasingly prominent family. He became first a notary and later a castellan-officer before rising to the rank of regional captain in the Valais (F 63). In April 1544 (after the plague epidemic had ended in Basel), the effects of war elsewhere in Europe began to make themselves felt: the conflict between Charles V and Francis I had resumed some years earlier. Captain Georg Summermatter was a Swiss officer, and Swiss troops were fighting in Italy with a French army under the command of a Bourbon, the Prince d'Enghien. At Ceresole Alba in the Piedmont, some 15,000 French troops, including 4,000 Swiss foot soldiers, clashed in a bloody battle with nearly 20,000 soldiers of the Empire, including 7,000 German lansquenets commanded by the Marquis del Vasto. The French victory cost Charles V 10,000 men killed or taken prisoner, against losses of only 2,000 dead on the "royal" side. The battle demonstrated the superiority of a force of infantry (especially Swiss infantry) equipped with harquebuses and pikes over cavalry. The victory at Ceresole enabled France to hold on to the Piedmont for another fifteen years (until 1559). The French held some of their Piedmont fortresses, such as Pinerolo, even longer, until the seventeenth century, when the Bourbons, successors of the Valois, finally gave them up—but then France's future did not really lie in Italy, not even northern Italy (if we exclude Savoy).

Of course Felix, at age nine, had no notion of such geopolitical considerations. He mostly remembered seeing the Swiss Confederates—
limping, ragtag veterans—marching up Bäumleingasse to the Cathedral
of Our Lady. The conquering troops' uniforms and banners were in tatters (*zerlumpet*). Among the soldiers was Captain Georg Summermatter,
Thomas Platter's kinsman and friend. Hence it was only natural that he
should give Felix a present of a doublet and a multicolored pair of trousers in the outdated fifteenth-century Roman or Florentine Renaissance
style—the fruit of his Italian campaign. Felix was quite proud of these
gifts. He wore them as long as he could, but he was a growing boy. Thus
the date 1544 stood out in Felix's mind as the year of the glorious homecoming of the veterans of Ceresole. It was also the year in which one of
the city's inner gates, the Aeschentor, was demolished. The bricks and
timbers from this structure, which formed part of Basel's wall, were re-
used in the construction of a new residence for a noble family.

⋏   ⋏   ⋏

From the colors of the clothing he wore as a boy Felix moved by analogy,
if not logic, to the changing color of his skin: epidemic, not to say epider-
mic, matters were once again on his mind. Felix came down first with
smallpox (certainly before 1544, when his father went out of the printing
business) and then with measles, two diseases that killed millions of
people at about this time: the natives of the Antilles and the Americas,
who were not immune to European "affections." In Felix's case, the diseases turned his skin many shades of red but did not kill him. When sick
he lay on a "couch" (*gutschen*) in the print shop (*stube*), a room that could
be heated in winter; apparently it was located toward the back of the Platter house. The typographers teased the sick little boy about his scarlet
complexion.

The child had a "sweet tooth," and people spoiled him by bringing him
sweets (*sieuss, siess, süss*), which apparently played an important part in the
dietary preferences of the middle and upper classes as early as the fifteenth
century. Sugar was imported from southern Spain, the Canary Islands,
and other islands off the coast of West Africa, but not yet from the Caribbean. Its production inevitably involved the use of black, or at any rate
dark-skinned, slaves to plant and cut cane. True to form, Felix also ate
fruit. While sick with either smallpox or measles, Felix was allowed as a
special favor to eat a superb pear brought to him by a noble lady, Magdalena Münch, the wife of Ludwig von Reischach. Reischach, a Protestant exiled for religious reasons, had been living in Basel for more than

fifteen years. He had been granted the rights of a burgher of the city in 1529, a turning point in the fortunes of "heresy" in Basel. He lived in a fine house on the cathedral square. As usual, Felix tries to impress us with his father's relations with eminent nobles while concealing his humble origins.[8] He mentions several times that Magdalena was a Valaisian: this was not true, but it allowed him to narrow the gap between the blue blood of this generous lady and the more rustic blood of his own forebears. But the child in him soon returns to the fore: like so many other children, Felix, at age eight, liked to be sick because it meant he would be pampered. "Would that you could stay sick for a long time," he told himself. "Then you could eat sweets." (When he talked to himself, he used the familiar form of the second-person pronoun: many people in southern France do the same thing today.)

Did smallpox and measles leave any traces? For a long time, when Felix worked outdoors, people noticed that his eyes were red and that he had red stripes on his nose (*rote strick über die nassen*). More serious were his urinary troubles, of which Felix, like Montaigne, does not spare us a single detail. When he urinated, he experienced a burning sensation. This was most often a problem in the afternoon. His acidic urine left a white trace, like the salt from seawater. Although there were privies on the second floor of Zum Gejägd, Felix urinated outside more often than not. His bladder frequently felt bloated, and as a result the child hopped from one foot to the other so often that he became embarrassed when people noticed. But with his travels in France, marriage, and quite simply the passage of time, his symptoms gradually disappeared. What had caused them? Much later, while in Speyer, he consulted Dr. Johannes Crato, a moderate Protestant who, after being educated in Lutheran Saxony and papist Italy, served as physician to two emperors: Ferdinand and Maximilian (F 65). Crato suspected kidney spasms, a diagnosis that thrust Felix into a depression that lasted all the way back to Basel. Although Felix no longer suffered from the problem, he continued to think about it, and it figured in the learned treatise on micturition that he published in 1614. Most likely young Felix had suffered from a urinary tract infection spread by dirty hands and linen.

\* \* \*

Thomas Platter's house was home to any number of boarders, who literally broke bread with Felix and other members of the family. Some of these boarders were the sons of nobles or other prominent individuals who went on to distinguished careers. One of them was Christoph

Efinger, the scion of a noble family and a man who would later father twelve children of his own (F 65). In 1552 his castle burned on the eve of his eldest son's birth. Thanks to primogeniture, his descendants remained major landowners in the canton of Aargau for three centuries. Another boarder was Ludwig von Diesbach, a scion of the Helvetic nobility who later sold his services as a soldier in Germany and France. He would enjoy the friendly patronage of the Duc d'Alençon and the Prince de Condé.

Then there were four brothers from the illustrious Truchsess von Rheinfelden family, which could trace its history in Basel back twelve generations. During the Renaissance, members of this family served Basel and other communities along the Rhine in various official and military capacities. One of the brothers, Jacob, a friendly practical joker, was especially close to Felix. To round out this survey, we should also mention Gedeon von Ostheim, whom we encountered earlier, and Ludwig von Schoenau, whose kinsmen held important episcopal and administrative posts. These students constituted the Platters' links to the aristocracy, of which they liked to boast (F 66). Felix above all prided himself on his frequentation of the "upper crust." These young nobles were more "suitable" than his previous companions, the crude and uncouth apprentice printers who were such a lively presence at Zum Gejägd until 1543 or 1544 and perhaps even longer.

*　*　*

Besides their democratic relations with typographers and their snobbish hobnobbing with bluebloods, Thomas and Felix also had dear friends of intermediate social status, among the (non-noble) patrician bourgeoisie. At Zum Gejägd, among Thomas's students, there were above all the brothers Paul and Johann-Ludwig Höchstetter, who belonged to a family of wealthy Augsburg merchants, dealers in "grains, fabrics, spices, and metals of all kinds" (F 66). The Höchstetters were ruined, however, by an economic crash that affected much of Europe in 1529, at which point the two boys bade farewell to the business world and made the familiar move into the more secure world of the professions (public or private): see Thomas Mann's *Buddenbrooks*. Paul took up law, while Johann Ludwig went into medicine. With Thomas, who, though well into his forties, still liked to amuse himself, the two boys liked to play *Spickspeck*, a game that involved throwing a knife at a board. The same trio—the "old" man and the two young boys—also shot at artificial birds on a pole with a small harquebus (or was it a miniature crossbow?): a game of "popinjay." The brothers also bet on who could knock the other off a table.

The room in which the two brothers played this rough game, as Felix looked on admiringly, also served as an aviary. One day, while fighting, the Höchstetters left the window open and allowed all the turtledoves to escape. Felix was wrongly accused of having opened the window and severely scolded (*übel gescholten*) by his father, but the truth came out later. Thomas, though a harsh and at times brutal father, was capable of acknowledging his mistakes. In any case, he was not the only person to try his hand at raising birds along with his other occupations: the printer Görg, with whom Felix had stayed during one plague outbreak, also kept birds in his house. But to get back to the Höchstetters, the episode in which they shot artificial birds with Felix's father must have taken place in 1548, given the date that they registered at the university and the periods during which they were students of Thomas's (F 66–67). Felix was then twelve or thirteen. Paul Höchstetter later embarked on a career in the judiciary, only to die of plague in 1563, before his fortieth birthday, in Thomas's house (F 66). Johann-Ludwig studied medicine at Montpellier with Felix, at which time the two became close friends. Having settled in Württemberg as a physician, Johann-Ludwig Höchstetter would drown himself in the Neckar three years after the death of his eldest son.

It is at this point in the memoirs, when Felix is twelve or thirteen, that he first mentions prayer—and shortly thereafter recounts a dream. Felix was a friend of another boarder in his father's house, a boy named Stelli (also spelled Stelle, Stölli, or Stellin—the spelling of proper names was not yet fixed). The boy was the nephew of the *junker* Captain Wolfgang Stelli of Solothurn, where he was a city official (*Obervogt*) in a family of officials (*Schultheiss*). He also owned a house in Basel known as Zum Samson. The two boys, Felix and Stelli, went almost every Sunday for breakfast prepared by Wolfgang Stelli's wife, née Salomé Baer (a "Berin," as people said—one of the Baer girls, in other words). She was the daughter of a hero of Marignano and of course young Stelli's aunt. A stubborn, authoritarian woman of breeding, she was not well liked by her neighbors. She became the butt of malicious laughter when she fell from a horse while crossing the Rhine bridge en route to her country estate and landed sprawling on the pavement with her skirts above her waist. Her foul temper frightened Stelli, who incurred her wrath frequently because he was often dirty—hygiene, as we have seen, was not the Platter household's strong suit. In the hope of warding off the usual scolding, Felix and Stelli prayed fervently on Sunday mornings before breakfast on wooden blocks set up in Saint Peter's square.

As for the dream, Felix dreamt that he had fallen asleep on a stone bench near Zum Samson where he often slept, and that he remained asleep there for years. Riders used this same bench as a convenient place to tie up their horses. (People in the past dreamt frequently of horses; in this motorized age we have lost touch with the connection between dreaming and horses, to which we owe the English word *nightmare*.) In later life Felix was able to decipher this dream easily. In 1574 he bought Captain Wolfgang Stelli's house, Zum Samson, and made it his home. Meanwhile, in 1565, having become one of Basel's leading physicians, he had treated the captain, whose wife had lost none of her irascible temper, for plague, from which he subsequently died, clearing the way for Felix to acquire his house ten years later. In his glory days, the captain had also been the owner of a noble estate not far from Basel in a place called Kliben or Klybeck. Salomé, who managed this estate along with her husband, invited Felix and Stelli to come work there during the harvest season. The boys expected to have a gay old time, but once the harvest was in, the mistress of the house sent them packing without so much as a crust of bread. Felix never again set foot in the inhospitable countryside. Had the aristocratic Salomé Stelli looked down on the young commoner whose father had been a beggar? Disagreeable as some of his encounters with the Stellis were, they were yet another link to the aristocracy and therefore invaluable as long as relations could be kept up. At their home Felix met another noblewoman, Catharina von Reinach, who was so tall that she had to bend down to pass through some of the house's doorways (F 68).

\* \* \*

The digging of a well at Zum Gejägd on Thomas's orders and before little Felix's amazed eyes provides an occasion with which to measure the differences in style and vision between father and son: Thomas is concrete, precise, and brief, whereas Felix often digresses to recall various details of his childhood. "At the time I had twenty boarders," writes Thomas in his characteristically concise style, "so that I was making a good deal of money." (The remark is worth noting: the boarders so improbably crowded together in the ramshackle house were crucial in allowing Thomas to amass enough of a fortune to suspend at least part of his activity in the risky printing business in 1544 and settle into the pedagogical branch of the more secure world of the gown). "I gradually paid off my debts. Immediately after buying the house [1541?], I dug a well.[9] Not counting the food for the workers, it cost me one hundred florins" (T 124). Thomas is just as succinct when he describes the construction of the second well (T 139), on his suburban property in Gundeldingen in the second half of 1549. "Shortly after buying the Hugwald estate in Gundeldingen, I began digging a well and then building, or rather rebuilding, the house, barn, and stable. I planted vines, I paid the workers, I bought three acres of pasture," and so on. Clearly the experience of the first well-drilling at Zum Gejägd served Thomas well in the second at Gundeldingen.

Felix, who revels in his memories and is more of a writer than Thomas, gives us a more detailed description of the scene. He was no more than eight and a half when the first well was dug at Zum Gejägd. Seven decades later, he recalled the extraction of sand from the hole, along with a few grains of silver and gold: he called the substance thus recovered *acrymoso*, embellishing it with a word taken perhaps from Pliny the Elder or Isidore of Seville (F 69). Felix fully depicts Thomas's understandable joy when his workers finally strike water: the elder Platter fills a fur cap with the fresh liquid and generously anoints his friend Lux Iselin, who came from a family of grocers and politicians.

Another scene connected with the well strikes a sadder note. It involved Gertrud (or perhaps Anna) Lachner, who had been the wife of two prominent members of the print trade, first the binder Hieronymus Frobenius and later Johannes Herwagen. Gertrud suffered from gout and was in the habit of treating the disease, as others treated gallstones, by drinking abundant quantities of water. She therefore had herself carried on a chair to the Platters' new well and eagerly drank the slightly carbonated water. The treatment proved ineffective, however: she died a few months later (F 69).

\*    \*    \*

Felix also remembered the mason Michael, whose job was to smoothe the inner wall of the well. While he was busy at this task, someone accidentally dropped a sizable stone down the well, grazing his head and shoulders. The workman was hauled up, and his wounds were dressed by the surgeon Franz Jeckelmann, Felix's future father-in-law. But the incident led to disaster: unable to work in the building trades after his accident, the handicapped former mason found work as a mounted courier. But his horse lost its footing on a narrow mountain trail and plunged, together with its rider, into a raging torrent. The man's body was never found. Divers later recovered his mail sack, still attached to the carcass of the horse, which had snagged on a rock.

According to Felix, the well also earned his father a certain amount of abuse from other burghers. One substantial citizen mocked the professor-printer for sinking a hundred gulden into an investment like a well rather than lending the money out at interest. With the interest rate at 5 percent, Thomas was forgoing an income of five gulden annually for the pleasure of drinking his own water. Thomas heatedly objected that he was no banker, that moneylending and usury were not for him. Felix's subsequent report of this virtuous indignation is all the more interesting in that a quarter of the substantial income he earned in his forty-four years as a physician in Basel came from interest on loans.[10]

Every year, Thomas organized a lavish dinner for his colleagues in the book trade, including Frobenius and many others. For some reason this was referred to as the "executioner's meal": perhaps the name had to do with some hazing ritual for apprentice typographers. Taken in by the name, the son of one of Platter's friends, a young man also named Thomas, went so far as to hide in an oven for fear that he would be hanged (F 70).

⅄   ⅄   ⅄

After the narrative reaches 1543 or 1544, Felix's chronological notations become considerably more precise. In the summer of 1543, he notes, an inn known as Zum Goldenen Kopf collapsed, killing several people. A little girl was retrieved from the wreckage safe and sound: a beam had protected her. The owners, a man and a woman, had the inn rebuilt, and it was back in business the following year as if nothing had happened (F 70).

*   *   *

Meanwhile, Felix's future—and even his future marriage—began to take shape. A sore toe and a toothache were the first signs. Jeckelmann treated him again, this time for an infected ingrown toenail. This probably took place before the fall of 1545, when Jeckelmann was still living in the Aeschenvorstadt district (F 70). He did not move to the more spacious house known as Zum Schöneck until October 1545. Slightly younger than Thomas, Jeckelmann, the son of a surgeon, was a member of the professional and municipal elite. He had at least five children, of whom three survived. One of them, a daughter named Madlen, would marry Felix in 1557, while the two sons, Franz and Daniel, became surgeons like their father. Daniel, while still young, tried his hand by pulling a tooth from Felix's upper jaw, an experience so traumatic that he refused to have a tooth pulled ever again. Was he immune to tooth decay despite his fondness for sugar? Daniel, who married fifteen years later, lost two children in the plagues of 1563 (F 70).

*   *   *

In 1543 or 1544 Felix took his first music lessons.[11] These suited his tastes and talents. His father sang, as we know. Felix, being the son of a prosperous man, learned to play an instrument. He was eight years old (*ich nur acht ieri wass* [F 71]) when Thomas paid for him to take lute lessons from Peter Dorn, a professional lutenist. Was this Peter perhaps a relative of the carpenter Ambrosius Dorn, whose shop, humming with saws and planes, adjoined the Platter house on the side of the Aeschentor? Or was he a son of the Flemish doctor Gerhard Dorn, a disciple of Paracelsus, who practiced medicine for a time in Frankfurt before coming to Basel (F 71)? There is no way to know for sure. In any case, Thomas hired Peter Dorn to teach Felix and other boarders at Zum Gejägd to play the lute. Together they formed a sort of musical circle, a hotbed of culture in which our budding music lover learned to play his first notes.

Felix's memoirs cast doubt on the standard view among musicologists that the lute was primarily a court instrument in the sixteenth century and did not gain popularity among the bourgeoisie until the seventeenth century, at which time it became common in salons as well as in theater and opera.[12] Clearly the instrument was already in widespread use among the middle and even lower-middle classes of Switzerland. The musicologists are right, however, when they say that in Basel and elsewhere the Protestant liturgy had a decisive influence on musical practice. But it was not the only influence. From early childhood, Felix was fond of hymns, but he also liked folksongs and mountain tunes. Unlike his father, Felix did not sing much, although he played a number of instruments. He was afraid that if he sang loudly he would show his teeth "to the back of his mouth." He would sing only when he was in a good mood or on horseback or accompanied by others in a choir. But he took great pleasure in listening to lute music during carnival or by moonlight after dinner, and he studied the instrument in depth under several teachers. He concluded his study in Montpellier, where other medical students called him *den Teutschen lutenisten,* the German lutenist (which proves that Occitan was not the only language in use in Montpellier, where many students chose to speak French). As an adolescent, Felix also played the lute for girls and at the inn for peasants; such evenings must have been reminiscent of a Brueghel painting. He also played at "concerts and banquets" (F 71). His lute cost him nearly two hundred crowns. In addition, he played other instruments such as the clavichord and possibly the spinet.

In Montpellier, Felix took harp lessons from a Dutch physician and anatomist and then from an Englishman whom he had cured of a bladder infection. When he died in 1614, Felix owned forty-two musical instruments (including seven violas da gamba), enough to equip an orchestra (F 73). As a child, he made and strummed all sorts of stringed instruments of his own design. Before 1541 (or was it 1544?) he liked to listen to his father's workmen playing the Jew's harp and dulcimer. A few years later, after the same typographers had benefited from the lute lessons of Peter Dorn, Felix delighted in their musical abilities. The traditional Swiss love of music runs in an unbroken line from Felix Platter to Frédéric Amiel.[13] Felix's musical memories from this period are more vivid than his memories of learning to read or write (the first book he mentions is not an ordinary printed book but a set of bound, illuminated parchments). What a difference from Thomas, for whom primers were precious objects, all the more so because in his life they were for so long forbidden fruit.

Felix's received instruction in the rudiments of Latin from a private teacher, Johannes von Schallen, a young man only a dozen or so years older than his pupil. The teacher was the bastard son of a notary-captain (in those days it was not uncommon for professionals to marry the pen and the sword). A former student of Thomas's, von Schallen went on to become a teacher in Platter's school, and it was then that he took it upon himself to teach the language of Cicero as well as the lute to Felix and Ursula.

*   *   *

It was also in 1543 or 1544 that Felix became aware of political and military matters extending beyond his local community. The battle of Ceresola Alba (1544), which he experienced intensely if at a distance, was a key factor in the child's politicization and acculturation. Meanwhile, in 1543, Vesalius, whom Felix had met, published his *Seven Books on the Structure of the Human Body*. To be sure, the great anatomist resorted to some unusual methods to obtain his cadavers, some of which were snatched from the gallows, others from their graves. As a medical student in Montpellier, Felix hastened to imitate the master's techniques: he frequently dug up newly buried bodies for use in his study of anatomy. Thomas Platter was a reader of Vesalius, and so was his son. Thomas was also Calvin's printer. In Geneva, some distance from Basel, the French reformer had inaugurated a theocratic government—or should we call it theodemocratic? In 1549 he reached an agreement with the Zwinglians of northern Switzerland about the theology of the Last Supper and the meaning of the Eucharist. In nearby France, which the two Platter sons would visit forty years apart (although their father would never set foot in the country), Francis I had resumed his war against Charles V in 1542, in alliance with the Turks and against the Anglicans of Henry VIII. The situation was perhaps less confused than it might appear, however. Along with this geopolitical maneuvering, the second "wave" of antiheretical repression is also notable for the massacre of the nonconformists of the Vaud and the execution of Etienne Dolet, the Huguenot and perhaps freethinker (1546).

Meanwhile, the workingman's standard of living fell as both prices and population increased. The French language made inroads among officialdom and the elite but failed to win the allegiance of the masses. The Protestant Clément Marot translated the psalms into French. The age of cathedrals was not yet over, as the continuing construction work on the steeple of Beauvais indicates. But the age of palaces had already begun: these new edifices symbolized the monarchy's assertion of sovereignty, although at this stage the monarchy was still relatively modest compared with what it became later in the age of absolutism. Construction and renovation were under way at the Louvre of Francis I; Henri II would continue what his predecessor began.

Felix, though an antipapist like his father, was more moderate on religious matters than Thomas. Had his travels taken him as far as Rome, however, he would have found numerous justifications for his congenital anticlericalism. Pope Paul III was in the process of reviving the Inquisition, the future Holy Office. His Holiness also approved—and who can blame him?—the creation of the Company of Jesus, that training ground for the Catholic teachers of the future. And last but not least, the pontiff convoked the Council of Trent. It was a time of feverish activity despite nascent or renascent manifestations of heresy and still fresh memories of papal revels from the time when the Borgias were in the Vatican. In a single year, 1541, Ignatius Loyola became leader of the Jesuits, Calvin settled in Geneva, and John Knox launched the Scottish Reformation. In Britain the antipapist offensive continued: the theological aims of the monarchy were modest, but in the economic sphere the government was resolute (it confiscated monastic property), and it was no less determined to have its way in the realm of liturgy and language (prayers were Anglicized). Out of these reforms came the "Anglican" Church, a narrowly nationalistic institution that also proved to be a useful tool in the hands of a monarch with hegemonic designs. Later, however, it would also demonstrate its capacity to shelter or tolerate new dissident tendencies. The anti-Roman offensive was also, to varying degrees, a confrontation between the central power of London and the Celtic or semi-Celtic peripheries (Ireland, Wales, Scotland). A certain papism often persisted in these regions—a papism that was also a reaction against English conquest. Henry VIII enjoyed moderate success in extending his authority to Ireland in 1541–42. English control of Scotland was far from assured despite frequent military forays. The Scots wavered between an old-line Catholic militancy and a new Protestant radicalism inspired by the preaching of John Knox and his notion of justification by faith. Would the Anglican Church be routed on its right (by pro-Roman, pro-French forces) or on its left (that is, before long, by Puritans and even Calvinists)? To ask the question is to answer it: Scotland, allying itself with England, chose the second path.

Henry VIII's goal was to build an insular monarchy. His forays on the Continent were risible: in 1544, the king of England, in alliance with Charles V, seized Boulogne—a precarious triumph that led nowhere. A more intelligent move was the decision to develop the navy, which Henry VIII took in 1545–46. Britain's future lay on the high seas, and it was a future that augured well in view of the country's already considerable demographic, cultural, and economic growth. Henry's bizarre behavior as an elderly, paranoid tyrant, when he imprisoned and executed former wives and allies, changes the picture only slightly. After his death, a brief resurgence of Catholicism under Edward and Bloody Mary soon subsided, leaving the Anglican Church dominant. Great Britain was thus able to develop peacefully on its own, on the fringes of a Europe often torn apart by warring dogmas and armies.

Thomas and his family, indifferent to these insular British concerns, saw themselves as "Alemannic," hence Teutonic and Continental. Charles V, the head of the Germanic Holy Roman Empire, is barely mentioned in the early memories of either Thomas or Felix. Still, it is convenient to use the emperor as a touchstone for discussing the fate of the German territories, among which confederated Switzerland, though not strictly speaking a part of the Empire, is always included.

The period 1542–44 was a turning point in the history of the imperial lands. After the failure of knights and peasants to enforce their claims, the period from 1525 to 1542 was the "age of princes," dominated by the landgrave Philip of Hesse and Prince Johann Friedrich of Saxony.[14] In 1542, the religious map of a Germany made powerful by its population, its precious and nonprecious metals, and its great merchants was already clear: the Prussian east was all Luther's, as were the center (Hesse, Thuringia, and Saxony) and the Hanseatic and lower-Saxon north, to which must be added the duchy of Brunswick-Wolfenbüttel, "evangelical" after 1542.[15] By contrast, the regions south of the Main and close to the Rhine had traditional ties to the emperor.[16] They have remained, broadly speaking, Catholic to this day. The religious choices made by the princes followed the old Roman *limes*.[17]

But the religious choices of the people were different, for the Reformation had flourished on both sides of the old frontier inherited from the Roman legions. The year 1543 marked the beginning of what Michael Stürmer and his collaborators call the "decade of the Emperor" (*das Jahrzehnt des Kaisers*). That decade began with two victories by Charles V. The first, over Wilhelm von Jülich, extended Hapsburg influence into the Netherlands, thus keeping "heresy" out of the lower Rhine region. Then, after the Treaty of Crépy (of 1544, in which Charles gave up his claims to the duchy of Burgundy, in return for which France ceded, along with other territories, Flanders and Artois to the Empire), Charles scored a major personal victory at Mühlberg, defeating the Protestant armies under Johann Friedrich of Saxony (1547). The landgrave of Hesse and the prince of Saxony were both prisoners of the emperor, who was further blessed by the death of his old enemy Francis I in 1547.

It would be a mistake, however, to exaggerate the consequences of the imperial decade. The Protestant princes had been humilated but were not permanently defeated. Furthermore, the Treaty of Augsburg (1555) consecrated the principle of *cujus regio, ejus religio:* "Tell me which prince or sovereign you are the subject of, and I will tell you which religion, Catholic or Protestant, you are firmly admonished to profess." The Treaty of Augsburg established a geographical equilibrium and more or less peaceful coexistence between the German Catholics of the west and south and the Protestants of the north and east. It fixed the balance of power between the territorial princes, who were much more powerful on German soil than in France or England, and the emperor, whose influence was limited but in principle unchallenged. All this took place through the mediation of the Reichstag: although its recruitment was narrow, this assembly was nevertheless one of the matrices from which today's parliamentarism emerged (though to a lesser extent, to be sure, than in Britain's House of Commons). This is not the place for subtle distinctions: however one sees the matter, the imperial star shone more brightly in 1543 than it had for a generation, and it would continue to shine for the next ten years, spanning roughly the middle of the sixteenth century.

To this point in his narrative, Felix (like Thomas) has said little about the great emperor in the first twenty-five years of his reign. Will he be more expansive about the remainder of Charles's imperial tenure, from 1543 until his abdication in 1556? For obvious reasons, the Platters have even less to tell us about the emperor's great enemy, the Turks, who were now close to the height of their power and whose sailors, allied with the French, were harassing the Mediterranean coast from Catalonia to Nice. The only sign of them thus far in Felix's text is the mention of his neighbor's having painted the head of a Moor on the wall of his house. Felix was also completely in the dark concerning another part of the Hapsburg domain (later to be known as Austria-Hungary), which in 1543 was also under attack by the ubiquitous Turks. Neither Thomas nor Felix knew anything about what was happening in Russia, which for the time being, until Ivan the Terrible regained sovereignty after his coronation in 1547, was subject to the anarchic rule of the boyars. The two Platters knew even less about China, about whose internal politics few Westerners had any inkling. Yet dramatic events were taking place there: in November 1542, several palace women attempted (unsuccessfully) to strangle Emperor Chia Ching, a startling crime that left its victim traumatized. In the following year, 1543, Mongolian cavalrymen launched raids into Shansi, with detrimental effects on trade and on an economy already suffering in the northern provinces from the effects of drought and famine.

Despite such setbacks, conditions in the Celestial Empire, as in Europe, were conducive to increases in agricultural output, textile production, and other craft and manufacturing activities.[18] Whether the Platters were aware of it or not, they were in indirect communication with the southern and eastern coasts of Asia via Portuguese vessels that had been transporting cargoes of oriental spices to Europe for decades. Thomas and Felix knew little about these expeditions, but thanks to their many friends among Basel grocers they were familiar with the taste of pepper. Over the past half-century ships from Lisbon had established a chain of ports and military and commercial bases along the coasts of India (Diu, Goa), Ceylon, Burma, and Indonesia, with Japan at the end of the line. In 1542, even as Felix was beginning to open his eyes to the wider world, a certain Francis Xavier was beginning missionary work in Goa, which had been in Portuguese hands since 1510. Meanwhile, a shipwreck led to the first Portuguese contact with southern Japan, and Portuguese businessmen then pursued this opening systematically from 1542 on. They introduced the Japanese to European goods and firearms and later to Catholic doctrine, which the same Francis Xavier preached in Japan after 1549. Across the Pacific, the Spanish had by now conquered Mexico and Peru and were pressing inland along the great rivers of North and South America, the Amazon and the Mississippi. Moving northward along the coast of California, they reached the places known today as San Diego and San Francisco and pushed as far north as Oregon.

The Spanish colonizers also explored Florida, the Mayan lands, Bogota, and Chile. On the microbial level the world was unified: smallpox, accompanied by other pandemics, wreaked havoc on Mexican plateaus. The Amerindians, who received no quarter from either microbes or con-querors, found a defender in Bartolomé de Las Casas, who, after de-nouncing the "destruction of the Indies" in 1540, was named bishop of Chiapas in 1544. In the meantime, and closer to home, in Poland (which Thomas had already visited), Copernicus published *De revolutionibus or-bium coelestium,* which dethroned the Earth, and man along with it, from their position at the center of the universe.

\* \* \*

Felix's reminiscences naturally fail to mention any of the major ideologi-cal and political "discontinuities" that emerged in 1543–44. If he was aware of the non-European world at all, it was chiefly through the "colo-nial" or tropical taste of sugar, which figures in an episode involving the boy's teacher, Scalerus (Johannes von Schallen [F 71]). Scalerus was es-sentially Felix's tutor. In addition, from 1538 to 1551 he was associated with the school of Thomas Platter, first as a boarding student and later as an assistant teacher. The episode I am about to recount probably occurred well after 1543: at the time in question, Felix owned books and had his own pocket money. Like most children, he also liked fruit. He was partic-ularly fond of exotic fruits, such as Corinthian grapes and figs, which his father's prosperity placed within his reach, to say nothing of juniper and other preserves that his mother made. Preserves were in any case one of the great passions of the sixteenth century.[19] It only stands to reason that little Felix was also fond of sugar and sweets. Since the sugar plantations of the New World (the Caribbean and Brazil) were barely established, most cane was still grown on the Canary Islands, Madeira, or Cape Verde.

Such geographic details were of little interest to Felix, who neverthe-less spent every penny he had on sweets. He became so dependent on the sugary drug,[20] in fact, that he fell victim to the blackmail scheme of a classmate, Amandus Langbaum, the son of a Basel bureaucrat (an official in the grain office), who went on to study medicine (F 74). Langbaum threatened to reveal the extravagance of Felix's craving for sugar to his father unless Felix turned over certain printed books from his personal collection. Scalerus settled the matter by persuading Felix to confess his peccadilloes to his father. The assistant teacher thus kept peace in the household.

Once, after consuming an overdose of sugar, Felix fell deathly ill in the bed he shared at night with his father. Thomas, who had no idea what was happening, became alarmed. Sometimes Felix ate candied fruits and bonbons colored with lead oxide, copper sulfate, and other chemicals, which probably killed other children with less robust constitutions.

\*   \*   \*

Writing later of his time in Montpellier, Felix frequently speaks of drunken German students who passed out, snored, pissed in their pants, and sprawled over kegs whose contents they imbibed straight from the tap. Felix, for his part, preferred sugar to alcohol. As a young man, he got drunk once or twice. His head spinning, he collapsed onto his bed and "puked his guts out." But such incidents were rare. In Languedoc Felix did not even count a wine flagon among his personal possessions (F 75). When he drank water tinged with wine (*drüncklin*), he sipped directly from a pitcher that his mother had given him.

\*   \*   \*

Sugar, wine, girls. One winter, Felix decided to build a snowman or snow fort in his father's yard. The two daughters of Thomas's friend Hans Rust, girls who bore the fine biblical names Sarah and Rebecca, made fun of his work from a turreted tower behind the house. Annoyed, Felix tried to run up the stairs to where they were but slipped on an icy step. Two of his teeth tore through his lip, resulting in a permanent scar. Incidentally, the father of the girls, and of many other children besides, was a poet, speculator in church property, and alchemist who made silver out of mercury (F 92). Another time, when he was fifteen, Felix injured himself in the thigh with a sharp instrument while visiting Rötteln in the Black Forest, where he had taken refuge from a plague epidemic in 1551 (F 75–76).

\*   \*   \*

Three years earlier, Felix may have had a crush on his cousin Margret Madlen Erbsin, a pretty girl from Strasbourg who was one of Thomas's boarders. This Madlenlin was the niece of Margret Erbsin, a widow, who, through another niece, introduced Basel to the beautiful yellow Strasbourg dresses that were a Lutheran symbol of sorts. Thomas and the widow Erbsin had secretly arranged a marriage between the two children, who soon suspected that something was up.

Felix's friends, who somehow found out about this premature romance, gave him a hard time about it. He was fond of the girl and liked to wheel her about in a cart. After returning home to Strasbourg, however, she died of the plague. Another wife would have to be found, and as it happens her name also turned out to be Madlen.

"Engaged" or not, Felix soon discovered a fondness for the caresses of beautiful women. While still very young, he allowed himself to be fondled by an attractive maid from Solothurn who worked for a time as a servant in his father's household. But he rejected the advances of his mother's lame elder sister, for whom Anna Dietschi-Platter had no use. The woman later disappeared without a trace, to no one's great regret. Family ties in these old Swiss clans were not always as important as some historians claim. In any case, the old hag, whom Anna always greeted with the words "Come in, by the devil,"[21] had predicted a brilliant future for the boy: "Felix, you will be an important person." Both father and son thus enjoyed rosy forecasts for their futures.

*   *   *

Optimism was vital for instilling confidence, but children were still treated harshly: punishment, maternal as well as paternal, was an integral part of childrearing. Felix mentions an extreme case: the printer Henri Aliot, who came from a family of Welch Anabaptists from Moûtiers, France, beat his young son, who then ran to the attic and hanged himself (F 79). Originally Felix concealed the name Aliot (suicide was dishonorable), but he later wrote it in the margin of his *Tagebuch*.

Felix's scolding by his mother had less dire consequences. One fall day, Thomas gave his son a quarter of a gulden to buy a dagger he had been eyeing for some time. Impatient, the boy hastened to the market and wound up buying all sorts of things in addition to the knife: dolls, toys, what have you. When he ran into his mother on his way home, she took him to task right then and there, after which she returned to the market and let the merchants who had taken advantage of her son have a piece of her mind before demanding her money back. Back home, the boarders, as usual playing the role of a Greek chorus, made fun of the boy. Thomas and his cousin (Aunt Margret) found the story quite amusing and managed to cool everyone's tempers (F 78). On another occasion, which must have been before Felix's eighth birthday because he was wearing a red tunic at the time, his mother slapped him for losing a small coin she had given him. He had tucked the money into his tunic and it had somehow disappeared. "You should have been paying more attention" was the philosphical advice he received from Chrischona Jeckelmann (the surgeon's wife), who did not yet know that she would become his mother-in-law *in partibus.*[22] In any case it is worth noting that Anna's outbursts against both her husband and her son chiefly concerned issues of money. The Platter household was heavily in debt.

* * *

His father's anger was a more serious matter, and Felix took it more deeply to heart even when the occasion was trivial. We are reminded of Henri IV whipping the future Louis XIII, or ordering him to be whipped, "for his own good."[23] Felix was punished by his father on at least three occasions. The first time was because he had thrown rocks onto the roof of the carpenter Philip, whose shop was located next to the Gymnasium, resulting in several broken tiles. Another time he was beaten for using chalk to deface the partition between two classrooms in his father's school. In both cases the malefactor was turned in by a class-mate, the snitch Langbaum, whom we encountered earlier in the role of blackmailer (F 80). In punishing these schoolboy pranks, Thomas was acting as both father and schoolmaster. Mama administered slaps at home; papa administered whippings at school. But the worst was yet to come. The date of the third episode is difficult to pin down: Felix, ad-vanced for his age, was already in his last year at his father's school. He may have been twelve at the time, in which case the incident would have occurred in 1548. In the middle of a Greek class, Thomas, standing at the podium, became incensed that his son knew nothing about the *alpha purum,* that is, the fact that in the Attic dialect one said *chora* instead of *chore* as in Ionian Greek. Such subtleties were beyond the boy, and Thomas felt called upon to beat the lesson into him. Although he aimed to hit Felix's back, his switch caught the boy's face, almost taking out an eye. Felix was left with a puffy, swollen face, which caused his mother to become incensed in turn at her husband's brutal conduct.

Thomas, overcome with remorse, never beat his son again. Until then he had not hesitated to whip or kick the child. Chastened by the event, however, Felix's father now gave in to his kindly natural bent. Was it com-mon for fathers to put away the whip when a son reached the age of twelve or thirteen? In any case, the headmaster of the Burgschule always treated Felix well when he was sick: the boy was his only son, after all. And after Felix went off to medical school in Montpellier, his father's let-ters revealed numerous signs of paternal affection (F 81).

Before that, his father had expressed his affection by buying the boy nice clothes. If children of relatively modest background often dress bet-ter today than do children of more prosperous parents, the same was true

in the sixteenth century. Thomas never forgot the rags he had worn as a
child and how they had stuck to his mangy skin. He therefore commissioned the tailor Wolf Eblinger, or Master Wolf, to make a tunic for Felix
in the medieval style, half in one color, half in another (F 81). When the
boy was a little older, Thomas had the same tailor make him two pairs of
breeches, one white, the other yellow. The boy paced back and forth in
the new marketplace, impatient for the tailor to arrive for his scheduled
fitting. This scene had to have taken place before March 1550, by which
time Eblinger was already dead. The new clothes evidently left an impression on young Felix, who in later life, whether studying in Montpellier or
traveling in the Valais, always liked to dress well. Indeed, he was so much
the elegant dresser that he was unpleasant if not downright hostile to his
distant highland cousins, who were hardly in a position to vie with him in
matters of luxurious attire.

A good father loved well and punished well; he dressed his children
appropriately; and he did what he could to provide them with a sound
religious education. Among the various paragraphs in Felix's memoirs
that begin with the words *mein vater,* symbolizing Felix's strong family
ties, those that deal with his father's role as a preacher could not be more
eloquent. In a time before Sunday services were customary in Protestant
churches, Thomas, the erstwhile itinerant beggar, read the Bible at home
and preached a sermon to his wife and children (F 79). This practice was
common to Lutherans and Zwinglians and soon to Calvinists as well.
Huguenot farmers were also great Bible readers.[24] Thomas's sermons
hinged on three main themes. First, the hardening of Pharaoh's heart: the
Egyptian ruler refused to allow the Jews to leave Egypt, and Jehovah was
obliged to visit the valley of the Nile with no fewer than ten plagues before the sovereign of the pyramids could be persuaded, temporarily, to
relent. The second theme was that of grace, or the absence of grace: for it
was God himself who had hardened the heart of a Pharaoh who was thus
excluded from the company of the elect. One is reminded of Racine's
hymn:

> Divin Sauveur, jette sur nous les yeux!
> Répands sur nous le feu de Ta grâce puissante.

> (Divine Savior, cast your eyes on us! Visit us with the fire of
>    Thy powerful grace.)

The third and final theme of the Platter sermons was really a set of
themes, a method of biblical interpretation based on types and antitypes:
the oppression of the Israelites, for instance, was the ancient type, or prefiguration, of the persecution of the Protestants in the Netherlands in the

early sixteenth century.[25] Felix indignantly notes that a number of girls were sent to the stake there on orders of Charles V (F 79). Such thoughts tell us a great deal about the spiritual evolution of the Platter family. Thomas, as we saw earlier, had been an iconoclast in his youth: he once burned a statue of Saint John, one act in the devastating wave of iconoclasm that engulfed parts of Switzerland and Germany and put an end to the great religious sculpture of the late fifteenth century.[26] Later, Thomas moderated these radical views, but he remained as pious as he had been, first in his clerical and Catholic childhood and subsequently in his Zwinglian Protestant youth. Felix, looking back on his long life, has vivid memories of his father's preaching. In retrospect, however, he sees himself as having been much more devout when he dressed in yellow trousers in the 1540s than he was later as a student in Montpellier or as a successful doctor caught up in a busy career. As a medical student in Languedoc, Felix seems to have been largely unmoved by the persecution of the "Lutherans" of Montpellier, or at any rate much less moved than he had been as a child by the story of the little girls consigned to the flames in the Netherlands—a story spread far and wide by Protestant propaganda at the time. Yet Felix would remain a Protestant.

\*   \*   \*

A lively, imaginative boy fond of amusements in which his family allowed him to indulge in the evening, Felix took advantage of the whole range of activities that urban culture made available to children of the middle class. When his father had been a poor country lad, he had played with hobby horses and pretended to irrigate miniature fields; a little later he had moved on to simple games involving red tiles and flocks of geese. Felix, a city boy from a prosperous family, had heard of the sea; he actually saw it for the first time at Palavas during the time he was studying medicine at Montpellier. He was already dreaming of ocean voyages long before that, however, and sailing wooden boats in the family well. His chief passion was the theater, and there was ample opportunity to indulge it in Basel. In this respect, Montpellier, though a large city, lagged behind. Felix was not impressed by the theater when he was there in 1555: executions of criminals were more entertaining. It was not until later in the century that his younger brother Thomas was able to attend decent productions of plays in the capital of Languedoc. Felix was already enjoying plays at home as early as 1546, however, and in Basel admission was free: was the Swiss city particularly advanced, or was the Languedoc metropolis particularly retarded?

The first precise date that Felix gives for a theatrical production in

Basel was May 23, 1546: he was nine and a half at the time. From his tailor's house he watched a performance of "Chaste Susanna" at the fish market (F 83). This biblical play features the misadventures of a pretty woman surprised in her bath by two randy old men ("elders" of the community). When they falsely accuse her of adultery with a young man, she is saved by the skillful arguments of a child, who grows up to be the prophet Daniel. The themes of the play, with its allusion to the Old Testament prophet, reflect some of the favorite themes of the Swiss Reformation: chastity, prophecy, reverence for the Bible, and so on. The play, now forgotten, was the work of one Sixtus Birk, or Sixtus Betulejus in Latin. A Basel schoolmaster and native of Swabia, Birk published the play (well before it was performed) in two successive editions, one of them in Latin, in the 1530s. The performance that Felix witnessed in 1546 was the work of a group of young actors. The director was a student in his twenties, Ulrich Koch, also known as Coccius and Essig, a native of Freiburg, who went on to a successful career as a teacher (F 83). He became a professor first of Greek, then of dialectics, and finally of theology (his talents as an impresario took him from the theater to the lectern). By his fortieth birthday he had also become a minister. For the role of Susanna, Koch chose his fiancée, Margret Merian, who was the same age as he and the thirteenth child of a sailor from Basel. According to the customs of the Renaissance, Margret should have played the role in the nude, but the Reformation did not tolerate such licentiousness. Ulrich therefore had his actress appear in a red costume in a zinc tub filled with water from the fish market fountain: since the performance took place in May, the weather was not so cold as to make this staging unbearable. The role of Daniel was played by a young boy (*bieblin*) not much older than Felix: Ludwig Ringler, aged eleven. He later became a glass-painter and sheriff of Lugano. The players were thus drawn from Basel's elite, or at any rate its middle class.

\* \* \*

Two weeks later, on June 6, 1546, another play captivated Felix: "The Conversion of Saint Paul" was performed at the grain market on a bright, sunny day. The city spared no effort, erecting wooden barriers around the space set aside for the players. The play is the story of Paul on the "road to Damascus," where Christ appears in a radiant vision to the young man of twenty-five, who is instantly converted from persecutor to apostle. The Alsatian Valentin Boltz, who had been a pastor in Württemberg and Basel, wrote and directed the work. Paul was played by Bonaventura von Brunn, aged twenty-six, a merchant who later became mayor of Basel. The glass-painter Balthasar Han, a militant corporatist not quite forty years old, played Hergoth, a character embodying, as Felix recounts it, both the Father and the Son of the Trinity. Finally, Captain Hans Rudolf Fry (or Frey), a robust man in his forties and a prominent member of the local elite, commanded a hundred burghers in colorful uniforms who, along with their standard-bearers, formed the saint's escort. Hergoth sat ensconced in "heaven," a round platform erected above the stage; thunder was simulated with stone-filled barrels. A flaming rocket launched from this firmament represented the apparition of the Savior. Unfortunately, the missile set fire to Paul's trousers, but the saint nevertheless managed to fall from his horse in panic at the miraculous sight. (One wonders if the mishap was in fact written into the script.) In any case, Felix took in every bit of the action from his perch at the home of his friend Hans Irmy, the eight-year-old son of a cloth merchant, who later went into the cloth business himself (F 82). Although a sudden downpour marred the end of the spectacle, good weather returned the next day, and the actors were treated to a joyous parade through the city. The occasion thus combined piety (Paul, the theologian of grace and faith, was one of the "patron saints" of the Reformation), urban military display, and pure burlesque typical of the late medieval and Renaissance theater.

"The Resurrection of Christ," performed at the *gymnasium* of the university, offered a similar mix of piety and clownishness (F 81). This play may have been written in Latin by Georgius von Langenfeldt, also known as Macropedius, a playwright and humanist born in the Netherlands in 1475. "The Resurrection" was one of a cycle of tragedies frequently performed in secondary schools in Switzerland and elsewhere. (Later, in the seventeenth and eighteenth centuries, the Jesuits would develop a Catholic version of the genre.) Young Heinrich Ryhiner, the twenty-year-old son of a municipal court clerk, played the Virgin Mary (it was not uncommon at the time for males to play female roles). Born in 1527, Ryhiner became a doctor after studying in Basel, Paris, Montpellier, and Avignon. In the end he converted to Catholicism and moved to Auvergne, where he was killed in 1584 while serving in the French army. For Felix, Ryhiner's indebtedness and papist marriage made him a model to avoid rather than imitate (F 128). Thomas's boarders also participated in the production, performing diabolical pranks and dances that may or may not have been part of the script: demons were an important part of these "mystery plays." Among the infernal pranksters was Jacob Truchsess von Rheinfelden, another childhood friend of Felix's, who, after a bibulous interlude as a courtier of the Comte de Montbéliard, was cured of alcoholism by his old friend, who by this time was a doctor well on his way to making his mark (F 93, 291).

*　　*　　*

"The Conversion of Saint Paul" was a favorite among mystery plays, for dramatic conversions were after all a part of contemporary history: the conversion of Basel in 1529 was in a sense a colorful "remake" of the conversion of Paul. Hence the old chestnut was periodically revived. Felix's friends put on an amateur performance at the home of the Langbaums, whose son Amandus the tattle-tale was Felix's friend and sometime enemy. Also participating were Lucas Just, aged twelve, who later served as a pastor in a number of parishes, including some in Basel, and Simon Colross, the valiant son of a poet and teacher, who died of the plague in 1552 at the age of sixteen or seventeen. He passed away in the home of yet another teacher and writer, Konrad Wolfhardt (Lycosthenes). Clearly, teachers and their children formed a distinctive social group, united in death as well as life. The Langbaum home, which Felix's youthful troupe used as a theater, would continue to play an important spiritual and cultural role in young Platter's life. In 1597 it became the home of Jacques Covet-Courtois, the deacon of the French Huguenot community in Basel.[27] (Both of Thomas Platter's sons were drawn to the French language.)

The young actors also attempted to stage another play at the Langbaums', but without much success: "The Ten Ages of Man" drew on a familiar theme of European culture (reflected in places as diverse as the friezes of the palace of Versailles, the popular images that appeared in the nineteenth century on mass-produced cards from Epinal, and the painting of the American Thomas Cole). All in all, however, "The Conversion of Saint Paul" seems to have been the favorite play of Basel audiences, to judge by the fifteen or so theatrical events that Felix mentions in his memoirs. The official staging of the play in June 1546, with its hundreds of volunteer extras,[28] apparently made quite an impression on the city's youth. Felix and his friend Roll, another of Thomas's boarders, decided to stage the play themselves in the courtyard of Zum Gejägd. Young Platter, tapped for the role of Hergoth, climbed up to the chicken roost with a log he intended to use as a thunderbolt (there seems to have been some confusion between Jehovah and Jupiter). Meanwhile, Roll, playing Paul on the road to Damascus, straddled a hoe representing the saint's horse. As the apostle passed beneath Felix's roost, Felix let go of the log, which hit Roll in the eye, drawing blood. The victim protested: "I'm a poor boy abandoned by my family, or you would never treat me so badly. You'll pay for this some day." Or words to that effect.

In fact, Roll's situation was more complex than his lament suggested. As a boarding student in Basel, he was indeed far from home, but he came from a noble (if impecunious) family. His full name was Gavin de Beaufort, Baron de Rolles, and his home on the shores of Lake Leman lay in French-speaking territory. His father, Count Amédée de Beaufort, was a war veteran who did his talking with gunpowder (F 85). Over the years, and notwithstanding young Gavin's complaints at the time of the incident with the log, a genuine affection developed between the boy known as "Roll" and the Platters. He was in fact the only boarder that Thomas kept with him when plague struck in 1551. For safety's sake all the other students were sent home, but Roll stayed on because he had no one to take care of him (*vil sich seinen nieman annam* [F 115]). Thomas even considered "adopting" Roll, and it would have been quite something if the scion of a noble family had become the "son" of a former beggar. Despite his family's neglect, Roll went on to a respectable career. Noble though he was, he became a burgher of Basel (there was no contradiction between the two conditions: the eminently proud Duke de Saint-Simon did not shrink from identifying himself at times as a *bourgeois de Paris*). In 1573 Roll married the daughter of a law professor, Gertrud Brand of Basel. It was not uncommon for the daughters of professionals to marry "above their station," taking husbands in the military nobility (the technical term for this is *hypergamy*).[29] The baron from Basel and Leman never renounced either his noble or his bourgeois status: he served as a French-Swiss nobleman on the Savoy state council while continuing to own a large house in Basel, of which he remained a citizen. Through him, the relatively low-born (though privileged) Felix made early contact with the nobility of Switzerland and Savoy.

Apart from "The Conversion of Saint Paul" (mentioned three times) and "The Resurrection" (mentioned twice), several other biblical passages figure more than once in Felix's memories of early theatrical experiences. One was the story of Zacchaeus. In Luke 19, Zacchaeus, said to be "little of stature," is the chief of the "publicans" and the man in charge of collecting taxes. His contact with money taints him.[30] Being short, Zacchaeus climbs a sycamore tree to get a better glimpse of the son of God, and Jesus, looking up, sees him and tells him to come down (Luke 19:5). Moved by the divine yet familiar way in which Jesus speaks to him, Zacchaeus promises to give half his belongings to the poor: if the Heavenly Father can convert a rich man in this way, he can do anything. The burghers of Basel—men who, like Zacchaeus, were accustomed to handling large sums of money—were not loath to see themselves represented on stage by one of their most illustrious forebears, a man who had distinguished himself in the cause of righteousness. "Zacchaeus" was performed in what had been an Augustinian monastery before the Reformation came to Basel, at which time it became either a school or part of the university (F 84). Included in the cast were the daughters of "Lepusculus" (or "little hare"), also known as Sebastian Häsli, who at the time was in his forties. He later became a professor of Greek and then a full-time Protestant ecclesiastic—yet another instance of a man who combined teaching with the ministry. Lepusculus, the Hellenist pastor, went to his eternal rest in a tomb shared with Felix's mother.

The author of "Zacchaeus," who also performed in the play, was Heinrich Pantaleon, a young man, not yet twenty-five, who wore a goatee and whose humorous expression was not without a malicious edge. A man of remarkable intellect, Pantaleon pursued his studies at the universities of Basel, Heidelberg, and Valence, the last a mediocre institution from which he received a doctorate in medicine in record time. At various times a professor of Latin, rhetoric, and physics as well as an administrator in his spare moments, he eventually became count palatine and poet laureate of the Holy Roman Empire. His "Zacchaeus," published by Cratander in Basel in 1546, was the first of a long series of his works and translations devoted to the Church and its martyrs, the knights of Rhodes, the Russians, the Franks, the Germanic heroes, and William of Tyre.

The theatrical life of the time was intense, and though many of the plays involved are forgotten today, they elicited the enthusiasm of their original audiences. Among other plays performed at the former Augustinian monastery was one about Esther, the Jewish beauty who outwits Haman, the vizier of Ahasuerus (Xerxes or Artaxerxes), and saves the Jews from slaughter. In the end, according to *midrash* (Hebrew commentary on the Bible), she even manages to cause the death of 75,000 of her enemies, would-be accomplices in the slaughter that is happily averted— at a heavy price. The episode is a religious apologia, an explanation of a miracle—yet another stroke of grace. Although the historical basis of the story turns out to be slight or nonexistent, it long served in Jewish tradition to bolster the confidence of the Jewish people in the face of persecution. The story was also exploited by the heirs to Jewish tradition: both Catholic and Protestant writers and artists identified Esther with the justice of their cause and Haman with the wickedness of the other side— Lutherans or papists. The story of Esther, well known to people of Felix's and subsequent generations, thus became a theme common to both Protestant literature (as in sixteenth-century Basel) and Catholic literature (in the work, for instance, of Lope de Vega and of Racine, who wrote to justify the Revocation of the Edict of Nantes). It also figured in a great deal of European painting: in the work of Rembrandt on the Protestant side and of Veronese, Tintoretto, Rubens, Poussin, and Lorrain in the Catholic camp.

The text used in the Basel performance was probably "Hamanus" by Thomas Naogeorgius, whose German name was Kirchmeyer or Kirchmair. This play was expressly described as a "new tragedy" based on the Bible, a tragedy that attacked the calumny and tyranny of the powerful in the hope of inspiring fear of God. It was first published in Leipzig in 1543 and reprinted in Basel in 1547 by Thomas Platter's friend Oporinus. Naogeorgius, who backed Luther and sometimes outflanked him "on the left," portrayed Mordecai in no uncertain terms as a good Protestant and Haman as a thoroughly wicked Catholic. In Basel the role of Haman was played by Cellarius (Isaac Keller), who as it happens went on to live a less than spotless life (F 169). The son of a cloth merchant, he became, at the age of eight, the stepson of Felix's godfather Simon Grynaeus. This symbolic genealogy created a spiritual kinship between the two boys, despite the fact that Isaac was six years older than Felix. Cellarius had lived in Basel for a time before continuing his studies in Strasbourg. It was while living in Basel in 1546 or 1547, at some time between his sixteenth and eighteenth birthdays, that he played Haman. Fate would later take him to England, Montpellier, Toulouse, and Valence, where he received his doctorate in medicine. Shortly thereafter, at the age of twenty-three, he was named to a chair in medicine at the University of Basel. A quarter of a century later he was implicated in a financial scandal and obliged to leave the city. He nevertheless remained a doctor and ended his career as a humble physician in Alsace.

"Hamanus," though full of Lutheran and indeed ultra-Lutheran propaganda, also had plenty of the usual tragicomic mishaps. Ludwig Hummel, a future pastor who was playing the role of executioner, was supposed to "hang" both Haman and his son, but he somehow slipped and left the actor who was playing the son hanging for real; he quickly cut the rope, however, and saved the boy, Gamaliel Gyrenfalck, a pastor's son who escaped with nothing worse than a rope burn on his neck.

Among the plays performed in Basel during Felix's childhood were also two classical Latin comedies, "Aulularia" by Plautus (the ancestor of Molière's "L'Avare") and "Phormio" by Terence (a foreshadowing of the "Fourberies de Scapin"). The themes of these plays, well known today because of their use by Molière, were thus already familiar to the urban audiences of the Renaissance.

Of the fourteen performances from the 1540s mentioned in Felix's *Tag-*

*ebuch,* eight were based on Bible stories, six from the Old Testament and two from the New. Six others had nonreligious themes, three based on Latin plays (including "Hypocrisin," in which Felix and the future humanist Theodor Zwinger performed) and two on "folklore": "The Ten Ages of Man" and a comedy written by Thomas Platter himself, entitled "The Innkeeper with the Dried Branch," which has not survived—a loss that we need not regret unduly. Thus 85 percent of the plays can be classed under the rubrics "humanism" or "Reformation." The directors and actors, many of them quite young, either belonged to or were descended from members of the interlocking worlds of Protestant pastors, bureaucrats, professors, historians, publishers, scholars, and printers of the city of Basel. In short, this was the local intelligentsia, the world of intellectuals and semi-intellectuals. Militant as well as learned, the theater was a spectacle that the elite staged for itself as well as for the common people. This was in no sense an authentically and totally "popular" theater, despite later stereotypes to that effect.

*       *       *

June 1546 was a high point of the theatrical season. Felix, born in October 1536, was nine years and eight months old at the time and already an occasional performer. In October 1552, when he left for Montpellier, Felix was just sixteen. The six years (or, more precisely, seventy-five months) that elapsed between the two dates, between childhood and adolescence, were shaped by family, school, and friends. They were marked by the seasons, current events, and brief journeys, as well as by history on a broad scale (viewed from afar) and, of course, by the plague and the need to choose a vocation. Felix's father is present on virtually every page of his autobiography. His mother seldom makes an appearance, but when she does her presence is strongly felt. Yet Frau Platter was not in the best of health. She was no longer a young woman. When Felix was ten, she was already in her fifties. Frequently bedridden, Anna appears to have suffered from pleurisy, which manifested itself in an irritating dry cough. Right up to the time of her death in 1572 at the age of seventy-eight, she was bothered by recurrent respiratory problems: frequent bronchopulmonary infections and asthma attacks exacerbated by the dampness of unheated rooms (only a few rooms were heated with ceramic stoves).

She also suffered, as early as 1549, from another ailment, possibly related to her pleurisy: *roten schaden,* or hemorrhagic tenesmus (a painful contraction of the anus or bladder) . This affliction made an impression on Felix, aged twelve or thirteen at the time, who remembered that it came in the same year as the fire that destroyed the Beckhenhaus, killing the baker Claus Peyger and his wife Ursula despite the organization of a heroic bucket brigade. Corpulent Claus became trapped in a window of the burning building and was unable to escape, and Ursula died when the rope that she, together with her son or a baker's boy, was attempting to climb down broke from the excess weight.[31] Thus the blaze claimed three lives: there was danger living in close proximity to a working bread-oven (F 108).

Despite her poor physical condition, Felix's mother was a strong woman (as Thomas's mother had been). Anna Dietschi did not shrink from telling off the Strasbourg-born sculptor Hans Tobell (or Tobel), who one day took after Felix with an ax and chased him right into the kitchen of Zum Gejägd (F 105). Did he intend to carve the boy up? Tobell was not just any artist: in 1547 he did the statue of an armed man that embellished the fountain in Basel's market square. After being taken to task by the professor's wife, he confined himself to amusements of a less violent sort. One day he perusaded Felix and his friends that an execution was about to take place. The boys ran as fast as their legs could carry them to the appointed place, but it turned out that the sculptor had made the whole thing up. In 1558, however, when Tobell fell ill, he begged forgiveness of young Dr. Felix Platter, who at twenty-two had just completed his medical education; Felix assisted the dying man in his final moments.

Anna Dietschi demonstrated her usual energy in another dispute, one in which Felix became embroiled with a man who sold gingerbread men that Felix claimed had broken several of his teeth and caused his face to swell. Anna found the man, called him a scoundrel, and refused to pay for what Felix had broken in the fight. Anna's ill temper occasionally sparked quarrels at home, especially during the spring and summer of 1552 (F 124). Felix, by then close to sixteen, was better equipped to grasp his family's material and moral situation. Although Thomas owned extensive property in land and buildings, he still had large debts, and these led to quarrels between husband and wife, which Felix, who loved and wanted to remain on good terms with both, found painful. It was Anna, of course, who criticized her husband for making foolhardy investments that had led the family repeatedly into debt. But relations between Felix's parents never became as bitter as the situation in the household of the late knight von Rufach, whose tombstone Felix was able to admire when he went to Alsace with his father in 1551 to buy a new donkey. For the stone covering his grave, the knight had commissioned a bas-relief depicting himself armed from head to toe and lying on his stomach with his face pressed to the ground and his (armored) back facing the starry vault above. This unusual posture was chosen because his wife had threatened to piss on his face if the artist depicted him in the usual supine posture. *Se non è vero, è ben trovato.*

\*　\*　\*

Ursula, Felix's sister, was the young woman of the house and the only surviving daughter. Her two elder sisters, Margret I and Margret II, born in 1530 and 1533, had died of the plague in 1531 and 1539 respectively (F 50). Born in 1534, Ursula was pampered by her father and mother as well as her little brother Felix, who was two years younger. In 1546, when she was twelve, Ursula had gone to Strasbourg to stay with Margret Erbsin, the widow of Simon Lithonius Steiner, Thomas Platter's cousin from the Valais who became the *famulus* (assistant) of the Strasbourg reformer Martin Bucer and later a professor in Alsace. In the capital of that province, Ursula found time to write charming letters to her family back in Basel, but she grew bored after her aunt remarried, choosing the Alsatian pastor Lorenz Offner, with whom she would have four daughters and a son. Thomas's only choice was to bring his daughter back home. She and her little brother had plenty to talk about: together they worried about their parents' quarrels over their debts. Concerned, Anna occasionally spoke briefly to the children about what was going on. The children's dismay about the small inheritance they were likely to receive only tightened the bonds between them.

In 1549 or 1550, Ursula, by now a young woman, attended at the bedside of her supposedly dying mother. (In fact, Frau Platter recovered "by the grace of God," *durch gottes gnodt*—again, the idea, typically Protestant, of divine grace [F 109]). Felix also stayed at his mother's bedside. The two children commiserated about their mother's affliction but above all about their fear that a stepmother would take Anna's place and surely, they believed, mistreat the children of the first marriage. This was a common refrain whenever a family was threatened with disintegration in the early modern period. Ursula was a cultivated young woman: along with her brother, she took Latin and lute lessons from Thomas's assistant, Johannes von Schallen (F 117). At age fifteen or sixteen she fell for a worthy young peasant by the name of Werlin Bur, who helped out with farm chores on Thomas Platter's country estate in Gundeldingen. He was an earnest, pious, hardworking young fellow, strong, skillful, and the son of a prosperous farmer as well as a member of the Anabaptist sect. Thomas Platter, following the lead of the tolerant Sebastian Castellion (F 89), hoped to convert "heretics" like the Burs to the official creed of Basel as set forth by Œcolampadius and Zwingli.

Things took an unforeseen turn when Werlin fell in love with Ursula too. He asked Thomas for her hand, but Thomas, despite his daughter's tears, turned him down cold. Did he refuse because of the religious difference (which in fact was relatively slight)? Or did Thomas and Anna have bigger things in mind for their children? Ursula was the attractive, cultivated, musical daughter of a man who was no longer poor. She had numerous suitors despite her lack of a dowry. The Platters were unwilling to marry their daughter to a mere peasant, even if he came from a prosperous family. In the end, the plague decided the lovers' fate. A local surgeon, Master Wolf, had indeed predicted "great misfortunes." In 1551 Ursula and Werlin succumbed almost simultaneously. Felix later renewed his acquaintance with Werlin's two sisters, Ann and Ketterin. He was even invited to Ann's wedding. But the newlywed treated him like a stranger, as was customary among peasant wives. Felix was disappointed: hadn't these pretentious farm folk ever heard of the relaxed ways of city women? If Felix is to be believed, Ann and Ketterin lived to a ripe old age and grew as wrinkled as withered apples (F 90).

*   *   *

Ursula had a curious influence on her brother during her brief life and even after her death. Knowing his fetish for cleanliness, for being as "clean as a cat" (*katzrein*), she one day made herself rings of flesh from chicken gizzards taken from her mother's kitchen. Then she chased after Felix and rubbed his face with the rings. The effect on Felix was extraordinary, especially when Ursula, despite her affection for her little brother, repeated the experiment. In a panic, he ran away and collapsed in a fit of vomiting. Although Felix was in general a well-balanced individual, the psychological trauma of this episode was so severe that throughout his life he could never bear to look at even a painting of a ring, and it made no difference that the painting was of a ring of gold or silver rather than chicken gizzard. His aversion became well known, and wherever he went pranksters were always putting gizzard rings in his food, even in the princely courts where the eminent physician later practiced medicine. His reaction was always the same: disgust, flight, nausea. Never having read Freud, Felix was able to write in all innocence that he was horrified by anything "round and perforated" (*rundt und gelöchert* [F 101]). Here is a symptom to be borne in mind as we seek to penetrate the depths of Felix Platter's mind. Even the bobbins of spinning wheels filled him with horror, and he would no doubt have been dismayed by the curtain rings our great-grandmothers used.

In light of this story, it will come as no surprise that Ursula, as well educated as she was, spent most of her time working in her mother's kitchen, while Felix devoted his time to nobler, more intellectual tasks, as well as to farm chores (which he disliked) on the Gundeldingen estate.

The account of Ursula's death is one of the most moving parts of Felix's memoirs. In March 1551, the plague, which had been lurking in the city for almost a year, at last struck the Platter household. One of the boarders, Niclaus Sterien, who came from a family of seigneurial officeholders, came down with the disease and took to his bed on a Sunday morning. He died that afternoon. Ursula found him dead when she took food to his room. Her fright was her undoing: people at the time believed that the plague could be transmitted by fear or even by a mere glance. Niclaus was buried the same day in the St. Elsbethen cemetery, where he would soon be joined by many other victims of the disease. Thomas immediately put emergency measures into effect: many of the boarders had gone to Gundeldingen to make whistles out of willow bark, and Thomas sent word that they were not to return to town for Sunday evening services. Some, including Felix, were evacuated to Rötteln, in Baden, which apparently was a plague-free zone. Two months later, in May, Werlin Bur developed plague symptoms, as did Ursula Platter. Ursula, with a bubo on her thigh, lay ill for several days. Despite the contagion she piously kissed her parents, whispering: "Say goodbye to my dear little brother" (*meinen lieben bruderlin*).

Then she died. She was seventeen years old. Her parents buried her at St. Elsbethen, where her elder sister Margret II had been buried thirteen years earlier, in 1539, when she had died in her seventh year. Thomas revealed the news to Felix, still in Rötteln, only gradually. Finally, in July 1551, two months after the event, he wrote his son informing him that his sister was dead. Sixty years letter, Felix still could not read this tender, affectionate letter without crying. History ordinarily takes little notice of such fraternal devotion. An exception is the case of Louis XIII, who revealed his genuine love, tinged with sadness, for his sister when she left France for good to marry the heir to the Spanish throne in 1615: she was "such a good sister," the sovereign observed simply.[32]

\* \* \*

Thus Felix's life at this stage was partly serious, partly playful, occasionally tragic. His year consisted of two distinct seasons: a snowy winter, which also included carnival time, and a lengthy summer. During the winter Thomas sometimes permitted snowball fights by the light of the moon. His son took part along with the students, who at this point ranged in age from ten to twelve. Among them were Ambrosius Frobenius, who in keeping with his family tradition became a printer, and Niklaus (or Niclaus) Kalbermatten, a strong lad from a family of seigneurial officeholders. Once, Niklaus was working in a heated room at the top of the spiral staircase when he was accidentally struck by one of Felix's snowballs, packed so hard that it had turned to ice. When there was no snow, the boys used carrots as projectiles (Anna Dietschi, who did not shrink from hard labor, dug carrots from her own garden). These scenes of boys on the loose (*meisterlos*) might have come from a painting by Brueghel.

At carnival time, the snowball fights continued. Occasionally Thomas was hit in the face by an errant snowball. The sight of blood made him angry. During one carnival season Felix made an important journey, to visit the von Andlaus, a noble family living in Neuenburg, some twenty miles north of Basel. Sigmund von Andlau was one of Thomas's boarders and a good friend of Felix's (F 87). He liked to grab Thomas's behind in the privy, and one day after playing this game he was obliged to wash his hands. Felix and Sigmund set out for Neuenburg with Balthasar Hummel, a future pharmacist who came from a modest family and would remain one of Felix's close friends. Balthasar had known Sigmund for a long time, because his father, Peter Hans Hummel, had been the von Andlaus' handyman (F 88). Although the boys were close friends, the social distance between them remained. On the journey Felix and Sigmund were allowed to ride Papa Hummel's horse, while Balthasar walked. His good humor was not diminished, however.

In this (Protestant) "evangelical" milieu, carnival meant among other things that the boys were encouraged to participate in anticlerical pranks by Sigmund's mother, née Eva von Pfirt. They made fun of the red-robed Catholic priest who ate the Eucharist at mass without sharing it with anyone (in fact he was offering communion to his flock, but Felix seems to have overlooked this "detail"; it may be that frequent communion was not the norm in "papist" circles at this time) Another time the trio of friends verbally assaulted a passing priest, thereby failing in their duty to show respect to their elders in general and clerics in particular—a corrosive consequence of religious mixing. Religious differences aside, however, the boys delighted in carnival treats, dances, and the sight of men dressed in women's clothing.[33]

The three von Andlau daughters, one of whom was married and the

mother of a baby, did not hesitate to show themselves to Felix almost naked or in their underwear (*underrock* [F 88]). Still a child, he told them
stories as they knelt before him, fascinated by his talents as a storyteller,
which manifested themselves early. Clearly Felix was a gifted child, who
spoke well and played the lute.

\*   \*   \*

Felix has less to say about the summer season. He and Thomas's boarders
often went to the Platter farm in the country, where they helped out with
the heavy chores. Felix's classmates frequently blackmailed him by threatening to tell his father about his candy binges and classroom mischief.
Sometimes they beat him. Once they cut the rope of his swing while he
was swinging. Looking back on these childish pranks, Felix had no hard
feelings. In some of his mischief he took after his father: once, while playing near a pond, he killed a goose with a well-aimed stone. Thomas was
obliged to pay the bird's owner. Always a stickler for cleanliness, young
Platter liked to swim in a tributary of the Rhine. One time he was nearly
carried away by the current, but fortunately a strong swimmer was there
to save him.

\*   \*   \*

In Felix's memories of his tenth to fifteenth years, the news of the day
occupies just as large a place as the routines of daily life, despite the fact
that there were as yet no newspapers or other media. And much of the
news was of a familiar sort, involving sex and violence. Living in Basel at
the time was a seamstress from Zug by the name of Regula (or Regel)
Rüttiman (F 102). Though an Anabaptist, she did not always abide by the
sect's rigid moral code. She lived alone, or at any rate she was separated
from her husband, who had been locked up as a lunatic. She did sewing
and cooking for the Platters and sometimes bathed little Felix. She also
made him shirts decorated with colorful birds and liked to banter with
the boarders. Everyone was fond of her. She fell in love with Paul
Höchstetter, who came from a notable Augsburg family that had turned
to the professions when the family business went bankrupt. This must
have happened sometime between 1544 and 1546, when Paul, approximately twenty-one at the time, was living with Thomas. But nothing
came of Regula's infatuation. When the object of her affections left Basel,
she set her sights on an older man: Franz Jeckelmann, Felix's future
father-in-law, who, well into his forties, had lost his wife in 1549. One
night at supper, while dining at Thomas's table, Regula declared: "I think

I've got a live one. He's a widower." A man, she hinted, likes to have a woman around the house who can sew. But Felix's father, no widower, did not altogether appreciate her manner. A short time later, she left the Platters to work in nobler households, where she apparently made a good deal of money—enough, at any rate, to buy herself a house in Basel, where she had decided to settle. She now had an affair with Conrad Klingenberg, the keeper of the Stork Inn (F 122). Conrad, also known as Küntz or Cunz, had a bad reputation, but no worse than that of his daughter Anne: both had been compromised in various marital and other scandals. From her liaison with Küntz, Regula gave birth to an illegitimate son, Georg Felix. Felix was one of the comely child's godfathers; the other, a tailor, was of course named Georg (F 123). Georg Felix proved to be a gifted lad, and with a good education he became a surgeon who treated Bern mercenaries for gallstones so that they could fight in France's wars of religion. He later returned to Basel, where, with support from Felix, by then an important doctor, he became a citizen. One day he decided to visit his mother, who had left Basel for Säckingen in the wake of persecution not for immorality but for Anabaptism. While there, he became drunk one night and agreed to marry the daughter of a minister in return for a promised dowry of 1,000 gold gulden. The girl was the product of an incestuous relationship between her clergyman father and his sister. Gossip had it that the randy young minister had also been to bed with his daughter. Marrying the girl off to Regula's son was a way of concealing the evidence of this presumed double incest. When Georg discovered the secret, he "died of sorrow." The girl went off with another man. The fornicating pastor, meanwhile, was strongly advised to leave town and not to stop until he reached Constance, quite a distance away. There we lose track of him (F 102, 122–23).

*　　*　　*

Georg Felix was the product of an extramarital affair. How common were such affairs in this segment of society? What might nowadays be called sexual harassment was tolerated: according to Felix, it was considered normal even in the most respectable households for the master to fondle the breasts of his servants at least once while they were in his employ.[34] Some people even felt that it was an honor for a girl to be treated this way. The fact that Felix underlined the qualification "even in the best households" (firnemmen hüseren [F 106]) suggests that in theory the dominant classes were expected to behave in a more ethical and civilized manner than others. When someone of the upper crust exceeded the tolerable limits, he was discredited in the eyes of society. Take the case of Dr. Hans Leuw: a one-time monk who became a Protestant minister and married an ex-nun, Leuw was also a doctor who treated the plague at Solothurn (F 103). Later he enjoyed a brilliant career as an anatomist and became an assistant to the great Vesalius himself in 1546. Ultimately, however, he was forced to leave Basel because of an adulterous relationship that resulted in two illegitimate children (F 105). The scandal was too great to tolerate.

\*   \*   \*

There were also love affairs among Thomas's colleagues. Take for instance the teacher of lute and Latin whose name we have already encountered several times. Johannes (or Hans) von Schallen, also known as Scalerus, was born in 1525. He was the bastard son of a notary and soldier. Hans began with Thomas as a boarder at the age of thirteen and went on to become his chief assistant. He had a (legitimate) brother, a certain Niklaus, who had been a student in Basel and later became the municipal treasurer of Sion. He and Johannes engaged in bitter brawls, sometimes in the Platter house, during which they exchanged blows, hurled objects at each other, overturned tables, and grappled in the dark. Thomas tried to stop them, while Ursula and Felix howled in fear.

In any case, Johannes von Schallen at some point fell madly in love with a beautiful young woman from Basel, who belonged to the municipal oligarchy. Either she or her mother sat as a model for some of Hans Holbein's Madonnas. Johannes used Felix as a messenger to send notes to this woman, who was married. Once, Felix found her, fresh from her bath, lying naked on a sofa (*gutschen*): Cranach's nudes were not simply evocations of antiquity. The beautiful lady accepted the love note without showing the slightest embarrassment in front of Felix, who at fourteen enjoyed the spectacle. Johannes Scalerus lived with the young woman and even had a child by her, a child that her "good husband" (*gut man*) raised as his own. Later, Johannes moved to Sion, where he became a teacher and eventually mayor. His former lover, desperate after his departure, wrote him ardent letters—very much in the manner of Madame Bovary—in which she spoke of leaving her husband and children to be with him. She even cried on Thomas's shoulder, but Thomas, stern puritan that he was, warned her against such foolish thoughts. In the end she died. Of a broken heart? Felix apparently thought so. Meanwhile, Johannes, on the other side of the Alps, was stricken with guilt and confessed his sins in a letter to his former employer. He, too, died at the age of thirty-six, according to Felix at any rate. According to other sources, he did not depart this vale of tears, spitting blood, until he had reached the age of forty-five and become a church deacon after living with tuberculosis for many years.

Another much more serious affair involving crime as well as sex concerned not Thomas's servants or colleagues but his extended family. This episode demonstrates Felix's memory and powers of observation at their best. Margret Erbsin, a "cousin" of the Platters by marriage and a true friend of the family, had lived in Thomas's house for a time after the death of her husband in 1543. While there, she aroused the passion of Niklaus Petri, a teacher from Lorraine living in Basel, who had divorced his first wife after she became pregnant in an adulterous affair. Niklaus married a second time, but his new wife also died. When Margret discouraged her lonely suitor's advances, he accused Thomas of having turned her against him and actually brandished a sword with murder in mind. Meanwhile, Margret returned to Strasbourg, where in 1546 she married a pastor. (Her first husband had been a professor: once again we encounter the endogamy of the professional classes, that is, their tendency to marry within their own social group.) Not discouraged by his failure, Niklaus now turned his attentions to the eighteen-year-old sister of his late wife. A pretty girl by the name of Maria, she had shown great kindness to the widower's children. When Maria also spurned his advances, Niklaus, after attending morning services at a Protestant church, plunged a dagger into her bosom on January 13, 1546. She collapsed at the bottom of the stairs of the house that she and her killer shared, but not before telling all the world, "He killed me" (*Er hatt mich gemördet*).

Meanwhile, Niklaus got rid of the murder weapon, fled to a nearby house, and leaped into the frozen Rhine through a privy hole. A blue and white flag taken from the enemy a generation earlier in the Battle of Novara (1513) hung nearby. Some fishermen fished the fleeing killer out of the river, wrung him out, dried him off, warmed him up, and helped him to escape to a forest in Alsace north of Basel. But soldiers from the city were in hot pursuit and soon caught the escaped murderer. His quick trial ended in a sentence of death: Niklaus was to be broken on the wheel. He had time to make a will, with Thomas serving as notary, and this proved to be of great solace to the condemned man. A week after his capture, he was put to death. Felix, aged ten, would not have missed this spectacle for the world, any more than he would have missed the theatrical performances that were staged in the city a few months later. The execution was an occasion for the boy to make everyone laugh with some bad puns on *hochgericht* (gibbet) and *gericht* (meal). The torture of Niklaus Petri could not have been more odious. The condemned man was attached to the wheel and stretched with levers until his limbs snapped, causing him to scream, in Latin, "Jesus, son of David (*sic*), have mercy on me!" The final blow, on his chest, caused his tongue to protrude from his mouth. The body was secretly buried at night.

So the criminal Niklaus Petri died as a pious scholar and Latinist, crying out *Jesu filii David miserere mei!* in the midst of his torture (F 96). A common thief of less exalted station proved less relgious and more down-to-earth. When one of a gang of sneak thieves from Rötteln was driven in a cart to the execution site, he kept repeating the same words over and over again all the way to the gallows: "I'm going to hang. The crows will get me." (Had he read François Villon, or was this a commonplace of the time, known to common criminals as well as to poets?)

Petri's long and painful torture seemed harsh, even to contemporaries not noted for shedding tears over the sufferings of criminals. Some said that the Basel authorities had been compelled by the muttering of the "common" people to impose an extremely harsh sentence. Apparently that muttering was the result of an earlier episode, which took place toward the end of 1545. A huge, fat carter from Brabant who was working in Basel had raped and committed other obscene acts upon a seventy-year-old woman, the mother of a country innkeeper. The elderly woman had made the mistake of traveling alone through the Hart Forest en route to the family inn. The carter had pulled her down from her horse before subjecting her to "vile crimes."

All but caught in the act, the Brabançon had been tortured by an executioner from Basel, a strong, conceited fellow who had torn out a piece of his victim's chest with red-hot pincers before hauling him, half-dead, to the chopping block to cut off his head. The man's body had then been impaled on a pike before being placed in its grave. Thomas Platter had insisted on taking his son to see the grave before it was filled in so that the boy might carry the memory of this edifying spectacle with him to the end of his days. But many people thought that the man had been cruelly and unusually punished. And it was whispered among the common people of Basel that Niklaus Petri, who was an intellectual (*gelerter*) judged by other intellectuals (the judges), might well be let off more leniently even though he had committed a worse crime than the carter from Brabant. Indeed, "class justice" does sometimes go easy on certain well-placed academics even when they commit crimes as heinous as murdering their wives. The Basel tribunal was therefore careful to mete out a particularly harsh punishment to Petri in order to prevent public opinion, always potentially dangerous, from getting out of hand. The use of executions as a pedagogical spectacle for the edification of children and the masses would continue, of course, to the nineteenth century and beyond.

*   *   *

Note, by the way, that criminals were often seen as foreigners: Petri, though from Lorraine, was viewed as a Burgundian; another criminal, a vintner by profession, was said to be a "Welch"; and the carter was a Brabançon. Is this tendency to see criminals as foreigners a deeply rooted prejudice or an accurate reflection of a persistent reality?

*   *   *

Children did not suffer when a father was disgraced. Was this a happy byproduct of the nature of Basel society, which did not place much stock in hierarchy or ancestry and whose *Genossenschaft* mentality was rather tolerant and democratic? Niklaus Petri's three sons enjoyed respectable if modest careers despite their father's tragedy. One was a tailor who received help from the generous Myconius. Another, Israel by name, became a painter who worked for Felix before dying of plague along with his wife in 1564 (F 98). It was only after his death that Felix learned of the elder Petri's threats against his father Thomas. People in Basel were capable of respecting the law of silence as long as necessary.

*   *   *

Felix later became a great traveler, but during childhood and early adolescence he journeyed only once to Baden and twice to Alsace. Anna Dietschi took her son to Strasbourg in 1550 or shortly before to visit a "respectable" family—of social status equal to the Platters—of preachers, teachers, organists, and clerks. Then, in 1551, after the plague season (during which Felix had been sent away to Baden) but before winter set in, Thomas and his son went to Rouffach, a town dominated by a huge castle in what is now the Guebviller district of the Haut-Rhin. The purpose of their visit was to purchase an ass, an animal disdained in Basel as old-fashioned or ludicrous for riding but less expensive than a horse for carrying fruit and other produce from Gundeldingen to town. Unfortunately, the younger Platter's memories of Alsace at the height of the Renaissance are slender. Upon returning from Strasbourg he recalled that he had found his father suffering from an accidental knife wound to the arm. And after the second trip, Thomas, who this time accompanied his son, had remarked, "Felix, you're glad to be home, but I'm not, because my daughter is gone." The dead child weighed on his mind. Thomas's words plunged Felix into distress. As hard as Ursula's loss was for Thomas to bear, he appreciated his son's active presence. His erstwhile severity lived on only in Felix's memory.

Before making the journey to Rouffach to buy the ass, during the spring and summer of 1551 (the period during which Ursula died), Thomas sent Felix to Rötteln in Baden where he would be safe from the plague (F 118). Unaware of his sister's death, news of which was kept from him for some time, the adolescent used his time in Baden to practice the lute. He also observed the amorous stratagems of a medical student who was courting the wife of an absent soldier. Along with a friend Felix stole pears and apples from the orchards of the Rötteln castle. This earned him some harsh words from the local sheriff, Ulrich Müllner, who seized the opportunity to rail against the Swiss—not much appreciated by certain Germans, apparently, despite their all being *Teutschen*. Later, this sheriff was dismissed by the nobleman who employed him and emigrated to Basel, where Felix treated him for an illness. A little later, Felix returned to Rötteln to launch his medical career after completing his studies in Montpellier. Ulrich meanwhile married and had a child but later "died and rotted along with his spouse and offspring." Such was Felix's brief obituary for a former patient whom he treated despite his personal dislike for the man.[35]

Felix knew more than just what was happening in his own life. News of the wider world appears in his memoir as early as 1544, when he was just nine years old. He reports, for example, on the expulsion of Swabian peasants from Munich: Protestants, they were forced to flee papist Bavaria for Swiss territory, where they lived hand to mouth. Thomas and Felix became acquainted or, more accurately, reacquainted with one such pair of Lutheran refugees, a husband and wife who had been members of the important soapmakers' guild in Munich. Once rich, they had used what remained of their fortune to buy a small house on "tanners' alley" in Basel in 1544.

The two refugees scraped by on their knowledge of soapmaking. The husband, Hans Schräll, an elderly man, made soap in his house, which also served as his workshop. His wife, "the old lady," whose name was Margaretha or Margret, sold what her husband produced in a tiny shop next to what had been an abbey. With their Bavarian dialect, dress, and belongings, the two passed for eccentrics. Hans got himself in trouble with the authorities for racist outbursts: "The Bavarians and Swabians could cook the Baselers and Confederates and eat them for dinner." Margret, for her part, never could get rid of her Bavarian dialect, to the great amusement of the Swiss. In all innocence she greeted Swiss children with words that sounded like "darling whoreson." Once she told the pharmacist who had sold her a laxative for her dog that "my pooch is shitting so much that he can't work anymore." Thomas recognized this impoverished pair as the generous couple that had saved him from starvation in Munich years earlier, in the days when he had had to fight dogs for his dinner and pick food out of cracks between floorboards. Hans, Margaretha, and their erstwhile protégé Thomas fell into one other's arms. From that day until the day he died, Thomas offered the two émigrés from southern Germany generous assistance, thus repaying them for the kindness they had shown him thirty-five years earlier when he had fetched up on the banks of the Isar.

* * *

Rumors of wars outside Switzerland also reached Basel, whose youth avidly seized on every scrap of information. Veterans fresh from battle in France and Germany had stories to tell or, if need be, to embellish with reconstructed memories. Felix, all ears, soaked these up and later poured them out in the pages of his memoirs. He was struck by the adventures of one of his neighbors, the cobbler Hans Bart, who owned the house across the street (F 106). Bart was a stout fellow, always ready to take up arms for the Protestant cause. At Mühlberg (1547) and Moncontour (1569) he came close to meeting his Maker. Through his hair-raising tales, Felix learned about the wars of religion in Germany and France. The flood of refugees from those wars, together with the work hastily undertaken to shore up walls around the city of Basel, persuaded eleven-year-old Felix Platter that his city and country were in grave danger, a conviction that would only deepen with time. In young Felix's mind it was entirely possible that one day Charles V would arrive with his cavalry to occupy the city and sleep with his boots on in the bürgermeister's bed.

* * *

Felix's fears proved groundless, but the Basel of that time was indeed a hotbed of anti-imperial plots, which Charles's secret agents sought to combat with whatever means were at hand, at times with ludicrous or tragic results. The episode that created the greatest stir along the banks of the upper Rhine was an attempt to assassinate Colonel Sebastian Schertlin, a charismatic soldier of fortune in his fifties who had amassed a fortune while serving under Charles V in the sack of Rome (1527). At midcentury, however, his loyalties were dearly purchased by the francophile or anti-imperial camp around Henri II. The imperial administra-

tion hired a spy to keep an eye on him, a man by the name of Hans Birkling, who, like many of his ilk, enjoyed the raucous company at an inn
called Zum Blumen, which was also a favorite haunt of the "felonious"
colonel. Did Birkling really try to poison Schertlin? In any case he was
arrested, forced to "confess" under torture, sentenced to death, and beheaded. Shortly thereafter, Colonel Schertlin headed up a troop of
twenty Swiss mercenaries who rode off to reinforce the French in the
siege of Metz. These events took place in 1552, when Felix was fifteen and
already deeply interested in medicine. He would have liked to dissect the
body of the executed spy, but it was said to be rotten with pox, the
"French disease" (*voller Franzosen*), so that Felix had to give up any
thought of dissection, while handsome Niklaus, the executioner of Basel,
strutted about in the Iberian mode in the clothing that had belonged to
his victim. No profit was too small.

*  *  *

When it came to the study of anatomy, Felix had a good model (F 103).
His father, a doctor *manqué,* loved dissecting things. Early in 1546 (when
Felix was nine and a half), Thomas Platter had participated in a dissection
with the surgeon Franz Jeckelmann, Vesalius's former assistant and Fe-
lix's future father-in-law. The two men, accompanied by the apothecary
Gengenbach, whose shop adjoined the cattle market, went to Riehen,
where they met the local pastor, a strange character known as Johan Jacob
Leu, alias Hans Leuw. A pseudo-physician and pastor of the Œcolampadian persuasion, soon to be defrocked, as well as an admitted fornicator,
Leuw had taken delivery of a decapitated criminal whose body the city of
Basel had donated to science. It was snowing. As was customary, beggars
came to the rectory in search of alms. Wolves prowled nearby. Back in
Basel, far from the out-of-the-way village of Riehen, Felix trembled for
his father's life: he felt a deep affection for the old man despite the whippings he had received. But Thomas, far from being afraid, was enjoying
himself. With the help of the apothecary and the surgeon, he chopped up
the cadaver obligingly furnished by the Basel authorities. He and his
companions then showed the body parts to the beggars outside the rectory, who fled in fear that the same fate might be in store for them. The
amused anatomists enjoyed the joke until one French vagrant, more courageous or perhaps simply more shrewd than his German confederates,
threatened them with a sword and swore to make mincemeat of them as
they had made mincemeat of their victim. Note, incidentally, that this
beggar (who admittedly came from far-off France) was equipped with a
sword.

The following night Thomas had a dream about cannibalism. When he woke up, he vomited. Shortly after the dissection, the authorities in Schaffhouse, a town not far from Riehen, charged the three anatomy students with murder: the local constabulary had bought the crowd's interpretation of the event. Not long thereafter, Reverend Leuw was obliged to leave town on charges of adultery. Although the morals of the age were sometimes loose, the morals of the clergy were no laughing matter. The departed preacher left the skeleton of the dissected criminal behind: reassembled bone by bone, it remained for many years in the basement of the rectory, where it could be viewed by the faithful (F 103).

"You will be a doctor, my boy": that was Thomas's implicit message to Felix, and it was also the message of the surgeon and the apothecary who had joined Felix's father in perpetrating a rather tasteless deception. Yet the young man's medical vocation was by no means an uncomplicated matter. It was closely associated with the boy's wish to make a good marriage and rise in society, a wish fostered in part by his mother. Anna Dietschi had not forgotten that, though born poor, she came from a distinguished line, which over the centuries had included various illustrious Zurich burghers and noblemen. She did not wish to see her son endure the social purgatory that she had known as a child. In 1549, as she lay on what was thought at the time to be her deathbed (in fact she was to live for many more years), she offered this advice to her almost adolescent son: "Don't be stupid enough, son, to marry a strumpet, as boorish students do. It would ruin you. All you could hope for then would be to eke out a living as a schoolteacher like your father's assistants [the delicacy of this advice has to be admired]. Or else you'll wind up as a wretched village priest or pastor" (F 109). This sage counsel did not fall on deaf ears. Ambition, a desire for luxury, a good career, a rich marriage—all these things entered into the fourteen-year-old boy's partially formulated plans. Here, after all, was a youth not unimpressed by the ostentatious weddings common among the cream of Basel society in the year 1551. What did it matter that one of the grooms was the son of a soldier who had fought on the losing side at Marignano, or that one of the couples thus joined in matrimony would succumb shortly thereafter to the plague of 1552 (F 112)?

*   *   *

Felix's medical vocation stemmed above all from his family environment. Think of the medical books in ancient tongues that Thomas Platter published or at any rate stored in his home and sold, copies of which were surely available to young Felix. And recall the (sad) story of Epiphanius,

Thomas's late physician and patron, who had rekindled Thomas's youthful passion for medicine, though by then it was too late for him to do anything about it. The tale of Epiphanius, retold a hundred times by Thomas sitting beside the fire, had been a constant presence throughout the first fifteen years of Felix's life. The ghost of the Venetian physician, resurrected by an old story, thus became a model for the future.

*   *   *

Felix's motives for studying medicine stemmed as much from the flesh as from the spirit, however. From early childhood (when he was no more than eight or ten years old), he loved to watch butchers at work, opening beef carcasses to remove the hearts. He spoke to the animals before they were slaughtered: "Tell me what miracle the butcher will find in you." He knew everything there was to know about slaughtering and butchering hogs at the farm in Gundeldingen. He played hooky so as not to miss a trick. He overcame the disgust that his sister's practice of making rings out of chicken gizzards aroused in him. With tears in his eyes he killed small birds so that he might dig out the veins in their thighs with a small knife. He dissected maybugs, flies, and burweeds (separating out the veins in the latter, as children do with chestnut leaves today). This was the origin of Felix's *Beruf,* his calling. *Beruf,* of course, was a word that Luther liked to use to speak of God's call to man to perform some particular mission on earth.[36] In short, God spoke to Felix through the entrails of cows and pigs. A haruspex of Roman times would not have been surprised.

Felix's down-to-earth (or down-to-flesh) motives were not incompatible with more elevated considerations. As a young man, his primary goal was not really to save his fellow man from disease and suffering. At any rate this was not a goal he wrote about, although he was clearly a compassionate person, ready to help anyone who was suffering and even to care for those close to him who came down with the plague. But when it came to choosing a profession, his concerns were not fundamentally charitable; he was motivated, rather, by admiration. Felix identified in advance with the professors of medicine, the deans and rectors who treated dukes and princes, important academics whom he saw strutting the streets of Basel in their velvet costumes, followed by servants on horseback. Thomas pointed out processions of such prominent citizens in order to remind the boy of the rewards of hard work. In a Protestant city already moving toward greater democracy and self-government, a city in which the status hierarchy was by no means frozen, a talented young man could dream of every sort of social advancement, however illusory such hopes might prove in reality. His father, moreover, encouraged Felix's hopes from early on by admonishing him to do well in school and if need be by cuffing him on the ear.

\*　\*　\*

Furthermore, when it came time ultimately to choose a profession, Thomas intervened. He did not conceal his joy at his son's choice of a medical career and encouraged him to read and take notes on subjects such as botany and therapeutics. Thomas (F iii) also confided in his boarder Höchstetter, a future prosecutor and physician: "The boy [Felix] will by the grace of God become a doctor. He will do what I was unable to do, and that will be his vocation, his calling [*Beruf*]." At the time of this pronouncement in the best Lutheran style, Felix was eleven or twelve years old. Over the next few years he realized that his future career disgusted him in some ways. As much as he wished to be an anatomist, he despised filth and disliked handicaps. When his sick mother vomited, he was a dutiful son and held her head, but he averted his eyes, for he was afraid he might faint. His father was obliged to scold him: "If you are going to be a doctor, get used to things that may disgust you."

Felix's decision to go into medicine was reinforced by his marriage plans. On New Year's Day, 1550 (when Felix was fifteen), Thomas stopped in to see his friend and fellow dissector, the surgeon Franz Jeckelmann. While there, he noticed a pretty girl of sixteen or seventeen, Madlen, who kept house for her widowed father. (Jeckelmann had lost his wife, Chrischona, the year before.) Thomas mused to himself that the girl would make a nice wife for his son and hinted as much to Felix, who was excited by the idea, as he confided to his friend Martin Huber, the son of the great Basel physician. But when he met the girl, he blushed, stammered, and was paralyzed with shyness, Madlen did not take it amiss, however, for she had already made up her mind. Felix immediately began dressing with even more elegance than usual, and he worked harder than ever at medicine with the idea of becoming a presentable son-in-law for "old Franz" (who was actually not yet fifty).

\*　\*　\*

Felix's marriage plans came up again in the summer of 1551, while he was away in Rötteln avoiding the plague. In Thomas's letters wishes became facts: Ursula was dead, so Madlen would one day become his daughter-in-law and take his daughter's place. The couple would live on Felix's earnings as a doctor. Felix's passion for Madlen preoccupied him: he wrote Latin poems to her and left them in the lining of his jacket, where a tailor found them and circulated them around town, to the amusement of all who knew him. But Thomas kept his head. He had dreamed up this marriage with God's help, and with God's help it would take place. Felix languished in Rötteln throughout the plague-ridden summer of 1551, while his father engaged in extended negotiations with Jeckelmann. The two men got on well together. Small gifts of wine and food passed from one household to the other. Nothing more needed to be spelled out. Everything was understood. The engagement became an open secret, about which Felix, far away in Baden, received news through his friends' mocking letters.

In September 1551 a new chapter opened in Felix's life: the plague was over (F 123). At any rate it was no longer a constant threat. Felix entered college as a freshman (as we would say) at age fifteen. Some of his classmates, drawn from the middle or lower-middle class of the city's intellectuals, were as young as eleven or twelve. Social classes were homogeneous, whereas school cohorts were heterogeneous. After a brief period of hazing or initiation, the young college student got down to work on Roman history, medicine, and Greek, which he studied under the aegis of Thomas, himself an excellent Hellenist. Sadness had descended on the Platter household since Ursula's death. The parents fought because Anna worried about the debts Thomas had incurred. Here was yet one more reason for Felix to work feverishly, taking assiduous notes in Johannes Huber's lectures on medicine. He also knuckled down to the study of Hippocrates, who was back in favor in the Basel region. These preliminary studies were to prepare him to study medicine at the University of Montpellier. Unlike Thomas, Felix was no self-made man, heading out into the wide world to seek his destiny. He was a well-educated boy, far better educated in his speciality than many college students are today. Felix left German territory and set out for the land of the "Welch," where he would discover French, Latin, and Languedoc culture in both the popular and academic spheres. Ursula, whom Thomas had hoped would make a grand marriage, was dead, so all his paternal hopes were now invested in his boy, on whom the future of the Platter line depended.

\* \* \*

In the summer of 1552, Thomas, who had been nursing his decision for a long time, therefore made up his mind. Felix was his only surviving child;

his three daughters were all dead. Hence it would not hurt anyone if he invested everything he had in his son. Sending his boy to Montpellier, one of the world's leading medical schools and certainly the best north of the Alps, would give him the best possible start as a doctor in Basel in the shortest possible time. Once established as a physician, Felix would help his father meet expenses and pay off the debts that had hung over his household for too long.

1. Portrait of Thomas Platter Sr. (1499–1582), in his eighties, by Hans Bock the Elder (oil on canvas). Oeffentliche Kunstsammlung, Basel, Kunstmuseum, Inv. 83. *Photo by courtesy of the museum*.

2. Portrait of Felix Platter (1536–1614). The great Basel physician is portrayed in a slightly pretentious manner among objects that reflect his passion for collecting items pertaining to natural history. This portrait is also the work of Hans Bock the Elder (oil on canvas). Oeffentliche Kunstsammlung, Basel, Kunstmuseum, Inv. 84. *Photo by courtesy of the museum.*

3. Portrait of Thomas Platter Jr. (1536–1614). To judge by this rather unflattering portrait, the youngest of the "great Platters" lacked the personal magnetism of his father and brother. The portrait is by Bartholomaüs Sarburg. Oeffentliche Kunstsammlung, Basel, Kunstmuseum, Inv. 42. *Photo by courtesy of the museum.*

4. Chrischona Jeckelmann (1577–1624), the wife of Thomas Platter Jr. and niece of Felix Platter's wife. The young woman is holding a small gold chain given to her as a gift by Felix Platter's wife, Madlen. Felix purchased the item in 1557 as a gift for Madlen, then his fiancée, from a shop in Paris located on one of the bridges across the Seine. The portrait is by Bartholomaüs Sarburg. Oeffentliche Kunstsammlung, Basel, Kunstmuseum, Inv. 43. *Photo by courtesy of the museum.*

5. Portrait by Hans Bock of Theodor Zwinger (1533–1588) surrounded by symbols of Time and Wisdom. Zwinger, a great humanist and physician, held the chair in Greek philosophy at the University of Basel and was a friend of Felix's Platter's, as well as the sixteenth-century thinker most responsible for the idea of the "scientific journey." Oeffentliche Kunstsammlung, Basel, Kunstmuseum, Inv. 1877. *Photo by courtesy of the museum.*

6. Portrait by an anonymous artist of the Anabaptist David Joris (1501?-1556). Joris, a resident of Basel, was a native of the Netherlands. The fate of this friend of the Platters is discussed in chapter 9. Oeffentliche Kunstsammlung, Basel, Kunstmuseum, Inv. 561. *Photo by courtesy of the museum.*

The following "urban" illustrations are taken from Georg Braun and Franz Hogenberg, *Civitates orbis terrarum* (Cologne, 1572) and, for later decades, from subsequent editions of the same work (more complete than the first printing), the last of which appeared in 1618.

7. Map of the city of Basel. On the right bank of the Rhine was "Little Basel," the city's "minority" suburb. *Bibliothèque nationale de France*.

8. Sion, or Sitten (*Sedunum* in Latin), was a large town in the Valais, Thomas Platter Sr.'s home territory. Thomas, Felix, and Felix's wife and father-in-law stayed here in June 1563. *Bibliothèque nationale de France*.

9. A pleasant, aristocratic view of Dresden. From his vagabond youth Thomas Platter remembered mainly having slept in a room here in which the straw was so full of lice that one could hear them moving. The harsh memory of the young "student" thus contrasts with the flattering image here of a "garden city," as conceived by a contemporary artist. *Bibliothèque nationale de France*.

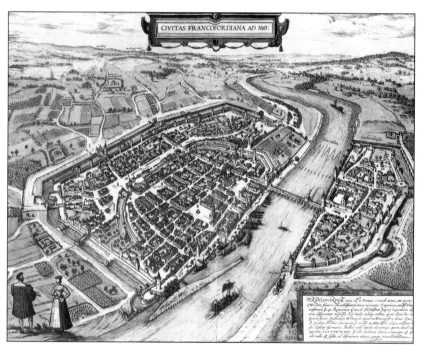

10. Thomas Platter Sr. transacted business at the Frankfurt book fairs during his years as a printer in the 1530s. *Bibliothèque nationale de France*.

11. Thomas Sr. and Felix had frequent contacts with Strasbourg both in youth and later. The city is mentioned at least fifty times in Thomas's *Lebenbeschreibung* and especially in Felix's *Tagebuch*. For the people of Basel, then as now, Alsace was just next door. *Bibliothèque nationale de France*.

12. Thomas Sr. and Felix went to Rouffach in 1551 to buy an ass. They visited the castle and admired the tombstone of a knight, a bas-relief in which the knight is lying face down in order to shield himself from "symbolic" revenge by a shrewish wife. *Bibliothèque nationale de France*.

13. The Platter clan had frequent contacts with Colmar and other Alsatian cities and towns. Felix's good friend Thomas Schöpflin, who also traveled down the Rhone Valley with him in 1552, became the municipal physician of Colmar around 1560. *Bibliothèque nationale de France.*

14. A famous theological colloquium was held in Baden in 1526. Thomas Platter followed the proceedings assiduously. This meeting had an important impact on the religious future of German Switzerland. *Bibliothèque nationale de France.*

15. Mainz: the Platters had little direct contact with this city, but it did provide Thomas Sr. with friends in his youth and Felix with friends later on. It was also the unique birthplace of printing, despite some scholarly claims to the contrary. *Bibliothèque nationale de France*.

16. En route to Montpellier, Felix Platter stayed in Lyons from October 20 to October 23, 1552. There he met the great physician Rondelet, who, at the University of Montpellier, would later teach him about medicine and show him how to dissect bodies. *Bibliothèque nationale de France*.

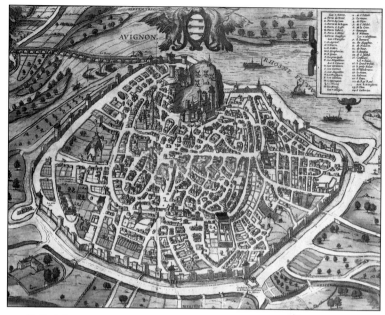

17. Felix Platter spent several days in Avignon around October 28, 1532. There he experienced fear and a brief depressive episode, but he also listened to hymns sung in a Catholic Church and began to moderate his hostility to Catholicism in his first authentic contact with the faith. *Bibliothèque nationale de France.*

18. Felix Platter passed through Nîmes on October 30, 1552. He cast an attentive eye on local antiquities. He also unwittingly came into contact for the first time with the pro-Protestant culture of Lower Languedoc. *Bibliothèque nationale de France.*

19. Montpellier, where Felix spent the years 1552 to 1557, remained a vivid memory when the elderly physician sat down to write his memoirs in 1608–13. His memories of the city as an attractive place were mingled with nostalgia for youth, the student life, and the pleasures of swimming in the Mediterranean. *Bibliothèque nationale de France*.

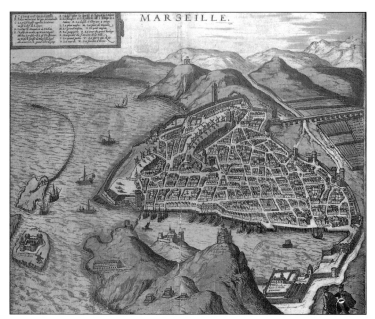

20. Felix visited Marseilles in 1555. He made detailed notes about his physical condition and appearance in this city. At the end of the sixteenth century, his brother Thomas Jr. gave a more objective account of the city and its port. *Bibliothèque nationale de France*.

21. Felix was in Bordeaux from March 11 to March 14, 1557. He viewed the Atlantic, visited Roman ruins, ate fresh fish, and participated in numerous musical activities, including small improvised concerts. *Bibliothèque nationale de France.*

22. On March 18, 1557, Felix visited Poitiers (his brother would later follow suit). He climbed a tower, visited a castle, and spoke with booksellers. *Bibliothèque nationale de France.*

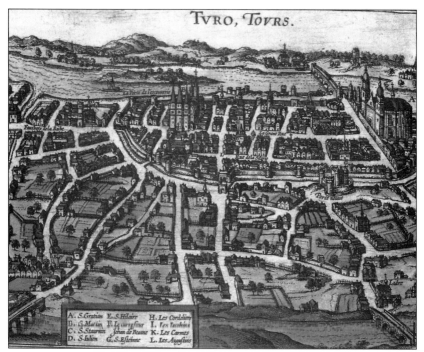

TVRO, TOVRS.

| A. S.Gratian | E. S.Hilaire | H. Les Cordeliers |
| D. S.Martin | F. Le curefuur | I. Les Jacobins |
| C. S.Staurin | Jehan de Beaune | K. Les Carmes |
| D. S.Iulien | G. S.Esteinne | L. Les Augustins |

23. On March 20, 1557, Felix passed through Tours, the first "jewel" of the Loire Valley, where Renaissance architecture was far more prevalent than in other regions of France. An industrial city, Tours specialized in the production of luxury goods (silk). Its fountains, marvels of city planning, and its castle made a particularly strong impression on the son of the Basel teacher. *Bibliothèque nationale de France.*

ORLEANS.

24. Orléans (March 23–25, 1557) gave Felix an opportunity to enjoy himself with the colony of German students at the local university. The student from Basel committed an egregious error of historical interpretation concerning the city's statue of Joan of Arc, however. *Bibliothèque nationale de France.*

25. In Paris, where Felix spent the first two weeks of April 1557, he visited important physicians, the Louvre, Notre-Dame, and the abbey of Saint-Denis in the northern suburbs and amused himself with shopping expeditions and revels with German and Swiss students. *Bibliothèque nationale de France*.

26. In Bourges, which Felix visited during hard times in 1557 and Thomas Jr. saw much later in the century, both Platters were drawn to the city's churches, to the "diamond-point" tower, and to the treasures bequeathed to the church by Jean de Berry. Felix also frequented the local German community, which at the time of his visit was still in mourning for a young Bavarian lord who had recently drowned while boating near the city. *Bibliothèque nationale de France*.

## CHAPTER FOUR

# Platter Enterprises: Thomas

Thomas's debts were long-standing. They went back to at least 1535 or 1536, when the family was reduced by plague to father, mother, and one daughter and then increased to four by the birth of Felix in 1536. The subsequent period, from 1536 to 1551 or 1552, is the one we have just examined through the inescapably youthful and often poetic gaze of Felix. "Old" Thomas offers us an adult vision of the same years—the view of a dynamic, active Renaissance man. His account is given in vivid prose, and the picture he paints contrasts with the verdant if sometimes tragic paradise described by Felix. Thomas, a man of learning, had reached a point in his life where he wanted to make money, or at any rate to earn a living, climb the so-called social ladder, and achieve a modicum of well-being, a respectable level of "comfort." His decision to take in paying boarders (*Tischgänger*) was an additional resource, a reliable if modest source of income. The regular payment of room and board by his students helped Thomas to meet his growing need for cash, for he had embarked on a plan to acquire land and buildings. The rent generated by the boarders only supplemented other sources of income, however—at least at first, for the situation would change later on. In Basel as in Lyons, the best prospect for an intellectual or semi-intellectual with a good knowledge of ancient languages like Thomas Platter—the royal road to a better life, if perhaps also a trap for the unwary—was for a brief time the printing trade, or, more accurately, the ownership of a print shop. Did printing provide Thomas with enough to live on? In any case it fed the dreams of a journeyman typographer who had not yet risen to the rank of master printer, or *Trukerr herren* (T 129). Master printers did good business and could amass a considerable amount of capital with a minimum of sweat. Such, at any rate, was what people said, and they may have embellished the truth somewhat. Wives of Gutenberg's allegedly well-compensated disciples pestered their husbands to take the books they printed to the Frankfurt book fair and sell them there, and then bring home nice cushions and pewter from the shops of that great German city (T 119). Many lived beyond their means. Even after he became the owner of a print shop, Thomas, who knew the value of a penny, contented himself with purchasing simple ironware on the banks of the Main (*ich koufft isin hä-ven*). But many printers' wives, once they were assured that their husbands' businesses would prosper, longed to move up in society, fighting their way upstream like trout or salmon desperate to reach the higher levels of the cascade of contempt.

This was the case with the wife of Andreas Hartmann, or Cratander, a native of Strasbourg who became a pious printer in Reformation Basel. The printer of Plautus, he had presented Thomas with a volume of that author's works whose printing he had overseen; this was the volume that Thomas had unstitched and hidden among the fibers in the ropemaker's shop where he worked, in the hope of combining mental with manual labor.[1] Cratander's success as a publisher proved to be brief. His ambitious wife persuaded him and their son Polycarpus to shun the scribbles and scrawls (*sudlery*) of the printing trade and take up the supposedly more respectable and certainly less grimy business of bookselling. True, Thomas did much the same thing some years later, when, his success assured, his capital amassed, his loans covered if not repaid, and his house bought and paid for, he abandoned the typesetter's chair and apron for the robes of a professor. An early mountain climber, Thomas-the-highlander inched his way up the social hierarchy by first establishing a foothold and then, with his free hand, searching the smooth rock face for the still higher protuberance, the small granite ledge that was all he needed to thrust his body up another notch: begging provided him with his first toehold, after which came literacy, and from there it was on to ropemaking, teaching, and printing and all the way to the status of boarding-school headmaster and leading pedagogue (even if his status was contested by the university).

Thomas was not only an intellectual but also a worker, a breadwinner. In the struggle for social recognition he had one big advantage: the physique of a soldier, a fighter. His son Felix knew this at first hand, having been at times the object of his father's beatings. But Thomas's combativeness, one of the many talents of this Renaissance man, was not directed solely against members of his family. In the very print shop in which he was a partner he fought a Homeric battle with Balthasar Ruch. Ruch worked for Episcopius as a typesetter until 1534, then, in 1535, joined Thomas Platter and two others to found a sort of printers' cooperative (T 118). Ruch and Platter quarreled over the financial details of the business, financial matters being something about which Thomas was always sensitive, as evidenced by his quarrels with his wife over his debts. To believe Thomas, whose version of the event portrays him, as usual, in an entirely innocent light, Ruch had attempted to bludgeon him from behind with a thick plank one night while he was reading proof, but he saw the blow coming and managed to avoid it. The two men fought, gouged each other, pulled hair, and went for the scalp. Thomas nearly lost an eye as the two exchanged blows. He then laid Ruch out with a punch to the nose. The loser's wife cried.[2] Employees of the two partners intervened: the journeymen evidently felt that their bosses had more important things to do than to put each other's eyes out. The results of this ferocious battle were as follows: Ruch was forced to wear a bandage on his nose for eight weeks, during which time he had to put in an appearance at the Frankfurt book fair, while Thomas wore a dressing on his middle finger for four weeks.

Did the two men make up after their fight? In his memoirs, at any rate, Thomas describes Ruch as a good typographer and a man capable of courage (obviously) and noble sentiments. He was also a good friend (*gutter gsell* [T 118]) with an eye to social advancement: in Thomas's book this was a point in his favor. Relations between the two men were disrupted briefly by the fight but improved later on when Ruch quit the partnership and went into business for himself from 1538 to 1541. The two had certainly had a good understanding earlier, around 1535, when they had formed the partnership with two other friends. (I arrive at the date 1535 for the formation of the partnership because it occurred after the birth of Ursula in 1534 and after Ruch quit his job with Episcopius but before the birth of Felix in October 1536 and the first joint production of books by Platter and Ruch in March 1536.)

Who else was involved? There was of course the ubiquitous Oporinus, who turned up at almost every important juncture in Thomas's life following his return from Germany and Alsace. Oporinus (whose German name was Johannes Herbster, "the autumnal one") was seven or eight years younger than Thomas and the son of a well-known painter (*verriempter Maler* [T 119]). This illustrious ancestry earned him the privilege of membership in his father's guild, Zum Himmel (In Heaven): guilds in Basel recruited on a partly professional, partly familial, consciously elitist basis (the consequent contradictions apparently went unnoticed). What Arlette Farge has called the "good fortune of being included" conferred considerable advantages. With his strong connections to the Basel middle class, Oporinus good-naturedly dominated his older friend, a country boy who was still something of a bumpkin, a "hick" according to urban prejudice. Of course such snobbish distinctions were soon blurred in a city ravaged by plague and religious upheaval: hardworking, talented new arrivals quickly filled the places that became available. The taint of low birth was soon effaced in the eyes of natives.

Oporinus never suffered from any such social stigma. An excellent Latinist, he had from the age of nineteen progressed steadily in his teaching career through primary, secondary, and university ranks. What is more, he had enjoyed the signal privilege of employment as Paracelsus's medical secretary. To supplement his income, he also corrected proof, and in 1535 he joined with Platter and Ruch in their print cooperative.[3] Fascinated by the printing trade, Oporinus quit the university altogether in 1542. It was a wise decision: in 1543 he produced his most important work as a publisher, a splendid edition of Vesalius's *Humani corporis fabrica*. A first-rate artist in the "graphical" tradition of the great dissector whose fame he helped to promote, Oporinus was not much of a businessman and regularly ran himself into bankruptcy. Although Thomas owed almost everything he achieved to Oporinus's influence, he nevertheless remarks acidly on his friend's penchant for burying himself in debt. Although one of Oporinus's two wives came from a wealthy family of goldsmiths, both proved to be spendthrifts, which did nothing to improve his situation. Toward the end of his life, however, a third and then a fourth marriage put him back on his feet. But was it really necessary to run through four women in order to end one's life in comfort?

Oporinus exerted considerable influence on a whole phase of Thomas Platter's existence. The younger man adored his older friend; he gradually transformed Thomas from a mangy, cloddish highlander into a respectable burgher. When Platter was still an ill-nourished, overworked ropemaker, Oporinus had made it possible for him to teach Hebrew to a class of twenty students at Saint Leonhard's school (this was at a time when Thomas, being something of a working-class militant ultra-Protestant with iconoclastic tendencies, took a particular interest in the Old Testament). Oporinus, with his bourgeois connections, also provided Thomas with a letter of introduction (*durch brieff Kundschafft*) to Heinrich Billing, the stepson of the bürgermeister of Basel; the Billing family subsequently took the ex-Valaisian under its wing (T 95). Somewhat later, after Oporinus had become the head of a prestigious school adjacent to the cathedral and settled comfortably into quarters in the former bishop's residence (the new Protestant teachers having snapped up the best jobs and apartments), he chose Thomas as his assistant at the unheard of salary of forty pounds a year.

We can now understand more fully why Thomas, whose Protestant convictions were no doubt quite sincere, had, if he wished to get ahead, no choice but to throw in his lot with the reform faction, which was Œcolampadian in Basel just as it had been Zwinglian in Zurich. It was either join the "heretics" or resign himself to being a nobody. Oporinus disapproved when Platter, on a whim, suddenly quit his relatively comfortable teaching post to become the valet and student of Epiphanius, the Bavarian-Venetian doctor, from whom Thomas had hoped to learn medicine and improve himself more rapidly (a miscalculation later redeemed by his son's success as a physician). Not one to hold a grudge, however, Oporinus cheerfully welcomed the disenchanted Thomas back to Basel after Epiphanius's tragic death in 1531. The two together then copied the precious prescriptions from the Venetian doctor's pharmacopoeia: their complicity, if not always scrupulous, was now complete.

Cooperation led to triumph when Thomas brought his old teacher and friend Myconius from Zurich, then under papist threat, to Basel and found lodging for him with Oporinus (T 112). In the following year Myconius inherited nothing less than the pulpit of the late Œcolampadius, the Protestant preacher who had converted Basel and become the city's foremost minister. From then on, things moved quickly. The two "scholars," Oporinus and Thomas, both taught in the city's *paedagogium*, switching from Hebrew to Greek and accordingly from iconoclastic (biblical) fanaticism to benevolent (Hellenic) humanism. Dissatisfied with their teaching salaries, our "duo" continued their progress by seeking part-time work as proofreaders (*Oporinus ouch . . . in den trukeryen corrigiert* [T 118]).

Hence there is nothing mysterious about the two men's later partnership in the printing business. Since Oporinus had for many years provided Thomas with bed, board, work, and all the rest, it is rather shocking to note the cold tone with which Platter describes his young friend's heavy debts, from which he escaped only by marrying a third and ultimately a fourth time. Such ingratitude or at any rate lack of concern is common in the writing of this successful social climber, who owed his good fortune largely to two men, Myconius in Zurich and Oporinus in Basel. Both were Protestants, and both—the strict preacher and the humanist aesthete—were destined to end their days as citizens of Basel: Myconius succumbed to the plague there in 1552, and Oporinus died in 1568.

There is no mystery about Thomas's two other partners in the printing business. Balthasar Ruch, whom we encountered earlier, and Ruprecht Winter both came out of the "stable" of Oporinus, who was not only the deus ex machina of the group but also by far the most talented printer. Winter was the son of a "good merchant" of Basel (T 172). He married a goldsmith's daughter, the sister of Oporinus's second wife. Though born wealthy, these women defied convention in their choice of marriage partners. Winter, examples of whose printwork from the middle third of the sixteenth century have survived, also ended up bankrupt. He spent everything he earned and had no head for business.

Ruch, despite his spectacular row with Thomas, was originally a friend of his as well as of Oporinus. All four partners were highly skilled printers. Separately and collectively, they produced a number of noteworthy books, foremost among which (apart from Oporinus's edition of Vesalius mentioned earlier) was Calvin's *Christianae religionis institutio,* which came off Thomas's presses in 1536. Their shop was one of the leading presses in Basel, a city that numbered among the publishing capitals of the world at that time. Oporinus, as was mentioned earlier, was a member of the guild Zum Himmel. Winter and Ruch belonged to Zum Bären (The Bear). At their request, Thomas was invited to join the latter in 1536, shortly before Felix's birth in October. Thomas also became a burgher of the city, a status that carried with it certain rights and privileges. Although he was now a citizen of some prominence, he felt himself under no compulsion to conceal his past as a poor highland boy. On the contrary, he told his story to anyone who was willing to listen. Early modern society was evidently not as closed and snobbish as one might think, at least not in the democratic cities of Switzerland.

The new printing business needed money and equipment. Providential assistance came from Cratander (Andreas Hartmann) (T 80, 163). Already in his fifties, Cratander had retired from publishing at the urging of his wife and gone into bookselling, which was less physically taxing than printing, a trade that required not only intellect but also physical stamina. His son Polycarpus helped out in the bookshop; the boy's name, like the father's, suggests that someone in the family knew Greek.

In about 1525 Polycarpus had himself been a boarder in the home of Collinus, also known as Rudolf Ambüel (also spelled Am Biel or Am Buol [F 259]).[4] Collinus, born in 1499, was an exact contemporary of Thomas Platter. Subtle and learned (*gelehrter*), this former student at universities in Switzerland, Austria, and Italy had been obliged to quit his teaching post in the Catholic city of Lucerne because of his outspoken Zwinglianism. As a refugee in Basel, he learned the ropemaking trade in 1524 and then, in 1526, opened a ropemaking shop. Meanwhile, he taught courses in Greek at the university, while Thomas, as an apprentice ropemaker in his shop, improved his Latin by reading the copy of Plautus that Cratander had given him. (It would be pleasant if today's workers felt driven to study Latin and Greek on the job.) Collinus also took in boarders to supplement his modest income. Both he and Thomas subsequently abandoned ropemaking in favor of full- or part-time teaching. The Am Buol family, through which the Cratanders made contact with the Platters (including Felix: see F 259), is particularly interesting because another member, Kaspar Am Buol, was one of the first learned apothecaries to extol the therapeutic virtues of hot baths, in his canton at any rate—and in Switzerland such priority is no small achievement. For Thomas Platter these men were models: scholarship, teaching, manual labor, and taking in boarders were all things he would try at one point or another in his lifetime. Here we see some features of Swiss humanism at its best.

Cratander stood at the center of a network linking the worlds of culture, printing, education, and craftsmanship. Besides having given Thomas the Plautus that he took with him into the ropemaking shop, he was in contact with Balthasar Ruch, the printer-pugilist, whose notes he sometimes countersigned. Another Basel printer linked in several ways to this network was Johannes Bebel, or Bebelius, who like Cratander came from Alsace. Bebelius was a friend of Thomas's and used the familiar *du* with him (although Thomas always called him Herr); he also considered him a *lantzman,* or countryman, although the reasons for this are not clear, since Alsace is nowhere near the Valais (T123, 137). Bebelius was also connected to Ruprecht Winter, whose debts he obligingly forgave (T 122). And he was a close friend of Cratander's. When Cratander died, Bebelius bought his bookshop, saving his heirs from ruin. Clearly this was a close-knit group, almost a holding company whose investors were "outsiders" rather than Basel natives: immigration has its rewards.

When Thomas and his partners set up shop, Cratander discreetly sold the new business certain essential equipment for the sum of 800 gulden. Did the money come in part from Ruprecht Winter, who had access to cash through his father and wife? In any case it was a loan that had to be paid off within a specified period (*uff ein gwyss zyt zu betzalen*). Besides supplying the partners with needed equipment, Cratander also rented them Bear House (the animal lent its name to the shop as well as the guild).

\*　\*　\*

The birth of Thomas's son in October 1536—the beloved only son of his first marriage—offers an opportunity to measure the strength of the ties that Thomas, a self-made man, had forged in the worlds of publishing, teaching, and the clergy in Basel. Indeed, the baby's first godfather was none other than Simon Grynaeus, or Grynaer, who grew up on the banks of the Danube and later pursued his studies along the banks of the Neckar. In Basel he taught Greek and later "biblical science." His relations with the University of Basel were stormy: the institution apparently challenged his academic credentials, or perhaps his lack of or failure to obtain such credentials (T 170). The *alma mater* had no use for autodidacts. In this respect Grynaeus held fairly radical views, which associated him with the working-class militancy or at any rate the anti-academic, "anti-prof" extremism that was shared to varying degrees by Myconius, Collinus, and Thomas Platter. Grynaer had a passion for teaching, however. It was he who, some years later, strongly advised Thomas to return to teaching, whose advantages and disadvantages he laid out in detail: "Become a schoolmaster, Thomas! No profession is more divine! None could suit me better! Ah, if only I didn't have to repeat everything I say!" The final sentence, which still rings true today, did not discourage Simon Grynaer's son Samuel (1539–99), who evidently remembered only the first part of the paternal paean. Samuel Grynaer, who became a professor of Roman law at the University of Basel (T 148 and 181; F 123), played a role similar to his father's vis-à-vis the Platters. On July 27, 1574, he become godfather to Thomas's second son, Thomas Jr., the fruit of septagenarian but still vigorous Thomas Sr.'s second marriage to a much younger woman. Thomas Jr., thirty-eight years younger than his brother Felix, would, like Felix and his father, also write his memoirs. But to get back to Felix's baptism, it was *Herr* Simon Grynaer (Thomas conferred this mark of social distinction upon him) who, upon leaving the church in which the sacrament had just been performed, remarked to Thomas that the child would indeed be *felix* (happy), "or else all my senses deceive me" (*oder all meine sin driegen mich*). Simon was not mistaken, except for the fact that Felix never fathered a child of his own. Thomas filled in for him, however, by remarrying at an advanced age and producing a second brood of sons and daughters. Apparently the name Felix was chosen primarily because Thomas's wife, who came from Zurich, respected that city's onomastic traditions: one of Myconius's sons was also baptized Felix. In this there is further evidence of Thomas Platter's fondness for his Zurich-based, "Myconian" connections, which had first allowed him to escape from the misery of his childhood.

Felix's other godfather was Johannes Walterus *typographus*. Everyone understood that this appellation referred to the typographer Johann Walter, who was active in Basel in the 1530s but has left no other trace in our sources (T 121, 173). Walter moved in the same professional circles as Thomas but at a lower social and cultural level. The fact that he came from Zurich argued in his favor, however, for Thomas continued to feel strong ties to the old Helvetic city on the banks of the Limmat and the Silh.

Ottilia Nachpur was Felix's godmother. The wife of a young and wealthy draper, Macharius Nussbaum, she evidently did not live long, for her husband soon took a second wife. The prestigious merchant lived on until 1553, long enough to offer Thomas Platter useful advice about investments in land and buildings (T 125).

* * *

Thomas's career as a printer, which extended from 1535 or 1536 to 1543 or 1544, had its ups and downs, which left their mark on him. In the summer of 1535 he paid an entry fee to join the Bear Guild, which accepted artisans in the trades of precious metals, coinage, typemaking, and printing. Oporinus, who like Thomas was also a professor and printer, remained a member of the Heaven Guild, a rather heterogeneous organization that accepted glassmakers, saddlers, and painters, including Oporinus's father, a celebrated local artist (T 119). In October 1535 Thomas also became a burgher of Basel (*ich ward burger* [T 119, 172]). Having risen in social status, he pursued his trade in partnership with his friendly enemy Balthasar Ruch until the spring of 1538, at which time he continued in business on his own. His partnership with Ruch had lasted nearly three years (from 1535–36 to 1538) and produced some two dozen books, including not only religious works but also secular humanist volumes and even medical texts, all bearing the mark of Ruch and Platter.

The peak of Thomas's career as a "typographer-intellectual" came early in his partnership with Ruch: it was nothing less than the publication of the first edition of Calvin's *Christianae religionis institutio* in March 1536. Was Thomas impressed by the mathematical precision with which the Huguenot leader set forth his thought, imposing a Cartesian clarity *avant la lettre* on the five hundred pages of the first surviving edition of his work—the masterpiece of Thomas Platter, printer?[5] Calvin takes up several subjects in succession: the law (an explanation of the Ten Commandments); faith (an elucidation of the Credo, a discussion of the importance of justification); prayer (glosses on the Lord's Prayer); and the sacraments (baptism and the Lord's Supper being the only ones that Calvin recognized, for he denied that the five other sacraments accepted by the Roman Church had any divine status). He concludes his magisterial if not always convincing work with some thoughts on Christian freedom, in which he relates the attributes of the two powers, ecclesiastic and temporal. Through many subsequent editions the thought of the "heresiarch" became considerably more ponderous, losing some of the joyfully militant simplicity of the first, "Platterian" edition of 1536. The whole work was suffused with the harsh principles of predestination, that divine forebear of royal absolutism (which had other antecedents as well): according to this formidable doctrine, the pot cannot complain to the potter (whose decision is arbitrary) of being a lowly chamber pot rather than a beautiful amphora (Romans 9:21). The artisan has power over his clay; he is the master.

More radical than Luther, Calvin rejected the mass, the real presence of Christ in the host, and the ecclesiastical hierarchy. The effect of his writing could only have been to confirm Thomas in the rather extremist attitude he had absorbed from his master, Zwingli. But Platter, unlike the Picardian theorist, was no ideologue. His fisticuffs with Ruch notwithstanding, he, like his sons after him, was throughout his life a nonviolent person in the mold of Montaigne, at least when it came to religion, politics, and intellectual discussion. One cannot help smiling at the *ad hoc* text that appears below the title of the *Institutio:* "Envisaging everything connected with the doctrine of salvation, a work worthy of being read by any student of pious subjects; with a preface addressed to the Most Christian King [Francis I] as an offering in profession of faith." In this, Thomas's first in-depth contact with French culture (albeit in its Latin form), it is also moving to read the final words of the volume: "*Basileae per Thomam Platterum et Balthasarum Lasium . . . martio 1536*" ("Basel, by Thomas Platter and Balthasar Lasius [Ruch], March 1536"). The two men were thus sanctified by the vast work whose reproduction they made possible. One suddenly finds it rather difficult to imagine them in their real lives as hardworking, hot-tempered printers exchanging blows and pulling each other's hair out by the roots. Astonishingly enough, Thomas's memoirs do indeed fail to mention the *Institutio,* a fact that suggests that the Valaisian's mystical period, which began with his conversion to Zwinglianism in 1520, was now behind him, even if he remained quite pious in his everyday life. By contrast, the memoirs deal at length, as is only to be expected, with the financial difficulties that beset the four partners, and particularly Ruch and Platter.

The partnership's business was conducted not only in Basel but also in Frankfurt, at the great book fairs that were held there. The assets of the business included the 800 gulden worth of equipment that Cratander had sold the partnership. The liabilities were increased by loans to finance the purchase of raw materials and other operating expenses. In addition, Ruprecht Winter had put up part of the partnership's assets as collateral for a loan he obtained to defray his wife's expenses. Trips to Frankfurt by one or another of the partners were also a drain on the business, and the money earned from the sale of books was often spent on trinkets and luxury items. Thomas was the only exception in this regard: of course his wife, though born a servant, harbored a few grandiose ideas, but she did not covet luxury as did the wives of Winter and Oporinus, who had been born into the Basel bourgeoisie. All in all, the partnership contracted debts of 2,000 gulden. Things got so bad that at one point it was feared that the partners would have to forgo their modest salaries, which had been set at 104 gulden annually for each of them and had at first been paid regularly (T 107). (For comparison, when Thomas became a school headmaster in 1540, he received a comfortable compensation of 200 gulden annually from the Basel authorities.)

In the spring of 1538, or more precisely sometime after the Frankfurt book fair around Easter of that year, the partnership dissolved, and Thomas became the head of his own business. Production immediately dropped off: the shop no longer turned out books as prestigious as Calvin's *Institutio,* which had been the opportunity of a lifetime. Calvin had literally launched Thomas Platter in 1536, though of course the religious leader had other things on his mind and had no idea what his book had meant to its printer. The temporary setback to Thomas's fortunes may have been more apparent than real, but the number of books produced certainly did decline: "From March 1538 to March 1543 [or perhaps 1544), the shop's imprimatur appeared on no more than thirteen or fourteen impressions," as compared with twenty-four at the peak of the Platter-Ruch collaboration (March 1536–March 1538), that is, twelve volumes annually in the peak period versus two to three volumes during the period in which Thomas was essentially on his own. At first sight, then, it would appear that Thomas was a much less substantial force in the printing trade than when he had been assisted in the management of the business by the dynamic if at times violent Ruch.

This hasty judgment is not entirely borne out by the facts, however, for it was during the second phase of his printing career that Thomas was able to buy a house and fair-sized farm in the nearby countryside. He enjoyed this prosperity, moreover, despite the fact that he was deprived, if we accept his side of the story, of one hundred gulden due him from the dissolved partnership (the money went instead to his hapless partner Ruprecht Winter). Is there something missing from his account? In fact, Platter probably made his way out of the cooperative venture with certain personal benefits about which he does not deign to inform us. His partner Ruch's desire to bash his head in may have had something to do with the anger of a shareholder and manager who felt swindled by a greedy "friend." Whatever Thomas may or may not have embezzled from the business, the fact remains that he was able to reopen the shop under his own personal management in 1538. The business was well equipped. Thomas had many friends among the city's diecasters, engravers, and manufacturers of type fonts who provided him with indispensable sets of carefully honed, aligned, and calibrated typefaces—all, he tells us, for a relatively modest price (*umb ein ring gelt*).[6] Among these benefactors, who may not have been as disinterested as Thomas maintains, was Martin Hosch, a typemaker formerly of Strasbourg who became a citizen of Basel in 1530. When he died in 1541, his widow married another typemaker, Christoph Behem: the trade was endogamous. There was also Master Utz (whose real name was Goruch Köpfle), a typemaker and engraver. Above all, there was the astonishing Peter Schöffer Jr., who owned a fabulous set of dies and whose perfectly honed typefaces nicely completed Thomas's equipment without costing him a penny. Schöffer came by his skills naturally, "for he was related to the early inventors of printing in Mainz itself" (*uss Welches gschlächt die trukery zu Mentz erfunden ist* [T 122]).[7] His father was Peter Schöffer Sr., the son-in-law and collaborator of Johannes Fust, a financier and aesthete typographer who had worked directly with Gutenberg. The three men, Gutenberg, Fust, and Schöffer Sr., collaborated on the celebrated forty-two-line Bible of 1453. Hence young Schöffer had quite an astonishing pedigree for a person in the printing trade.

After lending Thomas Platter crucial assistance in Basel, the younger Schöffer turned up in Venice in 1541, where he printed bibles and a work by Raymond Lull. By 1542 he was back in Basel, where he died in 1547. In the interim he was widowed and remarried and was accepted as a citizen of Basel.[8] In addition to a wide range of typefaces, Thomas seems to have obtained, without investing any large sums, the presses (*prässen*) essential for his business. "Young" printer though he was, he prided himself on his professionalism and his capital, both mechanical (the presses) and intellectual: his hardware and software. He never forgot that he had been a teacher (and would teach again). He therefore instructed his young apprentices (*lerbuben*) in the rudiments of Latin and even Greek (probably no more than the alphabet in the case of Greek, however), so that they could perform their daily work (*tagwerch*) under his supervision. Thomas's success in the book business was probably due to his striving for philological as well as typographical quality.

At various places Thomas alludes to the metals business and metalworking technology in typography. In fact, however, he had little detailed knowledge of metalworking techniques, for unlike Peter Schöffer or Martin Hosch he was neither a typemaker nor an engraver. Although he was a subcontractor in the world that revolved around Frobenius, he has little to say about the purchase of raw materials such as paper and ink. It has been found that centuries before the actual discovery of titanium (a metal used today in the manufacture of jet aircraft), there was titanium in the ink used by Gutenberg for his Bible. Thomas, who probably received helpful advice at the beginning from his partner Ruch, nevertheless solved many technical problems without being an expert himself. The pages of his edition of Calvin's *Christianae religionis institutio* have not yellowed after fifteen generations (see the fine specimen preserved at the Bibliothèque Nationale in Paris). Skilled workers did the rest, including members of the family: Thomas's children (Felix and Ursula) often prepared and folded paper until their fingers bled (*das inen die finger blutten*). Their mother, Anna, set an example for them to follow. Times were hard, but the business went well (*übel zyt, aber es gieng myr woll*).

\*   \*   \*

Thomas's early experience as a printer, particularly during the time of his partnership with Ruch (1536–1538), involved substantial risk from debt. He did not lack for good advice or cautionary examples. Among those from whom he received advice was Konrad Rösch, or Resch, a Basel citizen of Swabian origin, born on the banks of the Neckar (T 174, F 436). Resch was related to Wattenschnee, alias Johannes Schabler (T 123), for whom Thomas produced books as a subcontractor. Like Schabler, Resch had been a student at Tübingen. For a long time he had also sold books—in Paris, in fact, the Swiss having switched their allegiance after the Battle of Marignano (1515) to France and its culture, radiant with triumph and later with humanism (this despite, or perhaps because of, the massacre of French enemies on the field of battle). In Basel, Resch, a member of the Saffron Guild, lived adjacent to the fish market. He had successively married two sisters, as good a way as any of integrating into a society. In lengthy conversations with Thomas he delivered sermons against indebtedness, but he also described France and his stays in Paris. Was he the person who gave Thomas the idea of one day sending his son Felix to study medicine in Montpellier? Moreover, the unfortunate Cratander, who lay on his deathbed under a crushing burden of debt, revealed his financial woes to Thomas and warned him against burdening his business with too many liabilities.

How pertinent were Cratander's reflections on the eve of his demise? Thomas was trusted in Basel as a man of skill and know-how. Because he enjoyed solid credit, he eventually decided to move his business to more convenient and imposing quarters (still in rented space, however). The move took place in 1538, the same year that the partnership with Ruch ended (F 55; T 119, 172). Felix, Thomas's son, was two years old at the time. Thomas took advantage of the exodus of Catholic priests from Basel after the city adopted Protestantism as its official and compulsory religion in 1529. Ten years later, Thomas was able to rent two houses that had belonged to the former secretary of the local chapter of canons, a man by the name of Kächtler or Kechtler, who had arrived in Basel to attend the university in 1521 (T 174). A man of substantial means who achieved success in the city as well as in the church, Kächtler in 1524 purchased three adjoining houses at 90, 92, and 94 Obere Freie Strasse (according to the numbering on an 1859 map, drawn up well after the Renaissance, but residential addresses in the city had changed little in the intervening years). These houses were close to one of the city's gates, the Inneres Aschentor. They also abutted the Gothic apse of a church, the Barfüsserkirche. Together they defined a small triangular plaza extending beyond Freie Strasse (F 48 ff., figs. 2 and 3). Kächtler's influence in Basel and his extensive real-estate purchases reflected the economic and demographic growth of his native Alsace, both Catholic and Protestant. Alsace was the base that furnished Basel with both people and the cash that fueled its financial and real-estate market. After 1529, Kächtler, like so many other Catholic priests and laymen, was driven out by the Protestant revolution and forced to emigrate. But the Republic of Basel was not vindictive: it was not yet 1793! A regime of democratic or representative immanence rather than divine or royal transcendence, it did not in most cases confiscate émigré property. Hence the printer Platter was able to rent two houses from the "canonical secretary in exodus" for the not exorbitant sum of sixteen gulden per year (as a partner in a modest printing business, Thomas had an annual salary of one hundred gulden). Here we see how far Thomas had come between 1531, when he had not hesitated to accept a job as a physician's valet in order to sustain himself and continue his studies, and 1538, when he became an independent small businessman, in debt, to be sure, but still relatively prosperous. He was now able to move into substantial quarters, though of course his first order of business was to fill the space with as many beds as possible for boarders, and to fill the one-time clerical residence, whose facade he repainted, with new equipment for printing. Three presses were brought in. The shop took on work for Frobenius, or more precisely for Frobenius-Herwagen and associates, while Thomas continued to sell books that he produced on his own. At first twenty and later as many as thirty to forty noisy boarders—elementary and secondary school students—were accommodated on closely packed beds and yielded Thomas a good income (*so hat ich mer den zwenzig tischgenger, das ich do vill gwan*). This was makeshift capitalism, pay as you go: printing provided the means to expand into the operation of a boarding house, in which Anna played an important if exhausting role. Felix and his sister Ursula enjoyed a private, heated room of their own. In the attic, Kächtler, the absentee secretary of the canonical chapter, had left a storeroom filled with old clothes, unused cassocks, and the like. The stouthearted fellow still hoped that the Catholic, Apostolic, and Roman religion would one day return to its former glory in Basel, restoring him to his former glory along with it, and he was determined to be ready when the time came. Thomas, who maintained good relations with Kächtler (mainly by letter), paid no attention to these delusions. His chief concern was to repay his debts, and by some miracle he actually managed to do so. Indeed, he was so pleased with himself that in 1539, the year after he first took the lease on his new property, he had a hunting scene depicting a hunter, his dog, and the head of a stag with antlers painted on the facade of his new residence, the house at 90, Obere Freie Strasse, closest to Barfüsserkirche. Henceforth this two-story house was known as Zum Gejägd or Zum Gejegt (At the Hunt).

Was the mural intended to depict deer hunting? Did it suggest hunting with hounds? Did Thomas harbor seigneurial ambitions (for Felix, perhaps)? In any case, if Thomas believed that to escape from debt was ultimately a desirable goal, for the time being he had other projects to contend with. He had grasped the fact that in a time of inflation, borrowing, if done judiciously, is a way of getting rich over the relatively long run. No matter how much Anna harassed him on this issue, nothing could make him change his mind. Husband and wife might throw dishes at each other, but credit was credit. God took a hand in the matter. God was often present at important moments in Thomas's life: he who had cured his servant of illness in 1538 and had given him a male child now encouraged him to buy the two houses he was renting on Obere Freie Strasse. The year was now 1540, and poor Kächtler, the former chapter secretary, knew that there was no longer any chance of returning from exile to his former residence now that papism had been pulled up from Basel root and branch. He and his "woman," Ursula Güderin (who may have been a wife, a mistress, or merely a nurse or concubine), decided to sell all three houses. "On the advice of God and several other worthy people [sic]," Thomas initially bought the two houses he was already renting and then acquired the adjoining structure; this was to prevent a farmer from purchasing the property and using the building to house his livestock, which would have allowed him to pile manure on the triangular plaza in front. This would not only have created a stinking nuisance but, even worse, would have contaminated the subsurface water with urine (Basel's water table was high), thereby preventing Thomas from sinking a well. Once the three houses were his, Thomas was able to proceed immediately to the drilling of the famous well. The work cost him one hundred gulden, not counting the cost of feeding the well-diggers. This, as we have seen, was equivalent to his annual income as a partner in a modest printing business.

In order to acquire this block of buildings, the ex-Valaisian had to go into debt once again. No doubt he needed to borrow less than would have been the case a few years earlier, for the exodus of many wealthy Catholic clergy and laymen had led to a collapse in real-estate prices as many properties were put up for auction. What is more, Thomas was seen as a good risk: the sellers, the canon and his companion in exile, chose the dynamic Platter over more prestigious but impecunious and less adaptable buyers, including a noble by the name of von Offenburg belonging to a somewhat ridiculous family with which Thomas had come into contact on a trip from Zurich to Basel, and a city official, the head of the local mint (*Müntzmeister*). Having won this contest, Thomas spent the entire year of 1540 in negotiations over the purchase and sale. The deal was finally completed at the end of January 1541, with the purchase of all three houses for a total of 950 gulden, including deposits made (or promissory notes signed) over the previous several months. The terms were similar in some ways to a rental-purchase agreement or lease with option to buy and in some ways to an installment loan. Various agents served as intermediaries in the negotiations between the Catholic party (Kächtler) and the Protestant party (Platter); by this time religious antagonisms were of relatively minor importance in such matters. Thomas's days as a fanatic were over. He was prepared to tolerate the peaceful coexistence of the Œcolampadian and Roman sects, and indeed so were most other people, although beneath the surface considerable hostility continued to smolder on both sides. The Valaisian, who now enjoyed powerful connections, received advice from highly placed friends, including such "dear old gentlemen" (*die lieben alten herren*) as Bürgermeister zum Hirtzen and the draper Nussbaum.

Debts! The accounting that Thomas gives in his memoirs may not always be strictly accurate, but it seems that he paid 750 gulden for the first two of the three houses. His rent for the previous two years was 16 gulden per year, which works out to a relatively low return on capital of just 2.1 percent. True, the Catholic absentee landlord was hardly in a position to pressure his tenant and soon-to-be buyer, who enjoyed the support of powerful city officials. Kächtler, who felt he was being swindled by the printer, lost his temper at times: "Your collateral isn't worth a bucket of ashes" (*ein züber mit äschen*), he burst out one day after Thomas proposed to use his business assets as collateral to guarantee his loan (T 125). In any case, the sum of 750 gulden included not just the buildings but certain items of furniture, for Platter had agreed to pay 50 gulden of the total in compensation for Kächtler's old beds and other white elephants (actually not worth a brass farthing). Thomas bought the furniture only because he was forced to, or because he could fob it off on his two or three dozen boarders. From Thomas's rather esoteric calculations it emerges that on the 750 gulden that he owed the seller after closing the sale of the two houses, he paid only 5 percent interest on the first 500 gulden and 20 percent on the remaining 250, for a total of 75 gulden in annual interest, or an annual rate of 10 percent. This was by no means excessive, particularly when we take into account the fact that prices were rising intermittently or steadily over the long term, so that the seller was forced to charge a higher rate of interest to cover himself against the inflation that was "in the air." (The underlying causes of this inflation are still not altogether clear: Was it the first influx of precious metals from the New World, augmenting the traditional supply from Central Europe and the Sudan? Or the growing population, which exerted inexorable pressure on supply and hence on prices?) Bear in mind, however, that while the rise in prices that afflicted the sixteenth century may have been impressive to the early modern mind, it was moderate compared with the runaway inflation that the twentieth century has seen.

Platter and Kächtler soon agreed on the sale of the third house as well. Thomas's debts now rose to a grand total of 950 gulden (the equivalent of 120,000 Swiss francs of 1975): not an inconsiderable sum but not an excessive amount either by current standards (which are considerably more tolerant of debt, to be sure, than sixteenth-century standards were). Platter, after several stormy scenes with Kächtler in Freiburg, managed to come up with the necessary cash on his return to Basel. By 1542 he was able, through obliging intermediaries, to repay 300 gulden of the 950 he owed to the secretary in exile. Within five years he had paid off the entire debt (*ich hatt in 5 jaren gar zalt*). Thus by 1546 or 1547 he owned his property outright, fulfilling the dream of so many peasants of the past, who sank their hearts into their land (T 127). Thomas Platter remained a peasant at heart, and before long he became at least a part-time peasant in actual fact. Several things made this remarkable feat possible: Thomas's good connections with the Protestant bourgeoisie of Basel; his net profit of 200 gulden per year from the print shop; and the backbreaking work of Platter, his wife, and his children to make the boardinghouse work. Business was good, in fact excellent. In 1539 the Junker von Offenburg had been willing to pay 600 gulden cash (*bar*) for at least two of the houses. Within a few years, the master of the Basel mint offered Thomas 1,200 gulden for *just one* of the three houses he now owned. Housing prices were thus rising rapidly, doubling or tripling in just a few years. Indeed, the economic climate of the 1530s and 1540s was generally favorable in German-, French-, and Romansch-speaking Switzerland (although setbacks were not uncommon in the printing business). The age was thus propitious for the kind of speculation in real estate that gladdens the hearts and lines the pockets of born calculators like Thomas Platter.

\* \* \*

After buying his houses, Thomas went on to acquire farmland. His career plan was clear. Like so many citizens of Western cities then and later, this Basel burgher became a rural landowner. In the spring of 1549 he was still simply the owner, free of debt, of three adjacent houses on Obere Freie Strasse, but the time had come to make his move, even if that meant putting himself into the red again. In June of that year he bought several pieces of potential farmland and adjoining buildings, all close to various fortified medieval structures.9 None of the plots was more than a quarter of an hour's walk beyond Basel's old southern ramparts (on what is now Gundeldingerstrasse). The seller, not accidentally, was one Ulrich Hugwald Mutz, known simply as Hugwald. Born in the late fifteenth century and slightly older than Thomas Platter, Hugwald came from Thurgovia. As a young man he had been an enthusiastic manual laborer and farmer: "Thou shalt toil in the fields and earn thy daily bread in the sweat of thy brow" (F 103). He had even tasted the peasant life on occasion and in the end chose it as his own. Then, bitten by the bug to teach and join the elite, he became a teacher and taught at the Burgschule until 1540, when he became a professor in the Faculty of Arts. In 1549, he published a Latin history of Germany. (Did he pay for the publication himself or with money paid or promised to him by Thomas Platter?) In Basel, once one reached a certain social status that Thomas had already moved well beyond, everyone (with few exceptions) knew everyone else. But it was surely through the Burgschule that close ties were established between Hugwald, who had taught in the school and left his mark on it, and Thomas, who became a teacher there in the 1540s.

In order to purchase land, the printer-teacher short of cash was once again forced to rely on credit, which he obtained without difficulty (T 137, 178). He borrowed 500 gulden from the innkeeper of the White Dove, possibly a man named Hans Galle, and 200 additional gulden handed to him on the spot by Jacob Kannengiesser, a draper who at the time was probably engaged to Esther Frobenia, the daughter of Frobenius, the printer and bookbinder and Thomas Platter's friend and protector (T 137, 178; F 135). Jacob would marry Esther less than two years later in the winter of 1550–51. Here we detect the useful influence of the typographical network that grew up around Frobenius, Herwagen, and Episcopius, a network in which Thomas was still a relatively minor but already influential participant. Johannes Herwagen Sr. also played a key role in arranging Thomas's loans, not without reluctance, but it was the least he could do given that Thomas had done him an important favor by arranging a reconciliation between Herwagen and his wife (*ich im wider zu siner frowen geholffen han*), one Frau Lachnerin, the widow of the late Johannes Frobenius, who was the founder of the Basel typographical dynasty to which he gave his name (F 69, 357). And it has to be said that in this case the reconciliation was not easy, since Herwagen had put his wife in high dudgeon by having an affair with the wife of Frau Lachnerin's son by her first marriage. The ensuing scandal had set tongues wagging in Basel from 1542 to 1545. It took a man with the skills of Thomas Platter to rescue poor Herwagen from his plight (T 138, 179). The ex-Valaisian borrowed considerable sums not just to buy the land in Gundeldingen but to pay the cost of planting, digging wells, and building on his new property. Tears were shed and teeth gnashed before the deal was done, and Anna Platter, as usual, dismayed by the financial risks that her husband, much more imaginative than she, was willing to take, had lost her temper more than once. In any case, Thomas refused to find a co-signer to guarantee his debt to Hugwald, for he had no desire to be beholden to anyone. He therefore worked out the same kind of arrangement he had made to purchase his property in the city. After hard bargaining, he put up the land and three houses in the city as collateral for Hugwald's loan of the purchase price of the land. With hay in his boots, Platter was now a man of substance, who could gain the confidence of would-be lenders by pointing if not to a comfortable hoard of cash then at least to holdings in real estate.

Thomas thus did business with other people's money. At this stage of his life he was not yet a long-term lender (in contrast to his son, who became a substantial lender later on) or even a short-term usurer. He was rather one of the vast number of people who used other people's money to make more money for everyone concerned. Thou shalt invest! was the commandment that Thomas put into practice in school, boardinghouse, print shop, real estate, farming, and ultimately in securing a college education for his son, his only surviving child. He invested heavily in his new farm in Gundeldingen, using whatever cash he had on hand together with loans on which he paid sixty gulden in annual interest. He owed a thousand gulden all told to practically every burgher (*alle burgshafft* [T 138]) in Basel, by which he meant his friends and acquaintances, who were not always cordial when money was at stake. These people constituted a certain elite; they were among the Protestant city's secular and civic leaders. They included printers and innkeepers. Can this group be called a "bourgeoisie"? Certainly, but not the high bourgeoisie of aristocrats and big businessmen, for whom Thomas Platter was only a minor player. And not the elite of pastors and professors who, financially speaking, held the devil by the tail, even if God was on their side when it came to the spiritual aspect of things. And of course in all this business God marched as always at Thomas's side (T 138). But God helped those who helped themselves. Thomas fixed up the existing house, barn, and stable. As he had already done with his property in the city, he sank a well on his new farm. While not stinting on his own labor, he also paid and fed others to come work for him. For all this he needed to borrow. He planted vinestock on his property and in the best Valaisian tradition began to raise livestock. He purchased (for 130 gulden) three acres of pasture from the wheelwright Lux Dersam, who was also an official in various Basel hospitals and guilds (T 139).[10]

Thomas's return to the land may seem astonishing, yet it was in many ways typical. The peasant from the highlands of the Valais became a farmer in the plains around Basel. Geographically he had moved to a lower altitude, while socially he had moved to a higher one. In neither respect was he alone. Hundreds of thousands of residents of early modern cities, small businessmen as well as professionals, bought land as soon as they had the means to do so. They cultivated that land with their own hands and with the help of their families, servants, and hired hands. Their goal was to eat what they produced themselves; to ensure a supply of food in time of scarcity or crisis; and to satisfy a deeply rooted craving to live on the soil (a craving that would prove to be much less pronounced in Felix than it was in Thomas). And then, too, there was simply a desire to invest, even if the money for investment was borrowed, and to make more money by selling what one produced. These people did not "exploit" the countryfolk or the countryside—on this point a respectable historiographical tradition needs correcting.[11] On the contrary, they invested, increased the productivity of the land, diversified crops, and speculated on potentially profitable new ventures such as vineyards and pastureland. They also responded to the demands of the city, which consumed quantities of high-priced, high-quality products such as wine, meat, milk, and vegetables. Thus the fringes of the city were turned into a kind of countryside by the proliferation of suburban vineyards, vegetable gardens, orchards, and small farms. The monotony of lowland fields and meadows and highland pastures was relieved by these new ventures.

In this respect Thomas Platter can serve as a model. His was a successful resumé, one that could be copied by other members of the social groups through which he passed in his various capacities, sometimes with the slowness of a tortoise, at other times with the speed of a hare. He was of course one of a host of citydwellers who bought, worked, and improved rural properties, one of a host who renovated Gothic farmsteads that had survived the Middle Ages and who planted vineyards in weed-choked fields. He had been a highland peasant, a beggar, an urban craftsman, and finally a burgher. He had known the life of the poor peasant and the social outcast. He had been a worker and then a small businessman in the "manufacturing sector" (printing). And he had worked in the "service sector" (teaching) before returning to "agriculture" (with his suburban farm). Yet it is well to recall that his first vocation, by now largely forgotten, was to become a priest. In all this Thomas Platter was a Renaissance man, somewhere between Lazarillo de Tormes and Guillaume Budé, the beggar and the professor.

Before long, Thomas's suburban farm was thriving, and his investments in real estate were yielding a good return. He found himself briefly torn, however, between his most recent occupation (printing) and one of his earliest and deepest vocations (teaching). The printing business was quite profitable, generating a net income of roughly 200 gulden annually. But Frau Platter and her children were working their fingers to the bone. The journeymen printers, who shared the family's meals and quarters, were often incompetent or clumsy (*ungeschikt* [T 129]). Of course not everyone was capable of proofreading or even setting type in Greek and Hebrew: non-Latin characters held pitfalls for the unwary. Worse still, the journeymen sometimes displayed arrogance (*unbescheidenheit* [T 147]). They demanded higher wages in a crude manner: this, too, was a consequence of steadily rising prices. The great Lyons printers' strike, led by French workers, was not far off.

War also had certain negative repercussions on the market. The last clash between France and the Empire in the reign of Francis I took place between 1542 and 1544. It was marked by the "immoral" alliance of France and Turkey against Charles V, and by Charles's attempts to launch a "Germanic" invasion of French territory. The Valois monarch's victory at Ceresole, won by troops under the command of François de Bourbon, prince d'Enghien, in April 1544, had impressed the people of Basel because thousands of Swiss had fought in the battle.[12] Felix, eight years old at the time, remembered this episode and the veterans' war stories for a long time afterward. Thus various factors—the unpleasant wartime atmosphere, a restive work force, and a soft market—conspired in the end to drive Thomas out of the printing business and into the relatively calm world of teaching. There at least one was less likely to be disturbed.

\* \* \*

Nothing is simple in this story. The relationship between Thomas's diverse activities, including printing, and his permanent vocation to teach took various forms in the years between, roughly speaking, 1520 and 1555. Platter was not simply a man with two mistresses, the printing press and the classroom. The workaholic Sunday farmer always remained a teacher at heart. Just before becoming an apprentice ropemaker in the 1520s, he had taught his cousin in the Valais his *abc*'s. After that he became tutor to the two Werdmüller boys in Zurich, where he was able to eat to his heart's content (T 65). Later he gave private lessons in Hebrew to various preachers around Zurich. And finally, after a stint with Collinus, the Hellenist and ropemaker, he found himself employed by the "red ropemaker" in Basel, where he studied Plautus while braiding rope and in his off hours taught Hebrew to twenty-some students under the aegis of Oporinus at Saint Leonhard's. Shortly after that, he became a schoolteacher (as well as a small merchant, in business with his wife) back in the Valais (T 80). And then, after returning to Basel, he taught high school in 1531. Following the episode with Epiphanius and the death of Zwingli, he became Oporinus's colleague in the aptly named *paedagogium*, where he taught Greek from 1532 to 1540. Meanwhile, he and Oporinus became proofreaders in Herwagen's print shop. There was even talk of finding him a position once again as a schoolmaster in the Valais, but those plans came to naught when someone denounced him to the region's bishop.

Even as he worked as a proofreader, a partner in a printing business, and finally a self-employed printer, Thomas continued to take in boarders and to teach. All in all, Thomas's work as a printer was, despite the impressive feat of publishing Calvin's *Institutio* in 1536, an important though not a central episode in his life, even if it dragged on until 1555. The major story was not printing but teaching. And a major event in that story was a bizarre approach by a city official responsible for matters of education. This man, Heinrich Ryhiner, was not just anybody. A graduate of the University of Basel, he had served for a long time as the city's episcopal procurator and imperial notary (F 157). He wrote a chronicle of the Peasant Wars for the year 1525. In 1538, he summoned Platter, whom he regarded as an expert on teaching, for a consultation: "Can you explain," he

asked, "why things at the university are not going well?" The question
might well have been asked at many times in history. In any case, Thomas
did not mince words: his answer, in substance, was "too many
professors—more professors than there are students" (an answer that
points up the minuscule size of the University of Basel at the time, at least in
terms of the number of students). Thomas's advice continued: "Invite a
few good teachers from Germany, no more than eight. You'll have no trouble persuading them to come because of the religious upheavals there. Pay
them well, and you will attract a sufficient number [*gnug*] of students."
But, the official inquired, "What will become of our local teachers [*unsren
basleren*]?" His concern reflected the anxiety of a city whose academics
liked to think of themselves, not entirely accurately, as an established, ingrown group and did not relish either unemployment or competition
from outsiders. "If you find people from Basel, use them or keep them,"
Thomas concluded. "Otherwise, invite good teachers from outside for the
sake of your young students." Did Thomas see himself as an outsider,
someone from the Valais immune from the consequences of the treacherous advice he was giving? If so, he deceived himself. The city, having
consulted his opinion, changed its tactics (but not its strategy), leaving
Thomas in the lurch: he was dismissed, along with Oporinus (*gab uns
urloub* [T 129]). The authorities disapproved of the way the two men divided their time between printing in the private sector and teaching in
schools supported by public funds.[13] It was felt that they were neglecting
their teaching duties in favor of their work as printers, which paid better.
Thomas's dismissal probably occurred in the autumn of 1538, while
Oporinus's came in 1539; both men bowed to the decision of the authorities, if not without grumbling. The dismissals did not become fully effective until 1540.[14] This dispute with city authorities, though vexing, was
short-lived. The need for good secondary-school teachers was simply too
great. Thomas now moved back from the private to the public sector, in
1541 according to his text and surely no later than December 1544. On the
eve of this move, he was, of necessity, working essentially only as a printer.
By midcentury he was once again a full-fledged teacher and boardinghouse keeper; he now devoted only a small part of his time to printing,
while farming had become a major preoccupation, taking up much of his
time when he was not with his "beloved blond students." In the meantime,
the great strike in the Lyons printing industry had taken place (1539–42).
Did this have repercussions among print workers in Basel, whom Thomas
described as resentful and incompetent? Did they drive Thomas, whose
experience as a printer was relatively recent and who was not wedded to the
profession, out of the business?

The wars of the period, which choked off the market for books, did not help matters. The resurgence of conflict between France and the Empire between 1542 and 1544 has already been mentioned. And in the duchy of Cleves hostilities erupted in the same period between Charles V and the Protestants of Germany. The defeat of the German Lutherans at Mühlberg in 1547 was surely a blow to their coreligionists in Basel, and not just those in the printing business. As an experienced teacher with a knowledge of Hebrew and Greek in a time of difficulty in the book trade, Thomas decided to return to the world of education. Once again he demonstrated his old aptitude for mobility, for changing his line of work at a moment's notice. This time he benefited from the advice of friends and protectors, including Bürgermeister Adelbert Meyer zum Pfeil, now in his sixties, as well as the future bürgermeister, Theodor Brand, a man ten years older than Thomas and something of a father figure to him (T 176). Brand, the scion of a distinguished family of surgeons, was well known as a conciliator among city officials.

Felix's godfather, Simon Grynaeus, also urged Thomas to return to teaching and related lines of work, though his advice was tinged a bit more than that of some others with warnings against academic doddering. This mixed counsel had to have been offered sometime before April 1, 1541, the date of Grynaeus's death at the age of forty-nine. Joining the unanimous chorus of Thomas's admirers was the city clerk of Basel (*den herren Stadtschriber*), whom Platter, always eager to show off his illustrious acquaintances, does not fail to mention for the benefit of future readers. The only discordant voice was that of his old friend Myconius. Nevertheless, the city fathers sent Myconius to see Thomas and try to persuade him to quit the press for the lectern (T 130). Myconius, however, was only too aware of his former pupil's stubbornness: "I know that you're the best man for the job," he said. "But the thing is, I know you. You'll do just as you please [*du wirst dim kopf wellen nach gan*]. You'll quarrel with the university. They won't let you teach the way you want to."

Myconius's warning was to no avail, however. The offer was attractive. Thomas had had his fill of Gutenberg's noble art, which no longer appealed to him as a full-time occupation. What is more, becoming a professor was like the fulfillment of a dream to a man who had once thought of becoming a priest: to trade the priest's cassock he never wore for the cap and gown of a professor was an honorable transaction in the eyes of both God and man. Herr Rudolf Fry, a merchant and one of the leaders of the city council, put it this way when Thomas came to him on an errand (in addressing Thomas, Fry used the formal *Sie*): "My good man, become a teacher. You will enjoy yourself, and you will be doing a service

to the city council, to God, and to your fellow man." The purpose of education at the time was twofold: to turn out young Christians while at the
same time giving students the means to succeed economically and socially. The paradox was that their new secular knowledge carried with it
the potential of diminishing their Christian faith.

The errand that took Thomas Platter to visit Rudolf Fry is of some
interest, by the way. Hans Rudolf Fry, a native of Mellingen, had been a
Basel city councillor since 1529, the year of the Protestant revolution in
the city: Fry was thus a member of the group of Protestant militants who
had controlled the city ever since and whose backing Thomas Platter had
consistently enjoyed. Fry was a merchant who dealt in various lines, including parchment. It was precisely in order to buy parchment that
Thomas had gone to see him, for he had noticed the excellent quality of
the line that Fry carried, some of which came from the illuminated medieval texts that delighted little Felix Platter when he stumbled onto them
in the storeroom of his father's shop. Thomas bought parchment to use as
binding material for the books he printed. His boarders were pressed
into service as apprentice bookbinders. Many of these adolescents sprang
from the elite of the Valais and spoke Latin with Thomas, whom they
adored despite his occasional severity. The twenty or thirty boarders who
lived in Thomas's houses ate the produce of his farm, including vegetables, eggs, and milk. Not only did he benefit from their work as bookbinders, he absolutely depended on the money he received from their
parents for room and board, money that sometimes had to be dragged
out of them. Without this influx of cash, he could never have paid his bills
or met his debts.[15]

$$* \quad * \quad *$$

Rudolf Fry the merchant thus sold vellum to Thomas, the owner of a
print shop that turned out scholarly tomes. The same Fry, as a local politi-
cian in charge of funds for education, urged Thomas to become a full-
time teacher and forget about printing and binding books. Indeed, a fair
number of the local elite literally besieged the Valaisian immigrant with
requests that he change his way of life. They were determined to make
him headmaster of the Burgschule, and for the next several decades this
prestigious school, attached to an important church, did indeed become
his principal place of employment. The situation at the school had gotten
out of hand: there had been six headmasters between 1537 and 1541. Just as
governmental instability can be damaging to a country, instability of
leadership can be damaging to an educational institution. To many local

leaders, Thomas Platter seemed likely to be a disciplined leader and an excellent teacher. It was felt that, in a town where talented men did not grow on trees, here was someone who could put a dying school back on its feet.

But before he could close up the print shop (and set himself up in the teaching business), Thomas had to tie up loose ends and sell his remaining stock. He therefore went to Frankfurt to liquidate his remainders, which he sold by the pound for the paper they contained (*das myr Kum das papyr zalt ward*), or so he claims. The buyer was none other than Barthli Vogel of Wittenberg, who for twenty years remained an important associate of the leading Basel printers. A connection was thus established between the two men, the one a former disciple of Zwingli and the other a compatriot of Luther.

Thomas still had a substantial number of books back in Basel, which he sold to Jacques de Puys of Paris. He then unloaded his presses and other equipment on Petrus or Pietro Berna, originally of Lucca, who hoped to break into the printing business in a city where printers were not always receptive to new competition (Berna's efforts would prove successful in the second half of the sixteenth century). Pietro Berna enrolled in the University of Basel in 1542. Thomas Platter did not take up his post as headmaster of the Burgschule until the fall of 1544. Hence the sale of the presses must have taken place sometime between 1542 and 1544 (T 136, 178). The individuals involved in Thomas's farewell to publishing represented a good part of Europe, an area ranging from Wittenberg to Frankfurt to Basel to Lucca to Paris. Books published in Latin could be read anywhere on the continent, and the world of publishing was truly international: even a modest publisher like Thomas Platter was engaged in a cosmopolitan network.

\*    \*    \*

It is astonishing to see a man about to become a teacher selling off his books. True, his teaching required only a few works by major authors: Cicero, Terence, Homer, and so on. And in any case he needed the money, because he was still hungry for land. The liquidation of his assets in Basel and Frankfurt afforded him only brief respite. By the late 1540s he was once again in debt owing to the purchase of his suburban farm in Gundeldingen. By the end of 1549, he owed a hundred crowns (*Sunnenkronen* [T 137]). Herwagen had lent him money, it will be recalled, in gratitude for Thomas's help in reconciling him with his wife. Herwagen nevertheless proved to be an insistent creditor. And such important printers as Frobenius and Episcopius flew into a rage when Platter took the side of their former friend and partner Herwagen, who was now their enemy for having made a cuckold of Frobenius's son. They stopped sending work Thomas's way in the wake of the Herwagen affair, without which, Thomas insists, there would have been enough business to keep three presses running for a decade. He would have become a rich fellow (*ein richer gsell* [T 138]). But once the big printers turned their backs on him, he had no choice but to close up shop, or at any rate to shut down gradually. Here was yet another reason for Thomas to give up printing and go into teaching. In a sense he was driven out of the business by the Herwagen scandal, which became a Platter scandal when Thomas intervened. In Thomas's retelling, however, his banishment from the profession is presented as a personal decision on his part to return to teaching.

What became of Thomas's debt to Herwagen of a hundred crowns? Herwagen being a hard man despite all that Thomas had done for him, the debtor arranged to transfer his debt to Bebelius, another printer who remained on cordial terms with him and who was much more "pliable" than Herwagen. In other words, Bebelius repaid the loan to Herwagen and in turn became Thomas's creditor. Of course Bebelius did not have anywhere near this amount, so he actually borrowed the necessary hundred crowns from Balthasar Han, a glassmaker-artist and onetime student of Holbein as well as an influential member of the city council and the guild Zum Himmel (T 137, 178; F 82). Han seems to have regarded Thomas with the same immediate sympathy as did other open-minded members of the Basel elite: they sized him up as a worthy fellow who deserved their help. And indeed, the line of credit did not end with Han, who was short of cash himself and borrowed the needed sum from a deposit of 600 crowns entrusted to him by Count Michel de Gruyère of Freiburg, who, despite his mouth-watering name, was, aside from this propitious occasion, generally in debt himself (T 137, 179).

This old-fashioned system of loans thus depended on both the credit of the city and the often volatile fortunes of the old aristocracy. For the time being, however, it was Bebelius who held Thomas's note (on which he demanded no interest payment, by the way). Bebelius, a native of Alsace whose real name was Johann Bebel, did not die until after 1550. On his deathbed, he asked Bonaventura von Brunn, a friend of Balthasar Han's and of the Platter family, to summon Thomas. Brunn, a future bürgermeister, belonged to the circle of wealthy drapers, tanners, and butchers with whom Thomas had been on good terms since the 1540s. These men of substance treated the Valaisian immigrant familiarly but with respect. Bebel told Thomas that he was transferring his note to an honorable but less indulgent creditor, namely, his son-in-law, the printer Isengrinius, who, unlike his father-in-law, required Thomas to make payments of principal and interest on this and other, subsequent loans (T 138). The change in the terms of the loan was not pleasant for Thomas, but neither, apparently, was it usurious or catastrophic. Even if pressed (*ubertriben*) from time to time, he was reliable, intelligent, and hardworking and managed to stay on good terms with people in Basel. He gradually worked his way out from under his debt so that the sheriff was never forced to come to his door to confiscate bed, breadbasket, and china.

If only all his troubles had been financial. Twice, however, Thomas's house was visited by a scourge far worse than debt: the plague. Margretlin II (1533–39), Thomas and Anna's second daughter, died in the first epidemic, which lasted from August 1538 until June 1539 (T 128), just as Margretlin I had succumbed in 1531. At the time Thomas was involved in printing and managing a boardinghouse for the several dozen boarders whose rent kept him in the black. When the plague struck in August of 1538, no thought was given to sending the boarders back to the Valais, for they would simply have carried the disease with them. Hence the Platter family together with its young boarders—some forty people in all— moved to a place three leagues from Basel, where they remained for four months, well into autumn. Their temporary quarters were in the former episcopal town of Liestal (T 128). There, Thomas and part of his nomadic entourage lived perilously close to the cemetery in an inn run by one Ulrich Wentz, a former tanner who belonged to a family of textile workers (F 54). Since the "Platter group" occupied only one room, some of the boarders must have been housed elsewhere. Felix, aged two, slept in a cradle part of the time.

The death of little Margretlin II, briefly described, plunged Thomas and his wife into deep sadness. In reserved terms Thomas describes his dead daughter as a dear child (*lieb kind*) as well as a pretty one (*hüpsch kind*). Sixteen weeks after the exodus began, Thomas was back in Basel, where he immediately resumed his activity as a printer. A decade later, in 1551, another *lieb kind* would succumb to the series of plagues that ravaged Basel from 1550 to 1553.[16] Ursula (or Urselin), Thomas and Anna's third and only surviving daughter, passed away in 1551 at the age of eighteen (her father erroneously recorded her age as sixteen and a half).[17] Ursula's death disrupted life in the Platter household. To be sure, the neighbors accompanied the girl's body to its final resting place, but the boarders scattered like a flock of sparrows. One could live with the plague in a city, but when it struck a boardinghouse, the only wise course was to get out, and quickly.

\*   \*   \*

By the time school resumed in the fall of 1551, things had returned to normal. The plague had subsided. Thomas's school, despite his recent loss, reopened its doors. Its curriculum had at last been worked out, and the general outline of a system that would endure for thirty years was now clear. Of course Thomas had considerable experience as a teacher. As early as 1531 he had taught at the Burgschule. Over the next eight years he gave lessons in Greek at the *paedagogium*. And from 1544 on he became the most important, though not the only, figure in secondary education in Basel (1544 and not, as he misleadingly suggests, 1540, for he did not wish to lend substance to the accurate charge that he had been excluded from teaching between 1540 and 1544 on the grounds that his work as a printer conflicted with his teaching duties, and perhaps also for reasons of bad character).

Now that he was headmaster, Thomas supervised the work of three subordinates. Together, the four teachers taught four classes that met for four hours daily, two in the morning and two in the afternoon, with a period of supervised study in between. The alphabet and reading were taught in the first class; Latin authors and catechism in the second; the Bible, Cicero, grammar, the "science of fine language," and Aesop's fables in the third; and Ovid, Terence, dialectics, rhetoric, and music (in small doses) in the fourth, which also included translation into Latin. This four-grade system was less effective and less carefully designed than the Jesuit system of six or seven grades, however.[18] Hence there was room for improvement, whether one remained Catholic or converted to Protestantism.

Religious instruction, punctuated by attendance at Protestant services on Sundays and Tuesdays, was not neglected. The authors selected, including Cicero and, among modern Latinists, Erasmus and Castellion, were chosen for their humanism and tolerance. Thomas Platter had come a long way from the fanatical iconoclasm of his youth, a period in which he had suffered from the infantile disorder of hysterical ultradogmatic orthodoxy. By now his religious convictions no longer blinded him or confined him to an ideological dungeon.

His students ranged in age from six to fifteen. There was a span of ages in each of the four grades. The University of Basel kept a finicky eye on

Thomas's teaching, but the oversight was tolerable and easily circumvented. In any case, he was reputed to be one of the most reliable teachers to be found in Alsace, the Basel region, and the Valais, indeed one of the best secondary educators in all of northern Switzerland. When his students graduated, they went into various walks of life, including the crafts and commerce; some went on to the university. Thomas educated many of Basel's professionals in his time, including clergymen, teachers, jurists, and public officials.[19] Not surprisingly, his former students adored him. When they returned home, they sang his praises: Platter had friends everywhere.

Thomas would not have succeeded professionally or acquired so many friends without the important contribution made by Anna, his faithful companion and hardworking helpmate. Her management of the school helped spread the former Valaisian's fame far and wide. She ran the kitchen and dining room that served the boarders whose rent helped keep the Platter household afloat. When she died on February 20, 1572, neither Thomas nor Felix was short of memories of the "little housewife" (*hussmutterlin*) who for so many years had shared the bed of the one and the childhood and youth of the other. Of noble birth but an orphan and therefore *déclassée*, Anna had worked for seven years as a servant in the home of Myconius. The marriage of reason that the latter had arranged between her and Thomas Platter had developed, not without quarrels, into a solid mutual affection, reinforced by genuine love on Thomas's part (as his letters to Felix prove) coupled with a stoic acceptance of his wife's moods: "What do you expect?" he observed in a philosophical letter to his son in 1553. "She has worked hard and grown old, and she is a woman."[20] By 1564 she was an old woman with a cough, no teeth, illiterate, and six painful buboes from the plague. She had always worked extremely hard, whether in the print shop or spinning cotton to make thread, which she then sold for pocket money. Throughout her years in Basel, moreover, Anna Dietschi-Platter maintained her sense of humor. And once she even developed a crush on a boarder from the south of France with an attractive goatee, though nothing came of it.

Although she was illiterate, she dictated letters to her son when he was in medical school at Montpellier (1552–57); inspiration often eluded her, however, even if her gushing affection could hardly be concealed. She recovered her eloquence, however, when it came to urging her son not to fall for a French girl (his German-speaking fiancée Madlen was waiting for him in Basel) and not to acquire any debts. Her husband's debts were enough for one lifetime. Very ambitious for her brilliant son, she received tokens of his gratitude in the form of presents sent from Montpellier by mail, or at any rate what took the place of mail in those days. In 1555, for example, she received a crate of five dozen oranges. Felix's return to Basel in 1557 and his marriage the following year to a young woman whom Anna liked a great deal were great joys to her. Though emaciated, she continued in her fifties to sing like a girl of twenty, *ac si viginti esset annorum*.[21] Her death in 1572 came one year after her son was appointed professor of medicine.

\*   \*   \*

In any case, to return to the fall of 1551, it was a time for a new beginning. Although the plague epidemic was not over, it had subsided. Felix began a preparatory course at the University of Basel with the idea that he would soon go to Montpellier to study medicine, fulfilling the "Aesculapian" dreams of both father and son.

To find the young student a room in the capital of Languedoc took some clever maneuvering. This was always the case when a family in those days lacked cash to pay for the upkeep of a student far from home. The arrangements made to cover Felix's expenses are worth examining in some detail (F 128). Friedrich Ryhiner, the son of a Basel bailiff and a friend (and soon ally) of the Platter family, had gone off to medical school in Montpellier, where he had found lodging with the apothecary Laurent Catalan, in exchange for which Laurent's son Jacques was given a room in the Ryhiner house in Basel. But the younger Ryhiner, whose ambitions were increasingly centered on France (he eventually became a colonel under Henri III), left Montpellier for Paris. His room in the Catalan household was not allowed to go vacant. Jacques Meier, the son of a Strasbourg jurist, took his place (F 128). Meanwhile, Jacques Catalan left Basel for Strasbourg. Moreover, Jacques's brother, Gilbert Catalan, also went to Strasbourg, trading places with Hans von Odratzheim (the son of a Strasbourg city councillor), who lived with the Catalans while studying medicine in the southern French city. Thus the two Catalan boys went to Strasbourg, while two Strasbourg boys went to Montpellier: the score was even.

Eventually, however, young Odratzheim left Montpellier and returned to Alsace. Once again there was an opening, which was filled by Felix Platter. But Gilbert Catalan no longer had a place in Strasbourg, so he moved to Basel, where he became one of Thomas's boarders, filling the niche left by Felix's departure. Everything balanced out. Laurent Catalan now had two medical students living with him, Meier from Strasbourg and Platter from Basel. And the two Catalan boys were in the north, Jacques in Strasbourg, Gilbert in Basel. The arrangements were worked out by the German physician Heinrich Wulff, a graduate of Montpellier and a friend of both the Platters and the Catalans, families that traded sons as bankers trade letters of exchange.

# PART THREE

# Five Years in the Land of Oc
## (1552–1556)

## CHAPTER FIVE

# Traveling to Montpellier

The arrangements had been made; now it was time for Felix to depart. Preparations began in the late summer of 1552. The young man (he was just sixteen) needed someone to accompany him on his journey to France. Fortunately, the fairs in Frankfurt drew many merchants from Lyons, and perhaps one of them could be prevailed upon to take the boy in hand on the return trip from the banks of the Main. Of course someone else would then have to be found to accompany him the rest of the way, from the confluence of the Saône and the Rhône to Montpellier. The young student was not yet old enough to set out on such a lengthy journey alone. As luck would have it, Thomas Schöpflin, an Alsatian music teacher and (much younger) colleague of Thomas Platter's, was headed in the same direction. A friend who had taught harmony to the Platter family, Schöpflin was also about to embark on the study of medicine at Montpellier (he would later practice in France and Switzerland [F 73, 129]). His story shows how teaching could serve as a stepping-stone to other careers. Thomas Platter had started too low to make the jump to medicine, but Schöpflin succeeded. Schöpflin's background also exemplifies the close ties that linked Switzerland, Languedoc, and Alsace—a repeated refrain in Felix's memoirs.

Thomas still needed to locate a horse and other equipment for his son's travels. For seven crowns he bought the boy a small horse (*rösslin*) that turned out to be almost as sentimental as its youthful rider. The right man to serve as Felix's guide and mentor on his travels through France still had to be found, moreover. This took time. It was hoped that a printer from Lyons named Bering would pass through town, but he never turned up, perhaps because he was afraid of the plague that still lurked in the vicinity (F 129). Thomas was therefore forced to call upon the services of a certain Robert, a distinguished Parisian, possibly a jurist, who agreed to accompany Felix as far as Geneva, his own destination. After that, someone else would have to be found. In any case, the idea of stopping in Geneva appealed to Felix's father: a year earlier, when the plague was raging, he had thought of sending his son to live either in the city on Lake Leman or in Zurich.

*   *   *

As it happens, the plague returned to Basel in the summer of 1552. It was a relatively minor outbreak, but a decision had to be made. October 9 was devoted to packing, which was kept simple: the bags had to be carried, by horse to be sure, but still it was best not to overload the animal. Felix's father (and not, as one might expect, his mother) made up his bundle: he rolled two shirts and a few handkerchiefs in oilcloth. Not without anguish, Thomas parted with an écu and seven crowns, three of them gold; a part of this hoard was sewn into the boy's clothing. His mother contributed another crown: the difference between the maternal and paternal contributions reflected the respective share of each parent in the finances of the household. Whether poor or miserly, Thomas reminded his son that he had borrowed every penny of this money, including the purchase price of the horse. To Felix this was a familiar tune, but he took it to heart. "Work hard, take care." This shopworn advice was taken seriously by the young student for whom it was intended. On the evening of October 9, Thomas invited the surgeon Franz Jeckelmann and his son to dinner. The idea was still that Felix should eventually marry Jeckelmann's daughter, and the boy was only too glad to have his hand so sweetly forced. The dinner—rabbit and quail—was festive, a hunter's meal. The future nuptials were referred to often around the table, but the guests pretended not to understand what all the talk was about. At nine Jeckelmann had to leave the company: someone had come to ask if he could bleed a plague victim by the name of Batt Meier, a well-known debauchee (F 131). The quiet courage of a man ready at any hour to lance a contagious bubo elicited no particular comment from the assembled guests. Professionalism was taken for granted.

Early on the morning of October 10 two men on horseback appeared in front of the Platter house. Thomas Schöpflin and Robert from Paris were ready to go. Frau Anna Platter, who had been quite gay the night before, was in tears now. Would she ever see her son again? Although politics was not her cup of tea, she, like many others in Basel, was afraid: the emperor, Charles V, was just then marching on Metz with an army of more than 60,000 men. His objective was to reconquer the city from the French King Henri II and troops commanded by François de Guise. If successful, would the imperial army proceed to seize and destroy Basel? Such a prospect was the basis of Anna Platter's fears, which happily proved groundless when Metz held out against the besieging imperials. Nevertheless, the events of this period are important for understanding why the Platters and indeed all Basel were now Francophiles. Henri II was a Catholic, to be sure, but his alliances with the Protestant princes of

Germany made him a suitable ally for the Swiss in their struggles with the Holy Roman Empire. This latent francophilia was one of the ulterior motives behind Felix's departure for the University of Montpellier, an institution in the forefront of "Welch" medicine.

At last the young man was ready to climb onto his horse, but not before tripping over his spurs, which he was unaccustomed to wearing, and falling down the stairs. The first stage of the journey took the three travelers, accompanied by Thomas, to Liestal, the small town where Felix and his father had met Calvin some years earlier. The innkeeper, whose son was a student in Basel, offered them a free dinner. In Liestal Thomas Platter finally took leave of his son. He was so choked with emotion that he could only get out the first syllable of his Latin farewell: *Vale* became simply *Va*. At this point Felix's joy, like his mother's earlier, gave way to sadness. But young Felix had been well advised to put distance between himself and his native city: on the very day of his departure, his companion Schöpflin's maid and his father's servant, Anna Oswald, took to their beds with plague. Buboes once again erupted up and down Freie Strasse. Fortunately, Anna Oswald recovered, as she had many times before (F 131, 132). Felix heard all this bad news only afterward, in a letter from his father. After dinner the travelers rode a few more miles, and Felix suffered a minor spill from his horse but was not injured. They stopped for the night at the Stallion Inn in Langenbruck (F 132).

The next day (October 11) took the travelers as far as the "big" city of Solothurn, where they had lunch at the Lion Inn in the midst of the annual fair. Thomas Schöpflin, who ordinarily played the lute, tried his hand on the organ of the local church with the permission of the organist, Master Georgius. In the afternoon they continued past the former Abbey of Frauenbrunnen, which had been secularized since the beginning of the Reformation almost half a century earlier. In his first tourist's observation, Felix notes that in the twilight he was able, with difficulty, to decipher the medieval inscription at the top of a pillar of stone, which recorded for posterity the tribulations of a group of English soldiers in 1375. The young man was struck by this: he drew the column with its epigraph in his notebook—something he did only rarely. This is the first allusion in Felix's memoirs to "recent" history, in this case the fourteenth century. It is the only medieval notation among the miscellaneous observations collected in his traveler's *Tagebuch*. The day's ride ended after nightfall in a smoky inn that served a large peasant clientele, directly below the castle of Jegenstorf, only a mile from Bern (F 133). On October 12 the travelers stopped for dinner at the Falcon Inn in that city and visited its (now Protestant) churches, defensive walls, and bear pit. The afternoon proved diverting: along the way Felix drank from a bubbling fountain and traveled some distance in the company of a recent bride, who showed her legs when she fell from a horse. That night the men slept in Freiburg in "Welch" territory, that is, in what we would nowadays call Romansch- or French-speaking Switzerland. Crossing the linguistic boundary impressed Felix even more than the young lady's legs had done. The travelers bedded down "in the French manner." We know what this phrase means today: the French tuck in their covers, the Germans don't. Psychoanalysts have spilled a great deal of ink in their attempts to decipher the meaning of this. But what did the words mean in the sixteenth century?

*   *   *

We come now to one of the more dramatic parts of the journey, reminiscent of Thomas Platter's brushes with crime while traveling in Germany earlier in the century. October 13 started badly. It rained all morning. After a good ride, the three travelers stopped at the Lion Inn in Romont to dry out and eat lunch. The afternoon was even worse than the morning had been. It was still raining, and when Thomas Schöpflin wandered off the trail, it took his companions a good while to find him. Then all three riders became totally lost in a forest thick with thieves. After encountering some inhospitable villagers, they ended up at an unlicensed inn in a place called Mézières, where peasants and beggars drank themselves into a stupor on spiked wine while eating chestnuts and black bread. The night was difficult: tramps, soaked to the gills, snored in front of the fire, which died out. Meanwhile, the three visitors from Basel kept vigil, their swords unsheathed (this is Felix's first mention of the weapon he carried).

Three hours before daybreak, Felix and his friends made off on their already exhausted mounts. They plunged into the forest, but not before making several detours intended to throw any pursuers off the track, with the young peasant who had previously shown them the way to the despicable inn leading them. The guide, certain now of a fat tip, took them to the highway, and from there they made their way to Lausanne without further difficulty. At the inn in Lausanne they were congratulated on their narrow escape. The Jorat Forest had a very bad reputation. The men with whom the unfortunate travelers had spent the night were very likely criminals and, had the desperadoes not been drunk, might well have attacked or even murdered Felix and his friends. Apparently the area between French- and German-speaking territory was not very secure. Shortly after Felix's encounter, a bandit chieftain was put to the wheel in Bern after confessing to a number of crimes, including a plan to murder students staying in the inn in Mézières, whose keeper was apparently also a shady character. Had Felix had a brush with disaster? Or was he exaggerating the danger for the benefit of his future readers?

\*   \*   \*

At the time Lausanne was a large, semirural town of 6,000, squeezed between the vineyards along Lake Leman and the bandit-ridden Jorat Forest to the north.[1] Savoyard and episcopal influence in the town had been quelled by the powers in Bern since 1536. In religion the city inclined to a German style of Protestantism but with a liturgy in French. Two "depapalized" churches replaced the dozen or so Catholic churches that had served Lausanne previously. The Bern authorities were represented by a sheriff assisted by several locals, who shared power with a mayor and council drawn largely from the local elite. A Protestant academy for the training of pastors boasted as many as 700 students (a large number for a small town), but in 1559 it moved most of its operations to Geneva in order to bolster the "Welch" character of the Huguenot teaching it so generously dispensed.

For Felix Platter, Lausanne was a familiar and friendly place in terms of both politics and religion, if not language. He remained there only a few hours, however, just long enough to have lunch on October 14.

\*   \*   \*

When he arrived in Geneva from the east, Felix, as he conscientiously inspected the city's fortifications, could not help being impressed by the massiveness of the ramparts and other bastions erected in the 1530s.[2] The suburbs outside the walls had been demolished to enhance security still further. This had made it necessary to relocate 1,700 people, aggravating an already serious housing shortage within the walls. The city's defensive precautions were aimed essentially at the Savoyards. Between 1513 and 1532, Geneva had sought to divorce itself from its bishop and from the dukes of Savoy. After 1532, the combined effects of Farel's preaching and the insistent demands of Bern, a crucial ally, had transformed political emancipation into religious dissidence. When the mass was "finally" abolished in 1535 or 1536, the Genevans, or at any rate those who spoke in their name, decided to live under the law of the Gospel as interpreted and imported by Bernese reformers. The French influence became fundamental: after 1536, through thick and thin, exile and return, the destiny of Calvin was inextricably linked to Geneva.

Calvin's dominance in the city attained its doleful apogee shortly after Felix's visit with the execution of the ultra-Protestant extremist Michael Servetus: Calvin had no desire to be outflanked on his left. Geneva's population was increasing rapidly owing to an influx of Huguenot refugees not only from France but also from Italy and, briefly, from England and other countries as well. From a population of 13,000 in 1550 (the equivalent of Montpellier at the time), the city had grown to at least 22,000 by 1560. Additional stories were added to buildings, houses were divided, and new dwellings were erected in the courtyards of old ones. With the Catholic clergy barred from administering the sacraments, Protestant pastors performed marriages and baptisms as fast as they could. In the wake of the Reformation the local authorities set up German-style guilds of artisans and began regulating the grain trade, despite the fact that Geneva had previously favored a fairly liberal approach to manufacturing and food supply on the model of Lyons. The growth of the printing industry was of considerable importance for the purposes of Huguenot propaganda. Calvin's books became inspirational best-sellers. Among the new industries of the day were the drawing of gold thread and the confection of silk fabric and clocks, which required skilled artisans, many of whom, at least in the silk crafts, came from Italy. Along the northern and western banks of Lake Leman, small craft carried wood and wine to the port of Geneva.

Genevans still spoke a Savoyard dialect in reaction against both the many newcomers from France and their former Savoyard masters, who had spoken French as a language of snobbery and convenience. In Geneva Felix had the honor of meeting Calvin, with whom he was able to converse in Latin. As for French, he did not understand a single word of the sermon the great man delivered to a large congregation in the language of Ronsard. The supreme leader of the French "heretics" chose a new companion for Felix: Michel Héroard, later to be the father of Jean Héroard, Louis XIII's physician. The Parisian bookseller Dupuys (or de Puys), who had bought Thomas Platter's remainders some years earlier, also joined the group, which on October 17 set out for the Rhône and Montpellier. Clearly, Felix was going to have to learn French or else speak Latin. Before leaving Geneva he had spruced himself up with a haircut. Until then he had worn his hair long in the provincial manner of Basel. Short hair had become the custom in the cities of the Empire as well as France, but not in German Switzerland. Having shed his protective mane, he promptly caught a cold, and for several days his nose ran like a fountain.

\* \* \*

Five people set out from Geneva on the afternoon of October 17: Felix, Schöpflin, Héroard and his valet, and Dupuys. The route took the travelers straight to Lyons by way of Collonges and Nantua, with the southern elbow of the Rhône off to their left. In Collonges Felix suffered from nocturnal diarrhea and soiled the inn's circular balcony and freshly painted white walls. (He delights in intimate revelations of this sort.) The innkeeper was livid. The travelers blamed Héroard's valet, who had left early for Nantua to arrange room and board for the others. It is always easiest to blame those not present to defend themselves.

*   *   *

On October 18 the travelers found themselves on the road, or rather the series of wretched trails, leading from Collonges to Cerdon by way of Nantua. The steep paths took them past many mills powered by rapidly flowing streams. Outside one small town Felix for the first time observed hanged men dangling from gibbets. There were so many of them that to his horror he almost ran into one in the dark. His astonishment suggests that there may have been a difference between French and German customs in hanging, the French displaying the victims publicly outside city limits, the Germans taking a less exhibitionist approach.

*   *   *

To enter the extreme northern portion of the former Savoyard state in 1552 was to enter "French" territory, though it had not been French for long. The duchy of Savoy had been annexed by Francis I in 1536. The death, in 1535, of Francesco Sforza, the ruler of the Milanese region coveted by the king of France, had incited the latter to cross the Alps and attempt to seize Milan, which had required him to trample on the territories of the legitimate ruler of the north-Alpine state of Savoy, Duke Charles III. In this the French had been aided by their allies in Bern. His Most Christian Majesty the king of France had formed the habit of relying on the aid of Protestant principalities in his perpetual struggle with Charles V, the Hapsburg emperor.

The Bernese, for their part, had advanced as far as Geneva in 1536, thereby covering the northern flank of the French invasion. Seventeen years later, in 1552, at more or less the same time that Felix was beginning his visit to the regions of the Rhône and Languedoc, the victory of French troops under the duc de Guise over Charles V's besieging army at Metz would allow Henri II's agents to consolidate their control over the defunct state of the exiled Charles III. Indeed, the French agents, by no means dogmatic in their tactics, were all the more successful because of their decision to mollify the local populace by allowing them to maintain their venerable representative institutions (the Three Estates) and granting them a brand new Parlement located in Chambéry and of course loyal to the authorities transplanted from the banks of the Seine and the Loire. This Parlement confined itself to persecuting the small handful of local Protestants sufficiently to gladden the hearts of the Catholic clergy who held all the power in this mountainous region—a clergy increasingly inclined to collaborate with the French occupiers.[3] Thus the left hand of Henri II, allied with the German Swiss "heretics," ignored the fact that the right hand did not hesitate to send the Huguenots of Savoy to the stake in the region to the south and northwest of Lake Leman. Savoy—that bastion of the Counter Reformation—was only superficially French in the middle third of the sixteenth century. Its population was growing rapidly, and unlike many invading armies the Valois troops did nothing that might have slowed it down. It had grown 50 percent since the beginning of the century; some cities had doubled in size. As was often the case at the time, human proliferation went hand in hand with misery: in a classic Malthusian "scissors," economic growth and agricultural output failed to keep pace with the increasing population (rural industry was relatively rare in Savoy). Many small farms lacked even a single cow, and country folk reduced to wage labor crowded the roads leading to the cities, especially Lyons, where Felix Platter was also headed but for very different reasons.

In many respects, however, this demographic congestion hints at the powerful vitality of Renaissance Savoy. Nothing comparable would occur in this part of Europe until the nineteenth century. Content to reap the benefits of native energies, the French occupation did no damage to Savoy in the quarter century that it lasted. In 1559 it suddenly came to an end: virtually the entire duchy was restored to the legitimate heir, young Emmanuel Philibert. In command of Spanish troops, this brilliant general had earlier, in 1557, defeated the army of Henri II and his oafish constable Anne de Montmorency near Saint-Quentin. By 1559, however, with the French Wars of Religion already looming, Felix Platter had been back in his native Basel for some time. To him it scarcely mattered whether papist Savoy belonged to the king or the duke now that he had shaken the dust from his traveling boots and settled down back home.

\*   \*   \*

Felix's visit to Nantua in 1552 certainly caused less of a stir than the visit of Francis I. While passing through Bresse seventeen years earlier, the monarch had stopped in the town and stayed in the local monastery or priory.[4] François and Pierre du Breul, who served successively as priors, remained *savoisiens* at heart. They stood fast against agents of the Valois monarch dispatched by Louis de Lorraine, Cardinal de Guise, the titular possessor of the benefice and a friend of the French crown. In Nantua the Breuls' secret motto was, "Not one monk, not one *sou* for the clergy of France."[5] The town, which stood beside a fish-stocked lake, bore a silver trout upon a lake of sinople on its coat of arms; travelers from Germany, Switzerland, and Italy to the great city of Lyons passed by its gates. Owing to the ease with which brass could be imported, the townspeople had specialized in the manufacture of pins, which they exported to the south. En route, Felix passed trains of mules laden with shipments of these pins. North of Nantua he had unwittingly grazed the edge of a region in which freight transport was dominated by French carters. The narrow, bumpy trails here and elsewhere in the south were inhospitable to wagons, however, and suitable only for pack animals like the mule, or for that matter Felix's horse.

\* \* \*

On Wednesday, October 19, 1552, Felix slowly made his way out of Savoy, at that time under Valois administration, and into the kingdom of France proper. During the morning the travelers passed through a region of steep trails and chestnut forests. In this mountainous region, where grains, the normal source of carbohydrates, were much more difficult to grow than in the endless plains of the Saône and Seine to the north, chestnuts were a useful staple. Felix thus made his first discovery of the vast "chestnut zone" of southern France, which Olivier de Serres would describe a little later as extending through "Dauphiné, Haute-Provence, and parts of Languedoc, the Vivarais, Gévaudan, and Velay. Also Auvergne, the Limousin, Périgord, Guyenne, and several parts of Gascony."[6] In other words, the Alps, the Massif Central, and the southern Jura. At noon, having emerged from the forest of "bread trees," the travelers stopped for lunch[7] in Saint-Maurice-de-Beynost at the Cardinal's Hat Inn.[8] Already the influence of the big Italian bankers of Lyons extended this far into the countryside; later, these same bankers did not consider it beneath their dignity to extend usurious operations to such remote backwaters.[9] That night, after a further journey, Felix and his friends stopped in a small town, where they slept at an inn called the Crown, kept by a drunken German.

Despite this German presence, the travelers were now truly in France, in the kingdom of the Valois, which had been ruled for almost six years by Henri II. In appearance, at any rate, the kingdom was in great shape. Its population was greater than at any time since the Hundred Years' War. In 1552, some twenty million souls were encompassed within the borders of what is now metropolitan France, and perhaps sixteen or seventeen million within the borders of France as they then existed. The wars that French sovereigns had waged since 1494 had affected mainly France's neighbors, leaving French territory largely untouched. Agricultural production, fostered by this lengthy period of internal peace and regional development, was sufficient in most years to feed the bulk of Henri's subjects. To be sure, vigorous demographic growth coupled with rising prices and falling wages had had a deleterious effect on the standard of living of the *menu peuple,* those at the very bottom of the social hierarchy. But even the poor generally "got by," except for those who succumbed in brief periods of increased mortality. Reigning over the whole society was the king, who ruled with a relatively small number of functionaries (some ten thousand *officiers*[10] for the entire country, which is a very small number compared with the millions of civil servants employed by the French state today). The top "official," King Henri II, was a cultivated man, intelligent but not brilliant. He was a competent, decisive military commander. His achievements under the circumstances were quite as impressive as those of Francis I, who, for all his undeniable merits, ultimately suffered a greater number of disastrous reverses than his successor.

Whereas Michelet regarded Henri II as a sad figure in every way,[11] English-speaking historians, as always impartial because not caught up in our Franco-French conflicts, have recently offered a generally positive assessment of this king's activities.[12] Furthermore, his accidental death in 1559, which soon plunged France into a civil war that saw the country martyred by both its liberators and their enemies, in retrospect pointed up the usefulness of a vigorous prince like Henri, who reigned from 1547 to 1559. A certain balance between rival factions—that of Montmorency, more inclined to peace, and that of the Guises, more authoritarian and bellicose, the one and the other firmly associated with the power of the monarch—was essential for keeping the peace at home. It was a precarious peace, to be sure, but infinitely precious given the disastrous bloodletting to come in the period 1560–94. The "Henrician" state was traditional in structure, dominated by the court, the high nobility who were the provincial governors, and the magistrates of *parlement* and the other sovereign courts, who to all intents and purposes owned their offices. Despite the dominance of these archaic or at any rate traditional institutions, the king took steps to modernize his government: he appointed secretaries of state, remote but already powerful forerunners of today's ministers; he also created posts for *intendants des finances,* who functioned as undersecretaries of state in matters of finance, and *intendants de généralité,* still few in number but precursors of the celebrated regional *intendants* destined to play so important a role under Richelieu and an even greater role under Louis XIV. From a literary and artistic point of view, the ongoing Renaissance did not suffer from the death of Francis I, for all his remarkable achievements. Michelet hints at a cultural decline after 1550.[13] The work of the poet Pierre de Ronsard, already in full flower, along with that of the architect Philibert de L'Orme and the painter Primaticcio, among others, should suffice to prove him wrong.

Public order was strenuously maintained in mid-sixteenth-century France, despite some notable lapses. Peasant and urban uprisings in the southwestern part of the country in 1548 were harshly repressed by the royal army. Paradoxically, the rioters achieved their goal, which was to prevent modernization of the tax system in order to facilitate the financing of military operations. Henri had hoped to do this by extending the *gabelle,* or salt tax, to the entire country, including Aquitaine. Although the leaders of the rioting were put to death, the government was forced to abandon plans to institute the *gabelle* in the area between the Loire and the Garonne. Of greater consequence was the significant growth of Protestantism in the cities and even in certain rural areas, especially in the Cévennes. Henri met the wave of "heretical" conversions with harsh repression from which his "class brothers" in the aristocracy were exempt, however. The persecution thus fell on the middle and lower classes. Though strict, the king was by nature a committed Gallican and had no intention of permitting anything like a Spanish Inquisition run by the clergy and agents of the pope on French soil. Hence there was no inquisition as such in France, for which we can only be grateful, although the civil courts were often heavy-handed in religious matters. What is more, Henri was obliged to tread carefully with the Protestant princes of Germany who, like the Zwinglians and other Swiss "heretics," were his allies in his wars with the ultra-Catholic Hapsburgs.

Militarily speaking, the start of Henri's reign was a triumph. Piedmont, Savoy, and Corsica all fell into French hands. The Valois king also extended his possessions to Metz at the expense of Charles V and to Boulogne at the expense of the Tudors. There were disappointments to come, to be sure, but never a disaster as crushing as the French defeat at Pavia in 1526. With its 450,000 square kilometers of territory, its thousand "walled cities," and its big cities with populations as large as 350,000 in the case of Paris, France was the most powerful consolidated territorial state in Western Europe, even if it was surpassed in overall influence by

the heterogeneous empire of Charles V, whose far-flung possessions included, in addition to Spain, territories ranging from Germany to Italy
and from the Netherlands to the Americas.

But for his unshakable character, Felix could easily have found himself
divided between two loyalties: on the one hand his loyalty to the Germanic world of which he was already a distinguished member, *Teutsch*
to the very depths of his soul, and on the other his growing loyalty to
France, where he remained for more than five years a young man eager to
learn, to observe, and to wonder.

\* \* \*

October 20, 1552: "We reached Lyons after crossing a flat plain" (*durch
ein eben landt*). The city, in which Felix would remain until the twenty-
third, was large for its time and at the peak of its expansion.[14] Its population had more than tripled since the reign of Louis XI to 55,000 or 60,000
by the middle of the sixteenth cenutry, on a par with Florence, Rome,
Antwerp, London, and Seville. Italian merchants kept the goods flowing,
and trade was further stimulated by the expenditures of the French army
as the Valois attempted to make inroads into the Italian peninsula. In
printing and silk manufacturing, Lyons was the leading city in France.
The bankers of this city at the crossroads of the Savoy, Saône, and Rhône
regions lent money to princes bent on military adventures. And merchants, both Italians and to a lesser degree natives, ran things, occupying
the highest offices in the so-called *consulat*.

The poor and, more generally, the *menu peuple* certainly did not enjoy
their fair share of the growing collective wealth. Yet in the realm of social
policy the consuls took the bold step, quite in keeping with the spirit of
the times, of creating the Aumône générale, or General Alms, in 1531, to
ensure that the poor would always have bread. The city had previously
been shaken by popular protest in the *rebeyne,* or rebellion, of 1529, when
confraternities of artisans had rioted against high grain prices. After that
came the typographers' strike, the first important industrial conflict of
modern times. The repercussions of this event, which we detected earlier
in Thomas Platter's shop in Basel, were still felt in many Lyons print
shops at the time of Felix Platter's brief visit.

Despite the strikes, the vigor of the local publishing industry indicates
that Lyons was a city of culture, comparable in this respect to Basel but
much more populous than the Swiss city. Furthermore, most artisans
were literate, especially those employed in print shops. The city was also
distinguished by the work of great poets, among them Louise Labé, who

in 1555 published her *Elégies et sonnets,* culminating a long personal and
literary journey:

> Baise m'encor, rebaise moy et baise;
> Donne m'en un de tes plus savoureux
> Donne m'en un de tes plus amoureux
> Je t'en rendray quatre plus chaus que braise.

> [Kiss me again, kiss me and kiss me;
> Give me one of your sweetest kisses
> Give me one of your most loving kisses
> And I'll return the favor with four kisses hotter than burning
>    coals.]

In this warm (and not simply puritanical) soil, Protestantism took root
before and after Felix's visit. In 1546, the Pardon of Saint John, a summer
festival that was at once religious and communal, was disrupted, some
said polluted, by Huguenot demonstrations. In 1551, Henri issued the
royal edict of Châteaubriant, intended to stamp out heresy and the sale of
proscribed books. In May 1553, a half-dozen students educated in
Lausanne were burned alive on the Place des Terreaux in Lyons despite
appeals from the Protestant cities of Switzerland, Œcolampadian and
Zwinglian alike. In the spring of 1561, the Reformation was in serious
trouble up and down the valley of the Rhône.

Felix in 1552 had a front-row seat. In October, on his way to Lyons, he
saw a "Christian in a shirt," that is, a Huguenot, with a huge bundle of
straw tied to his back to fuel the fire in which he was to be burned to
death.[15] Felix's cool eyewitness account contrasts with the descriptions of
his suffering when, as a child, he heard stories of little girls being put to
death in the Netherlands for the good Protestant cause. At this point he
sees himself as an anatomist, a strictly objective observer. He became in-
ured to seeing martyrs on their way to execution, just as he had overcome
his fear after bumping into the hanged man on the way to Lyons (F 137,
138).

In Lyons, a great European crossroads, he also heard news of great
events connected with the history of the Reformation. He learned of the
victories of Colonel Schertlin, whose misadventures in Basel had kept
that city amused some months earlier. With his band of anti-imperial
Protestant mercenaries, Schertlin, in Picardy, had defeated a colonel from
the Netherlands in the service of Charles V. The defeated soldier was
named Martin Rossheim, and he had made a name for himself by laying
waste to Picardy, pillaging the countryside at will and wreaking havoc in

the rear of French forces. He also lined his pockets in the unscrupulous tradition of the generals and *condottieri* of the time.[16] The Rossheim-Schertlin battle was a minor episode in the vast conflict between Charles V and the Protestant princes of Germany, backed by Henri II of France. The French king had taken Metz from the Imperials a short while earlier. He now made ready to protect his conquest and in the final weeks of 1552 turned back the emperor's counteroffensive.

For Felix, Lyons was above all a stopping place, a way station on his journey southward. For lodging, he had the choice of at least fifty hotels equipped to receive numerous travelers, especially itinerant merchants who came to the city for its fairs or simply to trade.[17] The young man from Basel chose, as he often would in the course of his extended travels, to stay with a German host, with whom he felt safer. He therefore took a room, or at any rate a bed, at the sign of the Bear, an inn kept by a Swiss compatriot, Paul Herbelin of Zurich (F 138). The other guests were all German. There was even a stove, made of terra-cotta or tile, just as in Basel; such stoves were rare in France. The average price of lodging in a hotel of this caliber, neither overly luxurious nor unbearably bug-ridden, was fourteen or fifteen sous per night (for comparison, the average daily wage of a construction worker was five sous at midcentury).[18] This bears out Felix's statement that he spent fifty sous for three nights' lodging in Lyons, from October 20 to October 23, 1552. Fortunately, he had his own horse. Hiring a mount would have increased his daily outlay by half.[19]

When it came to horses, incidentally, the members of Felix's traveling party were not always lucky. One of them (Schöpflin) had purchased a mount in Basel from none other than Werner Wölflin, a draper and city council member with a good reputation among his fellow businessmen. The horse had seemed superb but soon proved to be lame and useless. Had the buyer been swindled? In any case, he was obliged to sell the horse for almost nothing in Lyons. True, horses, whether used by travelers or merchants, were often overloaded with heavy baggage in addition to their riders.[20] Schöpflin was forced to continue his journey down the Rhône by riverboat, aboard one of the countless vessels that drifted or were rowed downstream filled with donkeys, grain, and bundles of fabric. On the return trip they were hauled upriver by men or animals (horses or donkeys).

\* \* \*

Felix's "naval" experience on the Rhône was less extensive: he had only to cross the river, not travel downstream, to visit his future teacher, Professor Rondelet of the medical school in Montpellier, who was then staying in Lyons. But after boarding a ferry he found himself threatened by the woman in charge, who promised to hurl him into the river if he did not pay an exorbitant fare for passage. He had no choice but to fork over the cash. This is all we know about the strange company of *traversières,* or female ferry operators, who made it possible to cross the Rhône; none of the other sources mentions them.[21]

Dr. Rondelet, whose presence enticed young Felix to cross the Rhône, had come up from Montpellier to treat Cardinal de Tournon, lieutenant general of the province since 1542 and archbishop of Lyons since 1551. After suffering temporary disgrace following the death of Francis I, the cardinal, in Rome, soon contrived to patch up a rift between the pope and the king of France. On his return from Italy in September of 1552, he made a triumphal entry into Lyons.[22] He was welcomed by various official bodies, including the monks and the clergy, the corporations of German, Milanese, Luccan, and Florentine merchants, and, last but not least, the consuls of the city. All wore sumptuous costumes of satin and velvet, with black the predominant color. The cardinal, however, wore red and white. But his splendor proved ephemeral: worn out by old age and diplomatic vexations, the prelate was soon forced to take to his bed. On October 14 his condition improved, but the steadfast Dr. Rondelet was reluctant to leave his bedside. Felix was therefore obliged to go to the archbishop's residence to visit the already famous professor of medicine from Montpellier.

*   *   *

Guillaume Rondelet was born in Montpellier in 1507, one of many children of a man whose business was selling fragrances, a sort of olfactory apothecary.[23] Was it because he had been put out to nurse as an infant that Guillaume had been a weak and sickly child afflicted with every disease known to man other than elephantiasis? Or so he said, with the same playful sense of humor that had landed him a part, along with his fellow medical student François Rabelais, in a comic play about a doctor and a mute woman that was performed in Montpellier in 1530. An orphan from an early age, Rondelet was educated under the supervision of an elder brother and for a time supported and housed by his sister Catherine, the well-endowed widow of a wealthy Florentine merchant who had settled years earlier in Languedoc. As the University of Montpellier's *procureur,* or student representative, Guillaume soon took up Protestant ideas, but his religious convictions did not prevent him from associating with and treating prelates of the Catholic Church.

Like the Platters, Rondelet got around. He had lived for several years in Paris, where, like many of his contemporaries among the elite of southern France, he had become steeped in Latin and indeed in French culture. He had also attended the great Italian universities in Padua, Ferrara, Bologna, and Pisa. As a young man, he had briefly earned a living practicing medicine in the small towns of the Vaucluse and the Massif Central. In the French capital he had been greatly influenced by his friend Jean Gonthier from Andernach, a native of Germany educated in the Netherlands and in France and one of the foremost anatomists of the Renaissance. An impassioned anatomist himself, Rondelet would have dissected father, mother, children, and friends had the opportunity arisen (on occasion it did arise when a close acquaintance passed away). He made efforts, at times successful, to secure the patronage of various powerful lords, lay as well as ecclesiastic, including the bishop of Montpellier and above all Cardinal de Tournon, who became his primary patron. This achievement was all the more noteworthy because Tournon, since 1527 or 1528, had been, in theory at any rate, a fierce enemy of Protestantism in France and elsewhere. Apparently the prince of the Church whom Dr. Rondelet served as physician was not greatly troubled by the medical man's heterodox views in matters of religion. In any case, Dr. Rondelet frequently left his patron to resume teaching at Montpellier. He was appointed to a chair at the university there in 1545. When the cardinal fell ill in 1552, however, the doctor left Montpellier for Lyons in order to attend at his bedside. The great physician briefly interrupted his supervision of the patient's enemas to receive Felix.[24] Evidently the interview went well on both sides, for Rondelet, the eminent botanist and dissector, became the teacher who initiated Felix into the mysteries of human anatomy and the classification of herbs.

On October 23, 1552, Felix and his friends left Lyons for Vienne. Thomas Schöpflin traveled by boat on the Rhône. Felix and Michel Héroard rode along the left bank. Their route thus took them into the Dauphiné, a region that they would come to know better as they approached the city of Vienne. It was a rich province, of course, and one in feverish expansion following the (temporary) annexation of Savoy to France in 1536. The Chartreuse mountains and the Piedmontese marquisate of Saluces (Saluzzo) thus came under the jurisdiction of the ruler of Dauphiné, who saw himself as the inheritor of the old imperialist mantle of the Allobroges.[25]

That night the travelers arrived in Vienne, where they stayed at the Auberge de Sainte-Barbe on rue de la Chèvrerie in the Est district.[26] The morning of the twenty-fourth was devoted to touring the city; there was much to see. Vienne, the second largest city in Dauphiné, with roughly

8,000 inhabitants (compared with 12,000 in Grenoble, the provincial capital), deserved better than the Basel tourist's disdainful description of it as an *alt stettlin,* or little old city (F 139).[27] In truth, Felix was not very interested in the city's churches and chapels, of which there were dozens, along with hundreds of priests—a profusion of targets for the virulent propaganda of the local Protestants. The "heretic" Michael Servetus was living in Vienne at the time, quietly drafting a text of fire and brimstone. What caught Felix's eye, in any event, were the old Roman ruins: a theater, the temple of Augustus and Livia, the portico of the baths, a temple of Cybele, an odeon, and the pyramid of the circus, not all of which were identified. Of these he was most interested in the pyramid, of which he left a fairly decent sketch and a verbal description: "It is pointed, built by the Romans, and beautiful in its antiquity." He of course had no idea that in imperial times this pyramid stood at the center of a raised area in the center of a track around which chariots raced.

\*   \*   \*

The tour of Vienne was soon complete, and the travelers prepared to set out again later that same day, Schöpflin still traveling by boat, Felix and Héroard still on horseback. They exchanged loud greetings back and forth from towpath to river. After traveling a few miles, the two riders encountered a tributary of the Rhône that was swollen by a recent storm and impassable. Meanwhile, a "great lord" arrived en route to the south with five horses and a retinue of servants. It was Pierre Danès, tutor to the dauphin, the future Francis II (the Short). Since Danès and Felix could not communicate in French or German, they conversed in Latin. It was a stroke of good luck for the young man from Basel. Danès, born in 1497 to a family of Parisian drapers and furriers, had been a professor at the Collège Royal.[28] Now living on ecclesiastical benefices (as curé of Suresnes), he had enjoyed a long career as a humanist and royal functionary. Though he wrote little, he had produced an edition of Pliny the Elder. He knew Aristotle, Cicero, and Lucian like the back of his hand. And at one time or another he had been a disciple or friend of Budé, Dolet, Turnèbe, Marot, Oronce Finé, and many others.

Steeped in Erasmian evangelism, pre-Reformation ideas, Italian culture, and a Paduan rationalism that smacked of heresy,[29] but at the same time a zealous and obsequious servant of the kings of France, the excellent Danès was also the protégé of important prelates and cardinals such as Charles de Lorraine, Selve, Tournon, and Contarini—the elite of the conclave. The potential Huguenot in him never materialized. He rejected schism as he rejected the inconvenient rigors of the Augustinian-

Calvinist idea of grace. He was a Pelagian and friend of the Jesuits, and he ended up bishop of Lavaur and a rather hard-nosed Catholic militant. But in 1552, as he traveled in Dauphiné, he was at the midpoint of a lengthy career that had taken him as the French representative to the Council of Trent in 1546. In 1556 he would be appointed to the coveted position of confessor to his pupil the dauphin. At mid-century, however, Danès was still open-minded and tolerant and especially curious about the thinking of the young. He questioned Felix endlessly about political and religious problems in Basel, a notorious hotbed of heresy.[30] While waiting for the swollen tributary of the Rhône to subside, Pierre Danès took his new friend to see a local nobleman, a penniless petty aristocrat and gentleman farmer in the manner of Olivier de Serres, who cordially received the travelers in his humble farmhouse and served them lunch, for which he charged them—such were the straits to which the lesser nobility were reduced. After lunch the travelers returned to the river, having been informed by a servant that the waters had subsided. Danès's horse led the way across the submerged ford, and Felix followed. The caravan stopped for the night in Saint-Vallier, a small town of one or two thousand inhabitants that was one of many towns affected by the general growth in population.[31] The rising demographic tide stimulated consumption, commerce, and agriculture, strengthened local and fiscal authorities, and promoted education, all in symbiosis, in Saint-Vallier as elsewhere.[32] A population of drapers, papermakers (serving the Lyons printers), postal riders, carpenters, blacksmiths, locksmiths, masons, salt transporters (remember the *gabelle*), ferrymen, barbers, tailors, cobblers, weavers, dyers, mercers, and of course the inevitable butchers, bakers, and millers animated this tiny but lively town.[33]

Felix, not wanting to be left out of things, stammered his first words of French on the night of October 24: *"Donne-moi allons,"* he said at the inn to the servants of Pierre Danès, for he had somehow gotten the idea that the word *allons,* which he heard frequently, meant *drincken,* to drink (F 141). Sixty years later, having long since discovered his mistake, he was still laughing about it.

It was also later, sometime in the period between 1609 and 1612 when he was writing his memoirs, that Felix, then in his seventies, rounded out his account of the next stage of his journey down the Rhône in 1552 after leaving Saint-Vallier on the morning of October 25. The travelers passed close to a mountain, where they recognized, on their left, from descriptions they had heard, an old (Roman?) building known locally as the "house of Pilate." The legend that Pontius Pilate had died in the valley of the Rhône lived on in the memory of the people of Dauphiné as well as in

German scholarship. Pilate, Felix tells us, was supposed to have ended his days in misery in the house that the travelers recognized in passing. By the time the elderly physician completed his memoirs, however, he had gained further knowledge of the story of Pilate from a work published in Basel in 1610, which he read shortly thereafter. This text uses almost the exact same wording as Felix does, stating that Pilate had lived in the valley "in misery" (*ins ellendt* or *im ellendt*).[34] All of southeastern France was awash with folklore into which bits of biblical stories had been woven, so that people like Mary Magdalene and Pontius Pilate were associated with various places in the region.

Felix next crossed the Isère by ferry (*im schif*), complete with horse and baggage, and arrived in Valence on the night of October 25. The city, with its double walls and stout towers, its well-irrigated pasture to the east of the ramparts, and its grain, wool, and above all salt markets, was a sight to see. With 1,800 houses and five to six thousand inhabitants, it was much more than a *stettlin*, or small town, but rather, as Felix put it, a *statt*, or major city. A conscientious student, Felix noted the presence of a university, which was growing rapidly at the time and competing successfully with the efforts of rival intellectuals in Grenoble. Naturally the young traveler's attention was drawn by the medical teaching in Valence: by the late 1560s, when Felix's career was flourishing in Basel, Valence was awarding three to six doctorates in medicine annually.[35] In the early 1550s, however, the school was oriented more toward law than medicine owing to the influence of Italian universities in Bologna, Padua, Pavia, and Pisa.[36] At the noon meal our young traveler was approached by a servant in the inn who offered him a juicy pear in exchange for a little loving. The adolescent Felix turned red as a beet and took off. A hundred years later, in 1661, Racine had no better luck with another servant in Valence, who stuck a chafing dish under his bed in place of the chamber pot. Was this a linguistic misunderstanding, as Racine believed, or a pratical joke that the budding poet failed to grasp?

*   *   *

From Valence, Felix Platter and Michel Héroard continued on to the confluence of the Rhône and the Drôme, which joined the Rhône on its east bank. They crossed by ferry, which had its perils, but this time there was no mishap. Ferries remained in use in the area until 1789, when a bridge was completed, establishing a "veritable link between north and south."

The travelers passed Livron, a fortified city capped by a an enchanted tower complete with fairies overlooking the valley of the Drôme and the road to Marseilles; they stopped just long enough to await the ferry. Although Livron was a small town of 1,500, it boasted some twenty priests and other clergy distributed among its parish church and fourteen chapels. Apart from its walls, the town was also protected by drawbridges and massive gates. A castellan dispensed justice in the name of the bishop of Valence and monitored the activities of the consuls, who were more or less democratically elected—actually rather less than more. Felix noted the presence of a hospital, a grain market, several other markets, and a set of measuring stones. René Favier has classified sixteenth-century Livron as a "large town."[37] Nevertheless, the place made a strong impression on the visitor from Basel. When he wrote his memoirs some sixty years after his visit, he mentioned the siege of Livron, which, having been infiltrated by Huguenots, became Protestant sometime after 1560. In 1574 a royal and Catholic army under the command of the maréchal de Bellegarde laid siege to the town on behalf of Henri III. Three thousand cannonballs and numerous assaults failed to overcome the tenacity of Livron's defenders, including women who, distaffs in hand, mocked the enemy from the town walls and later avenged themselves in a deplorable way on the bodies of slain attackers. The arrival of reinforcements led by the young duc de Lesdiguières, who would go on to even greater achievements, forced the Catholics to call off the siege.[38]

\*　\*　\*

After a short additional ride, the busy day of October 25 came to an end in Loriol, a town of 300 houses and 1,500 inhabitants under the jurisdiction of the bishop of Valence. There the travelers bedded down for the night at the Three Kings, an inn whose name evokes the three magi of the Gospel. An impressive town of moderate size, Loriol did not lack for protection. A wall with fifteen towers was intended to dissuade the French army, which often passed by on its way to Italy, from disporting itself within. The century's prosperity had left its mark, even if the gains were not evenly distributed. Four annual fairs and a weekly market had been authorized or confirmed by letters-patent from the king since 1535. The people, however, especially the poor, were no better off than elsewhere. Yet they did enjoy the consolation—laughable, to be sure, in the eyes of a Protestant medical student like Felix Platter—of a collegial church containing the jaw of Saint Romain de Barral still blessed with all its teeth, a relic granted to the town by divine dispensation to offer healing to those afflicted with diseases of the mouth.

On the morning of October 26, Felix left the inn in Loriol. Proceeding without haste, he arrived a few hours later for lunch in Montélimar, a city of 6,000 with winding, narrow, filthy streets. Montélimar was famous for the manufacture of "Morocco leather" (and after 1759 would be famous also for its nougat). New vineyards and fields were clustered around the city's gates, attesting here as elsewhere in the region to recent growth typical of the Renaissance. Montiliens (as the residents were known) still shuddered at the memory of the German-speaking landsknechts (mercenaries) who had plagued the region in the second decade of the century. The city claimed exemption from royal taxes, but neither the sovereign on the banks of the Seine nor the parlement in Grenoble was impressed.

Our riders, following the course of the Rhône, crossed the city from north to south almost without stopping. They entered through the Porte Saint-Martin on Montélimar's northern edge, then proceeded along rue Droite, rue Alamanderie, rue Fruiterie, rue Saunière, rue Barute, and rue Charreterie to the Porte d'Aygu. Along the way they passed, on their right, the collegiate church of Sainte-Croix, then under restoration; and also on their right the Franciscan convent, where Huguenot influence had reared its head (urban women were particularly receptive to Huguenot preaching). Finally, toward the end of their route, they passed the Commandery of Saint John of Jerusalem on their left. That same evening, October 26, Héroard and Platter reached Pierrelatte, where they stopped for the night. The *bourgade* stood at the foot of a steep cliff topped by a pair of chapels dedicated to the Holy Angels and a fortress preceded by a gateway dating from the time of the Black Plague. Eleven years later, Pierrelatte achieved a modest celebrity that it could have done without: in July 1562, the baron des Adrets, commanding a small army of Protestants and cutthroats, massacred many local residents along with a royal and Catholic garrison composed mainly of *arquebusiers* (harquebus men) from Provence.[39] Felix, always curious about herbs and trees, noticed the many olive trees already in evidence here, at the northern extreme of the olive-growing zone, as well as further south along the flat road leading from Pierrelatte to Pont Saint-Esprit. Indeed, the growth of the economy, steady in the sixteenth century and intermittent later on, led to a gradual northward extension of the olive-growing zone.[40] In October of 1552, it was in Pierrelatte that Felix, traveling down the Rhône from Lyons, first encountered olive trees laden with green, red, and black fruit, already ripe but still quite bitter for his taste. Three centuries later, Flahaut encountered olive groves ten kilometers farther north, in Viviers. On the right bank of the great river one finds a similar progression: in 1595, according to Thomas Platter Jr., the northern tip of the olive region was located in Bourg-Saint-Andéol; by 1886 it had moved thirty-three kilometers upstream. The olive tree thus traveled northward at the respectable speed of one kilometer per decade, or ten kilometers per century.

In any case, it was almost time for the annual beating of the trees and gathering of olives. Meanwhile, poplar, elm, apple, pear, plum, cherry, and fruit-laden chestnut trees were beginning to shed their leaves. Beggars hastened to fill baskets with fallen chestnuts. The leaves on grapevines turned yellow, but the holly remained green. Turnip-digging time had arrived. Slugs devastated freshly sown wheat fields. Many children still went barefoot despite the autumn mud. And people faced the threat of pestilential fevers.

*　*　*

On October 27, after a brief excursion through the olive groves to the eastern end of Pont Saint-Esprit, the famous bridge across the Rhône, Felix, Héroard, and Danès arrived at the walls of Orange, which Felix described as a "little old city" (*gar alt stettlin*) despite the fact that its population stood at about 5,000—a sort of second Montélimar. Orange, administered by consuls and syndics, belonged in theory and occasionally in practice to the Dutch prince of Nassau, whose officials met with opposition, at times bloody, from elements of the populace and from a pro-French faction of the elite. In 1549 the ongoing struggle between the Valois and the Hapsburgs emboldened agents of Henri II to seize control. Vicissitudes of politics aside, cultural forces also propelled the city toward closer ties with France: minutes of council meetings had been kept in French rather than Latin since 1525. Some twenty years later, in 1547, the first Protestants began to emerge from a prolonged period of heretical ferment. The local bishop, Rostaing de La Baume-Suze, who had occupied the episcopal throne since 1543, responded relatively mildly, sentencing heretics, some of whom may have enjoyed the long arm of Nassau's protection, to prison terms on bread and water. During the few hours that Felix spent in Orange, he explored mainly the city's Roman antiquities, especially the triumphal arch, which was used as a target by crossbow marksmen, and the proscenium of the theater, which—progress being unstoppable—was used in a similar way by sharpshooters equipped with the more modern harquebus.[41]

On the evening of October 27 Felix and his companions reached Avignon, which our memoirist describes as a *mechtige stat*, a large and powerful city. Despite the departure of the popes, Avignon was still a fairly large city in 1552. Its population in the middle third of the sixteenth century numbered some fifteen or sixteen thousand, smaller, to be sure, than the thirty thousand of 1368 or the forty thousand of 1343, when the Avignon papacy was at its height. Still, in the reign of Henri II, the number of people living in the city was still almost triple the five or six thousand who had lived there when Clement V, the first pope to reside in Avignon, arrived in 1309.[42] In any case, by the time Felix visited Avignon, the human dimension of the city had shrunk owing to the papacy's return to the Vatican in the previous century, whereas the physical dimension remained as vast as it had been in the fourteenth century. By 1552 the visitor to Avignon did not feel cramped—certainly no cause to complain.

What is more, the city remained a business center for Italian merchants with connections in Lyons and Marseilles and export-import routes extending as far as the Levant. Not far from the city, mills on the Sorgue produced paper (supplying printers in Lyons, who generally drew their raw materials from the south). In the manufacture of silk and velvet for merchants in Milan and Lyons, Avignon was second only to Lyons. And money from Avignon was invested in farms throughout the Comtat Venaissin. Many people took a dim view of usury, a business in which Jews served as intermediaries—and as scapegoats.[43] Usury aside, we must be careful not to idealize this region's undeniable prosperity in the mid-sixteenth century. Hard times were frequent during and after the reign of Francis I, and falling wages imposed hardships on this Judeo-Christian community. At the time of Felix's visit, some of the most enlightened minds in Avignon were giving thought to setting up a central almshouse for the poor, a step finally taken in 1555.

Avignon did not live by silk, paper, low wages, and alms alone. The most important industry in this bustling city was still Catholicism, which drew in huge sums through the tithe and distributed equally huge sums in the form of prebends, contracts, and expenditures of all kinds, thereby exerting a tremendous influence on the local economy. The cumbersome papal bureaucracy was another source of profit: in the sixteenth century it included a cardinal legate, an archbishop, and several chapters of canons. Every year six hundred or more priests and deacons were ordained; the vast majority then left Avignon to find work (or unemployment) elsewhere. In addition, the municipal authorities subsidized frequent and impressive processions. Private devotional services created a demand for printed books of hours. In short, the religious life of the city was extraordinarily robust, even if some of the local prelates were known to keep concubines in their homes. Children's choirs were directed by well-trained singing teachers, whose efforts ensured that the musical life of the city could rival that of Basel and Nuremberg. When young Felix fell briefly into a deep depression in Avignon, he revived his spirits by visiting two suburban churches, where singing and organ music eased his pain. "God sustained me," he wrote (F 142). In this case God was not specifically either Huguenot or papist but an ecumenical Heavenly Father who presided over church music that enabled the young traveler to overcome his melancholy. When it came to religion, Felix was not a narrow-minded sectarian, as Montaigne would observe in 1580.

*   *   *

For a young man not previously troubled by adversity, the evening of October 27 and the entire following day in Avignon were painful and even depressing. Pierre Danès departed, on friendly terms to be sure, for his estate in Provence and a glorious future: within a few years he became confessor to the king's children and bishop of Lavaur. The adolescent traveler and the middle-aged humanist promised to see each other again, but their paths diverged: friendships begun while traveling are often short-lived. Felix also parted company temporarily with Michel Héroard, who advised him to find a room in Villeneuve-lès-Avignon. Accommodations there were less costly than in Avignon proper, and the churches were admirable. Héroard, meanwhile, went to comfortable quarters in the home of a friend of his, the master of the Avignon mint; a great deal of metal flowed through the city, some of it precious, some not, and much of it suitable for coinage. Héroard's friend tampered with the scales used to weigh copper for making the *billon,* a small, not very valuable coin of copper-silver alloy. Only later was this secret revealed.

At the Inn of the Cock, a second-rate hotel in the suburb of Villeneuve-lès-Avignon, Felix rubbed shoulders with rough (*rauwen*) boatmen wearing blue caps and bell-bottom trousers. Afraid of being murdered, he spent a lonely, sleepless night. He was completely miserable, and his horse, tied up in an adjoining stable, was no happier among the strange draft horses in the neighboring stalls. The next morning, Felix cried for a long time on his beloved horse's withers; he spoke to the animal in German, a language that the beast appeared to understand.[44] The clouds hanging over Felix seemed to dissipate, however, as the day wore on: the church music helped, and then he was invited to eat and sleep at the home of the mint official where Héroard was staying. Felix's "depression" was over as quickly as it began. In a good mood he set out again, at dawn on October 29, for Languedoc, accompanied by his friend Héroard. The two crossed the celebrated Pont d'Avignon and stopped at the wretched Inn of the Cock just long enough to pay Felix's bill. The hostess, a woman who knew how to do sums, totaled up the bill on a slate or board while Felix looked on: the total was twenty-one sous, two of which went for a tip. With her left hand the woman fingered her rosary. Arguing about the bill was out of the question: she spoke the *langue d'oc* (the dialect of the region), and Felix spoke German. It was the same difficulty he had faced earlier with the far more aggressive woman aboard the ferry. But the rosary is significant: it reminds us that Felix's visits to the Catholic churches of the Comtat had a radical effect on him. Henceforth, wherever he traveled as a tourist or on business, he deigned to take an interest in the churches of the Roman religion, whereas previously he had had eyes only for Protestant churches and Latin antiquities. His sensibility had evolved; his travels had made him more open-minded.

$$* \quad * \quad *$$

At the first rise in the trail to the west, Felix's horse began to limp. It had picked up a pebble between its shoe and hoof. With the pebble removed, the horse again moved at a good clip. The riders crossed the Gardon by ferry. At midday on October 29 they stopped at the Inn of the Angel in the large village of Sernhac (200 hearths, 1,000 inhabitants). The innkeeper's daughter attempted to greet Felix with the customary kiss, but our naive traveler spurned the girl's offer and immediately departed for Nîmes. As timid as he was, he was just beginning to learn the ways of Languedoc.[45] In general, conditions there were much the same as in Savoy and Dauphiné: demographic growth had led to crowding in many villages and towns; economic output had increased dramatically, but not enough to offset the concomitant increase in population; members of the elite had grown wealthy and cultivated; and a segment of the *menu peuple* had been reduced to poverty. At the time of Felix's visit, however, the food situation was not too bad. In October 1552, shortly before his arrival, the Provincial Estates in Nîmes had granted permission for free trade in grain between *sénéchaussées,* from Beaucaire to Carcassonne and vice versa. Export of grain outside the province was prohibited, however, which suggests that although there was a certain reserve of grain in storage, it was not sufficient to remove all worry about what might happen in future winters. War raged elsewhere, but it was not an immediate concern. Nobles did have to remain in readiness, however. In June 1552, the blue-blooded reserves of the region, the *ban* and the *arrière-ban,* had been summoned to fight the Spaniards, but in July it was learned that the Iberian galleys had withdrawn and there was nothing more to fear, even if some commoners may have felt threatened by the unruly behavior of the nobles who had responded to the call. Meanwhile, in October, came the first news of the siege of Metz, which Guise was defending against the forces of Charles V.

The progress made by the Protestant religion in Languedoc was as "worrisome" as in other regions, if not more so. A provincial council was therefore held in Narbonne in 1551; the failure of nearly all the bishops of the province to attend shows that certain abuses persisted. The council decided to prohibit the use of churches for celebrating the festival of fools and the festival of choir children, which were considered to be too profane. Dancing in churches and cemeteries was also forbidden. Priests were requested to decline invitations to so-called banquets *de fructu* at which people sang grotesque "psalms" such as "*Memento David sans truffe.*" But these measures came late. In Nîmes, Felix's destination on this stage of his journey, several heretics had been burned in August of 1551 and their property confiscated. Agents appointed by the parlement of Toulouse also tracked down Huguenots in Montpellier, Montagnac, Béziers, and Pézenas. There were well-defined limits to the persecution, however, as we shall see later on.

On the night of October 29, Felix and Michel reached Nîmes, where they stayed at the Red Apple Inn. The next morning they visited the Arena and admired the statue of Romulus and Remus. This work shows the two boys with the she-wolf, one leaning against her thigh, the other at her nipples and seemingly caressed by the animal (F 143).[46] The two travelers were also interested in another statue at the Arena, this one depicting a man with three heads, two of them bearded, all three surmounted by a crown. This "Tricephalus" can be seen today at the Musée de Lyon.[47] The amphitheater also contained a trio of priapic statues, one with birds pecking at its phallus "representing the passions that cause us to suffer a thousand pains." Much later, Thomas Platter Jr. would be quite impressed by this same statue.[48]

During the first three decades of the sixteenth century, the pious agricultural laborers who inhabited Nîmes witnessed innumerable impressive miracles at the city's Holy Cross. But times had changed. A plague of paupers after 1530 persuaded a ruling class steeped in Renaissance humanism that strict regulations had to be imposed on the poor. Beggars were compelled to comply with the new rules or else be thrown into irons or sent to the galleys. The authorities closed the local brothel in 1532 to prevent the spread of venereal disease. Although the municipal government was run by lay officials, it claimed the right to reform convents and monitor the activities of nuns. "Heresy," encouraged by the moralistic bent of municipal reformers, drew numerous recruits; its future was assured.

Several bishops of Nîmes belonged to the Briçonnet family of Tours and were protégés of Marguerite de Navarre, who was favorably disposed to Erasmian humanism; these absentee bishops favored church reforms so long as they remained moderate. The spread of Protestantism was further aided by the fact that the clergy in Nîmes were less vigilant against it than were their colleagues in Avignon, where agents of the pope kept a close eye on things. In 1534 a new *collège,* or high school, began to offer quality teaching, and this, too, aided, among other things, the Huguenot "sect." In this city of six to seven thousand people, proud of its Roman monuments but marred by a haphazard maze of fetid sewers and alleyways, traditional Catholicism was on the decline. Torture and burnings slowed the progress of Protestantism, but once incidents of rioting and iconoclasm broke out in 1561, a Calvinist seizure of power seemed inevitable. The growth of the wool and especially the silk industry lay in the future, primarily in the seventeenth and eighteenth centuries. In 1552, when Felix passed through Nîmes, times were good: neither plague nor famine afflicted the city. Things would change shortly, but the peaceful interlude is worth noting.[49]

The Swiss visitor's brief passage fell among a series of events that reveal something of the flavor of life in Nîmes in 1552. Pierre d'Airebaudouze, a prominent local citizen who had been converted to Calvin's new dogma by the secret teachings of the *collège,* fled to Geneva in that year. In June, sentinels were posted atop the towers of the Dominican church and the church of Saint-Antoine to watch for a possible Spanish invasion. Kegs of wine were laid in for a meeting of the Estates of Languedoc in October 1552. The new presidial (a court of justice) was installed in December. The cattle market, which had been banished for a time to a location two leagues from the city, was returned to a new suburban site near the Carmelite convent. And in what was apparently a sign of good economic times, a commercial exchange, providing such services as currency conversion, was established on a square adjacent to the cathedral, the Calade.[50]

Felix raced through the city's antiquities early in the morning on October 30. When his brief archeological tour was complete, he and Michel left for Montpellier. They stopped for lunch in Lunel, a small town (*stertlin*) of 2,500 inhabitants located between the two larger cities.[51] The route was bordered by olive groves set among fields of barley and wheat. In Lunel Felix drank his first mug of muscatel, which was either produced locally or imported from Frontignan. Although it was late October, the weather was hot, which surprised the Swiss traveler used to Basel's cool autumns. After lunch, the two young men, acquiescing in southern custom, bedded down on straw mattresses for a siesta at a local inn. Before long, however, they were on their feet again and ready to go. A livestock town with muddy streets, Lunel stood close to broad pastures and coastal salt marshes. Many of the buildings and implements in the town and the surrounding countryside had survived from the Middle Ages, predating the years of crisis (1348–1450). The ramparts, built in the thirteenth and refurbished in the first half of the fifteenth century, traced the limits of a town almost triple the size of the old Roman *castrum,* vestiges of which could still be seen in the pattern of streets intersecting the main north-south (Sommières-Mauguio) and east-west (Nîmes-Montpellier) roads. The banner of Catholicism still flew high in Lunel in 1552, perhaps owing to the memory of Saint Gerard, who was said to have belonged to a family of local nobles. And there was also the memory of Saint Anthony of Padua, who had allegedly performed the miracle of silencing frogs whose croaking had disturbed the prayers of the local Franciscans, or so the hagiographies reported a phenomenon that may have been a consequence of the destruction of a swamp ecology by urbanization. Yet all of these vestiges of Catholicism, starting with the monastery of the Franciscans, or *cordeliers,* which had been richly endowed as recently as the time of Francis I, would be swept away within a few years by Protestantism, which surely must already have been deeply entrenched at the time of Felix's passage.

In leaving Lunel, incidentally, Héroard and Platter escaped another rather dangerous band of professional thieves who plundered travelers in the vicinity of a suburban tavern known as La Bégude Blanche. This was another of the unlicensed inns that Henri II's agents had been trying to close down for years without success. Order was not established in this regard until the seventeenth century. The two young men proceeded toward Montpellier, their ultimate destination. In this large city the presidial, established only in 1552, had just asserted jurisdiction over the barony of Lunel, which had formerly been attached to the *sénéchaussée* of Nîmes and Beaucaire. Riding westward on the afternoon of October 30, Michel Héroard was pleased to think that he would spend the night in the city of his birth. En route the two riders passed through Sambres, which Felix, in his memoirs, mistakenly refers to as Chambéry. A little farther on, at the Pont du Lez near the inn of Castelnau, the young man from Basel again saw the bodies of hanged men whose souls had departed for a better world. Although the past few weeks on the road had surely hardened him, this sight made an unpleasant impression on him and made him feel strange (*seltzam*). The "depression" he had experienced in Avignon returned. He uttered one last prayer (whether silently or out loud he does not say); it is the first time he has mentioned praying since his departure. In his prayer Felix begged God to grant him grace (*gnodt*) —he was, after all, a Protestant—in his studies and his eventual return to Switzerland. From a hillside topped by a cross the two travelers enjoyed a panoramic view of the capital of Languedoc and—an important first for Felix—the Mediterranean to the south.

At the gates of the city, Platter again felt anxious, a feeling comprehensible in an adolescent entering a strange city for the first time—in this case a city capable of disconcerting even a native Frenchman, for the cities of southern France are not like cities elsewhere. Fortunately, the first sights Felix saw inside the walls were a pleasant change after the hanged men he had seen at Castelnau, and this revived his spirits. The two riders (who remained on their horses even inside the city proper) encountered a group of distinguished citizens, possibly nobles, all dressed in white and carrying banners and stringed instruments. They held silver shells and spoons with which they made a loud racket. With these spoons they also distributed candies and sweets to the well-born young ladies they passed along the way.

The explanation for all this is that it was the day before All Saints' Day, which is followed by All Souls' Day. And October 31 is also Halloween, once a pagan festival of death and witchcraft, which has been preserved in the Anglo-Saxon world but obscured in the Latin countries by a Catholic liturgy of much later origin. On these occasions one finds, on both sides of the English Channel, young people wearing masks and costumes, dancing, collecting candy, and engaging in other activities; Felix's account suggests that what was being celebrated was more All Saints' than All Souls': the festivities were gay, elitist, and socially acceptable. There were no *danses macabres* or other unruly or anarchic manifestations.[52]

*   *   *

Felix Platter and Michel Héroard parted company in the middle of Montpellier, not far from the Catalan pharmacy where Felix was to board. The shop stood alongside the residence of its owner, Laurent Catalan, across from what would become, in the twentieth century, the prefecture of Montpellier, itself adjacent to the present-day market. Michel Héroard rode off to his father's house alone. Felix, meanwhile, spotted the pharmacist Laurent Catalan and his wife standing on their doorstep watching the noble dancers in the street. It was Sunday, a day of rest for master apothecaries and shopkeepers. Felix jumped down from his horse and addressed the pharmacist in Latin before handing him a letter of recommendation that he had brought all the way from Basel. It was from a prominent citizen of Basel whom Catalan knew well. The conversation proceeded in Latin. Catalan gave out deep sighs (*seuftzget*) at the thought of his own boys far away on the banks of the Rhine, their lodging there obtained in exchange for the room to be placed at the disposal of the new arrival. Centuries later we can still hear those paternal sighs.

Felix's horse was led away to a stable. Johann von Odratzheim, a young Alsatian of good family and Laurent Catalan's apprentice, showed the newcomer to the tiny room that had been reserved for him through negotiations conducted by mail between Montpellier and Basel (F 128). All that remained was for Catalan's servant, Béatrix, to assist Felix in removing his boots. Felix's account of Béatrix's death a few years after this scene took place is rather curt, reading almost like a coroner's report: "On December 3, 1556, Catalan's former servant, Béatrix [Bietris], who removed my boots the night I arrived in Montpellier in 1552, was hanged on the square [in front of Montpellier's city hall and Notre-Dame cathedral] from a gallows with a single arm. She was hanged and choked to death. She had left the Catalan house a year earlier [in 1555] to go to work for a young priest [*pfaff*] who got her pregnant. When the child came to term, she threw it into the toilet in the priest's house, where its little body was found. The mother was sentenced to death and executed. Her body was given to the School of Medicine for dissection. Its uterus was still swollen and enlarged, because the birth had taken place only a week earlier. The executioner wrapped his victim's remains in a sheet and hung them from a gibbet outside the city."[53] Felix's text contains not a single word of reproach for the poor woman's clerical lover (who apparently went unpunished), except that the word *pfaff* as used by a convinced Protestant like Felix Platter was a term of opprobrium.

\*　　\*　　\*

Here it was, the end of October, and all that remained for Felix now that he had arrived in Montpellier was to total up his accounts (which the editors of his memoirs and I have corrected using information he provides). The trip from Basel to Montpellier took twenty-one days, sixteen of which were spent on the road and five resting in or touring cities along the way. His average expenses were eleven sous, sixteen deniers per day, compared with the average mason's daily wage of five sous. The young student, even as the son of a professor of no great fortune, was thus clearly better off than the average proletarian, as one would expect. Traveling by horseback one could cover an average of forty-five kilometers per day, with actual distances ranging from thirty to sixty kilometers depending on what there was to see, the winds, and so on. In sixteen days of actual travel, Felix covered a distance of slightly over 700 kilometers: 705 according to his own calculations, 720 if we correct his figures slightly. The distance between Basel and Montpellier if one travels by automobile today is 654 kilometers; modern roads make it possible to avoid certain detours that sixteenth-century riders were obliged to take (F 145). Thus a fairly fast driver can make the trip in a single day. Modern means of transportation accordingly reduce the length of the journey by a factor of only sixteen.

Felix thus went from a city of 16,000, Basel, to a city of 12,500, Montpellier. Once famous for its commerce, by the sixteenth century Montpellier had been displaced to some extent by Marseilles and other Mediterranean ports. Hence judges, lawyers and their clerks, and university professors and students (especially medical students) increasingly dominated daily life in the city.

## CHAPTER SIX

# Living in Montpellier

O
n November 4, 1552, Felix registered at the University of Montpellier. The night before, he had witnessed the burning in the streets of numerous secretly circulated "heretical" books and had not lifted a finger to stop the destruction. What good would it have done? Meanwhile, more prosaically, he had sold his horse for eight crowns, with which he was able to buy some clothes and a *flassada,* a type of Catalonian blanket (the November nights were already cold). His registration at the university brought him into contact with Dr. Honoré Du Chatel, a brilliant physician, womanizer, Catholic, and transplanted Parisian, who examined Felix and found his knowledge sufficient to begin a course of medical studies. Certain Marrano connections played a part in Felix's matriculation. His official academic patron, tutor, permanent advisor, and intellectual godfather (officially recognized as such by the local authorities) was Dean Antoine Saporta, a friend of Rabelais's and the grandson of Louis Saporta Sr., a Jewish doctor originally from Lerida who had been Charles VII's personal "caretaker." Louis's son, Louis Saporta Jr., the father of Antoine Saporta, had been a student at Montpellier before becoming a fashionable physician in Toulouse. Heredity in medicine? Yes, and also heresy: Antoine Saporta, a Marrano by birth, marriage, and numerous friendships, was a Protestant sympathizer. From the time Felix arrived in Montpellier, or perhaps even earlier, he was warmly recommended to Saporta by his landlord, the apothecary Laurent Catalan, also a Marrano with Lutheran sympathies (Catalan's son would later call himself a Spaniard by birth, a Frenchman by nationality, and a German—read Lutheran—at heart).[1] In Basel as well as Montpellier, in other words, there was a connection or association between Marranos and Protestants: recall that Catalan's sons were or would become boarders of Thomas Platter's and that Dean Antoine Saporta was a friend of Laurent Catalan's and in a sense a coreligionist. Catalan, moreover, was a complex individual: he had had his sons circumcised and felt drawn to Felix's Protestant, biblical, and anticlerical cultural background. Nevertheless, he paid for masses to be said in honor of the Virgin for the sake of his son Gilbert, a failure whom his father hoped to encourage through

pious prayer to return to the path of righteousness and hard work. Catalan was thus triply ecumenical, joining Jewish roots and new Protestant thinking to Catholic tradition—a man who wanted to cover all the bases.

The next five years of Felix Platter's life stand apart. A man who liked to avoid complications, he shunned Sunday and midnight masses like the plague, in contrast to his younger brother, Thomas Jr., who, out of an interest in folklore and perhaps a desire to edify his readers about papist superstitions, would latter attend Catholic Christmas Eve celebrations in Montpellier. As suspicious as Felix was of the Church of Rome, he nevertheless refrained from making the slightest gesture that might be interpreted as Huguenot. Felix Platter had no taste for martyrdom. He was living in Montpellier and working within a meritocratic system in order to prepare himself for a career in medicine, period. In childhood his heart may have bled for the victims of Charles V's persecution in the Netherlands, but as a mature student he seems to have calmed down. His response to witnessing the torture of Protestants in Montpellier and its environs is rather cool. His greatest involvement in religious conflict came one day when he tried to stop the executioner's henchmen from entering the pharmacy of his master Laurent Catalan in order to buy turpentine for the purpose of reigniting a bonfire (in danger of extinction by rain) on which a southern French heretic was being burned to death (F 190). On that occasion the apothecary's assistants immediately reminded the Swiss lodger that if he failed to mind what he said and above all what he did, if he dared to rebuke the executioner's aides, he might well find himself tied to the stake himself. No fool, Felix saw the wisdom of this advice and did not make an issue of the matter. Furthermore, he never attended a clandestine Protestant service in Montpellier: such an exploit, while dangerous, was hardly inconceivable at the time. Had Felix been eager for the opportunity, he surely would have found it. In his defense, however, we may note that he never dissected a Protestant, whereas he had no compunction when it came to cutting up papist cadavers.

For the young man from Basel temporarily ensconced in Montpellier, the years 1552–1556 were thus a period of religious hibernation. This did not stop him from continuing to hold firm "heretical," and more precisely "Œcolampadian," convictions or from forming solid friendships with "papists" such as Professor Honoré Du Chatel, whom he even addressed by his first name. Typical in this respect was his love-hate relationship with Brother Bernard, a lay brother who kept Felix supplied with *coq au vin* and cadavers surreptitiously exhumed for use in clandestine anatomy lessons. Not until 1557, on the eve of his return to Basel and after years of honest and loyal service, did Felix quarrel with Bernard, who had for so long been his accomplice and almost his friend.

As a student in the faculty of medicine of the University of Montpellier, Felix Platter reaped the benefits of the institution's growth and prestige (F 258 ff.).[2] The university had developed considerably in the wake of Charles VIII's decision toward the end of the fourteenth century to create four magisterial chairs. In making this decision, the king took note of reforms already accomplished at the university between 1462 and 1485. These measures, aided by the municipality, affected the faculties of law, theology, and liberal arts. The academies of Languedoc had suffered during the wars with England, but Henri II was determined to improve the quality of education, and by 1552 the decadence of earlier years was already a distant memory. Yet the city's hospitals, as active as they were, still played only a minor role in the training of future physicians. Medical students were more interested in diseases than in patients. To be sure, Felix saw the bedridden in the flesh in Montpellier, but he owed this signal favor to his good friend Dr. Du Chatel (alias Castellan).

In the city, a system of colleges similar to the one that used to exist at the Sorbonne and that still exists at Oxford allowed penniless students, primarily from Lozère and Catalonia, to enjoy the intellectual benefits of the alma mater. Student power was no idle phrase, despite opposition orchestrated as early as 1550 by Professor Schyron (whom we shall meet again). Students, even students from German-speaking countries, could compel their professors to attend to their teaching duties by threatening to obtain reductions of academic salaries or to go on strike against offending teachers. Willingly or unwillingly, Felix would participate in one of these work stoppages in the autumn of 1556, even though he risked disappointing his teacher and patron, Professor Saporta (F258). (Saporta, as was mentioned earlier, was a Marrano, but this caused him few problems in a society where racial prejudice did not exist so long as one adopted the Christian faith.) The entire administration of the university consisted of a secretary, a porter, and a treasurer, who between them managed to keep the whole apparatus running fairly smoothly.

When it came to "intellectual geography," professors at Montpellier looked down on the "universities" of Valence and Orange. Moreover, they knew themselves to be superior to their colleagues in Paris by virtue of the academic freedom they enjoyed, but, not being fools, they of course respected the natural preeminence of the capital. A Parisian was always an elder brother. Finally, our Languedocians showed a certain respect for the teaching offered in Avignon, which drew many students from Germany. Many of the professors in that papal city came from Montpellier. As for baths and other therapeutic facilities (other than hospitals) within Montpellier's sphere of influence (facilities that might have supported the work of the university), it must be said that the baths of

Balaruc a few leagues outside "Clapas" (as Montpellier was popularly known) did not achieve success until later, at the very end of the sixteenth century, as Thomas Platter Jr.'s visit would confirm. Ocean baths, which were sometimes used as substitutes for mineral baths, were not recommended by Montpellier physicians except for the treatment, always problematic, of rabies, as well as for scabies and another skin malady known locally as *grattadis,* which caused itching.

In "Clapas," the local Pantheon or collective Aesculapius comprised four regents, the professors who occupied the magisterial chairs created in 1498 by Charles VIII and who were in theory remunerated from the royal treasury. The creation of these chairs had marked an important step in the emergence of the leading city of Languedoc; further progress was indicated by the establishment of a Chambre des Comptes in 1523, by the translation *intra muros* of the bishopric of Maguelonne in 1536, by the installation of two royal treasurers in 1542, and finally by the inauguration of the presidial in 1552. Knowledge attracted power. The four regents of medicine elected the regent-chancellor, who answered only to God in the management of the university's affairs (the regulations limiting the number of electors had been adopted only a short while earlier). In addition, owing to another "Malthusian" regulation of 1554, only four or five doctors served as supplementary instructors. The senior doctor served as dean of the university, responsible for setting course schedules and ensuring that all required subjects were taught. The four regents were exempt from taxes, which caused some muttering among less favored fellow citizens, but they did not number among the wealthiest people in the city. They merely belonged to the middle class, distinguished by knowledge rather than wealth. At midcentury all the regents were Huguenots, or at any rate Huguenots at heart, except for Dr. Du Chatel, a confirmed papist. In general, they co-opted one another, sometimes with, sometimes without, competition inside or outside the ranks; after 1550 the leadership thus rotated among Protestants, which tells us a great deal about religious persecution under Henri II: it was limited in the main to outsiders or public figures imprudent enough to be caught.

Of his various professors, whether regents or doctors, Felix had particularly unpleasant memories of Jean Schyron, a native of Anduze (in present-day Gard), who was regent-chancellor and a Huguenot but also quite reactionary (he had worked behind the scenes to shape the restrictive regulations of 1550 and 1554). Schyron was "quite elderly" (in fact in his sixties) and reputedly unable to control his sphincters when he lectured, a matter of some mirth in a city where Christian charity was not the foremost virtue. His public courses, once a first-class source of knowl-

edge of Greek medicine, were no longer much good, if Felix is to be believed. About Rondelet, or *Rondibilis,* as he was known, a native of
Languedoc with a receding hairline, thick beard, and prominent nose
who succeeded Schyron as regent-chancellor, I shall have little to say
here, for we saw a good deal of him earlier when Felix called on him in
Lyons. The young man from Basel had boundless admiration for Rondelet owing to the latter's prodigious knowledge of zoology and especially
anatomy. In emulation of this teacher, Felix even dissected dogs, whose
remains he stored in Laurent Catalan's closets, to Catalan's utter dismay
(F 187). After all, had not *Rondibilis* himself dissected his own sister-in-law
and benefactress, his first wife, and his stillborn son, to say nothing of his
public dissection of the placenta of his twin children? An ichthyologist as
well as the discoverer of the mite that causes scabies, and the builder, in
1554, of a new and ultramodern anatomical amphitheater in Montpellier,
Rondelet would further distinguish himself in 1564, when Charles IX visited the city, by obtaining a quadrupling of the salaries of the four regents, whose pay had been frozen since the end of the fifteenth century
despite two- or three-figure inflation in the intervening years. True, the
professors also saw many private patients and did not live solely on their
salaries; furthermore, the salary increase reflected a trend evident
throughout Languedoc, for example in the increase granted that same
year to Montpellier nurses whose fees had also been frozen for almost
seven decades.[3] Pay was going up across the board for everyone involved
in the care of the sick. Still, pay increases had a hard time keeping up with
skyrocketing prices.

Antoine Saporta, who was named dean of the medical faculty in 1556
and went from Marrano-Catholic to Protestant back to Catholic again
after the Saint Bartholomew's Day massacre (one can understand why),
became, as planned, Felix Platter's patron and surrogate father. But Felix's great friend was Dr. (and later Professor-Regent) Honoré Du
Chatel, a Parisian of talent transplanted to Montpellier, who for a time
was regularly denied promotion to a professorship because of his Catholic views—and this was well before the death of the anti-Huguenot
Henri II. Du Chatel nevertheless obtained his promotion in the end: dis-
crimination had run its course. While Felix was in Montpellier, Dr. Du
Chatel often invited him to dinner and took him to see patients; once he
even obtained tickets so that Felix could watch, along with many noblemen and damsels, from a window with a view on the scaffold, the execution of an anticlerical peasant sorcerer who was hanged near city hall—
this, too, was an anatomy lesson. Du Chatel was firmly on the side of the
priests, indeed of the heretic-burners. He was also the lover of old Dr.

Griffy's wife, and he liked to take his mistress's pulse as she languished in bed in her husband's absence.[4] Meanwhile, Felix, like old Polonius, hid behind the arras—but the young medical student was there to play the lute: this was not Shakespeare but Marivaux. The young man from Basel, after all, had come to be on a first-name basis with the very Parisian doctor who had somehow landed in deepest Occitania. In the end Du Chatel became physician to the kings of France, one of the many Montpellier graduates whose careers culminated in an appointment as chief physician to one of the crowned heads of Europe. Indeed, thirty years later, after a splendid ascent up the rungs of the social ladder, Felix would become one of them.

For the time being, however, he was simply a student. Courses in medicine were offered by the professors free of charge from Saint Luke's Day (October 18) to Easter.[5] During the summer, ordinary doctors (not regents) were authorized to teach but without compensation. Meanwhile, the regent professors could continue to give lessons if they wished and were permitted to charge students. These courses were generally mediocre, in Felix's judgment, but the same can also be said of many of the courses offered in prestigious schools today, and despite this they remain the training grounds of the young elite. Some of the teaching may have been of questionable value, but it was nonetheless fascinating and of lasting impact. Sundays, holidays, and Wednesdays (Hippocrates' day) were free; otherwise the academic schedule began at six in the morning with the courses of Professors Sabran, Saporta, and Schyron. The young Germans, who were not impressed by Schyron's senile maundering, took advantage of his hour to drink excellent muscatel (a liter and a half's worth) and eat pork with mustard (no pork was eaten where Felix was staying, because Catalan was a Marrano and kosher to the tips of his fingers [F 163]). This breakfast was consumed at the Inn of the Three Kings in the suburbs below the medical school, which was located inside the city walls on what is now the rue de l'Ecole-de-Pharmacie. At nine the students hastened back up the hill so as not to miss the lecture of Professor Rondelet, who was still quite popular. After lunch came the lectures of Professor Bocaud, a Huguenot from Montpellier, and of Drs. Guichard, Fontanon, and Griffy (Du Chatel's "rival"). Only Guichard was not a native of Montpellier. So much for medicine proper. As for "chemistry" and pharmacy, Felix learned these subjects on the job, as it were, in the shop of his landlord, the apothecary Catalan, as well as by copying manuscript recipes from various countries that circulated among the students. In anatomy, the student from Basel, an excellent judge in the matter, delighted in Rondelet's practical demonstrations, to say nothing of his own

expeditions in the company of fellow students to snatch bodies from
cemeteries around the city. Felix was a man for whom dissection was
what breathing is to ordinary mortals.

The magisterial courses consisted essentially of more or less densely
commented readings of Greek authors. By midcentury the Renaissance
spirit had effectively conquered Montpellier. More and more of the
teaching concerned the Greeks. First came Hippocrates, whose reputation was firmly established and whose teachings were already appreciated
when Rabelais attended the university under Francis I. Then came Galen
and Paul of Egina, who made dazzling posthumous appearances in the
discourse of the professors after 1531 and 1545, respectively. Felix Platter
himself would turn out to be a diligent student of Galen, whose bound
volumes, imported from Lyons or Basel on muleback, adorned his modest library in the attic and back rooms of the Catalan home (F 186, 188).
Despite the reactionary recommendations of the Grands Jours of Béziers
in 1550, the books of the Arab physicians who had been so admired in the
Middle Ages were finally abandoned in Mediterranean Languedoc in
the middle of the sixteenth century. These disciples of Muhammad, the
*toubibs* (the word has survived in contemporary French as slang for doctor), were henceforth dismissed as poor interpreters of the Greeks who
obscured the purity of the original texts. One thing is certain: the reputation of the Muslim doctor Avicenna suffered a precipitous decline at
Montpellier in the years 1550–55. The reputation of Razi also collapsed at
about the same time; it revived somewhat after 1560 but only for a brief
time, and the ensuing obscurity was all the more complete as a result.

Montpellier progressed with the Renaissance, by leaps and bounds.
The revival of Hebrew and Greek learning had begun in the second half
of the fifteenth century with the invention of printing and the fall of Con-
stantinople. As a result of the latter event, the West came into possession
of manuscripts from ancient Greece, medical texts among them. Charles
VIII, back from Naples, encouraged French bookbinders and illumina-
tors to emulate Italian Renaissance models after 1495.[6] Between 1520 and
1535 the energy of the Renaissance spread from Europe to the rest of the
world. The conquest of Mexico and Peru, which has been described as
the true discovery of the New World, or at any rate the moment when the
Old World took possession of the New, spelled the end of the Middle
Ages. At the same time the ideas of Luther and Zwingli spread with
lightning speed, one consequence of which was that in the 1520s Thomas
Platter abandoned both his Catholicism and his traditional rural heri-
tage. The decade of the 1550s marked the triumph of Greek thought, not
only in the châteaus of the Valois but also at the University of Mont-

pellier, where medical Hellenism in all its purity scored triumph after triumph among both professors and students, Felix foremost among them.[7]

Students at the university worked extremely hard, at least if they were brilliant, conscientious, and motivated, as Felix was. They also engaged regularly in public and private debates. Felix participated in a *disputatio* every two weeks in 1556, af first among Germans but later with French students as well. Indeed, Felix was the only *Teutschen* who dared to cross the linguistic boundary to debate with the *Welches,* even though arguments were generally conducted in Latin.

Students also spent a great deal of time copying pharmaceutical formulas from Italy and Germany, which passed from hand to hand. They learned formulas for enemas, some of which were still unknown in Basel. They studied "topical" remedies such as pommades and carminatives (drugs that induce the expulsion of gas from the stomach) and wrote down mixtures of spices such as cinnamon and ginger that were said to reduce gas. At the same time they glued specimens of medicinal herbs and other plants to the pages of an herbarium. Felix also arranged for a secret copy to be made of a manuscript by Falcon, the great Marrano physician of Montpellier, who had died in 1540. Besides having amassed a fortune in his own lifetime (in this respect, too, he would be a model for Felix), this Jewish-Catholic doctor was also the author of a book about medicine and surgery that remained unpublished for some time after his death.

In preparing copies and editions of medical and pharmaceutical texts, Felix and his most diligent fellow students used a hyperanalytic method known as "isagogics," which involved compiling tables or outlines of major themes broken down into subthemes, sub-subthemes, and so on. This taxonomical method had been invented by Porphyry in Antiquity and had later been perfected and used by Raymond Lull in Catalonia, Ramus and Figon in France, and Fallope in Padua, as well as Zwinger and Platter in the German Swiss diaspora. When necessary, Felix pored over these texts by candlelight in his attic room in the Catalan house, beneath a starry sky that could be seen with great clarity through the unpolluted atmosphere of Renaissance Montpellier.

Finally, the students also engaged in practical work with patients. But one had to be careful. If caught, there was danger of being accused of treating patients by "cut and try" empirical methods and, until one had one's doctorate, of practicing medicine illegally. The punishment for breaking the law in this way was to be paraded through the city while mounted backward on an ass and to be subjected to the insults and brickbats of local ruffians. This tragi-burlesque ritual had a long history: it had been used in Rome in the year 1000 against antipopes accused of usurping papal sovereignty.[8] Felix was therefore extremely cautious about treating the sick. He chose the reasonable course of offering medical or paramedical advice only to his German friends, who he could be sure would not denounce him to the Montpellier authorities because of the language barrier if for no other reason.

All in all, the University of Montpellier resembled what would be called in France today a *grande école,* that is, an elite institution like the Ecole Normale Supérieure of Paris. In the sixteenth century the medical school served no more than 150 to 200 students at any given time, with 30 to 50 new students admitted each year. Students who had personally exercised a mechanical or artisanal trade were not accepted, moreover, although little attention was paid to the status of an applicant's father, mother, or other forebears. The bias against artisans and others of inferior social status concerned only the student's own generation.

For the purpose of comparison, it may be worth noting that the faculty of medicine of the University of Montpellier in 1950 still had only 700 students, and the course work was still as time-consuming and laborious as it had been four centuries earlier. The main difference was that instead of spending all day in lecture courses, medical students in the 1950s divided their time between the hospital in the morning and lectures in the afternoon.

Felix Platter arrived in Montpellier when the student population was at its height: in the 1550s fifty-two new students were admitted annually, compared with thirty or forty in each year of the five previous decades. After 1560, admissions again dropped to thirty or so because of the Wars of Religion and eventually to fifteen as the turmoil continued. Admissions did not return to the previous level of thirty until the end of the century when Thomas Platter Jr. came to Montpellier (1594–1600). This return to normality would not have been possible without the restoration of peace under Henri IV.

Students at the university were a cosmopolitan lot. Of 3,366 students enrolled in the sixteenth century, 692 were foreigners. Of these, 270 were Iberian, mainly Spaniards, and for a long time they lived apart from their classmates from north of the Pyrenees because the wars between France and Spain poisoned relations between the two groups. What is more, the "extreme southern" Catholicism of the countries subject to the Inquisition was different from French Catholicism. Further evidence of this split would emerge during the Wars of Religion, with the development, typically French, of the Catholic party known as *les politiques,* who were in fact moderates, unlike their Spanish coreligionists or for that matter their adversaries in the French Ligues. From Germanic regions and Central Europe came another 315 students, counting natives of the Netherlands, Scandinavia, and Poland, who can hardly be considered "Teutons." There were also 75 Italians.

One of these "East Peninsulars" was a certain "Flaminius," or Flamini, about whom we have no further information (F 191). Flamini achieved posthumous celebrity in 1554 owing to an event that caused something of a stir in Languedoc. After a wedding ball marking the marriage of the son of Professor Fontanon, whose forty-year-old mule had made him famous throughout the province, the Italian, quick with a dagger, became involved in a brawl in the course of which he rather foolishly impaled himself on the sword of one Le Beau, a (noble) medical student from Tours. Le Beau was arrested for murder after a chase across the rooftops of the city. After languishing in prison for a time, the young murderer (whose crime was almost inadvertent) was finally liberated. He went on to a medical career in Tours, where he was still doctoring in the early seventeenth century. In addition to the 75 Italians (for the whole of the sixteenth century), there were also 27 students from the British Isles (including Ireland as well as England). In general, the foreign localities most amply represented in Montpellier were Basel, Constance, Geneva, Utrecht, Liège, Tournai, and five Spanish dioceses. Clearly, Felix was a typical foreign student in two senses: he came to Montpellier in the 1550s, when the student body there was largest and the university was in fashion throughout Europe; and he came from Basel, a Swiss city with strong connections to the academic and medical institutions of urban Languedoc.

\*   \*   \*

But it was not only the academic and medical institutions that interested Felix. The young man from the north was also fascinated by southern life and Mediterranean customs in general, which stood in sharp contrast to the customs of the Upper Rhine that had shaped the first fifteen years of his existence. The whole atmosphere of Montpellier and its environs was new to him, as he became acutely aware in the spring of 1553, in late March and early April, when the broom and narcissus and almond blossomed and the alder sprouted catkins and the willows grew leaves and the box trees bloomed on the limestone plateaus known as *causses;* when the big flies became annoying, and snakes and lizards emerged from the earth; and when bats filled the evening sky. Already the young thrushes were plump; the sap was up in the chestnut trees, from whose bark barefoot children made trumpets, while men in shirtsleeves hoed the vineyards. In March seeds were laid in for peas and wheat, lambs were shorn for slaughter, and one ate salads of fresh greens.

As the good weather returned, the young man from Basel longed to see the Mediterranean, which he had already glimpsed once from afar from a hilltop between Sambres and Castelnau on his way to Montpellier. The sea had been flat, stretched out like a vast bolt of fabric all aglitter with flecks of gold. His temptation was compounded by the fact that from his half-timbered room atop the Catalan house (not far from the present-day prefecture), Felix caught almost daily glimpses of the sea that filled his dreams. He claimed that on certain days he could even hear the sound of the waves in the middle of town (F 173). Unable to keep his impatience in check, he and several friends visited the shore south of Pérols (not far from present-day Palavas) on February 22. It was a beautiful, hot day. In Pérols, Felix and his friends, all German-speaking students, observed a mineral spring whose "poisoned" water had killed one of the king's lackeys as His Majesty (we do not know which one) looked on impassively (F160). Using a small boat without oars, the group of students had crossed a salt pond to reach the beach: a few pulled the boat along with ropes, while the others kept dry inside. The beach, between the salt pond and the sea, was covered with seaweed, shells, cuttlefish, and fish bones—enough to make a wagonload (F 161). The waves filled the visitors' shoes and socks with water. Without hesitation they stripped down and went swimming. To these young men from the north the water seemed fine. The tourists then covered themselves with hot sand. This was a sort of medical treatment: it made the skin dry, hard, and firm, and was indicated in cases of scabies, ringworm, and various allergies at a time when people rarely washed. The young Germans collected shells of various colors and round crabs before returning to Pérols for lunch and on to Montpellier by nightfall.

During Lent, the sea was present on every table in Montpellier, and particularly on the table of Laurent Catalan: the apothecary's windows looked out on the cramped, foul-smelling fish market in the center of town. The market lined the narrow streets in the neighborhood of the butcher shop and the flour and herb markets. Catalan, a Marrano, had no reason to offend devout Catholics, some of whom were customers, by eating meat during Lent. Hence in February and March there was dried cod at every meal, or sole or tuna (the tuna transported to the fish market for cutting measured up to fifteen feet in length). The family also ate fried mackerel and sardines; quantities of eel; lobsters up to two feet long; and occasionally shrimp by the basketful. Everything was cooked in oil (butter was never used in Montpellier). In the evening during Lent, one also ate lettuce, endives, onions, and chestnuts, but not cheese or fruit.

On April 7 Felix made another trip to the sea. In the company of other German students he traveled to Villeneuve-lès-Maguelonne, where a fortified, Roman-style church had been erected on the coast to deter corsairs from the Maghreb. This time, however, no boat was available for crossing the salt pond to Maguelonne, and the students returned to Montpellier empty-handed. The coast offered little in the way of services to would-be tourists and swimmers. Those who lived inland feared the malaria that lurked in the coastal swamps. They rarely swam more than a few times a year, if that. In Montpellier the brackish marshes were thought to be filthy and disease-ridden. Felix and his friend Melchior Rotmundt, who had studied in Tübingen and Paris and who later practiced medicine in Saint-Gall, learned this the hard way when, while wearing white trousers, they tried to cross a muddy stretch of coast on the way to the city of Aigues-Mortes, already celebrated for its walls and its lighthouse. The excellent partridges that the two friends consumed at a local inn were scant compensation for the damage done to their wardrobes.

After Lent, on May 22, Felix again returned to the sea (F 197). After emerging from the water, he decided once more to bury himself in the sand. Three days later, he came down with bronchitis and a head cold and a terribly runny nose and felt as if he might die. A purge put him back on his feet. Eventually his father became alarmed by Felix's repeated trips to the insalubrious coastal marshes. By letter from Basel he offered his son this unforgettable advice: "Felix, be careful about swimming in the sea. Remember that you almost drowned in the Rhine a few years back. And beware of any French girls who might try to lead you on" (F 185). On August 30, 1553, Felix made another excursion to the beaches, as usual in the company of other *Teutschen,* in this case students who had not yet seen the sea because they had just arrived in Montpellier (F 222). They collected herbs, shells, and seaweed and went swimming. Among the newcomers was Johann Wachtel, the son of a Strasbourg apothecary who had come to Montpellier to apprentice in pharmacy and who would soon have his own shop in the Alsatian capital at the sign of Chapelle Saint-Jacques on the rue des Piques. Felix played a rather rough game with Johann, who did not know how to swim: the two tried to dunk each other's heads in the water to the point where they were blowing sea water out of their nostrils.

Young Platter's last "beach party" was also the best. In late September 1553, two noted German writers asked him to take them to the beach at Maguelonne so that they could round out a collection they were making of zoological specimens. The principal collector was Heinrich Pantaleon, a small man with a flowing beard, a round head, and intelligent eyes set in a wrinkled face. A theologian, he had been disappointed in his hopes of becoming pastor of Saint Peter's in Basel as a result of political maneuvering. A brilliant, highly cultivated man and a Latinist in the style of Montaigne, Pantaleon had thrown himself into the study of medicine at the age of thirty. He had hastily completed his coursework in a few semesters at the mediocre University of Valence, which was a kind of diploma mill, and graduated toward the end of 1552 or the beginning of 1553. The news caused something of a stir in Basel, where it was feared that physicians already in practice would suffer from the competition (F 286). Of course Pantaleon was no newcomer to the field, for in the 1540s he had attended the lectures of his friend Alan zum Thor, the disciple and friend of the two greatest Basel physicians, Paracelsus and Vesalius.

With his new doctorate in hand, Pantaleon had gone to Languedoc in the fall of 1553 to make the acquaintance of medical authorities there, both French and German, as well as to recover an old debt owed him by a recalcitrant debtor living on the banks of the Hérault. Heinrich appreciated pretty women and bacchic songs. Though a connoisseur of partridges, he could not tell a fig from a pomegranate. Until the collectors and their guide reached Maguelonne, Pantaleon had no complaints about Felix's services as a guide. A distinguished writer of prose, he was accompanied on this journey by the German-Latin poet Peter Lotich, a talented improviser of verse. The son of a peasant, Lotich had been around any number of universities. A former soldier, he was also reputed to be a secret agent. In any case, he had earned his living for a number of years as tutor to a family of German nobles, the Stibars. He traveled with the Stibar children and accompanied them to the leading French schools, including Montpellier. Perpetually in love, Lotich sang of his doomed passions. En route to the coast he celebrated the alluring qualities of one Claudia von Wittenberg, who had been unfaithful to him, as well as Tunicata of Montpellier, alias Kallirhoe, the wife of an Auvergnat jurist, who had fallen ill and died despite the ministrations of Dr. Rondelet—she could not have expired in better hands (F 214). Nor was Lotich any more successful with the women of Italy, where he had pined after a shepherdess who had unfortunately been determined to enter a nunnery and die a virgin. On the way to Maguelonne the two writers exchanged pedantries in Latin: *Germani socii tendunt ad litora maris* (the German friends are headed for the seacoast [F 184]). Felix did not hesitate to join in. Periodically the three travelers sang the "Song of the Knight von Steurmarck," a tune that became popular in Germany in the sixteenth century. On the beach they filled huge crates with shells. Looking out at the Mediterranean from atop the church of Maguelonne, Felix thought of Africa (*Aphrika*), which he knew lay off to the south even though he could not see it (F 256). Later, Pantaleon, having had his fill of maritime scenery, continued on toward Pézenas in the hope (ultimately disappointed) of recovering the money owed to him.

After 1553, Felix's enthusiasm for the beach and swimming seems to have cooled, although he did like to watch fishermen working with the *bouliech,* a long net that required twenty people to drop into the water and then drag it back, full of fish, including the *pastinaca marina,* or *boug-nette,* which Rondelet loved, onto the beach. The bougnette is a Mediterranean fish with poisonous stingers that are dangerous to touch (F 179). Was he now tired of the sea, whose charms he had appreciated numerous times? Was he afraid of contracting malaria, a disease that modern medicine had yet to banish to the tropics? Or was it simply, now that his return to Basel loomed nearer, that he was now devoting himself primarily to his studies in order to avoid the unemployment that awaited many graduates after they received their diplomas? In any case, drownings were frequent, as he was well aware, and perhaps in the end he took all the warnings to heart. In August of 1555, moreover, the medical student in "exile" from his native Basel received a salvo of letters from Switzerland, concerning his fiancée, various musical instruments, and that mischievous scamp and indefatigable womanizer Gilbert Catalan, the son of Laurent the apothecary. And then there was also the Flemish humanist Utenhove, who had recently become a boarder in Thomas's house. One of these missives came from Albrecht Gebwiller, the bürgermeister who had given Felix a place to stay during the plague of 1551 that had killed his sister Ursula. The municipal official told his correspondent in Montpellier about the most recent drownings in the Rhine on April 5, 1555: young boys from Basel had been competing with one another by diving from the main bridge, and spectators had gathered on the bridge to watch. A railing had given way, and several dozen people had fallen into the water. The locksmith Heinrich Sprenger had "broken his back" when he landed on a raft of logs caught between bridge pilings. A little girl, sent by her parents to buy mustard, had miraculously survived. When rescuers fished her out, unconscious but still alive, she was clutching the mustard pot and the four sous she had been given for her purchases at the grocery store— obviously a well-trained child.

Despite these dissuasive object lessons, Felix risked one more swimming expedition the following year, this time in fresh water. The summer of 1556 was one of the hottest and driest that Western Europe has ever known, comparable to the summers of 1718, 1794, and 1976. Forest fires damaged woods as far north as Cotentin, usually exempt from such disasters.9 Even pastures went up like straw mattresses. In Montpellier, which had suffered from oppressive heat (*grosse hitz*) since the end of April, a merchant's house burned down on Place Notre-Dame, not far from the cathedral of the same name (near the present-day Place Jean-Jaurès) (F 246). It was a stone house, not all that common in a city built mainly of wood and cob with many structures dating from the fifteenth century. The walls remained standing, but the whole interior of the building was destroyed. While it burned, the real show was in the street. Onlookers were enchanted; they came close to applauding as they enthusiastically watched the progress of the disaster. In Basel, where corporate solidarities were more robust than in France, citizens would have formed a bucket brigade. The authorities would have seen to it that water was hauled to the scene. During the heat wave, Felix sensibly set off for a dip in the Lez, despite his recent decision to give up swimming altogether. The poor boy just couldn't stand the heat any longer. Indeed, the ground was so hot that dogs could barely stand to run along the ridges between furrows in the freshly-plowed fields. Felix hurried across the same fields and felt the burning through the ultrathin soles of his shoes.

This torrid swim came in the midst of a desiccated harvest. The heat wave, which had begun in April, ended in a series of substantial storms, which refreshed the entire countryside (F 244). Feet no longer burned but sank into the mud. On June 15, lightning destroyed the steeple, altar, interior decoration, and door of the Saint-Hilaire church near the Dominican chapel, not far from the present-day Jardin du Peyrou. Reconstructed at the behest of the city council, Saint-Hilaire would be destroyed again by Huguenots in 1561. Another storm on June 25 unleashed hailstones the size of chickens' eggs. This was followed by an especially violent storm on July 11, 1556, which produced still further damage. Streets were turned into dangerous rapids by the runoff, and a person could easily have been swept away by the current. Felix was now afraid of drowning if he tried to swim.

Credulous citizens seized on an apocalyptic prophecy that had been making the rounds in Montpellier and elsewhere for some time.10 The end of the world was supposed to arrive on Magdalene's Day, July 22, 1556. Feverish interpreters had a field day with a host of supposedly premonitory signs. Fortunately, however, the appointed day came and went without any notable disaster, although the heat wave did continue for a time in Switzerland, where Thomas Platter complained of losing a number of recently planted young trees (*junge beum*) (F 254).

*   *   *

End of the world or not, Felix, as a medical man, associated summer with death from heat stroke, fever, and even plague, which struck Toulouse, "not far from us" (F 221), in the heat of early August 1555. City-dwellers did not remain passive in the face of the annual summer ordeal: apartments in Montpellier were sprinkled with water, and leafy branches and strips of canvas were hung to shade narrow streets (F 175). The custom of shading streets and squares with fabric awnings has all but vanished from southern France today, but one still finds shaded patios in Italy and Spain. The grain harvest in the south, which began earlier than the August wheat harvest in the north, was a period of intense activity on the land. In addition to getting in the wheat, laborers also picked hemp and cut the fresh growth of alfalfa (*auzerda*); they planted turnips and dressed vines. Peasants were so busy they didn't know which way to turn. Highlanders came down from the Cévennes into the plains of lower Languedoc in search of employment. Meanwhile, sheep from the plains moved in the opposite direction, up into the Aigoual to summer in the highlands. The herds of humans and the herds of sheep crossed paths, as it were. Meanwhile, wasps grew particularly aggressive in the summer heat, as did fleas and bugs. Stalks of wheat stood out among thick weeds, while thistles blossomed and poppies faded. Raspberries and *bon-chrétien* pears ripened. With an eye to the future, vine growers gauged the size of maturing grapes: did they resemble chickpeas, peppercorns, or lead shot? Quail and locusts raised a ruckus. Young blackbirds already as big as the parent birds attracted the attention of the local nimrods.

Although Felix was aware of the rural world through his parents, his view of the harvest was rather remote: he was no Brueghel. His chief interest, whether looking down on the countryside from the ramparts or observing the scene in the suburbs of Montpellier near the church of Saint-Denis, was in the threshing of the wheat in one of the large threshing areas reserved for local grain growers (F 209). There, teams of half a dozen mules trotted around circular tracks like circus animals to crush the sheaves of grain and separate the wheat from the chaff. Thomas Jr., although less intelligent than his older brother, was also more of a geographer and quicker to generalize: he noted threshing areas next to nearly every large barn in the southern countryside. Both Platters remarked on the striking differences between French and Swiss threshing techniques: in Switzerland, threshing was done in the winter, inside the barn, with a flail, whereas along the Mediterranean the "treading out" (*dépiquage*) was done in the summer, outside on the threshing ground. An Italian-

French artist of talent, influenced by the School of Fontainebleau, later had the idea of depicting both the northern and the southern techniques on a single canvas, a masterpiece of ethnographic insight even though the painter lacked the realistic touch.[11]

*   *   *

Weeks passed. Everyone in Montpellier, residents and students alike, closely followed the progress of the grapes. Everyone kept one foot figuratively in the vineyards, which grew close to the ramparts and in some cases even within the city walls. Several years in a row, on or about August 10 (August 20 according to our modern Gregorian calendar), Felix went to help his master Laurent Catalan harvest grapes for the table (what is properly called the *vendange*, or harvest of wine grapes, took place somewhat later). The apothecary's vineyard was located in a rural suburb of Montpellier. At this time of year the nearby pastures were full of crocuses and fat white caterpillars with mottled yellow markings and no hair. Small gray grasshoppers jumped about everywhere. Peasants harvested black figs and mowed the second growth in irrigated meadows.

Besides his landlord, Felix's usual companions on these grape-picking expeditions were Balthasar Hummel and Jacob Myconius (F 175, 202). Hummel came from a Basel family of nine children, including two pastors and a supervisory teacher in the school run by Thomas Platter Sr. The father of this large brood, Peter Hans Hummel, was a native of Little Basel who had been a mercenary (F 87). A childhood friend of Felix's and longtime apprentice in various pharmacies, Balthasar Hummel went on to become an apothecary in Basel in the latter part of the century. As for Jacob Myconius, he was the adopted[12] son of Oswald Geisshüssler, also known as "Bald Head" (Myconius), a self-taught Basel pastor and the successor of Œcolampadius as the city's spiritual leader, as well as Thomas Platter Sr.'s teacher and close friend (F 51, 166). Jacob went from being a student in Montpellier to being a doctor at the mediocre University of Avignon (the papal city had nothing against young Lutherans) and later became the municipal physician (*stadtarzt*) of Mulhouse. Jacob was by nature less "puritanical" than his father. He often joined Felix and others in nocturnal drinking bouts; the young men drained kegs of wine stored in the cellars of Laurent Catalan, who did not make a fuss since his wine never lasted more than a year anyway.

During the August grape-picking, Catalan liked to pick on young Hummel, for the boy had yet to master the languages of the Welches, the *langue d'oïl* and the *langue d'oc*. The apothecary therefore addressed the Swiss student in bad Latin: "Use your sword [*gladium*] to cut the grapes." Hummel took out his dagger. "You want to fight [*vis pugnare*]?" the apothecary then asked. And then he would explain that of course he meant not a dagger but a vine knife for sawing stems and separating them from their stalks. The vines in question were not espaliered, as in Lausanne or Geneva, but allowed to run along the ground, as was customary in Languedoc. When the harvest was done, Madame Catalan hung bunches of grapes from the ceiling of Felix's room to keep the rats from eating them. Felix claimed that these grapes were so fat and juicy that one a day was enough to assuage his passion for the fruit of the vine.

The *vendange* came in September, often in the second half of the month (by the Gregorian calendar). There was much to do besides cutting and pressing grapes. Acorns had to be gathered for the hogs. The bushes were thick with blackberries. Walnuts were shaken from their trees and chestnuts knocked loose with long poles (*gaules*). The pears were excellent, so long as they were not worm-eaten. Radishes were juicy and good to eat, but aphids went after the leaves of turnips left in the ground. Pigeons and slugs battened on the freshly planted seeds of wheat. Moles left trails in fields and meadows. Spiders worked day and night. Wasps and thrushes descended upon the vines. Wolves came down from the mountains. Snakes did not yet carpet the earth. And the children, still barefoot despite the first autumn rains, continued to swim in the river.

Felix, absorbed by his schoolwork now that the new term had begun, did not participate physically in the *vendange;* the work he had done earlier, during the academic vacation in August, to gather grapes for the table was enough. He did, however, note that his landlord Laurent Catalan was very busy: "On September 13, 1552 [September 23, new style], my master harvested his grapes. The fall weather is generally quite humid. It rains a lot, considerably more than during the winter" (F 181). He also described, as his younger brother would do toward the end of the century, the process of harvesting grapes and making wine in Montpellier. Donkeys (1553) or mules (1555) were used to carry *comportes,* or tubs of grapes, two per animal, into the city. Their braying warned people to get out of the way, and since the streets were narrow and there were no sidewalks, anyone who failed to heed the warnings risked losing an eye. A naked man hanging by his arms from a beam in the wine cellar trampled the grapes in their tubs; care had to be taken lest the trampler succumb to the fumes of carbon dioxide given off by the first fermentation of the grapes. Special porters hauled wine barrels from place to place. The first wine to be drawn was the light-red *clairet,* then the dark red, and finally the poor-quality *aiguade* or *piquette,* which was served to the servants of the vintner's family.[13] The wine of Languedoc, an urban product par excellence, or, rather, a symbol of a certain urban-rural synergy, points to a characteristic type of environment. Vine-growing areas, even those like the region around Montpellier that produced a diversity of crops, relied primarily on donkeys and mules for transportation and traction, whereas the Massif Central depended on oxen for plowing and the Swiss plateau and northern France used horses.

The earth beneath medieval as well as modern Montpellier was as full of holes as a Swiss cheese owing to the many vaulted wine-cellars. In 1553, the city was one huge wine-making factory comprising many individual operations that functioned in part independently, in part collectively. A fifth of the city's population lived off of agriculture, primarily the fruit of the vine. Streets and squares were riddled with holes for manure, as Felix discovered in January 1553, when people of high society began to enjoy themselves at carnival dances. The Swiss student went to one such dance with the daughter of Professor Griffy, a Protestant, of course, and an important figure in the faculty of medicine. The girl was also the granddaughter of a former chancellor of the university. While attempting to guide his companion around a pool of manure, Felix slipped in himself, splattering the young lady with filth from head to toe. His friends joked that he had been trying to anoint the girl with holy water.

Two drinking cultures coexisted in Montpellier. The majority of the natives drank regularly but not to excess. The minority of German students drank irregularly but immoderately, without limit. In the home of Laurent Catalan, a true man of the Mediterranean, people drank substantial amounts without ever getting drunk. Red wine was always available but generally mixed with water. It did not go to one's head. The pharmacist's boarders drank to console themselves for the modest fare. They ate stew at midday, and salad and roast meat for dinner (except during Lent, when only fish was consumed). Wine was also commonly drunk at student breakfasts. Sometimes there were also midnight suppers: on one extramural grave-robbing expedition by medical students eager to perform dissections, the students' accomplice, a monk, prepared a meal of *coq au vin.*

The drinking bouts that remained most vivid in Felix's memory were strictly German affairs. In Marseilles in September 1555, Felix was introduced to two German nobles, landsknechts in Captain Reckenroth's company, which had fought alongside Henri II's troops around Siena in association with Blaise de Monluc (F 226).[14] Felix and the two men together quaffed a substantial number of flagons of wine, so much, in fact, that someone had to undress the young student from Basel and put him to bed. His head was spinning. That night, the two gentlemen pissed in their violet breeches, leaving large stains on the fabric.

The rest of the trip was filled with similar adventures, and the students (commoners) behaved themselves no better than the professional soldiers (aristocrats). On the way back to Montpellier, Felix and his friends, all medical students at the university, stopped to admire the Pont du Gard (F 230). At an inn in the village of Sernhac where they spent the night, the band of students drank each other under the table while shooting dice and playing cards. Stephan Kunz, alias Contzenus, the nephew of a Protestant reformer in Bern, who was studying medicine in Montpellier while awaiting a doctorate from Avignon that would allow him to become the municipal physician of his native city, became increasingly aggressive. He threatened to go on a rampage and shoot the place up. Tension grew between Kunz and Benedikt Burgauer (F 203). Burgauer, the son of a pastor from Schaffhouse, was also studying in Montpellier while awaiting a doctorate from Avignon and a post as municipal physician in Schaffhouse, where eventually he became justice of the peace. The two came to blows, and it proved difficult to separate them. The next morning, Kunz woke up early; in the meantime he had sobered up. Disconsolate because everyone blamed him for the fight, he left Sernhac and returned alone to Montpellier (this took place on September 25–26, 1555).

There were other monumental "drunks" as well. After a night of drinking, Johannes-Ludwig Höchstetter and Melchior Rotmundt were completely "sloshed" and decided to pull a practical joke. Melchior, a "milk face" (that is, a beardless novice), cut off Johannes-Ludwig's thick beard and stuck it inside his jacket. Without his beard Johannes-Ludwig was unrecognizable and passed himself off as a Teutonic knight who had just arrived in town. He was received with all the honors due his rank. When he revealed his true identity, everyone burst out laughing, including Felix, who laughed himself silly. It is worth noting that Höchstetter, who came from an important but bankrupt family of patrician merchants in Augsburg, had studied or would go on to study in Tübingen, Montpellier, and Heidelberg. He became the municipal physician of Esslingen but ultimately drowned in the Neckar in 1566. Rotmundt, the son of a bailiff, had studied in Basel, Tübignen, Paris, and Montpellier. He became a justice of the peace, city councillor, and municipal physician in Saint-Gall. His brother Kaspar, for the time being in Lyons, later founded an important commercial house and dynasty (F 55, 239). These young men of "good family" were sowing their wild oats.

In that vein the ultimate was no doubt Hans Brombach, who came from a family of gunsmiths and was a student or at any rate former student, landsknecht, and indefatigable drinker. In 1553 or 1554 he was expelled from the University of Basel for drunkenness. He then became a bodyuguard of Antoine de Bourbon, king of Navarre (and the father of Henri IV), a position that allowed him to rub elbows with many Huguenot coreligionists in the king's entourage. On a visit to Montpellier on April 18, 1554, Brombach, elegantly attired in slashed breeches and armed with halberd and sword, was welcomed by Felix and his compatriots and treated to a feast. Moved by all this hospitality, he swore to champion the cause of the Swiss students, in exchange for which his new friends poured a glass of wine over his head as he rode out of town (F 196).

The drinking customs of those who came from German-speaking countries (as well as from Brittany, Normandy, England, and Poland) contrasted sharply with native customs in the grape-growing south: the natives were generally moderate drinkers, although excesses were by no means unheard of. The north of Europe discovered wine much later, centuries or perhaps even millennia after the Mediterranean. Hence northerners had not learned to master it, assimilate it, or civilize it to the same degree as southerners had done through Dionysiac or Christian cults with their rationalizing, moderating influence. Recent studies of the geographic distribution of alcoholism in France and Europe tend to bear this out, and so do the memoirs of the Platters. In Barcelona, according to Thomas Platter Jr., one found hundreds of prostitutes in the dives along the waterfront but not a single drunk. And consider what Felix has to say about the countryside around Montpellier in 1552: "My master Laurent Catalan owned a house and some land in the village of Vendargues [a few miles from Montpellier]. His steward [*meier*] there was a man named Guillem, who secretly subscribed to our religion [Protestantism]. He often spoke out against the papists as well as the Marranos, especially when he'd had a snootful (F 166). This was behavior that Guillem had learned in Germany [that is, in German Switzerland], for Laurent Catalan had sent him to Basel to deliver his two sons, Gilbert and Jacques, in baskets on a donkey's back [so that the two boys, thus conveniently transported, could pursue their studies and complete their apprenticeship]. In fact, I have seen very few people in Montpellier drunk on wine except for our Germans."

This passage is worth pausing over. It is unlikely that Guillem picked up his anti-Semitic or at any rate anti-Marrano attitudes exclusively from his travels along the Rhine. This was simply his way (shared with other members of the lower strata of Languedoc society) of pursuing the "class struggle," admittedly at a rather low level, against his employer Catalan, a Marrano. Guillem's contact with German culture did, however, turn him from Protestant sympathizer into active Protestant. And his alcoholism, while not necessarily of German origin, followed a pattern that in Felix's opinion was much more prevalent in German-speaking areas than in the south of France.

Taking things a step further, let us ask whether, in the eyes of a young man from Basel studying in Montpellier, it was possible to be a good, decent, middle-class German without also being an honest-to-God drinker, an unabashed consumer of fine red wine? Felix raised the question in May 1554 in connection with the case of Hans Beat Häl, or Hel, a contemporary of his in Basel, about which he learned by letter. Hans Beat was the son of a shopkeeper and the pretty daughter of a surgeon (F 198). He had been a classmate of Felix's and had gone on to the University of Basel in 1547–48, but his behavior there soon caused problems. He was a good-looking boy with a fine voice who was an only child; for a long time people made excuses for him precisely because he was an only child. While a student, he endlessly wandered the streets of Basel playing the lute, an instrument whose intricacies he had mastered. He chased girls and got involved in all sorts of masquerades. On occasion he fought with his fellow students. Eventually, however, he beame engaged to a seamstress, the daughter of a fisherman, whose first name was Barbara and who came from a respectable family in Little Basel. The two married in January 1551, the very year in which Hans was to become a member of the Saffron Guild. Marriage did not put an end to his disorderly ways, however (F 199). In August 1553, "he was even thrown in jail for six days and six nights" for instigating a rather scandalous "mummery" (masquerade). What is more, he did not obey his parents, with whom he continued to live after his marriage. He was ordered to swear that he would avoid suspect places and boardinghouses in the future. Henceforth he was supposed to eat only at his wife's home or his parents' home. The young couple apparently got on well enough, for they produced two sons, Hans Beat Jr. and Jacob, who went on to fairly good careers: the former became a secondary school teacher and the latter a pastor. They were raised, however, by their grandfather rather than by their father, who abandoned them when they were still quite young. The erratic youth had fallen in love with Anna Bottschuh (who was seventeen at the time). Anna, or Annette (Annline to her friends), was the daughter of a deceased keg measurer and the stepdaughter of Gregor Wentz, who kept an inn at the sign of the Salmon off the grain market. Hans Beat had deceived young Anna in the time-honored if indelicate manner of promising to marry her as his first wife lay dying. He had gotten Anneline pregnant on a pile of Catalan rugs in the course of a long evening of music and dancing. The rugs were there to muffle the noise so as to spare the neighbors downstairs.

Word of the girl's pregnancy got out, however, and Hans Beat landed in prison, where he attempted suicide. In July 1554 a court banished him from Basel. Anneline also tried to do away with herself, but in vain. She (along with her mother and accomplice) were let off with a fine of fifty gulden; then she gave birth. She went on to marry two or three husbands. The first, whom she wed in 1557, was an innkeeper at the sign of the Star, in the same line of work as Gregor Wentz. In the course of her various marriages, Anneline was convicted of adultery several times. Meanwhile, Hans Beat, having left Basel, went to Lorraine. Being an incorrigible sinner but of ecumenical disposition, he there seduced a well-born nun from the convent of Remiremont, whose inmates were reputedly of noble descent but loose morals. The girl was caught first, then her lover. He was tied up and placed in a wagon. While crossing a river, he fell in and was drowned, headed feet first for a better world. His death may have been an accident, or he may have been pushed: no one ever found out for sure. There were good reasons, Felix gravely noted, to have been suspicious of this fellow for a long time, for "he did not drink wine, except for sugared wine on rare occasions." The very idea of behaving in such a way!

*　　٨　　٨

In Languedoc, all roads lead to wine, or start from it. Not much was exported northward, however, because wine in those days was hard to preserve. Felix, who bankrupted himself sending packages of all kinds to his parents, never included fine wine in his expensive shipments. But he did send fruits that tasted exotic to their Swiss recipients, along with his collections of plants and of animal skeletons, as well as raisins, which he had often admired as they lay drying on beds of chalk when he passed by on trips like the one to Villeneuve-lès-Maguelonne in the company of the two German nobles. His mother was particularly appreciative of these packages, especially those containing fruits. Thomas, if we are to believe his son, retained the tastes of a peasant and often left oranges and other mouthwatering deserts to his wife. But both Thomas and his wife greatly appreciated the raisins their son sent from the land of Oc.

*　　*　　*

After the grape came the olive: the olive harvest in late fall or early winter was also a sight to see, though less fraught with social symbolism than the grape harvest. In "oil season," Felix, though still a fledgling student, found himself drawn into the German community the moment the olive picking began in early November 1552. He joined a band of students that included Jacob Baldenberger, or Baldenbergius, from Saint-Gall, who had studied in Basel before coming to Montpellier and who later practiced medicine in Switzerland (F 147). There was also the Saxon Gregor Schett, who, upon completing his studies in Montpellier, easily landed a job as professor of anatomy and surgery at the University of Leipzig. Johann Vogelgang of Flanders, an old hand at medical studies in Languedoc, was also part of the group, as was Hans Odratzheim, the son of a Strasbourg city councillor and an apprentice apothecary in the shop of Laurent Catalan, as well as Felix's roommate in the Catalan house. In the wee hours of the morning of November 2, Hans jumped out of the bed he shared with Felix and told him not to worry about the Don Quixote-esque presence of warriors armed with lances in the street below the pharmacy window: these were olive pickers equipped with the long poles that were the tools of their trade. Now that the olives had changed color, these harvesters had come down from the mountains in search of work. The oil content of the olives was already 19 percent and would increase to 25 percent at maturity over the next few weeks. Following the harvest, the olives were subjected to a first pressing or grinding by means of granite millstones turned by donkeys. Then, after the pure initial juice was drained off, the pulp was scalded, and a second pressing was obtained. The oil was then stored in large terra-cotta pots for household use or poured, as in Roman times, into goatskin bottles for export on the backs of donkeys or mules.

In Montpellier, the production of olive oil in the period between Toussaint (November 1) and Easter was largely an urban affair, conducted by hurried entrepreneurs and workers who did not complain about their heavy workload. They slept little (to the astonishment of the doctors), ate constantly, and worked hard for their wages. In the off-season, olive trees served another purpose: they played an essential role in a macabre display whose objective was to deter criminals. On July 22, 1553, a handsome young man, the son of a bread baker, having been convicted of a crime, was sent for execution on the Place Notre-Dame in front of Montpellier's city hall. A wooden scaffold supported a long chopping block covered by a wooden roof. The executioner blindfolded the condemned man, had him lie down with his neck on the block, and then took from beneath his robes a large hunting knife normally used for butchering deer. With two blows to the back of the neck, he deftly removed the man's head, then cut off his arms and legs and arranged all the pieces on the floor of the scaffold, with the head set among the severed limbs. There the dismembered body was allowed to remain all night. In the morning the pieces were hung from an olive tree outside the city and allowed to rot. The whole punishment was pure Machiavelli, except for the "oil tree," a local addition.[15]

*   *   *

Olives, grain, vines: all of these could be drawn together, as they were, for instance, on the Catalan farm, which was not very different in principle from the *meierhof,* or suburban farm, that Thomas Platter kept in Gundeldingen. In this respect Felix was in familiar territory. In Vendargues, a village about six miles from Montpellier, Laurent Catalan owned what was called a *mas,* or diversified farm producing a number of crops as well as livestock; it also served as a country home. His two sons sometimes rode out to the property on donkeys, each with a girl riding behind—a Marrano girl, naturally. The landlord's steward (known as a *payre* or *ramonet* in the local dialect and *meier* in Felix's German) was the same Guillem whom we encountered earlier, an astonishing and alarming mix of anti-Semitism, alcoholism, sputtering antipapism, and crypto-Lutheranism.

*   *   *

What would the *mas* have been—the land, the olives, the vineyards, and the gardens—without the men and women who cultivated it, the Languedocian peasants and gardeners whom Felix frequently encountered? We have seen something of Guillem the steward. Thanks to Felix's *Tagebuch,* we can also become more closely acquainted with the gardener Antoine, or rather Antony. Felix generally uses Occitanian first names (Guillem, Antony) when referring to common folk while reserving the *langue d'oïl* for members of the elite (Gilbert, Laurent, Jeanne, and so on), whether Marrano or pure Christian. This bilingualism was so embedded in the soil and so spontaneous that it seemed almost natural: the young man from Basel studying in the south of France felt no need to explain himself. For him, both were "Welch" dialects: what did he care whether a first name or anything else reflected the *langue d'oïl* or the *langue d'oc?*

Antony first appears in Felix's journal on January 28 or 29, 1554. A professional gardener who worked in both urban and rural settings (a true "rurbanite," as Renaissance men so often were), he was employed at the time by Laurent Catalan, who owned *ortalisses,* or gardens, in the suburbs.[16] These gardens were useful to the apothecary both for feeding his family and for growing certain medicinal herbs from which pharmaceutical products could be prepared. In the off-season, Antony, with his employer's consent, supplemented his income by traveling back and forth between Montpellier, Switzerland, and Alsace, carrying packages and mail for German students. The postal service established by Louis XI had yet to supplant rival private services.[17] The latter would subsist until the time of Henri IV.

On his first trip to Switzerland, Antony sold his services to two young clients (F 192). The first of these was Jacob Huggelin, a student of twenty-four and the son of a Basel tailor (F 152). In the winter of 1554, Jacob found himself in need of cash. He gave Antony a message for his mother, asking her to send the money he needed. Meanwhile, Felix asked Antony to carry a package of precious pharmaceutical products to his father. The most important of these was a universal antidote and antiplague formula prepared by Rondelet himself from powdered viper, vipers being more plentiful in the *garrigue* (scrub) around Montpellier than in Basel. The package also contained tincture of violet prepared from violets grown in Antony's gardens.

The gardener-messenger took four long weeks to make the round trip to Basel and back on foot. Felix, anxious for his return, took late afternoon walks after class but before dinner along the road to Nîmes, as far as the olive groves in the suburban village of Castelnau (olives were ubiquitous in southern France in the sixteenth century). This was the route by which Antony surely must return. Finally, on February 26, Felix could just make out Antony's stout silhouette in the distance as he returned safe and sound from his trip to German-speaking lands. In Basel the emissary from Montpellier had been welcomed with open arms by Felix's parents and their friends. The visit was celebrated with red wine, but Antony managed to avoid drinking to excess, unlike his colleague Guillem, who apparently contracted the German national "vices" in the course of his northern travels. The gardener returned from Basel with a thick packet of letters, but good manners prevented the boarders in the Catalan house from opening their mail during dinner. *No reading at the dinner table.* But Laurent Catalan, the master of the household, did not deprive himself of the pleasure of opening letters from his sons, both of whom were studying in Basel. Felix rushed through dinner so that he could at last set eyes on the news from his family, which proved to be good. But Huggelin's mother had not sent him one sou. It was therefore decided that the "traveling gardener" should be sent to Basel one more time to extract the needed cash from the coffers of Frau Huggelin.

The summer of 1554 passed without mention of Antony. There is nothing surprising about this: it was the growing season, and he was too busy with farm or garden work. He reappears in our source on November 14. On that day, Felix sent his father a crate of "exotic" fruits (oranges, figs, and pomegranates), together with a crayfish without pincers and a large crab shell to use as a dish. He also sent a cactus from America that had reached him by way of Spain and Italy (Felix mentions only Italy, but the rest of the route can be inferred), and with it the skeleton of a mouse and a letter. Antony contributed several pomegranates from his garden (*uss seim garten*). He was good with trees as well as vegetables. Was the gardener himself assigned to accompany this crate, loaded on the back of a donkey or mule, on its journey to the northeast? A letter from Thomas to his son suggests that this was the case. In any event, Antony left Montpellier on November 16, bound for Strasbourg (perhaps by way of Basel) on a mission for another German student, who as usual needed money. The loyal Antony wore himself out with the burden of so much traveling with so much freight; Thomas, who welcomed him warmly whenever he came to Switzerland, never failed to sing the gardener's praises in his letters. It was through a letter from Felix that Antony delivered to Basel in late 1554 that the elder Platters learned of the presence of forty or so Turkish galleys (allied with France) at Frontignan and Aigues-Mortes. Henri II's Ottoman alliances were of course destined to counter the power of the Hapsburgs of Austria as well as Spain.

Antony returned from Alsace (via Switzerland) around Christmas of 1554. The journey from Basel to Montpellier took him two weeks (F 211). He brought letters from Felix's friends as well as from the humanist Castellion and from Thomas himself (Thomas's letter was dated December 10, 1554). Lengthy journeys remained possible for Antony so long as the weather stayed cold so that there was little gardening to do. On February 28, 1555, the gardener again departed for Strasbourg, with a stop in Basel. He returned in April, carrying a letter from Thomas dated March 28 (this time it took him twelve days to walk from Basel to Montpellier). In addition to this letter, Antony brought Felix two beautiful pieces of hide, from which the student had two pairs of trousers made (F 214). These earned him the admiration of the young nobles of the region with whom he went dancing. Nothing like these pants had ever been seen in Montpellier. Unfortunately they were too tight for Felix, for the thoughtless tailor had taken part of the skins to make a stunning bag (*seckel*) for his wife (F 217), which meant that he cut Felix's trousers closer than he should have.

Antony's last trip, or at any rate the last excursion of which we have any knowledge, began on November 1, 1555, when he was once again sent to Strasbourg by a German (*Teutsch*), as Felix calls him, or, as we would say, an Alsatian (F 233). On his way north, he delivered to Thomas a letter from Felix concerning the fall term just under way at the University of Montpellier. The gardener returned on December 13 after visits to Basel and Strasbourg (F 236). He carried with him a long letter from Thomas to his son, bound in leather: Thomas expressed pleasure at the relatively tolerant attitude toward German Lutheran students in Montpellier and also discussed his confidential and rather promising negotiations with the family of Felix's intended, Madlen Jeckelmann. These discussions were carried on through an intermediary, Frau Frön, Franz Jeckelmann's godmother, a blind woman probably in her seventies.

We have enough information to attempt a portrait of Antony as he was in life. A peasant (*buren*), he was also a highly qualified urban artisan and a skilled gardener capable of performing grafts and cultivating fruit trees like the pomegranate. An affable fellow, he was also as strong as an ox, capable of walking more than thirty-five miles a day to cover the distance between Basel and Montpellier in thirteen or fourteen days (for comparison, it took Felix sixteen full days to cover the same distance on horseback). He was not only a cultivator of the soil but an active participant in the pharmaceutical industry of the day. Although not gifted in foreign languages (he needed an interpreter to converse in German or Latin with Thomas Platter), he acquired a remarkable knowledge of the geography of southern France, Alsace, and Switzerland. Although he was a sturdy man, we have Thomas Platter's word for it that he did tire after his long journeys. Despite being illiterate, he was in his way a Renaissance man of the "lower classes."

\* \* \*

Felix knew the world of the peasant mainly through people such as Guillem and Antony. He was familiar with the major crops—grains, grapes, olive trees, and vegetables—but has little to say about farm animals or, for that matter, about plants and animals considered individually, unless they differed from what he was accustomed to in Switzerland. For example, he frequently remarks on donkeys and mules, which were rare in Switzerland (although his father kept donkeys) but common in southern France. Conversely, he was struck by the relative absence of cows in Languedoc. At the Catalan farm in Vendargues he saw many goats of a type quite common in this region known as *cabrils*, distinguished by long, floppy ears—a trait unheard of in the northern goat. In Marseilles he saw another exotic species, this one from Africa: Barbary rams with plaited tails (which he describes, rather implausibly, as being several yards long), intertwined horns, and thick body hair that hung down to the ground. He also saw ostriches; Arabian horses capable of lifting building blocks; and pieces of intricately ramified coral.

*　　*　　*

Still more exotic were the turkeys of Vendargues, which fed on grass and made their way to market on their own, almost without supervision (F 166). These fowl, whose presence in Languedoc at such an early date was not known until the Platter memoirs were published, had only recently been imported from America. So had the Indian cactus of which Felix sent cuttings to Basel and the wood from Brazil that Felix must have seen because he says that the wine he used to write his journal (*biechlin*) on a trip to Provence was "redder than Brazil wood" (April 1555). Last but not least, all young men were aware of one poisoned gift from the New World: the treponema of syphilis, which Felix mentions in passing in connection with the death of Captain Niklaus Irmy (May 1553). Irmy, who succumbed to the new disease "in a secret part of his body," was a merchant's son and city councillor who had married beautiful Anna Meyer, the daughter of a Basel bürgermeister, whom Hans Holbein had painted in a kneeling posture when she was sixteen as the "Madonna of Darmstadt." The widow, apparently uncontaminated (Niklaus having contracted the "French disease" in Paris), did not have much trouble finding another man: Captain Wilhelm Hebedening married the former madonna but left her a widow a second time when he succumbed to a more honorable death in battle five years later (F 107, 168, 223). Turkey, treponema, cactus, Brazil wood: America is present in Felix's text mainly by way of its biological imports, both animal and vegetable. Neither the influx of precious metals from Mexico nor the growing Spanish power over the West Indies captured the memoirist's attention.

*　　*　　*

Wild animals figure only incidentally in Felix's prose. A visit in 1553 to one corner of the garrigue with its typical vegetation of holm oak and rock-rose provided him with an opportunity to sketch the many rabbits that scampered about at his feet as he walked. The flesh of these rabbits, which fed on fragrant herbs, was considered a delicacy, but hunting them was a privilege reserved for the "priestlings" (*pfaffen*) of a small nearby monastery. By 1596, when Thomas Platter Jr. visited this same spot, known as Grammont, between Montpellier and Pérols, the priestlings had fallen victim to the Wars of Religion and disappeared; the monastery had been deconsecrated and now served as a storage shed where peasants from the area kept plows and other implements; but the rabbits were still there, more active and tastier than ever. Partridges were also abundant, as well as excellent, and were often served for dinner, particularly in the villages of the plains that were located close to swamps (F 184, 256).

Penniless German students such as Sigmund Weisel from Breslau, who arrived in Montepellier on August 26, 1555, often poached herons and other shore birds commonly found in the coastal marshes. Weisel, who hadn't a sou to his name, was a real lout (*grob*) but an excellent shot who bagged a good haul of waterfowl with the aid of his dog Fasan. The other *teutschen* students in Montpellier took up a collection to help him out, and he ended up practicing medicine in Silesia. While living there in the early seventeenth century, he liked to spend winter evenings telling the Germans and Poles of the region stories about his past exploits as a hunter on the shores of the Gulf of the Lion.

\*    \*    \*

When Sigmund Weisel arrived in Montpellier in 1555, Felix was beginning to ask himself if the time had not come for him to leave. He was fed up with the teaching available at the university, most of which he found mediocre. In any case, he had overcome his first hurdle: on May 28, 1556, in the midst of a severe drought, Felix Platter passed his final examination for the baccalaureate in medicine (F 245). His patron (*praeses*), Antoine Saporta, had lost his wife the year before, and Felix, together with a few friends, had accompanied her remains to their final resting place. During the examination, Professors Schyron, Griffy, Fontanon, and Feynes had challenged young Platter's views. The exam had lasted three hours, from six in the morning until nine. Afterwards, Felix put on a red gown. He recited a speech and some doggerel of his own composition in Latin, in which he included a few thoughts for his German classmates at the university. He disbursed the sum of eleven livres three sous to cover the cost of his examination and received in return a diploma with an enormous seal and writing in Latin done by an Alsatian calligrapher by the name of Johann Sporer, who had been a student at Montpellier since May 1555.

The seal was affixed to this parchment in the church of Saint-Firmin, where the seals of the university were kept. This symbolic act was a reminder of the nominal authority of the Catholic clergy over the medical school, an authority that was in fact much diminished in comparison with the past. With his diploma in hand, Felix briefly considered making a pilgrimage to Santiago de Compostela in Spain—purely as a tourist of course, but one never knows what can happen. This idea had come to him in late April, when he had encountered five pilgrims of Saint James from deepest Switzerland—in fact, from the rural, old-Catholic canton of Zug. One of them, Caspar Fry, a man with only one arm, was actually a professional pilgrim. He had already made the round trip from Switzerland to Spain and back fifteen times for the purpose of expiating the sins of people who did not wish to make the journey themselves and who paid him to take their place. The five nomads all sported beards and were covered with medals and cockle shells (symbols of Saint James). They were traveling at the time with five pious old hags, also beggars, who gave the Welches unfortunate ideas about the beauty of Swiss women. But Felix's plans to travel to Spain came to naught. The extended heat wave of 1556 discouraged him, and so, perhaps, did fears of the Spanish Inquisition, whose harshness stood in sharp contrast to the tolerance of the French toward German Protestant students (F 236). In the end he decided to forgo the trip across the Pyrenees. In any case his thoughts were turning more and more toward Basel, where his young and virtuous fiancée awaited him.

PART FOUR

# The Year 1557

## CHAPTER SEVEN

# Going to Paris (Spring 1557)

Months passed: it was now January 1557. Felix's spirits revived. Many signs, not all of them favorable, indicated that the moment of departure was near. On January 12, during the winter dance season that preceded the Carnival, the young man from Basel was invited with a few friends from the local nobility to a masked ball at the home of a socially prominent family. This ball was to be the culmination of several masquerades, otherwise known as "mummeries" (*mumerien*). In the course of the evening, the mistress of the house, reputedly a lady of no great virtue, lost a precious rosary. Felix was suspected of having stolen it, a charge that filled him with revulsion. In fact (or so Felix alleges), the lady had secretly given the sacred object to her lover, a "priestling." She was merely trying to pull the wool over her husband's eyes by diverting suspicion from herself. Disgusted by the whole affair, Felix decided not to attend any more balls as long as he remained in Montpellier. He bluntly dismissed an emissary from the lady in question, a sort of monk, who came with the intention of searching him (in fact the so-called monk was the lay brother Bernard, the grave robber who had supplied Felix with anatomical specimens).

Before departing, Felix had letters to write and a few last packages to send off to Basel by cart or mule, including a crate crammed with books together with some skeletons of fish and land animals. The young man understood his father's psychology. Knowing that Thomas was anxious that he might not find work after returning home, he sent a letter with the crate: "I am now twenty years old and full of experience. I shall find a way to treat the city of Basel with Montpellier's excellent pharmaceutical remedies, which are vastly superior to those of my Swiss homeland." The young man calculated that he would be home by May at the latest. And indeed, he did reach Basel on May 9, 1557, after traveling through Aquitaine, the Loire Valley, Ile-de-France, Burgundy, and Franche-Comté. He knew, however, that he would need financial assistance en route. He therefore asked Thomas to arrange from Basel for an agent in Paris by the name of Martin Betschart to provide him with the funds he would need when he reached that city.

Felix also wrote to his father on behalf of Laurent Catalan to arrange for Jacques Catalan, Laurent's son, to return home to Montpellier for Easter. He also suggested that Jacques travel with the son of a friend of the Platters, a defrocked canon from Basel who eventually married and had a son, Sigmund von Pfirt, who was about to begin medical studies in Montpellier. Felix found a Montpellier businessman who was willing to give Sigmund lodging and return his horse to Basel (using it on the way). By this time, Montpellier's networks of exchange, which Thomas had exploited in 1552, held no further secrets for Felix.

Felix's final weeks in Montpellier were marked by several incidents that left a bad taste. On January 18 the city was treated to the spectacle of a pregnant woman walking a high tightrope (F 262). On the evening of January 21, Felix's German classmates stood him to a round of drinks to wish him farewell and treated him to a rabbit pâté—which turned out to be not rabbit but cat. The butt of this practical joke was none too happy about it.

On January 26 Felix received Thomas's final letter, which had been dispatched almost a month earlier, on December 29. He learned that three of his classmates had been appointed "municipal physicians" in Bern, Mulhouse, and Colmar (such posts were more common in Germany than in France). All three had studied in Montpellier, but two, Stephan Kunz and Jacob Myconius, had received their doctorates from Avignon. The third laureate, Schopefius or Schöpflin, was the former schoolteacher who had accompanied Felix from Basel to Montpellier in 1552; his doctorate was merely from the University of Valence. Thus the signs were good for Felix, whose Montpellier degree was more prestigious than these degrees from Avignon and Valence and therefore likely to win him a better reception back in Switzerland. (What is more, Felix later received a second doctorate from the University of Basel, in 1557.)

All that remained was to find a traveling companion for the journey from Montpellier to Basel by way of Toulouse, Bordeaux, and Paris. Such a decision deserved to be weighed carefully. Fortunately, Felix chose Theodor Birkmann, a young man who was completing a two-year stay in Montpellier (F 218). Theodor came from Cologne, from a family of printers of markedly higher status than the Platters; for all his youth, he was a man of learning steeped in the traditions of Greek medicine as well as a highly accomplished musician. Felix, anticipating the kinds of distractions that his coming journey would require, expected a great deal of such a friend.

An even more important choice was that of a mount. As it happened, a horse was up for sale not far from the Catalan residence. It belonged to a neighbor of the Marrano pharmacist, the noble Simon de Sandre, who had bought it from a young pharmacy student from Strasbourg who was apprenticed to Catalan. The sturdy animal thus began its life in Alsace, spent several years in Languedoc, and would ultimately end up in Basel.

With traveling companion and horse both lined up, it was time for Felix to sell his lute, which pained him greatly. Then came a farewell dinner with classmates, most likely of German extraction. He also said goodbye to his teachers (*doctoribus*) and good French friends from both the north and the south. And he bade farewell to a couple of young ladies, passing fancies, apparently, about whom we have no other information.

At about ten in the morning on February 27, the caravan left Montpellier. It included Birkmann, Gilbert Catalan, Felix, and several German friends who came to escort the travelers a part of the way before bidding them a final adieu. The preliminary farewells were lengthy and heartrending: Laurent Catalan stood on his doorstep and cried, flanked by his wife and his entire family, including the servants. Felix was "heartbroken" at the thought that he might never again see the city he loved so well (*geliepten statt* [F 263]). The first half-day's journey, to the southwest along the Pézenas road, took the youthful travelers to Fabrègues, an old *circulade*, or circular village, of a few hundred inhabitants. This embryonic Protestant community cultivated a variety of crops on the fringes of the garrigue.[1] After lunch at the inn, the group continued on to Loupian, a parish of roughly the same size as Fabrègues located near coastal marshes and the "mountain" of Sète. The next day they covered the final stretch of the ancient Roman road known as the *via Domitia*, arriving on Sunday, February 28, in Béziers right in the middle of carnival season. Located in the heart of a plain that in those days was devoted primarily to wheat, Béziers had benefited from the broad economic upturn of the 1550s. The year before Felix's visit a weekly market had been established or confirmed there: every Friday merchants came to the city from a radius of more than sixty miles.[2] The city was controlled by the local bishop (who belonged to a prestigious Italian family), by royal agents (who maintained a discreet presence), and by the consulate (which kept minutes in French from 1540 on).

As in other cities, the magistrates of Béziers had recently gained control of the consulate and asserted their priority over the merchants, who, despite their energy, were relegated to a secondary place in the common body. The "*bonne ville*" in which businessmen had once claimed seniority was gone. In the small world of local officialdom, the recently established *présidial* snapped up what had been the functions of the *sénéchaussée*. The presidial thus created a judicial core of some fifty officeholders of modest to high rank in a city of fewer than ten thousand people. Out of this group grew several new lineages of nobles who owed their nobility to the law or to royal office. Did this create a certain climate of conformity? Although Huguenot tendencies were not unknown in Béziers, the city lay outside the central area of Protestant influence, which included the Cévennes, Nîmes, and Montpellier. Felix found nothing to compare with this zone until he had traveled further west and northwest, to Montauban and the mid-Garonne, and even there the Protestantism was relatively attenuated.

In Béziers, Felix and his friends, young Germans from Alsace, Switzerland, and the like, were greeted by masked carnival dancers. These were young Jews, or rather Marranos, belonging to the family of Isabelle Catalan, the daughter of Felix's former landlord. Isabelle had married one of the dancers, the son of a Marrano merchant of Béziers, who that night held a banquet and ball. Gilbert Catalan, the black sheep of his family, who accompanied Felix on this first stage of his journey, danced with his Béziers cousins, who also encouraged the attentions of the Alsatians in the group. Felix spent a pleasant evening almost alone in a corner by the fire with a Marrano girl who wore yellow silk trousers. In those days yellow was a Lutheran color in Languedoc.[3] The girl teased her Swiss companion about abandoning the young ladies of France. She did not think of herself primarily as Jewish (though her remote ancestors were Jews) or Occitanian but rather as French, or at any rate "Welch," that is, part of the community of Romance-language speakers, probably with Huguenot sympathies. Between lunch at the inn and the evening banquet, Felix had had time, as was his custom, to make a brief tour of Béziers. As so often, he was interested primarily in the *Antiquitäten* of the city.

He expresses no admiration at all for the cathedral of Saint-Nazaire, even though the place was known as the site of an all too famous massacre.[4] The cathedral sits on a spur of land overlooking the Orb, standing as a bulwark against invasion from Spain by land or by river. By contrast, he was fascinated, as all Béziers had been fascinated for a thousand years, by an ancient statue, unfortunately mutilated, of Emperor Augustus, alias Pépézuc [*sic*]. In the Baroque Era this colossal marble torso served as a pretext for comic plays in the vernacular, including one featuring funeral orations by Pépézuc's ambassador.[5]

Before leaving Béziers, we should mention a minor but irritating incident, which Felix, who like Montaigne is always keen to impart news of intimate physical matters, duly reports. In the course of his conversation with the girl in yellow trousers, the young man from Basel broke a small piece off one of his back teeth (*ein kleinem sticklin von einem hindesten zan*

[F 264]). This frightened him, and he began to worry about further injuries to his jaw. Was Felix's habit of consuming large quantities of sugar to blame for his decaying teeth? Was it sugar from Spain or Sicily? Or, more likely, Iberian sugar from a more remote source such as Madeira, the Azores, the Canary Islands, Cape Verde, or even São Tomé in the Gulf of Guinea? The range of possibilities is broad, for this was a time when sugar from Spanish-Portuguese or offshore African sources accounted for 2 percent of French imports.[6] One thing is certain: the sugar could not yet have been Brazilian.[7] At this date only small quantities of Brazilian sugar had yet appeared on southern European markets.

On the morning of March 1, 1557, the group of travelers left Béziers. All were now German speakers, Gilbert Catalan having chosen to stay behind and spend a few more days with his cousins. At around noon, after a quick ride of almost thirteen miles to the southeast, the travelers reached the walls of Narbonne.

In 1557 Narbonne was only a modest or even small city of six thousand, governed by a consulate. Elections to this body had been held most recently in February 1557, and everything had proceeded normally, as it had in previous elections and would in subsequent ones. In order of precedence, the consuls were a doctor of law, two bourgeois, an apothecary, and two merchants.[8] Like Avignon, Narbonne had been decimated by the plague: the present population was a far cry from the thirty to forty thousand people who had lived during the "pre-plague" period from 1300 to 1340 in prodigiously crowded conditions in what was then one of the largest textile centers of medieval Europe. The sixteenth century, with its usual contradictions, had left an indelible mark on the large Languedocian town, really a frontier city holding the key to Roussillon and Spain. Between 1490 and 1560 Narbonne surrounded itself with impressive modern fortifications in "the Italian style."[9] These cost a fortune and were paid for out of the *gabelle,* or salt tax, hence ultimately by taxpayers. The new fortifications were the material embodiment of a largely harmonious collaboration between the agents of the kings of France and the consuls of Narbonne. The consuls, in the years since 1537, had accomplished the kind of municipal "revolution" that one finds everywhere in southern France during the Renaissance. Nobles, notaries, and magistrates loyal to the monarchy supplanted the merchants and textile manufacturers who had long constituted the cream of the local elite. The sixteenth century also did much to restore the city's prosperity, though the population never returned to the levels achieved two centuries earlier. It did increase but peaked at a relatively modest height. New dwellings rose on land that had gone vacant a century or more earlier under Charles VI and Charles VII, the monarchs who reigned over the difficult years.

The "merchant's bridge" across the Roubine, which linked the two parts of Narbonne known as *le bourg* and *la cité,* had been filled with merchants' houses since the time of Louis XII. The city had tamed the waters, equipping itself with an aqueduct, fountains, and mills. Immigrants from the Massif Central, eastern Aquitaine, and even northern France had swollen the population. By contrast, the Spanish presence was negligible, apart from a few "outside" nobles from nearby Catalonia. This lack of a Spanish influx reflected the fact that relations between France and Spain were not good and would not improve for some time. Intensive cultivation of the flat land around the city supported the revival of the urban center. Olive groves spread rapidly, as they did all along the Mediterranean. Wheat, which remained the principal export crop of the Narbonne region in the early modern era, flourished. Villages in the area kept faith with the civilization of the *agora,* in which the spoken word played a key role. The use of the written word for administrative and other purposes was largely confined to the principal town in each region. Exploitation of the local salt marshes was at its height, rivaling that of the marshes of Camargue. The proceeds from the salt tax paid for the city's fortifications. Urban aristocrats owned vast stretches of these profitable marshlands. At this point Narbonne was cut out of direct trade with the Levant, which had been responsible for its prosperity as a textile center in the thirteenth century. But it was an integral part of a vast network of coastal trade dominated by Provençal (and especially Marseilles) shippers, a network that extended from the Andalusian coast to the Roman *campania* and included Barcelona, Aigues-Mortes, Genoa, and Livorno. Woad (a plant from which a blue indigo dye was obtained) from Toulouse was one of the principal export goods, along with iron, linen, broadcloth, honey, and wine. In the city a new aristocracy emerged, composed of natives together with a handful of Iberians and Italians; many of the latter were former merchants or sons of merchants who had come as part of the entourage of Florentines whom the Valois monarchs had chosen to serve as bishops of Narbonne and Béziers.

In many respects the city in the Aude developed a reputation for an Italian-style *dolce vita,* a reputation reflected in Italian Renaissance literature by writers who visited lower Languedoc to see for themselves. Tuscan touches can still be seen in the marble ornaments and moldings on fountains and facades. At this distance from Geneva and the Cévennes, Protestantism had little chance of establishing a permanent foothold. It had largely run its course, hindered from further progress by a vigorous

Catholicism that was buttressed by devout Spain and, as in Carcassonne and Toulouse, was stubbornly resistant to the new faith.[10]

\*　\*　\*

Felix and his German friends stayed in Narbonne for one day and one night, March 1–2, 1557, a Monday night and the following morning, which happened to be Mardi Gras. Upon arriving at the city walls at noon on March 1, they had been greeted rather coolly. The sentinels, guarding the gateway to France, refused to allow the German quartet to enter on the grounds that they were subjects of the Hapsburgs (France was at war) and therefore accomplices of the Spanish enemy. Felix pointed out that he was Swiss. Indeed, this was the first time since his arrival in France that he had boasted of his Swiss identity. Among his Welch friends he usually identified himself as *Teutsch*, or German, which in a sense he was. In the present situation, however, it was better to be a Confederate (*Eidgenosse*), because the Swiss Confederation and France had signed a treaty of perpetual peace in 1516. Felix's protests succeeded in assuaging the sentinels' fears, and the travelers were allowed to enter the city, where the governor, a man of Italian descent by the name of Four-quevaux, personally arranged for lodging at an inn. Once again they enjoyed the carnival festivities, which as it happens were presided over by a masked German nobleman living in Narbonne.

The traveler from Basel was once again attracted by the city's Roman antiquities. Vestiges of ancient white marble had recently been incorporated into the gray Renaissance masonry of the renovated city walls. Felix even had time to visit the cathedral of Saint-Just. Papist though it was, it was well worth the detour. The student went into ecstasies over giant candles so high that one had to climb a ladder to light or extinguish their flames (he was not so ecstatic, however, that he failed to add ironic afterthoughts to his commentary). By contrast, he did not so much as glance at (or at any rate record having glanced at) Sebastiano del Piombo's *Resurrection of Lazarus* (today in London's National Gallery), which, some forty years later, his younger brother Thomas Jr. would admire down to such details as the hands and hair of the figures portrayed. On Tuesday morning, as the last fires of the "fat days" waned, Felix burst into tears in his bed, just as he had done before in Avignon.[11] This time, however, the tears flowed at the thought that he might never again see Montpellier, a city that had come to occupy an important place in his heart. He was also worried about the dangerous journey ahead of him through south-western and western France. He and Theodor Birkmann left Narbonne

alone, the other Germans having turned back. Felix and Theodor took
the right fork toward Toulouse; the left fork would have taken them toward Spain.

The first stage of the journey took place on the morning of Mardi Gras
(March 2), but there was nothing festive about it as far as the two young
travelers were concerned. By noon they had reached Moux, a small parish
(population 300) typical of a border region, for while it lay in the diocese
of Narbonne, it was "positioned" in what would later become the district
of Carcassonne.[12] It being early March, the broom had sprouted new
shoots and the cherry buds were about to open. Plenty of bees were in
evidence, along with flies, ants, and butterflies, some lemon yellow,
others orange spotted with black. Mushrooms were ready to be gathered,
the apricot trees were in flower, the peach trees showed new leaves, rushes
had returned to the meadows, and new leaves had appeared on blackberry
bushes. Lilies of the valley were up more than an inch. In Moux, Theodor
and Felix replenished themselves at an inn, for the younger Platter was
one of those people who, when traveling, prefer to dine only in restau-
rants if they can afford it. The picnics in the country that nineteenth-
century landscape painters were so fond of depicting held little appeal for
our Renaissance traveler. After lunch, the two *Teutschen* continued on to
Carcassonne, where they arrived late in the afternoon and remained for
the night.

Carcassonne in 1557 was a busy textile town. Indeed, business was so
good that there had been talk as early as 1547 of opening a third mint[13]
there to supplement the two already in existence in Montpellier and Toulouse.[14] Carcassonne was not an intellectual center. Its gifted students left
at an early age to pursue their studies and careers in Toulouse and its environs. By the late 1550s the city had only barely been touched by the Reformation: Huguenot propaganda had been spread among the local artisans
by ex-monks and other emissaries from the entourage of Marguerite de
Navarre, who had set up headquarters first in Nérac and later in the
Béarn. The clergy of Carcassonne were quite fond of missions, miracles,
and other syndromes of religious "panic" and not at all fond of the queen
of Navarre even though she was the king's sister. When she visited Carcassonne in 1537, the only gifts she received from the consuls were a few
cases of candles, preserves, and refreshments, whereas not only the king
and queen of France but the merest seneschal or governor of Languedoc
who visited the city in this period were likely to be heaped with expensive
gold and silver drinking vessels and dinnerware.[15]

The consuls of Carcassonne, long suspicious of heresy, were also "roy-
alized." It was the same story as in other cities: the power of the mon-

archy had long allied itself with local magistrates, who championed their cities' affirmation of a new identity. By 1547, the magistrates, with their flair for statecraft, had pushed the merchants aside as they had done throughout the Midi and seized the post of first consul. The "community" of Carcassonne was in fact not much of a community: it had been ravaged by persistent conflict between the natives of the "High Town" (*la Cité*) and the residents of the "Low Town" (*le Bourg*), whose population was less clerical and less "Ancien Régime" than that of *la Cité*. In the period 1555–65 *la Cité* was conformist; it counted few Huguenots among its residents, even fewer than in *le Bourg*. The two parts of the city also fought over the location of important institutions, especially new ones: the presidial, which was created in Carcassonne as in other southern cities in 1552, became a political football to be kicked back and forth between High Town and Low Town.[16] At first it seemed natural to locate it in the fortified High Town, the noble quarter and the normal location of anything bearing the hallmark of official state business. But by May 1553 the new court had been moved to the Low Town.[17] In September a council decree ordered it moved back to the High Town. In December, that order was reversed by letters patent. In February 1554 a new decree again ordered that the presidial be moved to *la Cité*. Then, in the month of May, a royal edict reversed that order. In September the King's Council sent the court back up to the heights while initiating an investigation into the *commodo et incommodo* of the affair. In December, new letters patent authorized yet another move to the "*bourg neuf*," or Low Town. The struggle continued for three generations (though not all of these orders were actually carried out).

Felix in his own way took note of Carcassonne's obviously schizophrenic identity. The city, he wrote, "lies partly on low ground, partly on the hill" (*liegt zum theil im boden, zum theil auf den Berg* [F 266]). He also recorded that his journey from Narbonne by horseback had covered eight leagues (Felix had his own notion of what a league was). He left Carcassonne on March 3. Eight months later, a plague struck the city and continued to rage until Lent of 1558. It was said to have caused 2,500 deaths, probably a good third of the total population. For once, Low Town and High Town were fraternally united in disaster.

\* \* \*

At dawn on Ash Wednesday, March 3, 1557, Felix and Theodor left Carcassonne. Lent had begun (F 266). For the next forty days, until the two young men reached Paris in the first fortnight of April, they would eat no more meat (*kein fleisch mer*). People along the way seemed to observe Lent properly, even in towns touched by Huguenot influence. *La France toute catholique* was no myth, at least not on the surface.

The first stretch of the trip to Toulouse proceeded over bad road. In Castelnaudary, where the two riders stopped for the night, Felix hit his head against an iron hook projecting from the wall of a butcher shop as he rode down a narrow street in the dark. His blood ran down a side of beef hanging from the hook. The next day, west of Castelnaudary, the travelers bade farewell to the last stretch of lower Languedoc and glimpsed Aquitaine just ahead. The countryside was unquestionably making rapid strides as diversified farming took hold, although some smallholders suffered cruelly as a result of the change.[18] Farmers grew woad (for dye, but in small amounts), grains, and grapes. There were of course no olive groves, because the local climate was too damp and subject to frequent frosts. Forests survived but suffered from excessive land-clearing. The growth of the population was not always compatible with ecological sensitivity: in extreme cases, peasants short of wood (because of overcutting of the forests) were forced to burn straw in order to bake bread.

The valley of the Ariège lay just ahead: there, mines and forges catered to the needs of the north, both civilian and military. Gunpowder was produced at Le Mas-d'Azil downstream from Ariège, where there were caves filled with saltpeter. Huguenots, encouraged by the local dynasty of Marguerite de Navarre and later Jeanne d'Albret, were not uncommon among the people. There was no shortage of silver. Attempts were made to extract it from "foxholes" (supposedly mineshafts) in the county of Foix, but after 1549 and the "silver rush" in the north of Mexico, most silver came from the south. The precious metal traveled across the Atlantic through Spain and into Aquitaine by way of Narbonne, Bayonne, and the passes of the Pyrenees.[19] At first Felix noticed little of the vitality of southwestern France. Shortly after leaving Castelnaudary with his companion, he deviated from his route to escape the ominous attentions of a pair of highway robbers. Later, while galloping once more along the road to Toulouse, the two students met up with a compatriot who seemed friendly (F 267). The man was a German, part highwayman and part tramp, and accompanied by a puppy on a leash; while carrying a sword on his shoulder, he sang at the top of his lungs. His name was Samuel Hertenstein, and he was the son of Dr. Philipp Hertenstein of Lucerne. Samuel had been a student of Thomas Platter's in Basel from 1546 to 1549 and had known Felix as a small child. Later he had practiced "empirical" medicine in Toulouse, where he was well known in all the gambling dens. After that he had fought in the Piedmont. Now, dressed in tatters, he was on his way back to Toulouse, where he hoped to earn enough money to pay for his return to Basel. After stops in various taverns in which Samuel joked with the innkeepers, the three travelers entered Toulouse during the evening of March 4 and rented a room at the Saint-Pierre inn.

Toulouse, with a population of 30,000 or more (the exact figure is unknown), was at this point probably the fourth or fifth largest city in France after Paris, Lyons, Orléans, and Rouen. In the 1550s the economic influence of the capital of Aquitaine extended over an area of some 15,000 square kilometers, roughly the size of three French *départements* today.[20] To get an idea of the material progress the city had made, a brief look at the history of the grocery (and cookware) trade is worth more than a long-winded description. In the second half of the fifteenth century, the leading staples were somewhat different from what they are today. The most important items were such basic ingredients as olive oil and sea salt from lower Languedoc and salted fish from the Atlantic. Spices and non-ferrous metals were still of minor importance. Things changed somewhat in the second half of the second decade of the sixteenth century, however: there was increased commerce in copper from Central Europe, tin from the British Isles, and wax (for candles, a sign of "enlightenment" in a university town). There was also increased trade in dyestuffs and related substances such as Flemish madder and alum. Sales of spices increased, as did the consumption of Portuguese sugar. The years from 1527 to 1531 were crucial in a number of respects: the issue of how to deal with the poor came to the fore, and southern France began to feel the first rumblings of the Reformation. On the other hand, consumer society was just getting off to a modest start, limited primarily (though not exclusively) to the elite: the influx of wax from Germany, salted fish from the Atlantic, and wood from Brazil increased, as did trade in sugar and dried fruit.

Between 1540 and 1560 Toulouse consolidated its position as an exporter of agricultural products, such as prunes, goose feathers, and above all woad (the source of indigo), which formed the basis of many fortunes. Trade was encouraged by the fact that Toulouse enjoyed substantial tax privileges. In 1558, the year after Felix's visit, the residents of Languedoc paid 562,282 *livres tournois* of the tax known as the *taille,* but Toulouse, one of the province's leading cities, contributed not a *denier* of that total because it had been exempt from taxes since the great conflagration of 1463. The flames had been a blessing. The city paid the king only one small tax of 2,500 livres.[21]

Felix's visit to Toulouse on March 5, 1557, concentrated on theological and military matters. He toured the city's ramparts of brick, or "baked stones" (*bachenen steinen*), and inspected the recently reconstructed walls, equipped by engineers from Italy with defensive structures known as demilunes or ravelins. In the construction of defensive fortifications, the great French military architect Sébastien Le Prestre de Vauban (1633–1707) was, to judge by the many cities already fortified in the mid-sixteenth century, more of a continuator or end of a line than he was an innovator. Felix spent most of his time in Toulouse visiting churches. In these pages of his memoirs he "softpedals" his anticlericalism, although it never altogether disappears. Despite the presence of eight hundred actual or potential Huguenots within its walls, the city remained a bastion of Catholicism thanks to its parlement, which countered the influence of a municipal government sympathetic to Protestantism.[22] The young man from Basel was particularly interested in *la Daurade* (from *deaurata*, the "gilded temple"). This was an unusually well-preserved Visigothic or Frankish monument in the shape of a regular decagon with a central altar "topped by a cupola with an opening in the center."[23] The structure stood close to the river, virtually with its feet in the water, as it were, between the court known as the *viguerie* and the fish market.

The inside of *la Daurade* was notable for its mosaics interspersed with marble columns. Dating back to Merovingian times, these mosaics, which stretched from floor to ceiling, were composed of small silvered and gilt stones and offered a compendium of Judeo-Christian theology, ranging from Abraham and Moses to the Archangels and the Apostles and the Virgin and Child. The whole church was dedicated to the cult of Mary, which held little attraction for a convinced Protestant like Felix. What is more, the future doctor, interested as always in Gallo-Roman and neo-pagan archaeology even when he toured churches, confidently maintained that *la Daurade* was originally a non-Christian construction, a temple of Isis. (Thomas Platter Jr. would later call it a temple of Jupiter [T2 409]). Anything but Catholic, in short: not for nothing was our author a Swiss humanist and Protestant. On the eve of the Wars of Religion *la Daurade* was occupied by a Benedictine community, which the Cluniac chapter had tried to reform by proposing a new set of statutes in 1535.[24] Under Richelieu, it would host a group of Benedictines from Saint-Maur, who supplanted the order of Cluny and who became noted for their scholarly researches. In the eighteenth century, unfortunately, *la Daurade* was destroyed, thus depriving France of a rare jewel of late antique or very early medieval religious art. Felix's account focuses mainly on the mosaics. He reports an oral tradition that he picked up in Toulouse in 1557: if one pressed one of the small colored stones into the walls or floor, it would make its way back to the surface in the space of a single night, returning infallibly to its appointed place in the intricate and sacred puzzle.

Even more impressive to the traveler from Basel—who had become a decided fancier of churches, if not of the papist religion—was the immense basilica of Saint-Sernin, the model of a whole tradition of Romanesque architecture in southern France. In the sixteenth century Saint-Sernin was still an important financial and religious power. Felix, focusing on the essential, went straight to the crypt, which contained twelve silver sarcophagi in which were preserved, supposedly, the bodies of the twelve apostles, including the decapitated skeleton of Saint James. Accordingly, Felix reports, pilgrims on their way to Santiago de Compostela still marched in procession through Saint-Sernin, just like their medieval predecessors, who, having been gouged on prices for wine and oats provided by crooked horse dealers who also sold them blind and decrepit animals, nevertheless passed through the church, content, their eyes fixed on a faraway tomb.

Felix's tour of Toulouse was concluded with breakneck speed. His memoirs make no mention of the *parlementaires* of the city, despite their important role, or of the highly militant local Huguenots (who were in the minority, however, and soon marginalized). Nor does he mention the University of Toulouse, where intellectual life was intense. Following the lead of Coras, learned jurists were there putting the finishing touches on theories of legislative sovereignty in the monarchical state, theories that would soon be taken up by Bodin.[25] The university of the "pink city" specialized in law, counterbalancing the University of Avignon, which was dedicated to theology. All that Felix later remembered, however, was that he had visited a print shop in Toulouse where there was a typographer who had once worked as an apprentice and messenger for his father. He also casts a brief glance at the mills on the Bazacle with their stone pillars, wooden frames, and tile roofs. These mills were kept supplied by endless trains of mules, which brought wheat in and carried flour out.

If we believe Thomas Platter Jr., this "factory" was capable of feeding 100,000 people in the city and surrounding plain (T2 422). While this figure may be exaggerated, Toulouse's future as a flour producer was foreshadowed as early as 1557. But none of this seemed important at the time. There were more pressing matters to be considered: the ground was burning beneath our travelers' feet, because the city had been stricken by plague. Four hundred fifty houses were already infected.[26] On March 6, 1557, after the noon meal, Felix and Theodor left Toulouse for Montauban. They had previously paid the innkeeper at the inn of Saint-Pierre.

Generous but penniless Samuel Hertenstein bade the two travelers a heartfelt farewell after signing Felix's remembrance book. Felix never saw the paramedical tramp again; he died in France without ever returning to Switzerland.

\*　　\*　　\*

The usual route from Toulouse to Agen and Bordeaux passed through Montauban, which meant leaving the towpath along the Garonne and making a small detour to the north. In Montauban a sixteenth-century bridge with seven pointed brick arches made it easy to cross the Tarn.

The route in general turned out to be secure, which would not have been the case a century earlier, when brigands set loose by the Hundred Years' War still roamed the area. In all his travels in francophone territory, Felix had encountered truly dangerous criminals only rarely: once north of Lausanne in 1552, a second time at an inn in the Comtat Venaissin, and a third time after leaving Castelnaudary. Each time he was frightened but not hurt. On the whole, the France of Henri II was not overly plagued with crime, particularly in view of the weak constabulary. Montauban, which had grown rapidly in the twelfth century, had long since recovered from the afflictions of the late Middle Ages, when the community, practically ruined, had been little more than a support base for the English forces of the prince of Wales in fourteenth-century Aquitaine.

In the age of Henri II, the city, refurbished from top to bottom, still surrounded by impressive ramparts, and embellished by a new pilastered square in the Florentine manner, served as a port of transit for wine and wheat being shipped to the lower Garonne by way of the Tarn.[27] Manufacturing of common textiles and coarse fabrics such as burlap and caddis developed around the center of town in the middle of the sixteenth century. The work force grew, replenished from such "demographic reservoirs" as the Massif Central, the Rouergue, and the dioceses of Mende and Saint-Flour. From the time of Louis XII on, Renaissance architecture left its indelible mark on the *hôtels particuliers* of Montauban in the form of "basket handle" motifs over doorways in place of the traditional ogee lintels typical of late Gothic architecture and once quite common in the south of France.

Control of the city was divided among three powers: the bishop, the *quercynol,* or seneschal's lieutenant, and the consuls. The latter were the most active, and as in other cities magistrates were more influential than merchants. The consuls formed a republic of minor municipal sovereigns, micro-potentates whose principal merit was to be present in the street whenever anything happened.

The consular authorities took a favorable attitude toward Protestantism in Montauban, all the more so since Bishop Jean de Lettes, the nephew of the previous prelate, Jean des Prés, and uncle of the subsequent diocesan Jacques des Prés, was involved in a romantic idyll with a young noblewoman. He married her in 1556 and spent the last quarter of his honeymoon between Geneva and Lausanne. Had it not been for the ever-vigilant parlement of Toulouse, "heresy" would have found few impediments in Montauban. It had deep roots among the city's artisans, having first gained a foothold through teachers in the excellent local schools with support from the middle-ranking clergy of the diocese, including a clerical judge, an "administrator of episcopal property," and a preacher in the mold of Savonarola.

Felix thus came into contact with the ribbon-like Huguenot stronghold of the central Garonne region. The contrast between this and the area between Béziers and Toulouse, where heresy lacked vitality, was astonishing. In Montauban Felix found himself once again in reformed territory such as he had known in Nîmes in 1552 and suspected in Montpellier in subsequent years. Just outside Montauban, in the suburban church of Saint-Jacques, a dog named Poclès who had been following Felix for months staged a sort of pro-Protestant demonstration. The Lutheran animal somehow got the idea that the ciborium on the altar cloth contained food and tried to wolf it down. On its first attempt the dog was beaten by a sacristan who happened to be present. As a result of this experience, Poclès conceived a holy horror of the papist cult. The dog never missed an opportunity to yap loudly at Catholic altars and ciboria in France and Switzerland. It thus boldly proclaimed the reformed opinions of its master Felix. The dog was truly a *bouffe-curé,* or priest-eater.

Felix and Theodor spent March 7 and part of March 8 in Moissac, a town notable for the astonishing doorway of its Cluniac abbey, its houses with dovecotes, and its old bridge of brick and wood. The travelers then crossed an ecological divide: cows (of which Felix had seen few for years) suddenly became plentiful and the countryside became moister and greener as they traveled toward the northwest. On the afternoon of March 8, the two riders, accompanied by Poclès, reached Agen (F 270). A flourishing town with a population of 14,000 (6,000 of whom were Huguenots), Agen, with its cathedral of Saint-Etienne whose radiating chapels had just been vaulted, rivaled Montpellier despite the lack of a university. The city's new quarters, with their recently built houses of red brick and exposed framing, gave evidence of a flourishing commercial vocation: Agen exported prunes and *minots* (barrels filled with flour) by way of the Garonne.

Numerous colonies of Italian merchants lived cheek by jowl with a variety of immigrants from Poitou, Brittany, and southwestern France. Agen, important as the site of one of sixteen tax collection centers (*recettes générales des finances*) throughout France,[28] stood at the crossroads of two principal transportation routes: the Garonne river and the land route linking the Swiss cantons to the Basque region by way of Auvergne and Gascony. Not only merchants but to an even greater degree prelates from Italy had opened the way for the Italian intelligentsia: "A monk approached us in the street and asked us if we wanted to meet Julius Scaliger, an illustrious resident of Agen. But this was a joke [*spot*] directed at us, and we dropped the subject" (F 270). It may well have been a joke, but the monk was indeed correct that Scaliger, a gladiator of humanism, was an active member of an important and creative network of literary figures. Born in Riva del Garda, Julius Caesar Scaliger, erstwhile soldier of Italy and former monk as well as a great collector, had followed the bishop Della Rovere to Agen. Scaliger took a wife in the city and became a consul. In 1561 he published *Poetics,* one of the works that later inspired the classicism of Boileau. He was the best known of a whole constellation of writers associated to one degree or another with Agen. Among them were Julius Scaliger's son Joseph Scaliger (all of Julius's children went on to brilliant careers in the nobility, magistracy, or commerce), Bernard Palissy, and the two Marguerites, Marguerite de Navarre (who played a crucial role in the Huguenot politics of the central Garonne) and Marguerite de Valois. Others included Monluc, Nostradamus, Belleforest, and above all Bandello.

Matteo Bandello, a writer of tales and friend of Scaliger, enjoyed the protection of the Fregosos, a family with episcopal claims that came originally from Genoa but had been living in gilded exile in Agen since 1542. During the twenty years Bandello spent in Agen (1542–61), he wrote and published the best of his fiction, the *Novelle,* or tales, one of which inspired Shakespeare's *Romeo and Juliet*. In 1554, shortly before Felix's visit, Bandello had just completed six years of conscientious service as bishop of Agen—an astonishing performance for an outspoken advocate of ribald hedonism, a man closer in spirit to Alfred de Musset than to Bishop Bossuet. Of course the writer had merely been keeping the episcopal throne warm until the titular bishop, a Fregoso of tender age, was old enough to succeed him. When Bandello tired of the job, a second place-warmer by the name of Corniolio replaced him as bishop from 1555 to 1558, a period that spanned the time of Felix's visit.

On March 9 and 10 the itinerant students covered the distance from Agen to Bordeaux in two stretches. While crossing the Garonne, Felix came close to drowning, along with horse and baggage, when the boat carrying the travelers capsized, fortunately close to shore. In Aiguillon near the mouth of the Lot, the travelers had to swear that they had not come from Toulouse, where the plague was raging. Their false oath was accepted all the more readily because they stated, as they had already done once before, that the were Swiss and therefore allies of the French. At the inn in Aiguillon they had ample time to appreciate the plumage of an immigrant from the tropics: a parrot. They also had a new linguistic experience: their first contact with the French of the "masses," which took place near Marmande, in an area recently repopulated by "*gavaches d'oïl*" (southern dialect for "skunks" from the north) from Saintonge and Anjou. They then passed through the heavily fortified town of La Réole; after that came Saint-Macaire, one of the few communities that had refused to join in the first anti-salt-tax revolts in the 1540s.[29] Between Saint-Macaire and Bordeaux they had to pass through the Cap de l'Homme forest, which was apparently a den of thieves. In Felix's mind, forests (not only this one near Bordeaux but others outside Basel, Lausanne, Lunel, and Toulouse) posed a threat of violence, whether real or imaginary we cannot say. Did cutting down trees therefore mean greater security? In any case, Felix's fears of the Cap de l'Homme proved as groundless as most of his earlier fears.

When the two students reached the walls of Bordeaux on the night of March 10, they were forbidden to enter the city. It was nighttime and the gates were closed. Security was of paramount consideration. Felix and his companion dined at a suburban inn. The menu included squid (*sepia*) and spider crabs (*merspinnen*): they were close to the ocean. On the morning of March 11 the travelers entered Bordeaux. There was no shortage of hotels: the new arrivals were free to choose among the Quatre Mendiants and the Ecu de Bretagne, the cosmopolitan Monde qui tourne, and the rustic Autruche, Cheval Blanc and Trois Lapins.[30] But the lure of the harbor drew them to an inn on the waterfront: the Chapeau Rouge, also known as the Chapeau de Cardinal, which stood adjacent to a forest of masts and hulls. In the 1550s, the mouth of the Garonne, as vast as it is, was crowded with ships, and collisions were inevitable. There were good reasons for this crowding of the harbor. It was easy to transport wine from throughout Aquitaine to Bordeaux by river, and from there it was carried to the thirsty drinkers of northern Europe by ship via the Atlantic. Felix watched barrels of wine being loaded aboard an English ship. Other export commodities included woad, hemp, honey, and tar from the moors; foreign sales of all these items were soaring. Imports (from the Netherlands) included furniture, paintings, tapestries, and copper kitchenware (from Flanders). From the British Isles came fabrics, tin, lead, and alabaster. Other imports included salted and smoked fish rich in iodine (hence a remedy for goiter); oats and salt from Saintonge; and, from the Basque region and Spain, smaller amounts of iron, weapons, anchors, pottery, bundled wool, barrels of sardines and whale meat, and Portuguese silver.[31] From the more or less recently discovered colonies came sugar (from Madeira), wood (from Brazil), and above all cod from Newfoundland. Cod, imported since 1517, arrived in substantial amounts, especially in the decade and a half after 1546.

During the reign of Henri II high-risk loans sustained the Newfoundland shippers, who in good years sent twenty or more vessels across the Atlantic. Trade rose substantially under the last five Valois kings. Exports exceeded imports in both weight and value, to the benefit of the Atlantic port. As a result, the docks were soon covered with piles of ballast, and no one knew what to do with it all. With the increase in business the port tended to expand beyond the ramparts into the area downriver around the port of Les Chartreux. Inside the city Felix rubbed elbows with substantial numbers of northerners who mingled with the 45,000 native inhabitants.[32] To be sure, there were also large numbers of visitors from the south, Basques and Bayonnais and Spaniards. But they were eclipsed by Normans, Bretons especially, and Englishmen. By 1550, moreover, there was a noticeable influx of people from Germany and the Netherlands, especially Flanders, as more and more of the city's trade was with the Low Countries (this trend would continue into the next century). Drinkers in Amsterdam were fond of their *brandwein* (brandy), which had been exported from Bordeaux since 1513. Aquitaine thus had a lead of a century and a half over lower Languedoc, whose glorious career in distilling did not begin until the age of Colbert. Historians are always quick to refer to "Marignano, 1515." But other dates also have their importance in the history of Bordeaux: the first local production of brandy in 1513;[33] the first Lutheran book in a canon's library, 1521; the first case of clerical syphilis in 1514; and the first cod from Newfoundland in 1517. These last two dates are the first signs of American influence for good and for ill.

The host of ships crowding the harbor included countless small "tramps," or coastal vessels of forty-five tons or less. These, according to Felix, were simply allowed to rest on the bottom at low tide; their keels suffered less than would have been the case with large ships weighed down by ballast and cargo and moved about by the shifting tides.[34] These smaller vessels carried diverse cargoes and could sail just as easily over shallow lobster beds as they could on the deep sea. Most ships' captains, or "masters," made do with very little specialized equipment: a compass (in common use in Bordeaux since 1500), a chronometer, and a sounding line; marine charts were virtually nonexistent. The Bordelais themselves were not great navigators and let foreign sailors take the lead in shipping even in their own port. There were no more than six hundred ablebodied seamen and mates in the substantial population of this port city—a very small number indeed. And half of these were freshwater sailors who piloted barges along the river or fishermen who went after lamprey, a river fish in season in the spring. During his three days in Bordeaux, Felix ate lamprey for lunch and dinner at the Chapeau Rouge. The Garonne, unpolluted in those days, was as well stocked with fish as anyone could wish. Those Bordeaux sailors who had direct experience of the sea belonged to religious confraternities rather than to the trade guilds that were common in northern Europe. Bordeaux merchants were wine shippers, just as their counterparts in Toulouse shipped woad and those in England shipped fabrics and fish.[35] Speed of travel depended on whether one was a sailor, rider, or spirochete. It took Felix five days to ride from Toulouse to Bordeaux on horseback. The same trip by river would have taken him four days going downstream but eleven days going upstream. Biological journeys were not as rapid. It took syphilis twenty years to reach Bordeaux from Naples (1494–1514).[36]

Owing to chance encounters and Felix's personal predilections, his seventy-two hours in Bordeaux were largely taken up with music (*wir musicierten* [F 272]). A shopkeeper from Berne who dealt in stringed instruments kept the two young travelers company. He lent Felix a harp and Theodor a lute. The Swiss trio spent much of their stay giving modest concerts that attracted crowds of natives. There is nothing surprising about the musical interests of the Bordelais: under Louis XII and Francis I, Bordeaux had been the residence of Clément Janequin, who, under the patronage of the archbishop, had composed twenty-odd polyphonic songs, 80 percent of which were devoted to themes of love and the remainder to war.[37]

In Bordeaux, a community open to currents from the four corners of the earth, Latin literature provided a shared culture, a frame of reference that loomed large in the minds of men like Etienne de La Boétie and Michel de Montaigne, who, still young in 1557, was just beginning a new term in the parlement of Bordeaux. The Swiss visitor was well aware of the depth of Bordeaux's Latin culture. He made an excursion outside the walls in the company of a guide from Bern to visit the Palais Gallien, a stadium in the shape of a vast oval—Thomas Jr. would later describe it as an elongated egg (T2 411). Built in the time of the Severi (after 193 C.E.), the amphitheater sat atop an underground prison. Originally it could accommodate 15,000 spectators for gladiatorial combats.[38] By the time of

Felix's visit, the still majestic and well-preserved ruins had become a sort of lover's lane. Amorous couples barely moved when riders, barrel-laden ox carts, or curious visitors passed by.

Forty years apart, Felix and Thomas Jr. also visited the "guardian pillars," another impressive relic of Gallo-Roman times that had become a destination for curious tourists and moonstruck couples. The two brothers independently counted seventeen or eighteen columns still standing, complete with acanthus-leaf capitals, architrave, and caryatids. In the sixteenth century a square garden (replacing the old imperial forum) in the center of the open area enclosed by the columns covered a series of vast wine cellars. Small houses with tiled roofs stood nearby. The great architect and jack-of-all-trades Claude Perrault observed the "guardian pillars" still standing in the time of Colbert, but they were destroyed under Louis XIV after a major local rebellion in 1675 so as to discourage future rebels by extending the defensive glacis of the Château-Trompette. To the Sun King's way of thinking—and dismay—Bordeaux was indeed a city of "powder and saltpeter," prone to rebellion and therefore to be taken firmly in hand. This was already the case in the "time of Platter," that is, during the reign of Henri II, who took a rather repressive attitude toward the people of Bordeaux.

\*   \*   \*

Apart from the monuments of Antiquity, which lay outside the city proper, Felix explored the city thoroughly (*überal*) in the company of his guide from Bern. He inspected the building in which the parlement of Bordeaux met (*das haus do das Parlament wird gehalten* [F 272]), the old Palais de l'Ombrière, where there is today a street of the same name, at the southeastern corner of the old Roman *castrum*.[39]

L'Ombrière, a medieval building ensconced in an ancient setting, was none other than the palace of the dukes of Aquitaine, which in the thirteenth century became the headquarters of the pro-British seneschals of Gascony. It stood at the southeastern entrance to a first line of fortifications, which followed the boundaries of the *castrum*. In the sixteenth century, the decrepit former palace became the home of the parlement of Bordeaux. The magistrates of parlement, wealthy vineyard owners, resided in the vicinity of the high court, whose filthy appearance set off their splendid houses. Felix noted the poor repair of the prestigious symbolic building, the structural defects, and the "filth" of the court chambers. Yet lucid observers, Thomas Platter Jr. among them, were not deceived by the wretched appearance of the place. The parlement had certainly suffered from the popular anti-tax rebellions of 1548 in the Gironde, in the wake of which a furious Henri II had temporarily suspended its normal judicial functions. But after 1550, things resumed their normal course.

The sovereign court (which had tripled the number of its magistrates in response to demographic, economic, and governmental growth between Louis XI and Francis I) was still the arbiter of justice in Bordeaux and Aquitaine. The magistrates were highly cultivated men. Parlement dealt with the royal governor and his lieutenant general as peers. It set the tone for other official institutions of the municipal and royal government: the *jurade* (aldermen), the *amirauté* (admiralty), and *les finances* (fiscal authorities). Despite the growing influence of Protestantism among intellectuals and aristocrats, parlement kept the city and the port, with its ships named for the Virgin and the saints, obediently Catholic, much as the parlement of Toulouse did in that city, where Papism was even more firmly ensconced than in the lower Garonne. Thus Bordeaux, which willingly or unwillingly kept faith with the traditional religion, experienced none of the Calvinist upheaval that occurred at this time in places like Nîmes and Agen, two among many communities in the Cévennes and central Garonne region where, in the absence of a sufficient institutional counterweight, the propaganda of a few preachers ultimately sufficed to win a majority of the population and personnel in key institutions over to the "heretical" cause. Nevertheless, the durable, persistent Catholicism of certainly highly placed people in Bordeaux remained open-minded and evangelical, even if it was tainted by the tortures inflicted on a number of Calvinists in Guyenne. Despite such bloody stains on its escutcheon, Bordeaux's "papism" was closer to the thinking of Montaigne than to that of the papists of Toulouse or to the fanaticism of the followers of the Duc de Guise or Cardinal de Lorraine. The humanist Platter was in his element among the men of letters of Bordeaux even if he was not aware of it. Later, in 1580, he would actually meet the author of the *Essais* during Montaigne's pilgrimage to Basel and Italy.

\*   \*   \*

On March 14, Felix, accompanied by Theodor (F 272), boarded the ship *Aquilon* (or *Aiguillon:* for once, a ship from Bordeaux had a name having nothing to do with the Virgin or a saint). They embarked near the Chapeau Rouge, which simplified matters. At around noon, after an untroubled crossing, the ship landed at Blaye, a small town on the right bank of the Gironde estuary consisting of a city proper, a fortress, and a suburb, all controlling an extraordinarily profitable customs post where duties were levied on ships sailing to or from Bordeaux. Felix located Blaye incorrectly as lying midway between Bordeaux and La Rochelle; in fact, it is close to Bordeaux and relatively far from La Rochelle. When Thomas Platter Jr. visited Blaye at the end of the century, he was less close-mouthed about it than his brother and more informative about local legends. He reports, for example, that locals believed, rightly or wrongly, that their town was the site of the tomb of Roland, the hero of the famous *Chanson,* who, with Herculean might, had supposedly hurled a heavy lance into the middle of the Garonne, which was in fact quite broad at the site of the fortified toll station (T2 449). After a stop at a tavern in Blaye for the inevitable noon meal, Felix and his friend crossed the border between Guyenne and Saintonge and headed for Mirambeau, where they arrived by early evening and spent the night.

In passing from Guyenne into Saintonge, moreover, the two travelers also crossed, apparently without noticing it, the linguistic boundary between the *langue d'oc* and the *langue d'oïl.* Indeed, this was the first time that Felix had really set foot in "France" (that is, in the France *d'oïl*), but of course Saintonge had still been "English" little more than a century earlier. The road north took the student past almost new Saintonge-style manors distinguished by their circular or polygonal towers with pointed roofs—a signature of the reconstruction of the region in the wake of the Hundred Years' War. Saintonge had also recovered from the more recent ordeal of the rebellions that had erupted against the salt tax in 1542 and 1548 in Charente as well as Bordeaux.

\*   \*   \*

On the morning of March 15, as Felix and Theodor rode north, they witnessed a genre scene: a *prévôt* (sheriff) accompanied by a squadron of mounted police captured an alleged criminal before the very eyes of our travelers. The prisoner was tied to a horse and taken off to an unknown destination (F 272). The arresting officer was one of a number of provincial and special *prévôts* whose posts were created under Charles VIII and Francis I. They patrolled the highways, collared suspects, and meted out summary justice, which may have been effective but drew much criticism from the regular courts. The question of whether judicial powers should be granted to policemen was an old one. The *prévôts* were still active in 1557 in Saintonge and elsewhere. There were not very many of them (Felix had not seen one since Montpellier, or for that matter since Lyons). Henri II had made a move to eliminate the office a few years earlier. Perhaps he meant his order to be enforced, perhaps not, but in any case it had no effect. The *prévôts* continued their itinerant, provincial careers under the royal aegis.[40]

On March 15 the two students passed Pons, an important stop on the way to Santiago de Compostela. Pilgrims traveling from north to south could find food and shelter in a vaulted hospice built in the town between 1157 and 1192. Felix and Theodor had just enough time to cast an eye on an imposing keep that dated from around 1185. This rectangular fortress, thirty meters high, was augmented by a tower built on its north face in the fifteenth century.[41]

Shortly after noon that same day, the two travelers approached Saintes, a city of four to five thousand people on the banks of the Charente. As they drew near the ramparts, they passed on their left an amphitheater built in the time of Tiberius—a perfect oval that adorned the Valley of Arenas. To the west they saw the suburban church of Saint-Eutrope, a sanctuary for pilgrims in transit.[42] Saint-Eutrope featured a flamboyant steeple barely a century old—the Gothic work still looked new. The two young men now crossed the five-meter-wide moat around the city, whose fortified walls followed the contours of the old Roman *castrum* everywhere except for an enlargement by the river. Passing through the Porte-Evêque, situated in the jurisdiction of the local prelate, they proceeded along narrow streets, rutted by iron-clad cart wheels. The streets were flanked by houses with sculpted beams, double-gabled facades, mullioned windows, and turrets with spiral staircases.[43] The students' route, though sinuous, corresponded more or less to the old *decumanus maximus*, which divided the Roman *castrum* along a north-south axis. They passed a stone's throw from the residence of the bishop, the astonishing Tristan de Bizet.[44] The bishop displayed a certain laxity ( perhaps owing to lack of zeal) toward local Huguenots, among whom dynamic artisans played a leading role.[45] He was on hostile terms, however, with the various local authorities, both civil and ecclesiastic, on account of certain dark tales of murder involving his nephew. Felix's route, and for that matter the entire bishopric, lay in the shadows of the cathedral of Saint-Pierre, a vast forest of Gothic arches that had been entirely rebuilt in the time of Louis XI and his successors. Although almost new, the cathedral had only a dozen more years to live: it was largely destroyed when Protestants seized the city in 1568.

The two *Teutschen* also passed close to some of the community's defining structures on their right: there was the great bridge designed in the late twelfth century by Isambert, the head of the cathedral school, and dominated by the thirty-meter-high Tour Mausifrote (whose name al-

ludes to the motto of Louis XI, "Qui s'y frotte s'y pique," touch here and
be stung). A chapel of the Virgin stood nearby. On the other bank of the
Charente stood a triumphal arch from the time of Tiberius. As an amateur archaeologist, Felix normally would have been interested in this two-
bay arch, but on this day he was in too much of a hurry. On both sides of
the bridge were landings for barges, which traveled upstream laden with
salt and downstream with wheat, wine, tiles, ceramics, and wood for barrels. Immediately north of the Tour Mausifrote stood one of the towers in
the city wall. This tower, with its views of Gothic and ancient architecture
and aquatic scenery, contained the studio of an illustrious Huguenot,
Bernard Palissy, who on this very spot had recently discovered the secrets
first of white enamel and later of colored enamels. The riverside fish market a short distance away inspired the pisciform reliefs of Palissy's colorful
dinner plates. What is more, "Master Bernard" was at the heart of an active circle of Calvinist intellectuals.[46] To exit the city one passed by the
communal building, where in 1557 Antoine Ogier (by profession a *re-
ceveur de la gendarmerie et des aides,* that is, a sort of tax collector) became
the latest in a series of mayors, all of whom had been, since 1492 and probably much earlier, nobles or magistrates.[47] Here as elsewhere, merchants
had been driven out of the highest offices. They did not lose their rights,
however: city hall stood adjacent to a series of long market buildings in
which meat, bread, and textiles were sold beneath the walls of a machico-
lated keep, the Capitole, which anchored the western wall of the ramparts. Now that Felix had made his way from one end of Saintes to the
other, he had only to exit the city through its northern gate, the Porte
Aiguière, beyond which lay the road to Poitiers.[48]

Soon the travelers would be in Poitou. But for the time being they were
still in Saintonge. Along the way, the two friends ran into an amiable fellow, a citizen of Saint-Jean-d'Angély (their next stop), who waxed ecstatic
about Felix's good looks: "You have a handsome nose," he told the young
man, who was flattered by the remark (F 273). Felix, after all, was from
Basel, where between 1517 and 1532 Hans Holbein the Younger had
painted portraits of Erasmus and the bürgermeister Jacob Meyer in
which the promontory of the nose became what André Chastel called
"the decisive argument of the face."[49]

This episode also gives us a rare record of a dialogue between Switzerland and Saintonge on the road to Poitou: the pleasant acquaintance described various particularities of the region for the two wandering
students. His account made them regret that they did not have time to
visit the free port of La Rochelle, a city of twenty thousand. It lay to the
left of their route as they deliberately headed inland toward the Loire Val-

ley and Paris, thus bidding farewell to the shimmering image of a city
already in contact with America, a city whose new and renovated streets
were lined with passageways, arcades, and houses of stone that replaced
the shanties of the previous century, as well as with fine aristocratic *hôtels*
adorned by Doric columns and bucranium friezes. The port exported
brandy (already), wine, salt, and wheat and imported spices (which now
arrived via the Cape rather than by way of Venice), drugs, sugar, textiles,
and salted fish.[50] The Catholic priests in La Rochelle were at this point
not particularly well educated (things would improve in the future), and
they found it difficult to hold their own in argument with Huguenot militants whose propaganda was readily received in this economically bustling, highly religious city.

By the time Felix reached Saint-Jean-d'Angély he had crossed not only
a linguistic but also a juridical boundary separating the south of France,
where written law prevailed, from the north, which had long been governed by customary law. Indeed, it was only in 1520 that the three orders
of Saintonge, convoked by *commissaires* of the parlement, had met in
Saint-Jean to cast the customary laws of the province into the titles and
articles of a written legal code.[51] Saint-Jean was also the place to which
another Felix, a monk by profession, had brought the head of Saint John
the Baptist, which he had stolen in Egypt, to the site of a future monastery; this was in the time of Pepin the Short. Other illustrious heads of the
decapitated (Saint Reverend, known in local folklore, and Saint Mark)
were eventually added to the collection.

In Toulouse Felix had shown an interest in reliquaries, but in Saint-
Jean he ignored the skulls of Reverend, Mark, and John the Baptist. They
were soon gone, in any case, destroyed five years later by Huguenots. Was
the loss irreparable? Actually, remains of holy personages were so abundant in Saint-Jean that in 1539 the local monks did not hesitate to trade in
holy relics, much to the horror of the parlement of Bordeaux.

March 16, 1557: the travelers covered a long (sixty kilometers) and not
very interesting stretch of road, with a stop for lunch at Villedieu
(twenty-two kilometers north of Saint-Jean-d'Angély) before continuing
on (another thirty-eight kilometers) to Chenet, where they spent the
night. This dreary day had nothing but the fatigue of travel in common
with the next, a brilliant March 17, which took our travelers to Lusignan,
the home, as Felix noted, of the fairy Melusina. Indeed, he was so impressed by this fact that he miscalculated the distances he had traveled and
misrecorded the places he had passed through.

Lusignan, a fortress that dated back to the tenth or eleventh century
and that would soon become a target of Huguenot attacks, had once be-

longed to the noble Lusignan family. In the late Middle Ages it had fallen to the English before finally being captured by the French crown. Felix had a good view of the huge castle perched on a hill (*uf dem Berg*).[52] The fairy Melusina had supposedly lived in this fortress (*gewont soll haben* [F 273]). That illustrious tourist Charles V had visited Lusignan seventeen years earlier and heard the old-wives' tales about Melusina, the fairy-serpent, stories that many people took to be literally true.[53] At the end of the century, Thomas Platter Jr. also described a part of the Loire Valley near Poitou where the nobility and country people alike took the Melusina stories absolutely seriously (T2 490ff.). At Cinq-Mars-la-Pile,[54] Thomas Jr. gazed at length on a castle so imposing that only *phées*, or fairies (the spirits or ghosts of gods), could have built it. Even the largest cannon was of no avail against these indestructible walls. One of the towers of this fortress was indeed supposed to have been the refuge or prison of a fairy, again named Melusina: the same Magical Woman about whom, according to the Platters, so much had been written, published, and printed in German as well as French since the last quarter of the fifteenth century (these publications were based on much earlier manuscripts). The two brothers took a keen interest in this body of fairy tales because they were aware of Melusina's role as patron of the building trades (T2 471). She herself was supposedly a mason capable of building walls stout enough to withstand artillery barrages—an indication that Melusina was a modern and not simply a medieval legend. In Poitou, moreover, she was reputed to have imported the green bean from America: in other words, this legendary figure was not scrapped in the sixteenth and seventeenth centuries but recycled in new myths that continued to depict her as a servant to the people of the region.

The Platters were not unaware of Melusina's totemic role.[55] Flying in the face of the Church, which held that man had been created in God's image, Melusina was part reptile, part human mother. She gave birth to quite a number of vigorous male offspring, who became the founders of aristocratic lineages for which she stood as totem, among them the Lusignans (Poitou) and the Sassenages (Dauphiné). Because the Platters were interested in Christian and pagan myths generally, they occasionally mention various other totemic mother figures. In addition to Melusina, Thomas Jr. discusses the Porcelets of Camargue, an astonishing family of aristocrats celebrated in Lorraine as well as in Provence: this noble lineage, while not actually descended from a sow (T2 134), did trace its origins back to a medieval lady whose vile behavior had led to her being compared to the "female of the boar." Her offspring, all nobles of good stock and illustrious lineage, were therefore referred to as *porcelets*, or piglets. Similar fantastic matriarchies figured in the foklore of Lorraine, a region with which the Platters had many connections.[56]

The travelers covered the distance from Lusignan to Poitiers on the afternoon of March 17. Along the way they encountered ironic peasants (did this mark the end of a certain southern cordiality?), peasants not quick to give directions but always ready to ask questions—"Oh, you want to go there? It's pretty there, I've been there. You must be foreigners. Where do you come from? The weather's nice. The road is nice. Why are you alone?"—and similar foolishness before telling the visitors what they wanted to know. The poorer peasants tilled the soil by hand, the wealthier ones with oxen. Most were armed with sticks, a few with rusty swords or *braquemarts* (short, double-bladed swords). Felix and Theodor (and Thomas Jr. later on) expressed their pleasure at the huge numbers of barely tamed donkeys, the poor man's stallions, which were bred with mares to produce Poitou mules for export as far away as Spain.

According to Thomas Jr., moreover, these donkeys earned good money, for at the rate of four or five daily matings they could make as much as four or five crowns a day, whereas their market value as reproductive males was only 120 crowns. The return on capital was therefore quite good. The two *Teutschen* also expressed surprise at the extraordinary number of birds and rabbits that the locals caught with snares or ferrets. They were entering game-rich northern France. There was no shortage of protein in the wild, although at a time of overall prosperity and demographic growth the poverty of a portion of the lower class was becoming a problem. Our travelers passed small castles that, with the king's permission, had been fortified in the fifteenth century through the addition of machicolations, watch towers, turrets, stairs, loopholes, and moldings.[57]

The years around 1557 were something of a golden age in Renaissance Poitou. By then, the Hundred Years' War was almost forgotten, but the Wars of Religion and the capture of La Rochelle in 1628 had not yet cast a dark pall over the brilliant successes of the sixteenth century. A three-year crop rotation cycle was generally observed in Poitou. This was no longer the sunny south, although the travelers did see numerous almond trees, a sign of a slightly warmer climate, perhaps, than today. Natives of the region spoke a bizarre dialect, definitely not Occitanian but not quite Parisian French. Death was still an obsession, and the old Romanesque churches in the villages were flanked by new funerary chapels built by the elite. Imperceptible but powerful transformations affected the environment: *Champagne* (open fields) gave way to *bocage* (fields enclosed by hedgerows). Noble landlords pieced together estates through entail-

ments (*retraits lignagers*) on tenant titles. They also turned recently re-
claimed heath and gorse barrens into additional enclosed fields. The
manor system had substituted a contractual (though not yet capitalist)
relationship for the whole feudal system.[58]

On the morning of March 18 our travelers were ready for a brief tour
of Poitiers. Felix climbed the towers and admired the city's gardens. It
was a large city, of fifteen to twenty thousand inhabitants, a population
that, following the painful hiatus of the Wars of Religion, would not be
equalled again until the beginning of the seventeenth century. In 1557 the
demographic pressure was apparently strong: landlords in the region
were therefore able to rack temporary tenants with high rents. Paradoxically, however, the city, which lacked an adequate building strategy and
was badly paved to boot, floated in the midst of its vast fortified enclosure: gardens and empty and cultivated fields occupied as much space
inside the walls under Henri IV as under Henri II. As for the urban landscape proper, although much of it was quite filthy, the city had been reju-
venated by the construction of *hôtels particuliers* with new facades in the
Renaissance style, with oblique windows following the turns of spiral
staircases. The city was surrounded by thick ramparts some seven kilometers in circumference and flanked by seventy towers or "turrets." Here as
elsewhere, the protective walls were paid for by local taxes on wine
known as *souquets* or *chiquets*. The protective walls were also protection-
ist, serving to enforce the payment of customs duties as much as to discourage would-be attackers. The city was strong, hence its *pucelage* (or
chastity, as the contemporary expression had it) was guaranteed. Thirteen years after Felix's visit, in 1569, the city held out against a siege by
Coligny, despite the admiral's establishment of bridgeheads on the left
bank of the Clain River. Thanks to this successful resistance, Poitiers
gained prestige as a Catholic stronghold.

No Platter could visit a city like Poitiers without contemplating at least
once the vestiges of Roman monuments. Felix probably and Thomas Jr.
certainly cast a ritual glance at the local amphitheater, which dated from
the end of the second century C.E. and was one of the most important
amphitheaters in ancient Gaul.[59] The two Platters might also have seen
sections of sewer and the crumbling arches of aqueducts that once supplied the city with water. In the sixteenth century, however, the job of
carrying water was assigned to donkeys rather than to the lead pipe of
Gallo-Roman times; the city lacked fountains and cisterns, and the water
hauled in by endless trains of donkeys had to be purchased from sup-
pliers. Indeed, one of the Platters stayed at an inn called At the Fountain,
a sign that such an obviously useful public source of water inside the city
walls was a remarkable rarity.

To jump from Antiquity to the Middle Ages and from amphitheater to princely palace, the Platters also showed great interest in the triangular castle that Jean, the duc de Berry and brother of Charles V, had built in the late fourteenth century on the edge of town, where it formed an integral part of Poitier's ramparts. Soon thereafter, the castle was immortalized by the illuminations in *Les Très Riches Heures,* a book of hours prepared at the duke's request. Jean de Berry had planned his *hôtel* to house the two hundred eighty persons of his retinue; by the time Felix visited, only a porter remained on the premises. Castles were no longer what they once had been, but the book business was booming. Felix looked up one bookseller, whose shop bore the arms of Basel on its sign; this man had once provided lodging to an old friend of the Platter family, none other than the law professor Bernhard Brand. This surgeon's son had connections with the best families among the municipal and corporate elite of Basel and Alsace. Six years earlier, Brand had temporarily left his young Swiss wife to do combat on French soil. Later, he returned to Switzerland to pursue a brilliant career, which culminated in his ennoblement by the emperor. In Poitiers, Sir Brand had been able to choose among any number of erudite hosts: in the 1550s there were three print shops in the city and twenty-three bookstores. Such a flourishing book trade was perfectly normal in an academic city boasting some two thousand students of all ages, or 12 percent of the total population. The schools were a training ground for future local officials.

While a segment of the lower class wallowed in misery, the city's officials, prosecutors, and attorneys prospered. Poitiers was primarily an administrative center, hence a city that consumed rather than produced, and a place where money was easy to come by, at least for members of the elite. To the Platters it seemed a lot like Montpellier: in the capital of Poitou the rich danced in the winter and the poor in the summer, marking, respectively, the end of cold weather with the Carnival and the happy conclusion of the harvest. Poitou's dances easily found their way to court and became the rage throughout France. And yet this city, charming in so many ways, was not ripe for antipapism. The view from here was very different from the view in Niort, a lesser regional center, where the Calvinist Reformation would soon become hegemonic. In Poitiers, clerical, judicial, and state institutions (such as the *sénéchaussée,* the *présidial,* the tax collecting and disbursing *élection,* and the *hôtel des monnaies,* or mint) had been growing since the fifteenth century and were much too strong, as in Toulouse and Bordeaux, for Protestant influence to overcome. Calvin seldom if ever prevailed in the major cities of either the north or the south of France. In Poitou, Huguenots would never be more than an influential and active minority. All in all, the local intellectuals, who included magistrates and other jurists, chose to devote themselves to belles-lettres rather than to the stringent rigors of heresy.

\* \* \*

En 1599, Thomas Jr. departed Poitiers to the northeast, crossing the Clain by way of the Pont-à-Jaubert, a skillful construction capped by a pointed rectangular turret. Once outside the city walls the rider passed through the suburbs of Montbernage and Saint-Saturnin, the traditional home of the city's poorest residents (the average tax paid in these villages in 1552 ranged from six to twenty-five sous, compared with more than a hundred sous in the better sections of the city of magistrates on the left bank of the river). Felix's younger half-brother would later wax ecstatic over the huge neolithic dolmen that the Melusinian Saint Radegund, known like her sisters in Camarge and Anjou for her prodigious ability to move rocks, had dropped here before going on to build a church for herself inside the walls. At the end of the century, Thomas Jr. would proceed from the site of the dolmen to the Loire Valley. When Felix left Poitiers on March 19, 1557, he most likely followed a similar route. On first leaving the city, Felix and Theodor were fortunate enough to be accompanied by a third man, who would remain with them part of the way, thus affording the travelers an additional "security" they had not enjoyed since leaving Narbonne.

Later that day, the three travelers reached Châtellerault, a surprising city, which had benefited in the first half of the century from the installation of a sensechal's court and from work done to improve the navigability of the Vienne downstream.[60] In 1549 Henri II had pledged the duchy of Châtellerault to the Scot James Hamilton, count of Arran, as a reward for his important services to France in connection with the marriage of Mary Stuart. The young count of Arran, heir apparent to the new holder of the title, spared no effort to convert his new ducal city to Protestantism. Henri II thus involuntarily continued his perpetual double-dealing: with one hand he persecuted the Protestants, while with the other hand he encouraged them with sometimes ill-considered support for his "faithful nobility," whether Scottish or French, which included many people sympathetic to the new thinking.[61]

\* \* \*

En route from Châtellerault to Tours, the three travelers stopped, as everyone must, to visit one of the famous "chateaus of the Loire" (or in this case, almost of the Loire). The château in question was Candé, a fine early sixteenth-century residence located between Montbazon and Tours.[62]

This manor belonged to a marquis, who had an impressive collection of helmets and shields (F 274). This collection reminds us that a substantial armaments industry, inspired by Italian examples, had grown up in Tours, not far away, in the time of Jacques Coeur and, later, of Louis XI. In 1557 important vestiges of that industry remained, and samples of its past ended up in the chateaus of the region, which functioned as museums of armament.[63] The château also had its rural aspect: the trio climbed up to a dovecote in a large turret adjacent to the castle's farm. The dovecote was of course one of the classic feudal edifices of northern France: the pigeon's guano, which after all began as seed snatched from the fields of wheat surrounding the manor, officially belonged to the lord of the land. In the course of a single day Felix thus visited the farm and the manor, both typical of the land tenure system of the Loire Valley. Such was feudalism between the Loire and the Meuse.[64]

On the afternoon of March 20, the three men drew near Tours. The (rather poor) road from Châtellerault first traversed a swampy area known as "Les Boyres" and then continued on to Tours proper. The city sat on a sort of mesa some fifteen to thirty feet above the Loire, which paralleled the river over a distance of a mile and a quarter. Standing thus between the river and the alluvial plain, it was beyond the reach of high waters. Late March marked a time of transition in this industrial city: winter, with its short evenings (owing to the expense of candles) was over, hence so was the season of low wages and unemployment.[65] "October to May was the busy season only for shippers" on the Loire, who carried wheat and wine downstream from the Beauce (on a river whose current had become stronger during the Renaissance) and then returned upstream with slate and salt, a primary source of income for the social and fiscal elite. Freshwater fish such as pike, carp, bass, barbel, eel, bream, plaice, and lamprey were on many tables, and not just during Lent.[66]

When it came to the choice of a hostelry, Felix once again had many options: a city accustomed to royal visits, Tours boasted more than fifty inns. It was the sixth largest city in France, after Paris, Lyons, Rouen, Bordeaux, and Toulouse, with a population of twenty thousand in 1557 compared with around ten thousand at the beginning of the fourteenth century. By the time of Henri II, Tours was not nearly as prosperous as it had been at its peak, but no major upheaval had accompanied its decline. For eighty years, from 1444 to 1524 (with high points and low points in between), the Valois kings had made this one of their favorite stopping places. Lately, however, they had abandoned it in favor of other cities in the vicinity and in the Paris region: *centralisation oblige*. Lovely vestiges remained, however, at the confluence of the Loire and the Cher. Of all the cities that Felix had visited, except Lyons, Tours was one of the few that deserved to be called an industrial bastion: a third of the population depended on the silk industry; embroiderers, tapestry makers, goldsmiths, and deluxe armorers also flourished. The châteaus of the Loire were the work of a distinguished elite, including the Berthelots of Azay-le-Rideau and the Bohiers of Chenonceaux. Tours was the very prototype of the good city warmed by the rays of the monarchic sun while its buildings and ramparts looked down on the peasant frogs croaking in the nearby marshlands.

In Tours, Felix briefly visited the royal castle ensconced in the northeastern corner of the old city at the southern terminus of the bridge across the Loire, which had been rebuilt at the beginning of the sixteenth century. The purpose of the reconstruction was to replace the old beams and planks that had spanned the bridge's vaulted stone arches, for these wooden components had been vulnerable to damage from floods. The château, a rectangular structure with four massive towers, dated from the end of the thirteenth century and the reign of Philip the Bold. Kings Charles VII and Louis XI had not been terribly fond of the ponderous old castle, which they used only for brief stays. According to a "Trojan" legend, the old fortress was supposed to contain the tomb of Turnus, Aeneas's unfortunate rival. This story did not displease Felix, who had a weakness for Latin pedantry. The visitor from Basel also had time to inspect the city's beautiful fountains (*die schön brunnen*). These were worth a detour: in 1506, Mayor Bohier, who belonged to one of the most illustrious local families, had decided to pipe water into the city from the Saint-Avertin spring.[67] Thanks to the construction of an underground aqueduct and a siphon beneath the Cher, it proved possible to supply four fountains inside the city walls, and the best artists of the province, including the painter Bourdichon, were summoned to work on them. One of these fountains, underwritten by Jacques de Beaune-Semblançay, still exists.

At the same time, the fish market and slaughterhouse were moved outside the space enclosed by the ramparts. Because the authorities in Montpellier had not been able to accomplish this feat, Felix's nostrils had been offended by odors from the fish market for the nearly five years that he had been a student there.

On March 21, Felix and Theodor left Tours for Amboise. By this time the travelers were in the heart of the French breadbasket, a long way from the *pays d'oc*. They marveled at the many caves they saw in the region. These were of course very ancient, but increases in agricultural output and population had bestowed a new significance on them: people were now living in them. "Riding [along the left bank of the Loire], we passed close to many cliffs pierced by cave entrances. With rocky ceilings for roofs, these caves were being used as dwellings and sealed against the elements. There were many of this type" (F 274). Some caves were also used for wine storage. The very soft subsoil could be worked easily with a pick. Vinestocks grew out of the rock around doors and windows, and smoke from fires was vented through soft chalky slopes.

The limestone hills were riddled with caves of this sort, which were not very healthy to live in. But clearly they were lived in during the reign of the Valois, as certain architectural motifs indicate. Felix's text corroborates this physical evidence, showing that the Loire Valley was comparable in this respect to various sites in Aquitaine, Scotland, Camargue, and Cornwall.[68] On the eve of the Wars of Religion, in a time of economic prosperity, people who lived in caves should not be thought of as survivals of prehistoric troglodytes. The silk trimmers of the Tours suburbs and the peasants of the surrounding countryside were simply coping with rapid economic expansion in a perfectly reasonable if not entirely comfortable manner.

In 1599, the youngest of the three Platters was curious enough about these cave dwellers to visit their homes. "In this region," Thomas Jr. wrote, "I saw countless dwellings hollowed out of rock. I went inside a number of them. People live in these places like foxes in their lairs. Most of the residents of these wretched hovels are poor peasants [*arme bauren*]. The cave openings, situated either along the road or part way up the slopes, are generally no farther than a harquebus shot apart" (T2 498). In writing these lines, had Thomas Jr. forgotten that his own father had also been a "poor peasant?"[69]

The agricultural Loire Valley, which Felix would follow upstream toward Orléans, was a little like the Comtat Venaissin of the popes, another region exploited by a growing population (population growth led, in classic fashion, to an increase in the number of farms at the expense of common lands).[70] Here, however, planting became increasingly sophisticated, as the royal court insisted on a variety of luxury products such as melons and asparagus. From Tours to Amboise and beyond, Felix, riding along the south bank of the Loire from west to east, could see the great earthen levee of 1480 along the right bank.[71] In fact, the word *levée* was of recent coinage: in the Middle Ages the river had been lined not with levees but with *turcies,* dikes constructed of pilings and gravel and planted with trees to protect the farmland while occasionally allowing water laden with fertilizing silt to pass through. After the end of the Hundred Years' War, these were gradually replaced by levees made entirely of earth, without stones, trees, or pilings. The new structures were tall enough to be insubmersible. They constituted a modern, rigid form of embankment whose purpose was to channel the Loire, facilitate navigation, and provide a commercially useful roadway along the levee's crest. In short, the *turcies* were the work of peasant artisans, whereas the levees were designed by the royal engineer. The purpose of the levees was to boost the economies of the cities, where the demand for them originated, rather than to assist in the fertilization of fields. The definitive change in vocabulary from *turcie* to *levée,* from countryside to city, occurred in the 1550s, during Felix's visit to France.

On the subject of urbanization, of such obvious importance to the prewar Valois reign, it is worth noting that the Loire Valley contained a string of cities of which Felix was able to visit only a few. The section of the valley from Tours to Orléans through which he traveled between the twenty-first and the twenty-sixth of March boasted a number of sizeable cities: among them were Gien, Sully, Jargeau, Orléans, Meung, Beaugency, Blois, and Amboise.[72] Several of these were river ports controlled by a company of merchants. Half-a-dozen of them had built stone bridges across the river. These cities were the hubs of a network of roads linked to the central axis of the river, a network whose northern and southern extremities were, respectively, Chartres and Bourges. The Loire was a royal avenue, a vehicle of Italian influences, which brought silk workshops to Tours and, before long, ceramic workshops to Nevers.[73] It was also a vehicle for Protestant ideas, which passed through the royal court. Calvin came to the University of Orléans in 1530. Extremist antipapist placards were posted in Amboise in 1534, triggering repression of Huguenots. The peasants of the Blois region refused to pay the tithe in 1542. Duc Antoine de Bourbon "infected" his duchy of Vendôme with the spirit of the Reformation. And many converts to heresy were drawn from the ranks of urban nobles, priests, professionals, artisans and merchants, lackeys and domestics. Protestant churches, or more precisely communities, were "established" in Angers in 1555, Tours and Blois in 1556, Orléans in 1557 (the year of Felix's visit), and Beaugency in 1559.[74]

On March 21, Felix and Theodor traveled from Tours to Amboise. The "road" between the two cities, along the left bank of the Loire, was mediocre, despite a cash gift from the king in 1552 for the purpose of improving the roadways in this portion of the Loire Valley. Felix approached Amboise through the area around the church of Saint-Denis, which was situated to the west of town, outside the walls, near the Hôtel-Dieu. The church, built in the twelfth century, had recently been completed by the addition of a highly ornate collateral wing, justified by the recent growth of the city's population. Adjacent to the church was a cemetery, which served not only as a place to bury the dead but also as a source of trees for the local timber industry. Felix probably stopped for lunch in the faubourg Saint-Denis, in the square of the same name, where a number of regional highways converged.

Entering the city through the Porte Saint-Denis, Felix eyed one section of the city's fortifications. Well maintained, the walls were equipped with cannon, culverins, harquebuses, and sentry boxes, which made Amboise, a city dominated by an imposing castle, one of the staunchest fortresses in the Valois kingdom.

In 1557 Amboise had a population of fifteen or sixteen hundred. It began as an island between the Loire to the north and the two branches of a southern tributary, the Amasse, at a point where the great river narrowed sufficiently to facilitate crossing by those headed from far-off Paris to Spain; the east-west route along the left bank of the river intersected the north-south route here. Inside the walls, hogs, geese, and pigeons roamed the streets. Public buildings were built of white stone and covered with slate roofs. Private houses were built of wood and had tile roofs. Thatched roofs were not allowed in the city because of the fire hazard. Amboise boasted a primary school but no *collège,* or secondary school. A print shop is mentioned in 1557, the year in which, with encouragement from Henri II, the city gave itself a mayor, who in theory was supposed to be a gentleman of *robe courte,* that is, a nobleman.

Following the course of the Loire from southwest to northeast, Felix proceeded from the Porte Saint-Denis toward the center of town along Amboise's principal thoroughfare (what is today the Rue Nationale). He passed by the Tour de l'Horloge (Clock Tower), flanked by smelly tanneries. Then, as if wandering through a ghost town, he made his way among vestiges of the early Middle Ages and even Late Antiquity, which had been refurbished during the Renaissance: he had already seen the *ecclesia* (the church of Saint-Denis); now he discovered the *vicus,* or burg, extended along the river upstream of the gate; and finally, dominating this fortified town, was the *oppidum* or *castellum,* the high château that had become, since the time of Charles VII and Charles VIII, a powerful royal palace perched on its spur of rock.

Along the way he passed the great bridge across the Loire on his left, adjacent to which stood Notre-Dame-de-Grâce (1521), one of the many new churches that Amboise owed to the artistic, religious, and demographic Renaissance. Off to the right lay the *varennes,* land that had been drained since the Hundred Years' War and made good for farming; comestibles from the Cher valley reached the city through this former wasteland, which now sported gardens and orchards producing apricots, pears, cherries, morellos, carnations, and apples. Farther east, the young man came upon the port of Petit-Fort, squeezed between the river and the castle. This was a district of recently constructed buildings: the salt warehouse and the city hall. The memoirist mentions the château, which, with its casemates, deep moats, towers, arsenal, and thick walls, was still impregnable. But Felix left it to his younger brother to elucidate, some forty years later, the intertwined philosophies of the city and the fortress: at an inn in the city Thomas Jr. saw a deck of tarot cards depicting the pope (offering his blessing), a judge (deciding a case), a woman (being unfaithful to her husband), a peasant ( providing food for others), death, and, last but not least, the king, guarding and protecting all (*ich verwahre und beschirm euch alle*) by means of his monarchical power, which was both "coactive" and military. As depicted in Amboise, then, the function of defense, or, if need be, of making war, was no longer assigned exclusively to the nobles, whose role was at most to defend the city hall, but to the sovereign, the heir to the military and protective powers once reserved to the nobility. The king and his (standing) army controlled access to that "mega-casemate," the city and castle of Amboise. The deck of tarot cards thus illustrated one aspect of the "birth of the modern state," namely, the transfer of the monopoly of the means of violence from the nobility to the monarchy.

French kings before and after Charles VIII were fond of hunting in the forests of the Loire region, and signs of this predilection were abundant throughout Amboise, from the castle above to the city below. Adjacent to the esplanade of the fortress, an elevated parade ground large enough to accommodate three hundred soldiers in formation, Thomas Jr. discovered, in the balcony of the castle church, a set of stag's antlers fifteen feet long (?) and six feet wide. The antlers had twelve points and were as thick at the root as a man's thigh. The animal that had sported this marvelous headdress had been killed during the reign of Louis XI in the the Lutzelbourg wood of the Ardenne forest.[75] The giant stag allegedly wore a golden collar on which was inscribed the name of Julius Caesar!

Thomas Jr. also had a chance to feed sugared almonds to a tame stag that he found wandering on the castle heights. The "cult of the stag" was thus firmly established in Amboise. After the death of Louis XI, Charles VIII, also a great hunter, ordered a chapel built adjacent to the esplanade in honor of Saint Hubert, the patron saint of hunters.[76] Today one can still see a Renaissance bas-relief on a door lintel depicting a stag whose antlers are adorned with a glowing cross: the animal is an avatar of Jesus. This Christianized theme was borrowed, however, from a body of not very Catholic folklore from India or perhaps Armenia. Meanwhile, another chapel in honor of Saint Hubert was erected, also in the time of Charles VIII, outside the castle in the faubourgs of Amboise, across the bridge on the right bank of the river. This is a fairly large church, with a single nave of five bays, twenty-three meters long and nineteen meters wide.

What a convergence of influences: ultramodern sugared almonds fed to a live deer; pagan legends Christianized and embodied in chapels and churches; Germanic folklore from the Ardenne combined with Christian tales of miracle-working stags associated with Saint Hubert; and, on top of all that, remembrances of ancient times in the form of a collar supposedly bearing the name of Julius Caesar, who also knew a thing or two about the secrets of the Ardenne. Amboise's memorial to the great stag and its royal hunter surely fascinated the traveling Platters, who always showed a keen interest in cultural syncretism.[77]

On the afternoon of March 21, the travelers left for Blois, which they reached that evening. As they crossed the great bridge at Blois from south to north, they witnessed something quite rare in the sixteenth century: a suicide. To be sure, in Blois, a large city of almost 20,000, this rather "modern" form of self-destructive behavior was less infrequent than in smaller towns and villages.[78] The bridge was a constant temptation in this respect. As Felix watched, a woman jumped over the guard rail and into the river (F 274). The unfortunate woman was carried downstream by the current before rescuers could fish her out. Felix jumped from his horse and ran to the victim to offer his assistance. She was still breathing. An apothecary stuffed some pills into her mouth, but she could not chew or swallow them. The "therapeutic" lozenges stuck to her throat. The woman gagged and died. Felix was outraged.

He crossed the bridge from the right bank, passing first through the southern gate, next proceeding across the central span, which was lined with sentry boxes, mills, and tripe stands, then passing through the bridge's northern gate, flanked by two towers, and continuing on into the city. Veering off to the west, he entered a section of shops, grouped by occupation: first cobblers, then money changers, then butchers.[79] Blois, the central town of an important vineyard region, was also a major livestock center, and many buildings were devoted to the processing of meat and hides. Sporadic royal visits sustained a number of luxury craftsmen: there were a dozen goldsmiths in the city, for example, along with potters, tapestry makers, enamelers, glovemakers, cutlers, cabinetmakers, and ceramicists. The city was also noted for artisans in all the latest fields: clockmaking, for example, was represented by only one craftsman in 1528 (the first of this profession to be recorded), but by 1535 there were three or four horologists in Blois, then seven under Henri II, and ultimately seventeen under Henri III.[80]

Civil architecture: the route followed by our travelers took them past Gothic edifices with turrets for stairways on the facade. In the cramped city, which lacked public spaces and abounded in culs-de-sac, these still recent buildings stood among new noble and bourgeois dwellings that reflected the stylistic evolution of the Loire châteaus: regular facades, horizontal moldings, medallions, superimposed pilasters, and "ornamental lozenges and disks."

At the base of the château (which stood in the middle of the city), Felix discovered some of the new realities of power[81] as redefined by Louis XII some sixty years earlier in accordance with Machiavelli's idea that the best fortress for a king is the affection of his people.[82] Without being too sentimental about it, we can say that Louis XII, who commanded considerable authority and a strong army and no longer had to contend with the civil wars that had hampered his immediate predecessors, was able to afford the "luxury" of razing the manorial or castellar fortifications that had separated him from his subjects in Blois. For the first time in European history, he had (to the dismay of some observers) gutted or knocked down the ramparts of his manor and surrounded it with gardens, thereby transforming the old fortress into a glorious facility for receiving foreign princes. In this vast new dwelling, largely open to the outside world, and its immediate vicinity, he had made room for hundreds of servants and thousands of soldiers, who constituted a court that surrounded, glorified, protected, and ran the apparatus of state.

From the memoirs it would appear that Felix Platter mainly contemplated the loggias of the main facade, which dated from the time of Francis I. He described the royal château of Blois as powerful (*gwaltig*), meaning not impregnable (for it no longer was) but stunning, for the sight of such impressive architecture truly amazed the visitor from Switzerland. Amboise was a place that provided military security as well as room to house a growing court. Blois now met only the second of these two criteria. On the subject of the relation of castle and city to the central power of the king, Thomas Jr. was even more outspoken than Felix: "They say that when the king prepares to go to Blois, the women of the city laugh and scratch the fronts of their bellies (*das vordertheil des bauchs*), saying, 'My goodwife, the king is coming.' And when His Majesty leaves, they change their tune and say, in all sadness, while scratching their behinds, 'My goodwife, the king is going.'"[83]

On March 22, 1557, in the early morning hours, Felix left Blois.[84] He again crossed the bridge to the south, then headed toward Orléans along the right bank of the Loire. As the afternoon wore on, the two young men, having stopped for lunch in Saint-Laurent des Eaux, reached Cléry after a ride of almost thirty miles (F 275). This was a town of 154 houses (and roughly 700 inhabitants), 97 on the south side of the main street and 57 on the north side, with rudimentary fortifications.[85] At the center of town was the church of Notre-Dame, dedicated to the Mother of God, whose heavenly grace redounded to the prosperity of the local townspeople. Felix was always careful to record details about important pilgrimage sites (*grosse wallfarten*). Of this one, he notes that a statue of the Madonna with Child had allegedly been unearthed in the vicinity in about 1280 by local peasants; similar miracles were associated with many other pilgrimage sites. This statue, carved in rustic style from a rough-hewn log, was still drawing a Brueghelesque assortment of humanity to the site in 1557: among them, the ill and the mute, devout shepherds, hermits, and devotees of divine interventions of all sorts, including maritime miracles. Indeed, the Virgin of Cléry was credited with miraculous rescues of the victims of shipwrecks, even though she was located hundreds of kilometers from the coast.

Notre-Dame de Cléry was, to believe our two Teutonic travelers, something like a great, glowing ship in the night, with hundreds of tapers and candles burning in the radiant windows of its oversized nave. The walls of the church were literally lined, according to Felix, with mementoes of miracles: wooden legs, devotional objects in wax, silver arms; relics of Louis XI and Dunois, the latter emblazoned with armorial bearings in copper; the heart of Charles VIII in a box with epitaph; stained glass, paintings, gilt objects, statues, and sculpted plaques of bronze, marble, and alabaster. Vault intersections and pillars were covered with grotesque animals. There were images of an eagle snatching a sheep, canons playing the bagpipes, four-leafed roses, acorns, teeth, pearls, spindles, scalloped niches, leafy moldings, and carved pews donated by Henri II. There were also statues of Saint Sebastian, Saint James with a pilgrim's staff, and Saint Andrew.[86] Our two Protestants turned their backs on all these marvels, just a short distance from their path, and spurred their horses on to Orléans, only fifteen kilometers away. By the time they reached the city, it was pitch-dark.

Felix and his friend spent March 23, 24, and 25 in Orléans, They stayed at the Auberge du Lansquenet, a favorite of German students. Orléans was a large city, one of the largest that Felix had visited since leaving home. Its population was by now almost thirty thousand, compared with twelve to fifteen thousand in the time of Charles VII. On the eve of the Wars of

Religion, things had been peaceful in the region since 1429, when the city was saved by Joan of Arc; the capture of Calais in 1558 and the Treaty of Cateau-Cambrésis in 1559 ended a long war that had raged elsewhere without affecting the Loire Valley. From Louis XI on, the last Valois kings had collaborated in extending the city's fortifications, doubling the developed or developable area. Streets were relatively broad. Planning far in advance of other cities had endowed Orléans with numerous squares, including the *places du Martroi, de l'Etape,* and *de la Porte-Renard,* which became marketplaces for wheat, wine, and vegetables.

Orléans was one city that Felix felt he had to visit. It was home to a substantial group of his compatriots, some two or three hundred Swiss and German students. Most of these were law students who had arrived in town with a knowledge of Greek and Latin. Except for two from Saxony, all of the twenty or so students from beyond the Vosges and the Rhine whose birthplace or original residence Felix mentions came from the western part of German-speaking Europe: from Alsace, Zurich, Augsburg, Zweibrücken, and Bavaria—the Platters' regular haunts (F 276). A few were noble or on the way to becoming noble. Others had itinerant pasts typical of the Renaissance: Johannes Achilles Yllisung, from Augsburg, had been a student at the Universities of Padua in 1552, Freiburg in 1555, and Orléans in 1557. In 1572 he became an imperial councillor and bailiff in Swabia.

In Orléans, moreover, Felix was reunited with his childhood friend Sigmund von Andlau, now twenty-one years old. Felix had known Sigmund as a boarder in the Platter household twelve years earlier, at a time when both boys were intoning Latin verses (F 86, 87, 275). As a temporary resident of Orléans, Sigmund did not hesitate to spend money to "roll out the red carpet" for his friend. It was no more than Felix was due: as a student in Montpellier, he had always seen to it that Swiss visitors were received properly and had spent lavishly to keep his guests in drink. In Orléans, Sigmund arranged a splendid banquet (*panquet*) with other Germans, "who came from various social estates, high and low" (*von hoch und nider standts*). The meal included all sorts of preserves, a favorite of the time and the subject of a substantial portion of Olivier de Serres's *Théâtre d'agriculture.* Felix washed these sweets down with excessive amounts of an Orléans wine of which he thought quite highly (the city and nearby farmland were full of vineyards that produced quality wines, and vintners from the surrounding plains came to learn how it was done). There was a further "digestive" complication, however: it was Lent, and von Andlau's lavish banquet featured seafood that had gone bad. Felix had already consumed more than his share of spoiled fish during his long weeks of travel, which coincided with the forty-day Lenten fasts prescribed by the Catholic Church. The visitor spent the night of March 23–24 puking his guts out. By morning he was suffering the tortures of a martyr.[87] His German friends whispered that he might not survive. But the prospect of a midday meal put him back on his feet. Later, his illness forgotten, he went dancing at the home of German students. Before an audience of admiring Teutons he performed a series of typical French (*welsche*) dances. In gratitude the German colony lavished still further attentions on the travelers, to whom they lent harps. With these instruments the visitors became, for the next forty-eight hours, the official musicians of the German contingent in a city noted for its strolling fiddlers' guild. Foreigners though they were, the German students were an integral part of the University of Orléans, one of the foremost institutions of higher learning in France; they constituted one of its "nations."

The university depended on a network of print shops and libraries. It also relied on official and unofficial groups of legal specialists, scholars in various fields, and neo-Latin poets. In a city where the Reformation was the almost legitimate offspring of humanism, Calvin and Théodore de Bèze made brief appearances. Orléans, an intellectual way station between Paris and Lyons, was home to many cultivated men, and humanism's raucous squabbles with scholasticism continued throughout the century. A figure like Thomas Platter Sr., who taught courses in Hebrew and Greek for so much a head in Basel, would not have been out of place in Orléans, where one found many itinerant Hellenists competing for pupils and living on what they earned by giving private or group lessons. German-speaking Lutheran students felt at home among the native Huguenots, who were firmly ensconced in Orléans (but remained discreet about their presence, since it was still possible for Protestants to be burned at the stake).

The local German community squired Felix about the city's major tourist sites. Foremost among them was the summer meeting place of nude swimmers: the bridge across the Loire, with its statue of Joan of Arc. In fact, this was not a single statue but a group of several figures installed between 1502 and 1508. The ensemble contained a crucified Christ, a Virgin, a king (probably Louis XII), and the Maid of Orléans with her hair down and decked out with sword, spurs, lance, helmet, and plume. Felix had little time for the patriotism of the French, however; his primary interest was in ancient art objects. He therefore described the heroic young woman (about whom he knew nothing) as an "antiquity" carved in stone. He was mistaken on two counts: this image of Joan had actually been cast in bronze relatively recently, at the beginning of the sixteenth century.

From the bridge the city could be taken in at a single glance: in the center loomed the Tour Neuve, overlooking the ramparts; on the far right, the Tour de la Brebis, which commanded the southeastern section of wall; in the distance, toward the northeast, the church of Notre-Dame-du-Chemin, near the Porte de Bourgogne, which controlled access from the east; and finally, in the center background, loomed the Sainte-Croix cathedral, which had been renovated at the end of the fifteenth century. With Felix in the forefront, the group of young Germans visited the cathedral and were entranced by the sight of a holy measuring rod, which indicated the exact size of Christ's body and was revered as if it were a relic of Christ himself. As always when it came to relics, this elicited from Felix a brief outburst of Platterian (or Calvinist or pre-Voltairian) irony, after which he and his new friends climbed the stairs of the cathedral's bell tower, a sturdy structure completed relatively recently, in 1511. After a dizzying climb to the base of the lead-clad spire, the young man from Basel faced a shaky ladder leading to the very pinnacle. Some of his companions made the ascent, but the ladder swayed disconcertingly back and forth. Felix, looking down, saw the narrow alleyways of the cathedral quarter filled with people. A man accustomed to gentle terrain, he was gripped by panic. He climbed back down, unscathed by the taunts of his comrades.

\* \* \*

On the morning of March 26, Felix left Orléans and headed straight north through the forest of Orléans, where hogs were raised on acorns.[88] Before departing, he had purchased a new saddle for his horse, the old one having rotted (F 277). Like their compatriots in Languedoc, the Germans from the university formed an escort (*gleit*) and accompanied the travelers on the first twenty miles of their journey, until they stopped for lunch. Before setting out, they had signed Felix's notebook (*stammbiechlin*), which was filled with signatures of people he had met, sayings, inscriptions, and dedications.

\* \* \*

On leaving the forest, still headed north, the travelers discovered a region that was densely populated, or rather repopulated after having been reduced to near wasteland in the 1440s by war with England. In 1557, the rural population density increased, as one approached Paris, from 65 or 70 per square kilometer to 120 on the immediate outskirts of the capital.

These densities declined somewhat in the seventeenth century. Along the way Felix did not see a single donkey, but he did notice four-wheeled wagons with axles made of metal rather than, as in the past, of wood. Toward the end of the century, Thomas Jr. would follow the same route in a carriage traveling on paved road. On both sides of the road, peasants were busy with the spring planting, primarily of oats, as well as with various chores connected with fallow land. Fallow fields were not particularly demanding and could be maintained by allowing sheep to graze at the rate of one or two per hectare. The travelers also saw cows, mostly brown and black, some with light spots. Near Etampes, the grain fields (of winter wheat and spring oats) were separated by plots of garlic and onion. And there were some notable absences: no field beans or lentils and not even any sainfoin (yet), despite the market for horses in the capital. The slopes, covered with vinestocks, offered a sampling of the wines of the Paris region, which at the time was one of the most important wine-producing regions in the world (these vineyards have since vanished). The 350,000 residents of the capital had to be kept supplied. There were a few vast, open fields, but farming on this scale was still rare. Other fields were much smaller: some plots were in the shape of long, narrow strips, eighty meters long by five meters wide, and laid out like a parquet. Others were little more than small beds of wheat or vines, endlessly repeated. The mediocre wine produced by these vineyards rarely lasted more than a few months, and the yield was apparently miserable (ten to twenty liters per hectare).[89]

The villages of the region, composed of blocks of houses built close together, had replenished their population to the point where small, isolated farms began to spring up on the land between villages from the middle of the sixteenth century on. Rural churches had been restored or rebuilt over the previous century; the ogival and flamboyant styles still dominated. Local sculptors had carved countless altar tables and tombstones in these modest sanctuaries, a sign of the relative prosperity of a generation of farmers now dead; these were peasants who had enriched themselves under Francis I, when the rural economy was thriving. Clear glass windows flooded church interiors with light, helping those parishioners who could read to decipher the prayers in the relatively inexpensive missals that were Gutenberg's gift to the people of the Beauce and the Ile-de-France. Many of these peasants were devout Catholics, despite some Protestant influence in the region. Memories of the great drought of 1556 remained vivid; amid a forest of crosses under leaden skies, men from the villages had gone in procession to the Parisian shrine of Saint Genevieve to pray for rain.

In March of 1557 the road was crowded with prosperous peasant couples on foot, on horseback, and in wagons. The farmer "wore a great-coat that hung down to the middle of the leg" while allowing his carefully buttoned doublet to show through; his wife "wore a flat hood or bonnet tied at the neck," a rosary on her belt, and a gown and bodice adorned "with gorget and velvet trim." He was on his way to Paris to sell a load of grain and hay after making his way to market through traffic jams on the rue Saint-Jacques. His wife had many things on her mind: "cows, chickens, dairy, oven, cellar, bedroom, linen, sheep, garden, clothing, kitchen utensils." Such farmers formed what was almost a hereditary caste; they were nearly totally endogamous and lived on substantial two-plow farms of roughly seventy hectares per household. These entrepreneurs of the land were a prolific group: the women married young, were well fed, and lived longer than did female workers or "manual laborers."

In social terms, these well-to-do farmers rented their land from a class of landlords, including *grands seigneurs* such as the abbots of monasteries, illustrious magistrates, and other public officials—in short, the *Who's Who?* of Paris—together with a certain number of rural nobles with substantial landholdings.

Eager to reach Paris, Felix temporarily set aside the curiosity that had led him to spend several days with the humanist *grand seigneur* Pierre Danès when both men were traveling down the Rhône Valley. Only a week before his arrival in the Beauce, this same curiosity had impelled him to visit the Château de Candé, a veritable museum of modern weaponry. Between Orléans and Paris, however, Felix did not stop at a single one of the unpretentious manors that dotted his route, manors that housed the *hobereaux,* or country squires, of Ile-de-France, who either cultivated their fields *par valets* (that is, with hired hands) or leased their land to tenant farmers. Had he visited one of these lesser aristocratic manors, he would not have found the décor any different from that of a "substantial" farmer's farmhouse. In both he would have found two bedrooms, a downstairs room, and furniture of oak or walnut: "beds, tables, chests, benches, stools, and a buffet or sideboard." The real social distance between the "commoner" and the "man of privilege" revealed itself in the stable: a commoner might own four horses averaging seven to eight years of age, whereas the squire might own seven horses: as in the thirteenth century, every noble wanted to be a *chevalier,* or horseman (knight).

On March 27 the travelers reached Etampes. They passed through this long "street-village," actually a city of four thousand, repopulated in the period 1480–1520 by immigrants from both the north and the south (Au-

vergne, Limousin). Since 1514 or 1517 the city had had a dynamic municipal council, which took the lead in building new schools and hospitals.
Having achieved official status toward the end of the reign of the Louis
XII, the community sought and obtained designation as a *bonne ville,* a
recently created status that bestowed the privilege of electing aldermen
(from the beginning of the reign of Francis I) and a mayor, chosen as
usual from the ranks of the *noblesse de robe,* the royal magistrates and officeholders. Felix and Theodor followed the Orléans-Paris or Bordeaux-
Paris road through Etampes, the same route that pilgrims on their way to
Santiago de Compostela followed in the other direction. At the Porte
Saint-Martin, where northbound tourists entered the old city, the two
young men paid the traditional *droit de barrage,* or toll levied on riders as
well as merchandise. After that, they simply followed the city's traditional
central axis (their passage was marred by a few spills from their mounts):
first the especially tortuous ruelle d'Enfer, then the rue des Cordeliers,
which passed by the thirteenth-century Franciscan monastery. From
there, through the intersection with the rue de la Manivelle, they entered
the rue basse de la Foulerie (the name evokes textile manufacturing), then
rues Saint-Santoine, de la Juiverie, and de la Tannerie, and finally rue
Evezard, which led to the "exit," the Porte Evezard, flanked by two pep-
permill towers with loopholes for cannons. Were these ancient popguns
intended to ward off potential British or imperial attackers from the
north? Once outside the walls, Felix and his companion rode along the
port of Etampes, which had been growing since 1490, reflecting the prosperity of the new century. Barges that drew as much as three feet of water
and were all too prone to running aground in poorly dredged channels
choked with mud, filth, and sand (the famous sand of Etampes, prized by
glassmakers) stopped here to take on hundreds of sacks of grain for Paris.
Occasionally one saw an intellectual perched atop these sacks, taking advantage of the calmness of the voyage to finish a book. After passing the
leper colony, which by this time actually held only a few inmates, most of
whom were shamming, Felix, with a good lunch in his belly, was on his
way to Paris.

Etampes left our young man above all with the memory of a dozen
churches and bell towers carefully restored over the previous two generations. He also remembered (on his left as he rode through the city) a large
tile-roofed castle with a projecting keep known as La Guinette, which
appears in *Les Très Riches Heures* painted by the Limbourg brothers in the
previous century. Felix actually caught only a brief glimpse of "down-
town" Etampes and the new residences erected there for the royal mistresses of Francis I and Henri II.[90]

After leaving Etampes and riding through forests and vineyards, our travelers came to the populous farming region around Arpajon (which at the time was called Châtres). To the east of their route lay plains planted with wheat or oats, and just to the right stood a leper house known as Saint-Blaise, close to but outside of Arpajon. This was similar to the leprosarium they had passed on the way out of Etampes. Châtres offered the new arrivals the spectacle of a city whose ramparts had been refurbished over the past thirty years through the addition of new walls, towers, moats, gates, and drawbridges. It was a small town of at most 1,200 to 1,500 people, short of the 3,000 needed to qualify as a *bonne ville*. The influence of the municipal authorities, if any, seems to have been negligible. By contrast, that of the great lords, powerful investors, and rebuilders was apparently considerable in the eyes of the Eternal: among them were not only court aristocrats like Malet de Graville, who came from the *noblesse d'épée,* but also men like the Villeroys, typical of the new elite of *secrétaires d'Etat.*

Châtres gave these families a great deal and also owed them a great deal. Entering the city through a gate called, logically enough, the Porte d'Etampes, our travelers simply had to follow the one major street, which led (regional centralism *oblige*) to the Porte de Paris. The street was flanked by houses, including many inns (owing to the proximity of the capital). Even though these buildings were situated inside the walls of the fortified city, they were surrounded by shrubs, flowers, and vegetable gardens. Proceeding north past the almost new market shed, built after urban fairs were authorized in 1490 with a roof supported by twelve chestnut pillars, the two men crossed the bridge over the Orge. They glanced briefly at the urban castle of the Malet de Graville family, patrons of the local clergy as well as the wine market. The château looked out on a park of no less than seven hectares, as large as the courtyard of the Palais-Royal in Paris today. There was no shortage of green space in Châtres-Arpajon. Finally, close to the Porte de Paris stood the church of Saint-Clément. Once Romanesque, the church had been turned into a charnel house by the English (who burned nearly a thousand people alive inside it in 1360, much as the Nazis did in Oradour in the 1940s). In 1510 the church was rebuilt in the late Gothic style at the behest of the local lords.

Heading due north out of the city, Felix and Theodor rode along the park of the château de Chanteloup, a gift from Francis I in 1518 to Nicolas de Neuville, *seigneur de* Villeroy and *secrétaire des Finances,* in exchange for another house whose salubrious climate suited the king's mother, Louise de Savoie. Felix did not have time to visit Chanteloup, but his younger brother Thomas Jr. was in less of a hurry: on his way to the capital later in the century, he found a few hours to visit the splendid gardens adjacent to the manor. The youngest of the Platters admired the multicolored depictions of myths from Ovid's *Loves* that were created with flowering and leafy plants on the park's walls and in its flower beds. He especially enjoyed the walkways covered with thick sand from the quarries of Etampes. This made it possible to tour the garden even on a rainy day without muddying one's soles or heels (*man auch regenwetterszeit gar trocken darinnen gehen kan* [T2 543]). Thus the sandy walkways, which were carefully raked to remove all footprints, were a favorite with early modern gardeners not only because they were pleasant to look at but also because they were convenient for visitors.[91]

\*     \*     \*

On the afternoon of March 27, after riding for a time past vineyards to his right and the edge of a forest to his left,[92] Felix arrived in Montlhéry, a community of a thousand to twelve hundred people situated on a truncated spur of land dominated by a castle spread out along the northern slope of a vine-covered hill and equipped with a series of four enclosures culminating in a hundred-foot-high keep with a conical roof of slate and lead. The two riders entered the city through the Porte Baudry and then followed the Grand-Rue and the rue de la Chapelle, lined with inns and a dozen or so bakeries, to the Porte de Paris at the other end of town. The shops along the rue aux Juifs and the rue du Soulier-de-Judas, populated by drapers, corn chandlers, weavers, and grocers who shared a network of interconnected underground storage cellars, held little appeal for Felix. A city of fairs and markets that received a good deal of Paris traffic, Montlhéry in the mid-sixteenth century was afflicted by numerous "ills, robberies and larcenies by bad fellows," bold as brass, "men deliberately abiding in the fields," vagrants "who frequently assaulted, robbed, beat, and insulted" the natives.[93] Although this description may have been exaggerated, it gives us an idea of the state of mind that led the residents of Montlhéry to ask the king in 1540 for permission to spend their own money to enclose the city with a system of walls and barbicans—yet another enclosure. Despite the vigorous efforts of the local *prévôté*, crime was not entirely a myth. Late in the century, Thomas Platter Jr. would complain that one night as he lay sleeping not far from Montlhéry, he was robbed by a roving fiddler (T2 546).

## CHAPTER EIGHT

# The Spring of 1557: Anabasis

O n the afternoon of March 27, the two friends left Montlhéry and proceeded to Paris along the interminable rue Saint-Jacques (*durch S. Jacob Stross* [F 278]). Along the way they passed through Longjumeau and Berny and followed the triumphal route through the vineyards, a road that followed the same course as today's suburban rapid transit line, the Ligne de Sceaux. This brought them to the heart of the largest city on the continent, the "Great Beast," which had only recently displaced the Loire Valley as the seat of the Capetian kingdom.

From southern Paris the two visitors gazed upon the distant hill (*berg*) of Montmartre, atop which stood a Benedictine convent (*Kloster*) housing some sixty nuns, who had once (before 1503) been a subject of scandal but were now "reformed" in the Catholic sense of the word. This convent looked out over a large vineyard, beside which, halfway up the hill, stood the humble chapel in which Ignatius Loyola founded the Society of Jesus in 1534.[1] The big city seemed to be surrounded by windmills (*windt mülenen*). These were administered by a highly diverse group of millers dominated by a handful of wealthy flour wholesalers.[2] These businessmen played an essential role in feeding the capital's 350,000 people. Paris, already the most populous city in Christendom, was still growing. The two young men rode quickly through the rapidly expanding faubourg Saint-Jacques. Laid out in a thin line from north to south, the faubourg followed the street from which it took its name (like many another suburb or single-street village).[3] The travelers passed the chapel of Saint-Jacques-du-Haut-Pas on their left and proceeded on through the Porte Saint-Jacques adjacent to the recently rebuilt Convent of the Jacobins, which housed several dozen monks; a steady stream of new vocations kept the ranks replenished. The rue Saint-Jacques followed the route of the ancient Roman road from Paris to Orléans. This "vital artery" was lined with tall buildings crowded close together, along with bookstores and print shops. The inhabitants of the *faubourg* were people of modest station. Upon passing through the gate, Felix and Theodor found themselves in the university quarter on the south bank of the river. The Sainte-

Geneviève *quartier*—the Latin Quarter par excellence—stood off to their right; the Saint-Séverin *quartier* to their left. In between, still on the rue Saint-Jacques, they registered at the Auberge de la Croix, which they, translating into German, referred to as *Zum Kreutz*.

At this inn our travelers met the first of a long series of *Teutschen*, a certain Jochum, who was in fact a prominent citizen of Strasbourg by the name of Johann von Mundolsheim (F 278). That night (March 27) they looked around the city for the first time, just to get a feel for its "ambiance." Paris thrived, of course, on the centralized administrative apparatus of the monarchy. France was an *Etat d'offices*, or state of offices, typified by the Parlement and Chambre des Comptes, whose size, in terms of number of offices, increased steadily under Henri II.[4] It was also an *Etat de finance*, embodied in the coffers of the Royal Treasury at the Louvre, coffers that were empty more often than they ought to have been. His Majesty, in flesh and blood, might, if it pleased him, make war in the northeast or go hunting in the forests of the Loire, yet Paris could still say: *L'Etat, c'est moi*. This was especially true since the return from captivity in Spain of Francis I, who spent more and more of his time residing along the banks of the Seine in and around the capital, a choice symbolized by the commencement, in 1528, of work on the Château de Madrid in the game-rich forests of the Bois du Boulogne; in this Francis was followed by his son Henri. In the 1520s the whole system of royal finance was restructured; the decade was also decisive for Paris in other ways. The first serious plans for the capital were drawn up in these years: the celebrated woodcut by Truschet and Hoyau, an excellent map conserved among the papers of the University of Basel, has survived as a later reflection of these early plans; it has been dated, *a posteriori, circa* 1550. The resumption of economic and demographic growth in Paris probably began in the second half of the 1440s. By 1500 the city boasted a population of 200,000. By the time of Felix's visit, it had grown to 350,000: the pre-plague, pre-war high-water mark of the fourteenth century had been surpassed once and for all. Paris also left the cities of Italy in its dust: Naples had a population of 212,000 in 1547; Venice, 150,000 in 1557; Milan, 180,000 after 1550. And forget London, whose population rose from 60,000 in 1520 to 200,000 in 1600 but still, despite an extraordinary rate of growth, lagged far behind the capital of France.[5]

"Peace" had a major impact on the specific form that the growth of Paris took—this despite the fact that France was in fact perpetually at war. Its conflicts were modest ones, however, relegated to the borders of Italy, Lorraine, and "Belgium" and involving smaller armies than would be engaged in the next century. Between the Treaty of Crépy-en-Laonnois (1544) and the French debacle at Saint-Quentin (August 1557, not long after Felix's visit), Paris had nothing to fear from foreign invaders. In March and April of 1557, however, the city was still quite tranquil: no one had an inkling of the catastrophe looming on the horizon (the magnitude of which should not be exaggerated, however).

On the evening of his arrival (March 27), Felix took his first stroll along the banks of the Seine and was struck by the extraordinary array of boats of every description. Paris in those days looked more like Bordeaux than like Limoges or Clermont. The sea was not far off. Fish from the ocean made the journey posthaste, within twenty-four hours if possible; seafood was rarely spoiled when it reached the market stalls of the capital. The streets and quays along the river were a vital, almost tumultuous place, with some 5,000 porters, longshoremen, and warehousemen and some 10,000 water carriers to keep things moving. Poverty was everywhere; it spread as rapidly as wealth (at times fabulous), as wages in some trades went into sharp decline after the turn of the sixteenth century. The government had a hand in this: if the Renaissance monarchy took a relatively relaxed attitude toward assemblies of its provincial estates, it kept a close watch on the activities of the capital's aldermen.[6] In 1533, moreover, the monarchy initiated work on a major public project in the Italian style, with the construction of the Hôtel de Ville. Such public works would continue to the end of the century.

The *prévôt de marchands*, equivalent to a mayor, was generally (despite a 1547 edict to the contrary) a man of the *robe*, for the municipal government of Paris, like that of Montpellier and Béziers, was dominated by royal officeholders. The king kept a close watch on this official: since the days of Etienne Marcel (1315–58), the agents of the central government looked upon Paris as a potential powderkeg. The *prévôt* was elected, not without royal interference, by extremely limited bodies of electors. He presided over representatives of the city's sixteen *quartiers*, the famous "Seize" [Sixteen], who took on real political importance only in the last two decades of the sixteenth century (during the Wars of Religion). For the time being, the Sixteen were on their best behavior. The big problem of the moment was the growing Protestant influence among the citizens, *robins*, and nobles of the city. This would cause something of a stir five months after Felix's visit, in early September 1557, when 350 Protestants gathered on the rue Saint-Jacques, not far from the inn where Felix had stayed, behind the Sorbonne. They were arrested in the early morning hours of September 5 by the royal prosecutor of the Châtelet following a night of unpleasantness that might be likened to a minor pogrom. Among those imprisoned were several Swiss, who were soon released at the request of the Swiss cantons; some of them had spent time with Felix during his visit.

On the morning of March 28, Felix Jr., always ready to move on, decided to leave the Auberge de la Croix. Perhaps it was too expensive for him. In any case, he and his friend moved to the Mortier d'Or, a boarding house of dubious reputation on the rue Saint-Jacques. Despite the sonorous name, the reality was sordid. The two young men shared a minuscule room with one bed above a pharmacy (the *mortier*, or mortar, of the name referred to the pharmacist's mortar and pestle). There they remained for the next three weeks, until April 21. From this convenient base they fanned out to explore the various quarters of Paris, on the Left Bank, the Right Bank, and the Ile de la Cité. They soon made a new acquaintance: Carl Utenhove, originally from Flanders but German-Swiss by adoption (the visitors remained in the German orbit). Utenhove came from a good humanist family in Ghent. He called frequently on his two friends at the Mortier d'Or. To do so, he had to climb the spiral staircase to their room. Utenhove's family had connections to Erasmus as well as to the University of Montpellier.[7] The young man flirted with the neo-Latin muse. The Platters knew him well, because he had been a boarder in Thomas Sr.'s Gymnasium in Basel. Later, he continued his studies in England, where he prepared himself for a career in teaching and the study of Greek, which eventually took him to Cologne. Thus, in the person of Utenhove, the Flemish diaspora with its British and German offshoots touched the life of Felix Platter. The Flemish presence in Paris was even greater than in Montpellier.

At the Mortier d'Or, our Swiss traveler saw yet another (temporarily) uprooted countryman: Balthasar Krug, the son of the bailiff and half-brother of a future bürgermeister, also a Krug—the megalomaniac mayor who would become an important associate of the Platter family in years to come. Balthasar was an odd fellow, sociable and resourceful, with more friends in Paris than financial resources. Felix also met the French king's Swiss guards, whose undoubted Protestantism apparently bothered no one. The guards' headquarters when it came to reveling was the Auberge du Mouton, it, too, on the rue Saint-Jacques. One of the guards, from Zurich, had married a Frenchwoman, who invited Felix for an evening of drink. Another, a tall, slender fellow from Basel by the name of Jockel, had a pain in his groin about which he consulted with the traveling medical man, who offered his sage advice. Was this the same man who died of a groin problem a few days later?

Did Felix meet only Germans and their associates in Paris? Not exactly: he did also see Frenchmen, but, as was often the case with him, they were doctors, people who had things to teach him or who might be of use to him professionally. This was true in Montpellier and even in Lyons, where, shortly after arriving in France, Felix had been received by Dr. Rondelet. In Paris his first "medical" visit was to Jacques Goupyl, known as Gubillus, a Hellenist from the Poitou and professor at the Collège Royal who was responsible for translations of ancient Latin and Greek texts on medicine, botany, and zoology, including works of Alexander of Tralles, Aretaeus of Cappadocia, Dioscorides, Galen, and Paul of Egina, as well as Ausonius from the literary realm and Alessandro Piccolomini from the Italian. Most of these translations, particularly those on medical subjects, appeared prior to 1557, so that Felix would have known them. Even more important, Goupyl had the wisdom to publish, in 1554, a convenient student handbook containing the works of Rufus of Ephesus on the various parts of the body, the kidneys, the bladder, purgations, and menstruation in women.[8] Felix found this compendium quite handy seven years letter when a plague struck Basel in 1564: on July 26 of that year, Thomas Platter discovered a bubo on his right knee, as well as a boil, which Felix noted when he removed, without shame, his father's pants (F 435). He treated the older man with pills based on one of Rufus's formulas, a mixture of two-thirds aloe and one-third myrrh dissolved in wine. His brother-in-law, the surgeon Daniel Jeckelmann, lanced the boil without fear of contagion. Thanks to the ministrations of his son and his son's wife's brother, Thomas Platter was back on his feet a few weeks later.

Felix also met Louis Duret, a student of philosophy who hailed originally from the valley of the Loire and was destined for a brilliant career as physician to kings and professor at the Collège Royal. A good speaker who was popular with students as well as a competent specialist in the works of Hippocrates and Arab medicine, Duret was reputedly a traditionalist.[9] The same could not be said of Jean Fernel, a man of modernity, or, more precisely, of Antiquity, and therefore hostile to the intermediary glosses of Muslim physicians, to which he referred as "Arabic garbage" (sic). Felix's encounter with Fernel, a Parisian by predilection who became, in the year of Felix's visit, Henri II's personal physician, would prove crucial. It supplied Felix with arguments that he would use against the academics of Basel a few months later, when he defended his thesis on the controversial issue of native heat.[10] The fact that Felix was received without difficulty by three of Paris's most prominent physicians (Duret, Goupyl, and Fernel) suggests that he arrived on the banks of the Seine with a certain reputation, which persuaded his older colleagues to open their doors to him. Perhaps he carried letters from Dr. Saporta, his patron in Montpellier, who was well-known in medical circles in France and throughout Europe. Be that as it may, the religious scrutiny of the *sorbon-nard* theologians weighed heavily on the University of Paris, including the faculty of medicine. Felix was unable to find the climate of free research, open to Jews and Huguenots and ready to engage when necessary in dissections, that he had experienced during his five years in Montpellier. For any Protestant worthy of the name, the Sorbonne could only be the devil's own synagogue, an abominable intellectual bordello, the gateway to hell.[11] But Felix seemed not to care.

Dr. Jean Fernel, Welch though he was, had a Swiss cousin, Andreas Wechel, a bookseller and printer, who agreed to show Felix the interesting sites of the *Université, Cité,* and *Ville*. Andreas was the son of Christian (or Chrétien) Wechel, a Swiss native who had set up in business as a printer in the Ile-de-France and who had published, during the reign of Francis I, hundreds of scholarly works for the French market.[12] As successor to his father (who had himself succeeded Conrad Rosch, a Swiss-Parisian bookseller *"à l'écu de Bâle"* from 1515 to 1526),[13] Andreas continued a long Parisian publishing tradition. He liked to welcome foreigners to the city. His house was a meeting place for visiting Protestants from across the Vosges and the Rhine. Though a notorious Huguenot, the younger Wechel escaped persecution for a time, but in the end his luck ran out: his inventory of books was burned in 1569; in 1572, after the Saint Bartholomew's Day massacre, he was forced to flee to Frankfurt, where he lived out his days as a bookseller. In 1557, with this adoptive Parisian as a guide, Felix explored the vicinity of the rue Saint-Jacques and the banks of the Seine. One of their first excursions took the two men to the Louvre: King Henri II was absent that day because he was off visiting his estate at Villers-Cotterêts (which Felix in his *Tagebuch* spelled Ville-Accoustrée).

Henri II loved his grand château at Villers-Cotterêts. Although of recent construction, the castle was quite traditional, rectangular in shape with a long interior corridor, slanted roof, tall rectangular chimney stacks, park with evergreen shrubbery, and lanes lined with hazelnut trees, complemented by an *orangerie* and a wooded area for hunting.[14] The king had not gone to his palace in the northeast just to relax. He also wanted to keep an eye on the work of his masons (the château was still under construction). Most of all, he wanted to inspect for himself the next likely theater of military operations, where his prospects did not look good. The Truce of Vaucelles (February 1556) had just been denounced, and France had lightheartedly declared war once again on the Spanish Hapsburg Philip II, the son and partial heir of Charles V—that ever-troublesome House of Burgundy again! Having made a rather bizarre marriage with Mary Tudor, Philip II had secured the paradoxical support of the English for several years. This was a sobering prospect for Henri II, for in the face of the Madrid-Brussels-London axis that was thus created, France's northern borders were virtually undefended: François de Guise had just marched off to Italy with an army of thirteen thousand men, leaving the heartland vulnerable to attack. The remainder of the French army numbered only twenty to twenty-five thousand men, concentrated in Attigny (now Ardennes) and commanded by the not very capable Montmorency. This rump of an army was not up to the task of fending off Philip II's horde of forty-four thousand men under the able Emmanuel Philibert of Savoy. To make matters worse, the Hapsburg commander had it in for the French, who in 1536 had stripped him of his hereditary duchy in the northern Alps and Piedmont. Here was an opportunity for revenge. Philip II, sure of himself, took up a position in Cambrai and bided his time.[15]

In Villers-Cotterêts it was easier for Henri II to prepare to meet the peril than it was in Paris. The French disaster at Saint-Quentin in August would show how inadequate his preparations were, however. In early June, Henri held a council of war at Villers-Cotterêts to consider the British problem.[16] Although the whole situation was already clear by March, Felix does not breathe a word of it in his diary, which contains observations he wrote down at the time and recopied half a century later. Was this ignorance? Certainly. But it was also, no doubt, indifference, silence, and prudence.

Regardless of the king's absence, the Swiss visitor took an interest in the Louvre. Since 1528, when Francis I made a definitive decision to return to Paris, this palace had become a significant center of power; what is more, it was close to the Parlement of Paris, which did nothing to diminish its importance. The authorities reacted accordingly. The huge central keep was razed and replaced by a paved courtyard, now the Cour carrée. Like Blois before it, the Louvre began to shed its fortresslike character. It became a relatively open palace, more or less integrated into the city's ramparts and taking the friendly disposition of the capital's population for granted. The quays along the Seine had recently been straightened, paved with stone, and made fit for wagons. They ran along the edge of the palace, where horses once drank from troughs in the berm bordering the muddy towpath. Pierre Lescot and Jean Goujon were at work on the nascent Cour carrée, whose west wing was just being completed at the time of Felix's visit.[17]

On his way to and from the palace, the young man mingled with the population of the *quartier:* washerwomen, goldsmiths, leather workers, fishmongers, and courtiers with pointy mustaches and plumed hats. Despite the fact that the king was frequently out of Paris, the Louvre in its new form was by mid-century a major component of the machinery of power. Its transformation came after the Forbidden City of Peking and the Kremlin, two enclosed palaces that dated from the fifteenth century, but before the Escorial, a semi-abbatial residence that would be partly open to the public, as Henri II's palace already was.

After touring the seat of government embodied in the long building along the Seine, Felix went on to inspect the colleges of the university and the city's churches (*vil colegia, vil kilchen*). His German-speaking friend Wechel made up for his lack of a tourist guidebook. Their round of churches was purely for touristic purposes, since neither man cared for the papist atmosphere of these religious edifices. The tour sites ranged from the brand-new rood-screen of Saint-Etienne-du-Mont to the vast construction site at Saint-Eustache, where work was proceeding on the choir chapels and the final bays of the nave. The pace of construction matched the growing animation of the surrounding market district, Les Halles. Our tourists also visited Notre-Dame in the heart of the wealthy clerical and judicial quarter on the Ile-de-la-Cité. In order to reach the cathedral, Felix had to pass the Hôtel-Dieu on his right (the access was different from what it is today) and the church of Saint-Christophe, which had been entirely rebuilt in 1500, on his left. Once inside, he found the elite of the clergy, a class of priests far superior to those he had known as a student in Montpellier.

Visiting Notre-Dame later in the century, Felix's brother Thomas Jr., a confirmed anticlerical, insisted that the cathedral's choir was full of roving pimps and madams offering their services (*Diensten*) to anyone who happened by (T2 560). Around the pillars of the sanctuary, he also saw beds crowded with foundlings. As for prostitution, it is true that a *quartier chaud* (literally, hot quarter) had developed over the centuries on the Ile-de-la-Cité around the rue Glatigny and extending all the way to the Pont Notre-Dame, "even adjacent to the cathedral."[18] Some of this debauchery had apparently spilled over into the interior of the huge Gothic structure at a time when sacred and profane activities were less distinct than they are now. Felix mentions only that, as in Orléans, he climbed the bell tower so as to enjoy the spectacle of the huge bells and the lead roofs below. The entry, nave, and screen of the sanctuary were at this point much as the builder Jean Le Bouteiller had left them when the last major work was done on the cathedral in 1351. Overall, Notre-Dame did not change much from the time Felix saw it until the late seventeenth century, when certain architectural changes were made at behest of Louis XIV. The pure art of the Gothic arch, embodied in Notre-Dame, was thus frozen for three centuries, from 1360 to 1660, long enough for Felix and Thomas Jr. to appreciate it.

From Notre-Dame to the Pont au Change, which Felix calls the Pont aux Orfèvres, was but a short distance. Felix walked quickly because his purpose now was not to see the sights but to purchase gifts for his fiancée, Madlen Jeckelmann. The wooden Pont au Change, built at the end of the thirteenth century, was the oldest bridge in Paris as well as the most solidly built, to judge by the way it withstood time and the elements. To be sure, the low houses that lined both sides of the bridge were refurbished fairly regularly, every half century or so (*vast alle so jahr*).[19] Its sturdy architecture is confirmed by the fact that the structure bore their weight. Aligned with a major north-south thoroughfare (the rue Saint-Denis), the Pont au Change faced the threshing mills of the Pont aux Meuniers to the west. Some years before Felix's visit, there had even been a rather far-fetched proposal to install mills on the Pont au Change itself. Joining the wealthier quarters of the capital, the bridge passed close to some of the major sights of the Right Bank, among them the church of Saint-Jacques-de-la-Boucherie with its famous tower of the 1510s, a masterpiece of flamboyant Gothic architecture, and the stalls of the (dying) Grande-Boucherie; the fortress of the Châtelet, the headquarters of the *prévôté* of Paris and other regional authorities and thus the seat of power in the Ile-de-France; and the stone quays of the Right Bank, which Felix had seen earlier while visiting the Louvre. Built between 1528 and 1538, the quays served as conduits for long lines of wagons that stretched along the Seine westward from the bridges of the Ile-de-la-Cité to the royal residence and the site of the present and future Tuileries.[20]

The Pont au Change had once been an obligatory passage for joyous royal entries, but it had lost that role to the Pont Notre-Dame in 1515. It nevertheless remained a mecca for goldsmiths, a place to buy reliquaries, showpieces, monstrances, and even golden ship models.[21] Felix went "shopping" there for jewelry in the well-placed studio of Hans Jacob David, who came from a leading Basel family that included city councillors, exchange agents, and more or less noble knights. Hans, however, had gone to Paris to seek his fortune.

At a special price for friends and fellow Germans, Felix bought Madlen a gold chain, which eventually became a family heirloom: Madlen, by then the elderly Frau Platterin, gave it one day to Chrischona, the wife of Thomas Jr., a pretty woman whose portrait would be painted in the early seventeenth century with Felix's gold chain hanging from her belt. At

Hans David's studio our student met another young man of about his own age named Felix Keller. Keller, from Zurich, had come to the Pont au Change to apprentice before returning to his birthplace, where he became a jeweler, city councillor, and member of the leading municipal guilds (F 280). The city of Paris, with its deep traditions of craftsmanship extending back to the thirteenth century, was a remarkable school for training specialists in the fashioning of precious metals, some of whom went on to settle in the French heartland, while others returned to exercise their French-perfected talents in their native lands. Our tourist shoppers on the Pont au Change also enjoyed visiting the studios of the bookbinders, whose art reached a pinnacle of perfection under Henri II.[22] Felix, in the mood for gifts, purchased a pocket Bible (actually a half-Bible, a *Testamentum,* probably the New Testament) for his fiancée, whose name he had inscribed in gold letters on the handsomely bound volume. Was it the Latin Vulgate, that is, a Catholic Bible, or a German translation by Luther that had escaped the notice of royal censors unable to decipher the language of France's neighbor?

Felix's anticlerical tendencies made themselves felt in one way or another, even if the Bible he purchased was not a very Catholic one. A few days after his visit to the bookbinder, the young Helvetian visited the Cimetière des Innocents on the rue Saint-Denis, six or seven "blocks" north of the Pont au Change and the Châtelet. Somewhat further north along the same street was the Cimetière de la Trinité, where the dead from the Hôtel-Dieu were buried until 1554, when a royal decree put an end to the practice on hygienic grounds.[23]

Hygiene, or more accurately the lack of it, was in the forefront of Felix's mind as he walked to the cemetery. During the plague of 1531, the Cimetière des Innocents was literally gorged with the dead and gave off a pestilential odor that was seen as a danger to the public. The stench was almost as strong when Felix visited the cemetery a quarter of a century later. The surfeit of cadavers was greater than ever in this place haunted by the Angel of Death. The neighbors had made their peace with it: the *quartier* had its share of prostitution but was dominated by the textile trade (mercers, dyers, shearers, drapers). At the Innocents there was something for every taste, outside the walls as well as inside. Felix discovered various artifacts of late-medieval taste: an alabaster skeleton of Death from the early sixteenth century and a charnel-house gallery illustrated by scenes of the *danse macabre*.[24] The Renaissance was also present in the form of bas-reliefs of Seine nymphs and fluted arcades and pilasters on the new Fontaine des Innocents (1549), which was designed by Jean Goujon to resemble a royal tribune. The transition from the funerary ala-

baster of the early 1500s to the time of Henri II in mid-century dra-
matized the cultural transformation that had taken place. Yet a certain
clerical presence remained, hence an anticlerical presence as well: Felix
witnessed a procession of monks and "priestlings" (*pfaffen*) that went on
for an hour and a quarter. Felix meant the word "priestlings" to be as
disagreeable as possible: he despised these sovereign clerics whose word
would soon be law for the Parisians of the League (the Wars of Religion
were only a few decades away).[25]

Of course the man in the street in those days was still accustomed to
religious processions, especially when there were funerals. In March,
shortly before Felix arrived in Paris, the city had witnessed the funeral of
Cardinal de Bourbon, which had resulted in disputes over priority leading to fisticuffs between the canons of Notre-Dame and those of Saint-
Germain-l'Auxerrois.[26] As the persecution of Protestants continued
(Parlement recently having requested that the bishop provide information against suspect preachers), Henri II, reacting to this and other
scandals associated with ecclesiastical processions, issued an order establishing the priority of various official bodies: Parlement came first, followed by the Chambre des Comptes, the Cour des Aides, the Chambre
des Monnaies, the provost of Paris, the Châtelet, and finally the Hôtel de
Ville.

One Sunday morning (was it March 28 or April 4?), Felix faced the
problem of what to do with his time. Attending mass was of course out of
the question. His dog Poclès, more Calvinist even than its master, would
have forbidden it. From dawn until noon Felix therefore made a quick
tour of the circumference of Paris, which approximated the shape of a
pumpkin.

The German community in Paris was a city within a city, or, more precisely, a village, a very lively village. Felix rarely left the company of this
gregarious group, except when he called on the three leading French physicians at the beginning of his visit, which otherwise remained "ethno-
centric." A German injured himself on the inside of his knee, and the
young Swiss doctor was summoned. He found the wound still fresh
(*ziemlich frisch*). The next day, the man was dead: was it an embolism, a
hemorrhage, or a rapid infection? Everyone was overcome (*was uns allen
leidt*). The burial took place at night, by torchlight, with torches held
aloft at arm's length to illuminate the dead man's coat of arms, which was
displayed along with the body, for he was a noble. The German community of students and shopkeepers turned out for the burial, Felix among
them, even though he was only a migratory bird on a brief visit, an Alsatian stork ready to take flight at a moment's notice. Still, his compatriots,

well established in the Ile-de-France, adopted the young Swiss for the duration of his visit.

The Germans' communal sentiments extended, moreover, to the countries of Central Europe without regard for boundaries, just as in the time of Thomas Platter Sr. When a Polish nobleman died in Paris in the spring of 1557, "we accompanied him to his final resting place," wrote Felix, who was always fascinated by burials so long as the deceased hailed from "the other side of the Rhine," a geographical expression that has to be understood in the broadest possible terms as extending all the way to the Vistula.

*Crédit Suisse:* when Felix's money began to run out, he was obliged to call on a rather strange countryman, Martin Betschart, a native of Lucerne and former resident of Basel who had chosen Paris as his place of business: he was a pawnbroker and perhaps also a usurer. From 1557 to 1559 he served as agent or broker in northern France for a Zurich printer. In the time of Henri II he lived on a small street noted for its prostitutes (*gmeine wiber*) in a horseshoe- or crescent-shaped block of buildings known as Champ-Gaillard, situated between Saint-Nicolas-du-Chardonnet and rue Bordelle and between rue d'Arras, rue Saint-Victor, and rue Clopin. Champ-Gaillard had a bad reputation; the Parlement of Paris complained about it as early as 1555.[27] Betschart himself was a curious fellow, whose facial scars and the spicy stories they seemed to suggest made him famous among German visitors. Among other things, he was always rubbing his nose with saliva in the vain hope of getting rid of the striking scars that disfigured his face.

Betschart had previously tried his hand at various trades, including those of proofreader and musical copyist. Later, he moved up a notch to become the representative of the German nation in the French capital. From 1529 until his death in 1569, he served first as *procureur,* then as *questeur,* and finally as *doyen* of the Germans of Paris. One can readily imagine him as a secret agent of the Swiss. He did his best to find rooms at reasonable rents for students from the Alps and the Jura. He complained in his letters that the morals of young people were easily corrupted in Paris (and especially in Champ-Gaillard), while French husbands were tyrannized by their wives. He bailed Felix out by lending him twelve crowns on his father's credit. The young visitor was astonished by Betschart's house, a treasure trove filled with furniture, jewelry, and even food left in pawn by his clients. The Betschart pawnshop forged a kind of bond between the Rhine and the Seine.[28]

In early April Felix went to see the great abbey in Saint-Denis, a small town of two thousand that had come down quite a bit since the fourteenth century, when its population was said to have been ten thousand before the Black Plague. In letters patent issued in November of 1556, Henri II had only recently authorized the town to resume holding the Lendit fair within its walls, but this privilege could not compensate for the failure to thrive.[29] The declining population was reflected in the presence of large green spaces (cultivated fields, forests, and gardens as well as uncultivated land) within the fortified enclosure. The route from Paris to Saint-Denis had long been marked by the peregrinations of the saint himself (dead as well as alive); he was often depicted holding his severed head in his hands and washing it as he went, just as he was supposed to have done when he continued on his way to Saint-Denis after being decapitated in Montmartre. The road from the capital to the monastery was also the customary route of the *hanouars,* who in ordinary times hauled salt but who, when a king died, were charged with the mission of bearing the royal corpse to its final resting place.[30] Their last occasion to do so had been in 1547, on the death of Francis I. Felix and Theodor entered Saint-Denis through the woad market, then proceeded down rue Cordonnerie and rue Boulangerie, passing the Hôtel-Dieu on their right. From there they went to the abbey church of Saint-Denis. Since it was late, they took a room at the Auberge du Maure.

That evening they had time for a rousing tennis match at a local court. All the Platters took an interest in the game. Thomas Jr. counted eight tennis courts in Montpellier in 1595, seven in the city and one in the *vorstatt,* or suburb. In Montpellier recreation halls were frequented mainly by court officers and soldiers, bachelors fond of dancing, horses, and sports. In Paris, Thomas Jr. counted no fewer than 1,100 tennis courts (other sources report only 600, which still comes to one court for every four hundred people or one hundred households). Courts were so popular and so profitable that when the faubourgs of Paris were partially destroyed by cannon fire in the siege of 1590, damaged buildings were replaced by tennis courts, which yielded a better return on investment.

Felix, by now an accomplished tourist completing a long and educational journey, leapt out of bed the next morning and hastened off to see the sacred works and treasures on display at Saint-Denis, a stone's throw from the Auberge du Maure. He described and admired what he saw, distinguishing among three types of artifacts: religious and cultural objects (reliquaries and antiquities); funerary sculptures (such as tombstones); and precious objects, valuable in the world here below (*kostlichen Sachen*).

For once he looked at relics without his customary Protestant irony. He mentions the crucifixes of gold and silver containing fragments of the

True Cross, part of a gift from Jean de Berry, as well as a nail from the Crucifixion kept in a gilt vermillion reliquary that had been given to Charlemagne by Constantine (or so Felix quite astonishingly believed—yet another Donation of Constantine!). Saint Denis's head with its jewel-encrusted miter is supported by two gilt angels, while a third angel holds up a many-faceted reliquary containing the saint's jawbone. The reliquary bust of Saint Benedict, weighing more than a hundred and thirty pounds, contains pieces of the skull and arms of the founder of the Bene-dictine Order. The bust is covered with ancient cameos, including a Vic-tory, a left profile of Domitian, and two galloping horses, all given to the abbey in 1401 by the same Jean, duc de Berry. (Later, in 1804, some of these cameos were transferred for the anointment of Napoleon to the counterfeit "crown of Charlemagne" with which the emperor was crowned.)

A golden reliquary containing a hand of the apostle Thomas, also flanked by a pair of angels, was yet another gift from the Maecenas of Berry. Thomas's finger, which had once explored the wound in Jesus's side, "was covered with gold and wore a ring with a set stone."[31] Felix also reports finding a tooth of Saint John the Baptist (more "scholarly" sources speak only of a reliquary of John the Baptist containing part of the saint's shoulder along with a tooth from Saint Pancras Martyr, as well as two walrus tusks given by King David of Scotland). There was also the money that Judas had received for betraying Christ and the lantern that Judas had been holding when Christ was arrested. Antiquities consti-tuted a second facet of a certain Renaissance "ensemble" (ancient culture after Christian culture): in this case, according to Felix, there were cameos of Cleopatra, Antony, and Nero. These identifications are rather fanciful, because the actual cameos in the crypt of Saint-Denis would more likely have depicted emperors such as Claudius, Augustus, and Car-acalla. The last "antiquity" that Felix mentions is the "jawbone" or tusk of an "elephant": to judge from the surviving inventories, this can only have been the *olifant de Roland,* Roland's horn, actually an eleventh-century Hispano-Moorish ivory hunting horn, or perhaps another horn in the Saint-Denis collection, a fifteenth-century horn decorated with an ape emerging from a chalice to preach to an audience of birds arranged in two rows.[32]

Felix turns next to mortuary objects: the celebrated tombstones of Saint-Denis, which played a part in the royal funerals of the Renaissance. No monk disturbed the young man's thanatological explorations or in-quired in an inquisitorial voice as he peered at some funerary tile whether he was a Huguenot or a Papist. The two German tourists first visited the sepulchre of Charles VIII with its bronze mausoleum, which was destroyed in the course of the repugnant exhumations carried out in 1793. They went next to the tomb of Louis XII and Anne of Brittany. There, the Gothic arches of the dais were juxtaposed with ancient-style *tempietto*.[33] The young Helvetian saw the old theme of the king's two bodies brought to life in a striking new way: the sovereigns' naked cadavers, depicted with striking realism, are contrasted with images of them kneeling as they were in life. When the sepulchres were violated at the end of the eighteenth century, two crowns of gilt copper were found on the sarcophagus of the Franco-Breton couple.[34] Francis I could well have placed a solid gold crown on the tomb had he wanted to; in this instance he showed himself to be miserly. His prodigality was lavished, of course, on the visible structures rather than the hidden depths of the sepulchre, as Felix and his companion discovered when they inspected the white marble statues around the monument to Louis XII representing the mirror and serpent of Prudence, the sword and orb of Justice, the lionskin of Strength, and the clock and bridle of Temperance. As for the (mortuary) arch of triumph dedicated to Queen Claude and Francis I, whose figures were enveloped in a shroud of stone and carved into the stylobate, work was still in progress in the spring of 1557 (*doran man noch werckt* [F 281]).

Felix also mentions that attached to the cenotaph of Francis were statues of his mother, Louise of Savoy, and Charlotte, Louise's granddaughter. The modeling and realism of the figures, whether erect or recumbent, delighted our traveler. These cadavers were full of life. Felix's sensibility responded to the art of the Renaissance, which was being created all around him. But "medieval" sculpture did not leave him cold either: he noted the tomb of a fourteenth-century constable, possibly that of Louis de Sancerre, with its brutal expression, or Bertrand du Guesclin. In the abbey Felix marveled at the open book of French history, transformed into a heroic cemetery bristling with columns and statuary.

Leaving piety, classicism, and death behind, he next moved on to a more traditional sort of museum, filled with regalia, or symbols of sovereignty that played a role in the royal anointment ceremony, mingled with miscellaneous treasures. Among the regalia Felix mentions a golden scepter with a hand[35] on top made of "unicorn horn" (actually a hand of justice).[36] The visitor also saw three royal crowns that no longer exist: a Gothic "king's crown" with a bonnet "topped by the huge ruby of John the Good"; a queen's crown dating from 1250–1300 and encrusted with gold, precious gems, and *fleurs de lys;* and finally, a holy crown, contemporary with the queen's crown and embellished with a hundred and fifty large pearls as well as a sliver of the Crown of Thorns and hairs from the

Savior's head—still more relics. Of these three crowns, one vanished in 1590, when it was confiscated and melted down by agents of the League. The two others met the same fate in 1793–94. Among the other regalia in the abbey in the sixteenth century were three swords: that of Charles VII; Charlemagne's sword, the so-called *Joyeuse,* today in the Louvre; and, most important of all, the sword of Saint Louis, which vanished during the Revolution. Of these three weapons, Felix saw or at any rate mentioned only one, that of Saint Louis, about which he tells us only that he saw it.[37]

Felix also marveled at a plate or tablet (*tafel*) covered with precious gems, probably the red and white ornamental clasp with heraldic emblems that Charles V had made for his son to wear to his anointing; it was encrusted with forty pearls, nine red rubies, and four cut diamonds.[38] The Swiss visitor also mentions certain royal garments that were essential pieces of the regalia: pants and shoes (*Hosen und Schuh*) were a basic part of the anointing costume. In fact these "pants" were sumptuous breeches, decorated with pearls,[39] and the shoes were boots with spurs bearing dragons' and lions' heads (one of which was reworked in 1547, ten years before Felix's visit). Last but not least were two real conversation pieces. The first was a "unicorn horn" six feet long (*ein einhorn 6 schu lang*) preserved in a basin of water behind the altar. The water was to be ingested for therapeutic purposes. The horn was in fact one of the finest narwhal tusks in France. The second conversation piece Felix referred to simply as "Solomon's cup" (*Soll des Künigs Salomons gwesen sein*). It was in fact a Sassanian rock crystal cup with gold stem dating from the sixth or seventh century and either a gift of Charles the Bald or booty from a raid by Charlemagne: "This goblet was made of pure gold together with fine emeralds and garnets and beautifully wrought," according to the author of the *Grandes Chroniques de France* in the fourteenth century.[40]

Felix spent only about thirty hours in the abbatial town of Saint-Denis.[41] By mid-April he was back in Paris. Shortly after arriving, he made a brief excursion to Les Tournelles, the site of the royal stables. He thus explored two perpendicular tourist axes: an east-west axis running from the Louvre to Les Tournelles, the axis of (royal) power, and a north-south religious axis running from the Sorbonne to Notre-Dame to the Innocents to Saint-Denis. The two intersected at the Pont au Change, a place for shopping and buying presents.

Les Tournelles belonged to a vast ensemble of royal residences on the eastern fringes of the capital's circumference. Among these was the Hôtel Saint-Paul, which had not been used since the reign of Francis I or perhaps before. In this huge building, Charles V had allegedly lived such a democratic life, so close to the common people, that Louis-Sébastien Mercier, writing in the time of Louis XVI, was able to refer to his reign retrospectively as the "Popular Front" of medieval monarchy.[42] As for Les Tournelles, the shift of fashion toward the west end, a phenomenon observed in many cities over the preceding centuries, had gradually diminished the palace's value. In 1519 Louise of Savoy abandoned it, having found its stench unbearable. The royal family continued to reside here during the winter, but during the high season there was competition from Fontainebleau, Saint-Germain, and the Louvre.

Les Tournelles continued to be useful, however, as a site for equestrian exercises and military maneuvers. Its park, though inside the walls of Paris, was extensive and well suited to military drill. When Felix visited in the spring of 1557, he saw two figures silhouetted in an upper-story window of the big house: the dauphin François (the future Francis II) and Charles II, duc de Lorraine.[43] In the following year, 1558, Charles married Claude de France, the second daughter of Catherine de Médicis. But for now, as Felix looked on in April 1557, the dauphin picked up a dog and hurled it through the window at a page galloping past, who adroitly caught the animal as he rode (F 283). Forty-five years later, Felix would relate this memory to Duke Charles, whose official physician and friend he had meanwhile become.

Felix wrote about his reminiscences of Paris during the reigns of Henri IV and Louis XIII. But in 1557, when he was still only twenty-one, he faced a decision. Although Paris was by no means boring, it was time to move on. His financial resources were running low, and the presents he had purchased were costly. The longer the young man from Switzerland dawdled in Ile-de-France, the more likely it was that Madlen, his fiancée, would wind up in the arms of another man. Better get a move on! Before that, however, there was time for a dinner among *Teutschen,* a regular occurrence whenever it came time for one of them to head home. A group of twenty young tourists from Switzerland attended the banquet. They had just come through central and eastern France, hoping to see something of the kingdom and visit the great city. And since they happened to be in Paris, why not meet Felix, who, because of his long stay abroad, had become, *in absentia,* an almost legendary figure in his native city? Among the guests was also a part-time soldier named Hans. As luck would have it, he decided to accompany Felix on his journey home. And of course the cream of Basel's itinerant typographers and humanists also turned up. Among them was Basilius Amerbach, aged twenty-three, at one time a student in Germany, France, and Italy, the son of a jurist, and himself a humanist and soon to be professor and rector in Basel. His visit to Paris in 1557–58 is of historical importance because he returned home with the only surviving copy of the map by Truschet and Hoyau, which eventually became the jewel of the Basel University Library collection. Amerbach allegedly lent the map to his friend Theodor Zwinger for the printing of a work entitled *Methodus Apodemica*.[44]

Seated beside Amerbach at Felix's dinner was Caspar Herwagen, whose name calls to mind one of the leading families of Basel printers. This particular Herwagen belonged, however, to a bastard offshoot of the illustrious line: he was the illegitimate son of a Herwagen who had become a priest. Caspar, having distinguished himself as a student in France and Germany, served first a Catholic bishop and later a Protestant prince. Also present was Aurelius Erasmus Frobenius, whose name alone speaks volumes: he was the son of a printer (the publisher of Erasmus), the brother of another printer, and a printer himself. And soon he would father a brood from which would come yet another printer. Next to him was Eusebius Bischof, also a printer's son who grew up to be a printer and who, in his forties, would be ennobled by the emperor. Then there was Bernhard Burckhardt, aged twelve, who came from a family of drapers and aldermen and who would soon become a draper and silk merchant. It may seem surprising that Bernhard's parents allowed him to travel to Paris at such a tender age, but he was surrounded by staunch friends. Finally, to round out the guest list, let us mention the iron-monger's son Hans Jacob Ruedin, who, over the next few days, would make Felix a disagreeable companion on the road from Paris to Basel. Our banquet of humanists thus included a fair sampling of gilded or semi-gilded youth, friends and professional colleagues of the guest of honor who temporarily found themselves traveling abroad. This dinner capped Felix's weeks in Paris, one of the high points of his life. On April 22, having shilly-shallied for some time (Ruedin had injured his eye in a ball game), three men set out for Etampes, from which they would pro-ceed, not without detours, to Orléans, Bourges, and Basel: Felix was joined by the mercenary Hans, armed to the teeth, and by Herr Ruedin, who wore a patch over his left eye. They looked like a Renaissance engrav-ing of a trio of landsknechts—almost a Dürer.

The road from Paris took the three travelers first to Etampes (April 24), then to Orléans (two days later). Felix spent the night of April 26 at an inn in Pierrefitte, between Orléans and Bourges. Plague lurked in the vi-cinity, and the next day, after a hasty lunch, the three Swiss departed for Bourges, which they reached that evening. They had traveled through a region of hedged fields, heath, and vineyards before coming to the area of open grain fields interspersed with vineyards just north of the capital of

Berry. The revival of the countryside over the previous century leapt to the travelers' eyes. In the absence of other criteria, we can use the "white cloak" of new manors as a test: of 123 chateaus inventoried in Berry[45] (the list is incomplete), we "find 72 that had been enlarged or renovated between 1430 and 1550; of these 72, 62 had been entirely rebuilt." In other words, half of all noble dwellings were new in 1557. These sported Italian facades with medallioned loggias and finely wrought towers "with windows capped by stepped gables."[46]

The city of Bourges was not totally unknown to Felix. A year earlier, he had heard through the German grapevine about the disaster that had occurred there in early July: the duke of Bavaria, aged fifteen, a student in Bourges, had drowned while boating on the Auron river just outside of town. His accidental death had touched the people of Berry as well as German students all over France.

The young duke's drowning tells us something about the topography of the region: around Bourges one found, in addition to cultivated land, any number of swamps and small streams. Owing to the density of the hydrographic network, the moats surrounding the fortified walls were almost always filled with water even in times of drought, thus improving the city's defensive position. The heath and fallow land in the surrounding countryside provided good pasture for sheep, whose wool supplied the mills and studios that produced a much-prized woolen fabric. Solemn processions marked the importance of the local textile industry: in January 1544, when the future Francis II was born, Bourges celebrated not only with bonfires but also with a procession including (in order) students, officers of the courts, and vintners followed immediately by carders, fullers, and weavers. Bourges hosted half a dozen fairs annually, or so Felix reported in his memoirs, unaware that some of these fairs may have dwindled to a pale shadow of the splendid future envisioned for them by the Estates General convoked in 1484 by Anne de Beaujeu.

In 1487 a huge fire had destroyed half the city, seriously diminishing the size of its fairs and their likelihood of success. When Thomas Jr. visited Bourges in 1599, he counted eighty imposing towers along the ramparts (a 1567 map shows only fifty or so).[47] Felix, forty-two years earlier, approached the city from the north, crossing countless streams whose banks were dotted with grain and textile mills. Beyond the gate he passed a relatively new hospital on his right. Built in the 1520s, the Hôtel-Dieu attested to the city's thriving population and spirit of initiative. Bourges, having been designated a *bonne ville* in 1492, had enjoyed the privilege of a municipal government since that time. Demographic growth had also led to an increase in pauperism, however, especially after 1520. Veering toward the east, Felix headed up the rue du Bourbonnou, not far from the gate of the same name with its two slender towers. On this street, which skirted a section of monuments, Felix found lodging at the Auberge du Boeuf Couronné, where he stayed for several days.

His first venture out was for a meeting with German students, the elite of the University of Bourges, founded in 1463 by Louis XI and among that king's many successes. In 1517 the university moved to improve its legal and other faculties by recruiting teachers from abroad at the city's expense. Among the scholars lured to the banks of the Auron were Ferrandina from Portugal, Wolmar from Germany, Jacques Amyot from France, and above all the Italian Alciati, a fist-rate jurist and theorist of royal sovereignty. After a period of decline around 1530, order was restored early in the reign of Henri II: students were no longer allowed to participate in the election of the rector, and new faculty were recruited, including Le Duaren of Brittany, Cujas of Toulouse, and the "German-Parisian" Hotman. Representing two successive generations, these teachers trained such prodigious students as Calvin, Beza, and De Thou. A few scapegoats were sent to the stake in anti-Protestant persecutions, but the leading heretics were left untouched in their academic chairs or *hôtels particuliers*. In the 1550s, even before the death of Henri II, the University of Bourges, like that of Montpellier, went over to the Reformation bag and baggage. What is more, royal princesses extended their protection to the city's intellectuals. They contributed to the university's development and saw to it that its faculty and students were spared by rampaging inquisitors. The princesses in question were of course Marguerite de Navarre, the sister of Francis I, and Marguerite de Valois, the sister of Henri II, who took up residence in her duchy of Berry in the middle of the sixteenth century. It is easy to understand why German students would have felt "comfortable" in Bourges: many of them were Lutherans, hence all the more pleased to rub shoulders with their French-speaking Huguenot classmates and colleagues.

This religious tolerance did not keep the Teutons from attending papist ceremonies, however, as in 1556, when the young duke of Bavaria drowned just outside of Bourges. This was one of the rare occasions when the "German nation" (as the students from the east were collectively called) marched as a group. Felix reports some details of this occasion: a group of a hundred to a hundred and twenty Germans preceded the body of the prince, which was carried in great pomp to the church of the Jacobins in the center of town, west of the cathedral, which stood adjacent to the ramparts. Each of the marchers carried a torch bearing the victim's coat of arms. Behind them marched another German carrying a long lance, from the end of which flew black streamers bearing mottoes and encomia to the illustrious genealogy of the deceased. The prince's horse, draped in black cloth, was led by two young Germans; it carried the heart of the dead duke, escorted by two German noblemen, one on each side. Finally, the duke's body rested on the shoulders of eight or ten Germans dressed in mourning garb. This all-German part of the procession was followed by a substantial number of Frenchmen representing the municipality and the university. The size of the German contingent reveals the importance of the German influence in Bourges in the time of Henri II and young Felix Platter.[48] Note, too, that the contingent of visitors from the east was itself divided according to age and social hierarchy.

Felix's visits with the students of Bourges took place three hundred days after this funeral, on April 27, 1557. The next day was given over to visiting churches and chapels. The "great schools," as the faculties of the university were known, stood in a building adjacent to the cathedral of Saint-Etienne. Thomas Jr., who followed in his elder brother's footsteps forty years later, gives us some idea of what Felix must have seen when he visited the local churches. At Saint-Etienne—"the greatest French church," according to our author, who is exaggerating a bit—Renaissance architects were still at work in 1557, embroidering on Gothic structures inherited from the thirteenth century. The student from Montpellier enjoyed a fleeting glimpse of the tall, lead-encased spire topped by a twelve-foot bronze cross, which was still being installed high above the great nave.[49] Plunging right in, Thomas Jr. entered through the new portal of Saint-Guillaume with its hagiographic sculptures. The portal had been cut into the base of the massive Tour de Beurre, also built after 1506 and distinguished by a series of balustrades and interwoven blind arches marking the upper stories. The two brothers liked the windows of the huge edifice with their brilliant, sun-concealing stained glass. The colorful windows of the small Tellier chapel were just twenty-five years old in 1557 and still radiant; their painted figures illustrated the exploits of various members of the Tellier family, which had contributed six canons to the clergy of Bourges.

At the Sainte Chapelle, close to the cathedral, Felix and later Thomas Jr. retraced the princely path of the ubiquitous Jean, duc de Berry, who long after his death seemed to dog the two brothers' footsteps as they traveled from Tours to Etampes to Saint-Denis to Bourges. In the "princely" crypt of the Sainte Chapelle, which was consecrated in 1405 and modeled after the Sainte Chapelle of Paris, Thomas Jr. marveled at a priceless crucifix encrusted with rubies, turquoises, emeralds, and pearls as big as hazel nuts and covered with cameos, among them a veiled aristo-

crat in profile crowned in oak leaves that had been made for the duke.[50]
He also noted the presence of historiated chasubles, a gold crown donated by Jean de Berry, and a goblet carved out of a giant emerald. The
"museum rules" of the time were fairly liberal: these precious objects
were kept in locked chests in the crypt's vaults and displayed to any visitor
deemed worthy of viewing them. The Platters enjoyed a glimpse into the
ecclesiastical history of Bourges: the architecture of the Tour de Beurre
showed off the influence of the Renaissance; the treasures in the crypt
revealed the fifteenth century; and, to round out the tour of French history, the crypt itself dated from the twelfth century. The younger of the
two brothers paid tribute to the airiness and lightness of this underground church, whose capitals, like those of Notre-Dame of Paris, are
adorned with leaves of fern, water lily, and acanthus.

Students, priests, and finally soldiers: upon leaving the cathedral, Felix
headed south. He ignored the archepiscopal palace, a long building with
high gables and mullioned windows. Beyond Notre-Dame-de-Sales he
came to the ramparts, dominated by the Grosse Tour, which housed a
sort of siege engine. The tower was decorated with rustic protuberances
pretentiously dubbed "diamond points" (*wie die spitzen diamant* [T2
519]). It had been built in 1188 at the behest of Philip Augustus. The great
tower was still a considerable dissuasive force, with its walls eighteen feet
thick at their base (*Die wändt seyen 18 Schu dick*, according to Thomas Jr.'s
accurate observation). This fortress had been used to store arms and mu-
nitions, especially crossbow projectiles, since the thirteenth century.[51]
Behind one of the doors, Felix discovered an old crossbow, as tall and
broad as a man (*eins mans lang und gross*). Louis XI, who took an interest
in the Grosse Tour, had ordered an iron cell installed in the arms room
"above the first joists."[52] The cell was a square roughly three and a half
feet on a side, for a total living area of twelve square feet: prisoners were
definitely not indulged. The walls were of ironclad wood. This minuscule
prison did not escape Felix's notice; he claimed that a king had been incar-
cerated there for a lengthy period. As usual, his notions of French
history—even recent French history—are quite vague.[53] His brother
Thomas Jr., more scrupulous as to his sources, states that the unfortunate
prisoner was named *Sforcia;* in fact, it was Cardinal Ascanio Sforza,
brother of the Milanese Ludovico Il Moro, who had been a prisoner of
Louis XII at Saint-Encize in Lyons and later in the Grosse Tour of
Bourges.[54]

Thomas Jr. tells us little about the economy of Bourges, and Felix tells
us even less. Both confine themselves mainly to empty generalities. There
is one exception to this rule, however: Thomas was struck, during his

brief stay in Bourges, by the bell founders he saw at work in the street. Bell-casting was and is a sophisticated business; its techniques have been passed down through the ages largely unchanged to this day. Making bells was a current matter in 1599 because a decision had been made to replace those removed, destroyed, or melted down by Huguenots after 1562. Thomas noted that many onlookers tossed counterfeit or retired coins into the molten metal being prepared for casting. This was one not very scrupulous way of "contributing" to the common effort. Despite such indelicacies, the clergy did not hesitate to baptize (*tauffen*) the new bell a few days later, after the metal had cooled and the mold had been removed. Thomas, who was given to caricaturing the ways of the Catholic clergy, reports that this baptism was performed in highly ceremonious fashion. In fact, he was echoing his brother's sentiments, because as a young man he had carefully read the first draft of Felix's diary, and Felix had indeed been struck by the large bells (*gröste glocken*) of Saint-Etienne in 1557.

The two Platters' vision of Bourges is ultimately eclectic, even "impressionistic" in the best sense of the word, although it is not always profound or comprehensive. Felix missed one point entirely: 1557 was a difficult year for the city's "lower classes." From the journal kept by Father Jean Glaumeau, a rather odd Bourges priest who kept a concubine and ultimately became, logically enough, a Protestant, we know that the drought of 1556 had led to food shortages in Bourges and its environs in the spring of the following year: "This year, for eight or ten months running, corn was very dear, so dear that a bushel of wheat went for XVII to XVIII *soulz*. Oats, five *soulz*. The poor suffered a great deal, so much that, according to the elders, never in living memory had corn been dearer. Yet society [in the past] did not suffer as much, because other things were all less dear. This year, however, all things were dear, hence when August, September, and October came, the poor were afflicted with countless maladies, pestilential fevers and other incurable diseases, and many died."[55]

Father Glaumeau's analysis of the way in which a dangerous rise in grain prices, long-term inflation, and increased pauperization combined to cause suffering among the "little people" is quite astute. Notice that our tourist's financial resources, though modest, were sufficient to allow him to get by, while the plight of the poorest inhabitants of the places he visited eluded him. As a young man, Felix's father had shared the distress of the poor, but the old man's son now belonged to a sheltered segment of society. Felix does, however, allude briefly to an outbreak of plague in the village of Neuvy, just before Bourges; he seems to have been aware of the grain shortage and its connection with disease, the very connection that would later alarm Father Glaumeau. But let us not be too hard on Felix. As the municipal physician of Basel some years later, he did his best to cope with the epidemics that afflicted his fellow citizens. The good doctor's zeal would go a long way to make up for the tourist's inattentiveness.

\*   \*   \*

On April 29 Felix left Bourges, where the first covered tennis court in the city was under construction.[56] Our traveler avoided the normal route to the east, which led to Burgundy through Nevers. This road passed too close to the Massif Central, known to be a lair of criminals; in particular, it passed through the dangerous forest of Frétoy. Perhaps the drought and the ensuing food shortage made this route particularly hazardous in 1557. Hard times had driven more than one highwayman into the woods to prey upon unlucky travelers. Felix decided to head more to the northeast along the "big old road" or "high road" (*chemin de la chaussée*) that led through Sancerre, Clamecy, and Vézelay to Dijon. The first stage of the journey, on the afternoon of April 29, took him to Sancerre. This was an old *ville champignon,* or "mushroom city," of the tenth and eleventh centuries, which had grown into an oval-shaped town of three thousand perched on high ground a quarter of a league from Saint-Thibaut, a small port on the Loire that was inhabited by about fifty people. Sancerre contained approximately five hundred houses, half of which had been built or rebuilt in the Renaissance; these were arranged on the hillside in rows, as in an amphitheater. The place was dominated by a more or less rectangular citadel over three hundred feet long. Perched at the edge of a precipice, this castle was protected by an "iron gate" that opened onto the rabbit-ridden countryside: sentinels amused themselves by pelting rabbits with stones from the battlements. Ramparts, reinforced at intervals by nine towers, encircled the town, which could be entered through any of four separate gates. The approach took Felix through hedgehog-filled vineyards laid out on a gently sloping hillside; donkeys were used to work the ground. The fashionable grapes of the moment were the *chardonnay* (for white wine) and the *pinot noir* (for red). Both red and white wines were exported to Paris, Flanders, and Normandy, where they appeared on noble and bourgeois tables.[57] Felix entered the city through the Porte de Bourges, also known as Porte Vieille or Portevieil; this was also the outlet through which the town's waste water was discharged. He exited to the east through the Porte Oyson, probably a deformation of the word *portillon* or *porteson;* or perhaps he took the scenic route, which actually skirted the walls of the city from the Portevieil to the Porte Oyson. In "normal" times Sancerre had little use for its walls. The ramparts did, however, continue to have a function in peacetime under Henri II: they kept wolves out of the center of town. Without adequate walls, the wolves would soon have made their way into the city by night, attracted by the meat in the butcher shops.

The function of the walls would change after 1561, when Sancerre, which had long been full of neophyte Huguenots and had recently begun to welcome refugees of the same stripe, became one of the strongholds of the Reformed Church. Accordingly, the city was "predestined" to become the target of a terrible siege by royal and Catholic troops in 1573, as celebrated in its day as La Rochelle would be later on. In old age, Felix telescoped his own experience of Sancerre as a young man in 1557 with impressions he had gathered subsequently from reading the gazettes and listening to rumors. In his memoirs he mentions the harsh famine (*hungersnöthe*) that the papist siege produced in Sancerre's *annus horribilis*, 1573.[58]

On April 29, Felix crossed the Loire and headed north toward the city of Cosne. This was a small, rectangular town of 2,500 to 3,000 inhabitants adjacent to a château surrounded by ramparts from which at most four or five towers protruded. Felix, arriving from the south, crossed the Saint-Aignan bridge and then entered the city through the gate and along the street of the same name. Atop the gate was a conical tower and possibly a cross. Felix crossed the city in a northeasterly direction along the rue d'En-bas, rue Jean-d'Or, rue des Chapelains, and rue Bourgeoise. On his right he passed the church of Saint-Jacques with its corbelled facade. To his left he glanced at signs of recent construction reflecting Renaissance tastes in ecclesiastical and official buildings. These were especially evident in the chapel of Notre-Dame-de-Galles, whose almost new stained-glass windows bore the arms of a bishop of Auxerre, framed by dragons with silver banners.

The salt warehouse, adjacent to the chapel, had also been refurbished under Louis XI. Thus the two buildings maintained an architectural dialogue that paralleled the heraldic dialogue between the escutcheon of the canons of Notre-Dame-de-Galles (vert and sable—i.e., green and black—separated by a diagonal silver bar, or tiercé in bend) and that of their neighbors the *gabelous*, or salt tax collectors (gules and or—i.e., red and gold—also separated by a diagonal bar of silver). Cosne collected considerable tolls from traffic on the Loire, which supplemented its income from the salt tax. The city could boast of its social accomplishments: the transition, characteristic of the early modern period, from the medieval leprosarium to the modern hospital was already well under way. Religious turmoil was also in evidence: the quasi-public wedding of a priest caused a scandal in Cosne toward the end of Francis I's reign. This eventually led to the erection of a stake, followed by a public burning that reduced the unfortunate clerical bridegroom to ashes, but not before he had been strangled to death—a humanitarian gesture that the temper of the times demanded. A year before Felix's visit, the *maréchaussée*, or magistrate's court, had been obliged to hold hearings in Cosne to "root out the wicked," that is, to punish religious dissidents, despite the judge's evident inability to sort out doctrinal issues; the repression was not very successful. Felix does not deign to tell us which inn he slept in. The next morning, he and his companions left Cosne via the Porte d'Auxerre, headed for Clamecy.[59]

They passed through Donzy, where the local barony, a possession of François de Clèves, the first duke of Nevers, was transformed into a *duché-pairie* at midcentury.[60] From there they proceeded to Clamecy, a city of 2,500 on the Yonne, where all the teachers and students of a thriving school would be wiped out by plague in 1582.[61] Clamecy was a timbering center from which logs were floated downstream either singly or bound together in rafts. The destination was Paris, whose feverish growth was stoked by huge quantities of fuel from the forests of the Morvan and elsewhere.[62]

On May 1, after leaving Clamecy, Felix and friends passed below the former monastery of Vézelay, perched on top of a hill (*uf dem berg* [F 288]). This former Benedictine abbey with its tympanum bearing a huge image of Christ, high Romanesque nave, and linden-shaded gardens was by 1557 no more than a shadow of its former self, despite or perhaps because of its vast property-holdings and constant flow of pilgrims. With backing from Francis I, the erstwhile monks had secured Pope Paul III's approval for their secularization, that is, their transformation into a college of no more than a dozen purely secular canons, whose leader, the *abbé commendataire*, was appointed by the king.

In the community around the abbey, moreover, all roads led, however briefly, to Protestantism. A small Huguenot community had developed in the town in 1555. "Trouble" never comes alone: in 1560, Cardinal Odet of Châtillon, Coligny's brother, became *abbé commendataire* of Vézelay. He soon went over to Protestantism, with the incidental benefit that he was able to marry Isabelle de Hauteville, a woman half his age. Felix followed a street "under the walls" south of the abbey and at the foot of the hill. He crossed the Yonne and headed for Dijon. In the memoirs he wrote in 1612 from notes hastily jotted down in a notebook, he mentions his visit to Vézelay only in passing; he spells the name of the town "Verde-let," a slip no doubt linked to the word *verdet,* verdigris, with which he was familiar because of the custom among women of the bourgeoisie and common people in Languedoc of making small copper plaques, of which Felix had seen thousands during his stay in southern France.[63]

On May 2 Felix, while traveling from Précy-sous-Thil to Fleury-sur-Ouche, had a brush with danger (*ein grosse gfor*). Riding through moist terrain, he guided his horse onto a narrow high road that formed a sort of dike between two ponds (F 288). Eventually the path narrowed to the point where the horse could neither proceed nor turn around, and its rider could not dismount. Felix was afraid that he might fall into the water with his horse and all his belongings. He somehow managed to back the horse out without dismounting and then made a detour around the bad patch of road.

On Monday, May 3, Felix reached Dijon, a city built on marl and pudding stone from the Oligocene as well as on recent alluvial deposits lying at the base of vine-covered hills where, Thomas Jr. tells us, Gallo-Roman coins were still frequently unearthed (T2 906). The city offered a jagged skyline of tall monuments, mostly churches. The biggest were Saint-Philibert, Saint-Jean, and Notre-Dame, in whose belltower with skylight sentinels were posted. There was also Saint-Bénigne, where the kings of France stopped on their rounds of the country to swear that they would respect the privileges and liberties (*privilegien und freyheiten*) of the people of Dijon. And last but not least, there was the remarkable Tour de Philippe. The days when Brussels and Mechelen were the capitals of the dukes of Burgundy and Dijon was their official necropolis lay in the not-so-distant past. The population of Dijon, comprising Huguenot artisans and Catholic vintners, was roughly fifteen thousand in the time of Henri II, perhaps as many as twenty thousand, and conditions in the city had been fairly crowded since 1513, when the Swiss infantry, well equipped with cannon, had feigned a siege after a brief expedition. In preparation for such an attack, the local authorities had razed a number of suburbs in order to give the city's defenders a clear field of fire. As in Geneva, the population of these suburbs had had to be relocated inside the city, which had led to a housing shortage and to new residential construction.

There was also a certain poverty within what was apparently a thriving community. More than a thousand people, almost a tenth of the population, were officially listed as below the poverty line. Their care was entrusted to a *chambre des pauvres,* or poorhouse, that dated back to the famine of 1529, as in Lyons. Together with the parlement, municipal officials, and the *vicomte majeur,* the poorhouse administered alms and other funds collected for the poor.

The Swiss emergency of 1513 only increased Dijon's innate tendency to erect impressive ramparts and then hunker down behind them. Under the terms of the Treaty of Senlis (1493), the Burgundian capital remained a frontier city within reach of imperial (and later Spanish) outposts. The walls of the city were therefore strengthened through the addition of ten imposing towers with far greater dissuasive power than the medieval turrets punctuating the walls of many other cities. From these towers Felix enjoyed a view of Dijon almost equivalent to that of a print offering a bird's-eye view of the city that Edouard Bredin created in 1574 for Belleforest's *Cosmographie universelle,* which came out the following year.

The thick walls were backed up by a militarized city. The conical-roofed towers of the royal castle adjacent to the walls near the point where Felix made his discreet entry were manned by no more than eight or ten of the king's soldiers, but the local authorities could if necessary muster some eight to ten thousand men in arms, counting reinforcements from the surrounding plains. There was reason to fear, however, that this municipal militarism, coupled with Burgundian tradition, might some day pose a threat to the power of the French king. But already, only three-quarters of a century after the death of Charles the Bold, the memory of the "Great Duke of the West" was fading. Loyalty to France outweighed any nostalgia for an independent Burgundy.

The city of Dijon stood first and foremost for judicial power, which had grown steadily over the half century preceding Felix's visit. In 1511 the provincial parlement had moved into a palace of its own. In 1533 the Estates of Burgundy were depicted as a series of concentric circles, with financial institutions and the *chambres des comptes* in the center surrounded by city mayors, nobility, and clergy. In 1535 a complex system of municipal elections was established based partly on genuine elections, partly on municipal cooptation. In 1536–38, Francis I's ephemeral conquests in Savoy made it possible to expand the (scanty) jurisdiction of the parlement of Dijon as far as Bresse and Bugey. In 1537 the same parlement, accustomed to steady growth, added an additional chamber, the so-called Chambre Criminelle de la Tournelle. In 1542, Burgundy, along with its capital Dijon, was integrated into the system of *généralités,* remote ancestors of the provincial *intendances; other généralités* were set up at the same time throughout France. In 1553 the city's mayor and aldermen took advantage of the monarchy's war debt to purchase the local and royal *prévôté,* which exercised general police functions.

These developments were of interest to Felix only incidentally, insofar as they had already begun to give Dijon its distinctive character as a judicial city, a character that it would retain throughout the Ancien Régime. A clique of magistrates from parlement owned most of the surrounding flatland and dominated the peasantry, in enlightened fashion to be sure.[64] Felix had his own concerns. On May 3 he immersed himself in the past. Early in the morning, even before entering Dijon, he had visited the Carthusian monastery at Champmol, on the western edge of the ramparts. He had sincerely admired the tombs of the dukes of Burgundy (*schöne begräbnissen*) and appreciated the cenotaph of Philip the Bold, portrayed as a recumbent figure, almost life-sized, wrapped in an ermine-lined azure mantle and resting on the lion of Flanders—a typical product of the union of Capetian ancestry (the *fleur de lys*) with Flemish energy. Felix was struck by the sculpted figures of monks encircling a miniature cloister at the base of Philip's tomb. The monks' hoods revealed or concealed a wide range of personalities from preacher to dandy, ascetic to intellectual.

Felix also enjoyed a privilege we can no longer share: he was able to contemplate the entirety of the Carthusian calvary, a destination of countless pilgrims and source of innumerable indulgences, which had been built in the late fourteenth and early fifteenth century under the supervision of Claus Sluter. Here, a crucified Christ, man's intercessor with the hereafter, stands next to a Saint John, preaching the faith, a dolorous Virgin, and a sinful but repentant Magdalene. Felix, who knew his Gospels, nevertheless mistook this Golgotha for a Mount of Olives carved in stone (*gehuwener ölberg*). This error reveals the young Swiss traveler's devotion to the Last Supper and the anguish of Christ, for which the Mount of Olives served as a stage or witness in the time of the Gospel.

Of course one couldn't expect a "heretic" like Felix to express enthusiasm for the cult of the Virgin. When Georges Lengherand, the mayor of Mons (in present-day Belgium), visited Champmol in 1486, he noted that the Carthusian church contained "a gold and silver table marking the death of the Virgin Mary, a chapel of the Annunciation to the Virgin, quite beautiful . . . and a number of beautiful reliquaries, including one containing Our Lady's arm." Felix mentions none of these things. A full-fledged citizen of Basel, he had banished veneration of the Virgin from his mind. Yet when he mentions the monks, or rather the sculptured images of monks, he spares us for once his constant jibes at "priestlings," whether regular or secular. Perhaps the funereal grandeur of Champmol had touched him deeply.

At the end of this full day in May 1557, Felix may have spent the night at an inn in Dijon, a city whose textile and pewter industries had prospered, attracting new clients to local hostels. After all, the Rouen-Paris-Lyons-Dijon axis was a major trade route, further stimulated by France's annexation of Burgundy in the 1480s. The number of inns in the city had increased steadily, from thirty or so in 1530 to sixty-six in 1593; there must have been about fifty at the time of Felix's visit. Following the example of Lyons, the municipal authorities adopted a laissez-faire, antiguild economic policy. They could only approve of the consequent increase in the number of inns. Of course *hôtel* rhymes with *bordel* (bordello), and the disorderly conduct that frequently went along with such rapid growth triggered certain puritanical reflexes in Renaissance Burgundy. These were in part a response to the increase in veneral disease, one concrete result of which was an attempt to establish a home for repentant prostitutes on rue de la Poulaillerie in 1538.

Felix, however, was in no mood to linger in Dijon. Basel lay within reach. He stayed just long enough to have lunch with his young friend Caspar Krug, who was living in Dijon at the time. Caspar was just fifteen, as Felix had been in 1552 when he first went to Montpellier. He was the son of Caspar Krug Sr., himself the son of a locksmith and by trade an ironmonger who became a guild leader and bürgermeister of Basel. Krug Sr. was also a Latinist, and in 1563 he was ennobled by Emperor Ferdinand I during a stay in the Rhineland (F 299). About the great man's son we know only that he was raised in the splendor of his father's house, Spalenhof (which later became a theater), and that he had been in Dijon for some time (*ein zeit lang*), so long that he had practically forgotten his German (*Teutsch vergessen*), a circumstance that made conversation with Felix difficult. It is highly unlikely that Caspar Jr. was a student in the Burgundian capital. Francis I's efforts to found a university in Dijon in 1516 had not borne fruit, and the best the city could boast of was a *collège*, or secondary school, which had been in operation since the 1530s, having replaced a school headed by Pierre Turel, the Burgundian Nostradamus and author in 1523 of a work entitled *Grant pronostication*.

On the afternoon of May 3, Felix bade farewell to young Krug and left Dijon. His route took him near the old church of Saint-Michel: partially rebuilt, its triumphal facade, decorated with a Last Judgment in the latest Renaissance style, depicted a recent execution, which had taken place some time between 1547 and 1551. He also passed Saint-Pierre, a powerful if oddly round bastion which stood as a defense against attack from Franche-Comté. This fortress had been built in 1515 along the southern ramparts in conjunction with repairs to the city's walls. From there the two young men proceeded along the road to Auxonne and Dole. But first they had to cross the Ouche, which was well stocked with fish (*sehr fischreich wasser*).[65] They stopped for the night in Genlis, a few leagues from Dijon.

On May 4, Felix crossed the Saône. The bridge made an impression on him. Underneath its arches, traveling upstream and down, passed lines of vessels loaded with iron, wheat, wine, glass and wood from Lorraine, bundles of hide and wool, oil, and herring. That afternoon and evening he visited Dole, a city of 3,000 to 3,500 inhabitants. He briefly inspected the irregular, polygonal enclosure consisting of seven winged bastions connected by curtains "in the Genoese style," whose construction Charles V had ordered in 1541 as a defensive measure against a possible French attack from the west. Continuing along the logical route, Felix headed toward the center of town, passing Notre-Dame, a collegiate church in a heavy late-Gothic style on which construction had begun in 1509 and would end in 1557, the year of Felix's visit. The porch tower of this church, topped by a belfry and lookout post manned round-the-clock by a sentry, was not yet finished.[66] Dole lived in fear of French invasion, although in this era of regional peace that fear was seldom fulfilled. This small community could muster nearly a thousand men to defend it, including active soldiers and reservists, militiamen and arquebusiers, and residents of both the town itself and its adjoining suburbs and countryside.

The porch of the church faced a line of forty-eight shops. Next door stood the parlement, the seat of collective government, whose twenty magistrates, grouped in two chambers, represented the local elite of the Comté, or Franche-Comté as it was also known. The parlement of Dole embodied—constitutional patriotism *oblige*—the ideal of a government of judges, an ideal that the Paris parlement would never achieve despite its desire to do so in the period between the Fronde and the Revolution. Felix Platter paid a brief visit to the University of Dole, where he probably felt at home. The university dispensed knowledge to a hundred or so students from Flanders, the Tyrol, Saxony, and Pomerania—that is, to *Teutschen*, hence Felix's compatriots in the broad sense, many of whom retained their folk ways and were not terribly serious students.[67]

On the morning of May 5, Felix made his way on horseback across Franche-Comté from Dole to Besançon (which was not a French city at the time). In the countryside he saw houses with pointed gables and thick stone walls pierced by tiny windows; vast haylofts stored the land's produce. Towns were surrounded by ramparts of red brick lapped by a muddy stream or extended by a system of moats. After spending the night of May 5 at the Auberge du Bois de Cerf, Felix entered Besançon on May 6 via the Porte des Arènes, which involved passing through a double partition and a sort of obstacle course. Along the way he passed extensive vineyards both outside and inside the walls; these stretched north, south, west, and northwest of the city. In the streets Felix and his companion encountered vintners carrying sacks and two-tined pitchforks on their shoulders and picks or pruning knives in their hands as well as small kegs fastened to their belts.

Felix spent the entire day of May 6 in Besançon (population 10,000), where a statue of Charles V stood in front of the city hall. The emperor, revered by the local populace, was poised astride an eagle soaring off on the north wind. Hans Ruedin, the son of a Basel ironmonger and Felix's disagreeable companion ever since Paris, had lived near Besançon as an adolescent and had learned French there. Although the city's schools functioned only intermittently, they were not bad. A partially secularized *collège* had been in operation for a decade, offering courses in reading and writing, grammar, rhetoric, and Greek. Ruedin, a convivial fellow, took Felix to see his former landlords, who owned a house (*hus*) in town. The two young men spent the day dancing, playing the lute, chatting, and flirting with the daughter of the house, a certain Barbel. Forty-three years later, while traveling in Franche-Comté, Professor Felix Platter would again meet this same Barbel. Now past sixty, his former dance partner had grown old and ugly in Felix's eyes; no doubt he hadn't looked at himself in the mirror recently. In the interim she had given birth to two illegitimate sons, now grown men.

After supper, Felix and Hans, having left young Barbel, went for a walk with some young nobles who, in the course of their revels, tried to pass themselves off as peasants (*buren*). These aristocratic youths stemmed from a part of the Franche-Comté elite whose nobility was of recent date. They followed in the footsteps of two illustrious Franche-Comtois, Nicolas Perrenot and his son, Cardinal Grandvelle, in the sense that their roots were in the judicial bourgeoisie, which had supplanted the older noble lineages that once dominated the region. Felix joined his new friends in raising a ruckus in front of the houses of Italian merchants (from Genoa, Milan, and Florence) whose business had brought them to reside in Besançon, where they rubbed shoulders with German businessmen from Strasbourg, Wurtemberg, and Basel and with traders from Geneva. These businessmen were not averse to investing their capital in local vineyards. The presence of the Italians was due in part to a decision by the Republic of Genoa in 1535 to organize exchange fairs in Besançon. This fledgling financial market did not last long, however, because the Genoese soon came to feel that the Besançon arrangement was cumbersome and perhaps even harmful to their interests.

Still, the 1535 decision remained important: the term *bizensone* was still applied to foreign exchange fairs even when held in other places such as Poligny and Chambéry. The fact that the name stuck shows how significant the event was in people's minds as well as in the fortunes of the city on the Doubs. As for the confrontation between the young French-speaking nobles and the local foreign colony, whether from Italy or elsewhere, this was a common occurrence, not at all unusual in a city of any size, and not only in Franche-Comté. Sometimes students of different "nations" clashed, and at other times there were confrontations that were partly ethnic, partly social in origin. In this case it was local nobles versus merchants from across the Alps.

*   *   *

During his stay in Besançon, Felix was greatly concerned about the behavior of his friend Hans Ruedin.[68] After celebrating with the group of young nobles, Ruedin had become so drunk that he had collapsed fully clothed on the bed the two travelers were sharing at the inn. Annoyed at the prospect of a sleepless night, Felix undressed and placed his naked behind on his sleeping friend's face (F 290). Although he doesn't tell us what ensued, we shall refrain from making any diagnosis of latent homosexuality, that perennial favorite of psychoanalysts who pose as historians.

This scabrous incident temporarily put an end to two weeks of intense and very difficult relations with Hans Ruedin, from whom Felix had expected great things but who had in fact caused him no end of trouble since leaving Paris. The two had fought constantly on the journey home. We have only Felix's side of the story. Hans, who used the familiar *du* with Felix, was, according to young Platter, rich, pretentious, and much given to practical jokes, only some of which were funny. All in all, he lacked maturity and was woefully ignorant. At the beginning of their trip together, he had tricked Felix into contributing to the support of the mercenary who was traveling with them, a soldier of fortune who continually embarrassed the son of the old printer-pedagogue. Hans Ruedin also did not hesitate to mock the professional hopes of the recent graduate of the University of Montpellier by predicting that when Felix became a doctor he would have difficulty finding a job.

Furthermore, Ruedin coldly discussed the possibility of killing the dog that had followed young Platter all the way from Languedoc. Felix was especially disappointed in his friend because relations between them had been good when they had first met back in Paris. Still, Felix was not one to hold a grudge. Ruedin had an eye ailment that was slow to heal, and his companion, despite their differences, changed the dressings on the bad eye every night. In the end the treatment proved effective. Back in Switzerland, the two youths eventually made up. Ruedin, soon after arriving, married Rosina Irmy, the daughter of a Basel burgher. When Felix married Madlen Jeckelmann, Hans and Rosina gave the couple a rather handsome goblet in gratitude for the ophthalmological treatment Felix had dispensed on the road from Paris (F 290, 329). Hans died young, of plague, in 1564.

On May 7 and 8, 1557, Hans and Felix rode hard to cover the long distance between Besançon and Montbéliard. For a while they followed the Doubs Valley; they came close to the abbey of Baume-les-Dames but did not stop. On the morning of May 8, they took a room at the Auberge de la Tête de Maure. Montbéliard (population 2,000–3,000) was at this time the capital of a county in which both French and Romansch were spoken. Henriette, the countess of Montbéliard, had married Eberhard von Wurtemberg early in the fifteenth century, transforming her fief south of the Vosges into a possession of the Wurtemberg dynasty for several generations. In May 1553, Duke Kristof von Wurtemberg, preoccupied with his duchy, had ceded possession of the county of Montbéliard to his uncle, Georg von Wurtemberg. Two years later, in 1555, Georg, aged fifty-seven, married Barbe, daughter of Philip the Magnanimous, the landgrave of Hesse; Barbe was nineteen, thirty-eight years younger than her husband.

From this marriage was born Count Friedrich, who was destined to succeed his father. On the whole, Georg was an enlightened sovereign. He tried, without much success, to make the Doubs navigable; given the means available at the time, the job was impossible. As conflict gradually diminished, he respected the liberties of the city of Montbéliard, which enjoyed the privilege of self-government through its aldermen, while Georg retained responsibility for governing the vast county of which the city was the capital. The count's religious policy was of even greater importance. The county of Montbéliard, which lay in "Welch" territory, was the only non-German region to adhere to a fairly strict variety of Lutheranism. In 1550 the two religions, Catholic and Protestant, coexisted in Montbéliard on an "interim" basis decreed by Charles V. Soon, however, Duke Kristof and later Count Georg prohibited "papist" practices, abolished the mass, and banished priests. In 1552, the priests of Montbéliard were described in an official document as "animals, asses, public embarrassments, drunkards, blasphemers, and murderers who are only after their poor lambs' lips and fleece." Texts such as these tell us a great deal about a certain form of sixteenth-century intolerance. The logical cul-

mination of such attitudes came in October 1556, a few months before
Felix's visit, when Count Georg outright prohibited pilgrimages, masses,
baptisms, confessions, prayers for the dead, holy water, the ringing of
bells to ward off bad weather, the use of blessed candles and branches by
clerics, and other "superstitions." In contrast, listening to the word of
God was prescribed, and one version of Christianity was granted a monopoly.[69]

Exclusionary measures against the papists did not necessarily lead to
intolerance among Protestants: Georg and his friend Toussain, chief pastor of the county of Montbéliard, steered a middle course between the
Lutheran orthodoxy advocated by Wurtemberg and the Calvinist rigid-
ity that had taken hold in Geneva. They deplored Calvin's excesses, including his execution of Michael Servetus (whose path Felix had crossed
in Vienne in 1552, when the Jewish-born heresiarch was secretly preparing
his great treatise on unitarian, anti-trinitarian, pre-Socinian theology, a
theology that would come into its own in the twentieth century long after its author had perished at the stake in 1553).[70] In this respect, the ideas
of the Protestant humanist Castellion in Basel clearly had a calming influence on Count Georg and Reverend Toussain, as well as on the Platters,
both father and son. Calvin accordingly nursed a certain suspicion of the
authorities in Montbéliard. This made no difference to Count Georg: his
authority as "Protestant prince" gave him full power in religious matters,
and his response was to insist on the education of the young within his
principality. His hope was that this would not only contribute to their
earthly well-being but also familiarize them with the texts of the Gospels
and the Old Testament and those of their Protestant interpreters. Meanwhile, relations between the county of Montbéliard and the France of
Henri II remained friendly, insofar as Henri, while persecuting
Huguenots at home, sought alliances with Protestant princes to the east,
especially when those princes controlled territories in which Romance
languages were spoken, as was the case with the Wurtemberg dukes and
counts.[71]

We have two versions of Montbéliard, one from Felix, the other from
Thomas Jr. The younger Platter wrote his account in February 1600,
shortly after his visit to the region. He correctly noted the growth of the
population, not only in recent years but also over the past century and
more. Both city and county had gained in size, buildings, people, and
wealth (*grösse, gebeüwen, volck und reichtumb*). New mills had sprung up,
as well as botanical gardens and zoos in which deer gamboled inside city
walls. A new palace had been built next to the old château. All of this,
moreover, had taken place in a stimulating climate of bilingual Protes-

tantism, which left it up to the individual to choose between Welch and Teutonic traditions (T2 923). Although Felix's text concerned his exploration of Montbéliard in the spring of 1557, he wrote it much later, in 1612, and it was far more "existential" and personal than his younger brother's account.

At the inn where he was staying on May 8, Felix ran into a childhood friend, Jacob Truchsess, who came from a noble family in Basel, perhaps the most illustrious family in the city. Jacob had in the meantime been appointed to an important post as *Hofmeister* at Count Georg's court. He had made a good marriage, in 1555, to Salomé von Andlau, the daughter of Arbogast von Andlau and Eva von Pfirt—a whole series of *vons* that augured well for the young couple's future. The Hofmeister, a compliant courtier, decided to escort the young Swiss travelers out of the city on the last leg of their journey. He began by getting drunk at the inn (the Platters, as upstanding burghers, invariably poured scorn in their memoirs on the bibulous habits of the nobility). Already intoxicated, Jacob pulled on his boots with some difficulty and then got up to accompany his friends, who had not asked for an escort. At the first ford, Truchsess, unsteady on his feet, came close to drowning (F 291). Once again, we see the German penchant for drunkenness (from which Hans Ruedin himself was not exempt) in contrast to the relative moderation of the "Welches."

Fortunately, Count Georg had foreseen the difficulty. Well aware of his Hofmeister's chronic drinking, he had sent a small escort after him. The soldiers fished the drunken courtier out of the stream and carried him home, soaking wet and fully sobered up. Hans and Felix continued without stopping all the way to Seppois, the gateway to Alsace, between Montbéliard and Basel. Seppois marked the limit of the Romance-language zone, and Felix was well aware of having crossed a linguistic boundary the minute he set foot in Germanic territory. In contrast, his earlier passage from Catholic into Protestant territory (Besançon to Montbéliard) had not made any particular impression on him, Protestant though he was. The last stage of the journey, on May 9 (with a lunch stop at Waldighofen), was marked by yet another dispute between Felix and Hans, whose tattered felt cloak made him look like a beggar. Hans insisted on borrowing Felix's cloak and threatened to throw it in the mud if Felix refused. Felix wanted no part of this, but to mollify his companion he took from his bag, and risked soiling, the new Spanish cape that he had been keeping pristine for the imminent reunion with his family and fiancée. Did this quarrel spoil the homecoming? No, for Basel lay just ahead, beckoning to her prodigal sons.

At the first sight of the Basel cathedral, Felix felt himself bursting with joy, to which he gave vent by firing his harquebus. In his excitement he fired two shots into a garden gate. Spitting fire, the quarreling travelers thus arrived at the monumental Spalentor, the city's main gates. Along the walls were three rows of towers, rebuilt in the second half of the fourteenth century when the ramparts were repaired after an earthquake in 1356.[72] The Spalentor was the entrance to Basel for travelers from France and Alsace, and Felix's arrival marked the end of his Tour de France. On this trip from Montpellier through southwestern France and Paris and on to Basel, he had averaged more than thirty miles a day, roughly the same as on his trip from Basel to Montpellier five years earlier, in 1552. *O Basilea finis mea:* O Basel! End of my journey.

## CHAPTER NINE

# Summer and Fall: Thesis and Wedding

After passing through the Spalentor, Felix parted company with Hans at Gens ("Goose House"), the house that Hans's father, Jacob Ruedin, had enlarged and renovated. This construction work reflected Jacob's success in his career, which within a few years would take him to Paris as the official representative of the Swiss Leagues at the court of the Valois. Goose House would continue to occupy an important place in Hans's life. Even after his marriage, he came often to see his father and his eleven brothers and sisters (children of his own mother or of Jacob's three subsequent wives) as well as his forty-odd nephews and nieces. A good comrade who held no grudges, Felix walked a short way with his other companion, the annoying mercenary who had been with him since Paris. (To be sure, Felix and the two Hanses had made a well-armed trio, a daunting enough presence to discourage any French highwayman with larceny in mind). When it came time to part, Felix gave the mercenary his cloak. At last he was alone. But then he ran into Georg von Brück, still wearing mourning for his father, David Joris, who had died in late August 1556 and whose real name was Johann von Brück. A wealthy refugee from Holland, Johann had secretly subscribed to the ultimate heresy, Anabaptism, of which Protestant officialdom in Basel took a dim view. He had had eleven children, counting Georg, and had been a great friend of the Platters. Two years later, Felix looked on unflinchingly when the cadaver of Johann von Brück, freshly exhumed for the purpose, was consigned to the flames in a posthumous "execution" imposed by the Basel authorities for the grave crime of "Anabaptism."[1] The "condemned" man had successfully kept his heresy hidden until after his death. Despite the deplorable public incineration of his corpse, Johann's many descendants were not barred from pursuing successful careers in Basel once they had made their peace with the local religious authorities. The burning of the corpse was forgotten.

From Tanners' Alley to Zum Gejägd, the home of the Platters, Felix was tempted to take a direct route, which would have taken him past the home of his fiancée, Madlen Jeckelmann, in the middle section of Freie Strasse at the corner of Rüdengasse (F 294). But he chose a detour instead, for he knew that Madlen, a frightened doe of a girl if ever there was one, was modest and reserved. Perhaps he also wanted his own family to be the first to experience the joy of his homecoming. At last the not very prodigal son came to Obere Freie Strasse and stood before his father's house, where he found only a man carrying a urine pot and obviously in search of a doctor—possibly a good omen (*tütnus*).

Felix rang the bell, but the house was empty. It was Sunday, and his father was off working on his suburban farm. The servant was at church. Felix's mother, who had been gossiping with neighbors, ran over, burst into tears, and hugged her son. Thinner, older, and more wrinkled than Felix remembered, she wore a green cloak and fashionable white shoes. Eventually his father returned, accompanied by Castellion, the tolerant humanist. Thomas exclaimed at how much his son had grown. Indeed, in almost six years in Montpellier, he had grown taller by a head and a neck (*kopf und hals*).

By late afternoon Felix's homecoming had turned into a block party. The neighbors came—the same neighbors who would turn up six months later at the younger Platter's wedding. Dorly (or Dorothea), the servant, ran over to the Jeckelmanns to tell Madlen that her beau had returned. She made such a fuss that Felix's presumptive fiancée almost fainted. The young man's friends were invited that night for dinner. Among them was Balthasar Hummel, the son of the mercenary from Little Basel, a childhood companion of Felix's and a staunch friend during the Montpellier years. He had recently gone into business as an apothecary, and his shop, after struggling at first, was at last showing signs of life. Also present was Theodor Bempelford (Theodorus Pempelfurdus), a native of Düsseldorf and a student in Basel since 1556, after having been a proofreader in Lyons, Paris, and Basel. In April, Theodorus had carried letters home to Basel from Felix in Paris (F 285). Such favors could not go unrewarded. After supper, all the young people, including Felix, left to escort Theodor back to his rooms at the inn Zur Kronen. On Freie Strasse (Fryenstros) they ran into Madlen Jeckelmann. She recognized Felix in his Spanish cape and took off as usual like a frightened lark. During his six years in Montpellier, Felix had apparently remained faithful to his nervous young lady, preferring the prospect of a lifetime of happiness to the pleasures of a Mediterranean night. Madlen's skittishness did not offend him. Time had opened up before him: the future redeemed the present. At Zur Kronen the group of young men accepted a *drunck,* or round of drinks, from the innkeeper, Emmanuel Bomhart, who had taken over the inn from his father and had once been a classmate of Felix's. Unlike some of his colleagues in the tavern trade,

Emmanuel "had culture": he had received a bachelor's degree from the University of Basel in 1552 and a master's degree a short time later. The informal celebration at the inn was moving for Felix, because the guests included his future brother-in-law, Franz Jeckelmann Jr., and Franz's brother-in-law, Daniel Wielandt of Alsace, the son of a municipal official in Mulhouse who would soon succeed his father in office. Franz and Daniel had married the Schoelly sisters, Mergelin and Sophie, the daughters of a master saddlemaker. And they were not the only connection with Alsace and Mulhouse, a region and a city with which the Platters had deep affinities. The host, Emmanuel Bomhart, had married a wealthy Mulhouse heiress, Anna Wächter, in 1557. Other marriages subsequently united the pair's siblings, creating still further ties between the Wächter and Bomhart clans and hence between Mulhouse and Basel. Emmanuel Bomhart had been a suitor of Madlen Jeckelmann but had been rejected in favor of Felix. He did not pass up the opportunity to have some fun at Felix's expense. The younger Platter's "secret" if promising idyll with the Jeckelmann girl was hardly a secret any more. No one talked about anything else. Around midnight, Felix returned home, where his parents were still celebrating his safe return, which of course they owed to the grace of God.

From Monday, May 10, to Saturday, May 15, Felix paid courtesy calls, accepted dinner invitations, and made various arrangements. He repaired his father's harp and the cypress lute that he had received long ago as a gift from his music teacher Thiebold Schoenauer. He also took long walks with Thomas to the family estate in Gundeldingen. Thomas reminded him of the need to put first things first: his doctorate and his marriage, his thesis and his wife. Thomas also asked him to speak more slowly, for Felix had picked up the southern French habit of chattering at a rapid rate. There were inevitable encounters with Madlen in the streets of Basel. The most notable of these took place near the Marktplatz, just outside the huge Schol slaughterhouse. Felix, on his way home from church, was wearing a velvet cap and a dagger at his side, as was the custom among students at the time, even non-noble students of modest background such as the Platters. Madlen was standing in line to buy meat. When she spotted the fashionably dressed young man in the distance, she ran into the slaughterhouse and hid among the beef carcasses and pork bellies. For a long time thereafter she refused to set foot in the Schol, where all the butcher's boys were now on to her romance and wouldn't let her forget it.

Other encounters were more wrenching. When Felix went to the cathedral with Balthasar Hummel on Monday morning, he immediately ran into a Junker named Ludwig von Reischach. A German aristocrat in his seventies, Reischach had become a burgher of Basel because of his conversion to Protestantism. He gave Felix the cold shoulder and pretended not to recognize him because he took the young man's velvet cap and dagger to be aristocratic pretensions—a usurpation of the noble identity. On the plaza in front of the cathedral the former Montpellier student also encountered a trio of university professors, including his former teacher Hans Huber, to whom he presented a work of Clément Marot bound in Paris, where the bookbinding craft had reached a pinnacle of aesthetic perfection under Henri II. This work of Marot's was one of Felix's few contacts with the "Welch" literature of his time. It was of course a work by a Protestant author, and Felix in any case served only as an intermediary between author and reader. Was he perhaps more of a man of science than a man of letters? In any case, Huber continued to represent the francophone community of Basel, as he had done for many years.

Meanwhile, Felix devoted some effort to fixing up a small room for himself in his father's house, because he needed an agreeable place to study. This room was his father's, but since Thomas was busy with his teaching and with managing his boardinghouse, he let Felix use it during the day. Felix painted the bookshelves and turned wood under the supervision of a carpenter, whose wife taught him the art of mixing strong glues, though as the lesson proceeded she became totally confused. But Felix's major problems remained his thesis and his bride-to-be. The two were not independent: no doctorate, no wife. Jeckelmann would never give his daughter's hand to a man who was not a doctor, a good-for-nothing.

Felix took the first big step: he began courting Madlen. It was expected that courtship would lead quickly to a formal proposal to marry, after which the betrothed couple would be allowed to visit more frequently until the time of the wedding. To screw up his courage, Felix first went on May 10 to see his friend Jacob Huggelin, who, at twenty-seven, was older than Felix and already a doctor. Jacob had set up in practice in Basel. He lived with his father-in-law, not far from where Felix lived on the upper part of Freie Strasse, toward the center of town. The son of a tailor, Jacob had married a weaver's daughter (endogamy in the textile trade). For Felix he was a role model: married, in practice, and moving up in society. Huggelin had studied Greek, philosophy, and medicine in Basel and Montpellier and perhaps also in Paris and Valence. With strong backing from the Basel city council, he had embarked on a successful career and would soon go on to become official physician to the margrave of Baden.

Seven years later, however, in 1564, his remarkable career would be cut short by the plague, which claimed him and so many others. Tragically, the young made way for the younger. In 1557 Jacob Huggelin was already famous in Basel for his elegant dress and especially for his Polish leather shoes, known locally as "horned pumps." Once, when he slipped and fell flat on his back, the "horns" on his shoes protruding upward made a nice effect (F 308). After leaving Huggelin's office, Felix went to lunch with Sigmund von Pfirt. A noble and former Catholic priest, von Pfirt had married a woman of the aristocracy and become a burgher of Basel. He had been made a canon and been given a sinecure that the Protestants had taken over from the Catholics. In his sixties, he had hopes that Felix might marry his daughter Susanna. Unfortunately, the "pretty person" (*schön mensch*) was out of reach, boarding with a countess near Colmar, and in any case she was not long for this world. The beauty's brothers Sigmund Jr. and Solon had both been good friends of Felix's since childhood, when they had been part-time boarders at Thomas's Gymnasium. The elder von Pfirt was beyond prejudice: though born noble, he was willing to allow his daughter to marry Felix, the son of a man who was not only a commoner but had spent his early years in grinding poverty. Basel was a democratic place.

Von Pfirt and Huggelin were not the main issue, however; Madlen was. The campaign to win her can be divided into three phases: the introduction, the marriage proposal, and the romance. The introduction was in a sense an artificial rite of passage, since the two young people already knew each other. It was decided, however, to make a ceremony of the occasion: an official introduction would serve as a kind of initiation. Thomas Platter therefore proposed a luncheon for May 16, during which the couple would be formally "introduced." The guests were to include Felix and the young woman dearest to his (and his father's) heart, Madlen's father and brother, and the brother's fiancée, a woman named Dorothea, a lively girl who was the daughter of a leading blacksmith. The setting chosen for this ceremonious occasion was the Platter estate in Gundeldingen. To start things off, the guests took an invigorating walk around the grounds. Then came "luncheon," which was actually a formal dinner. Afterwards there was music and dancing, and Felix distinguished himself by playing the lute and dancing a very French dance, the *gaillarde*. Finally, the whole company returned to Basel on foot: the two prospective fathers-in-law, the teacher and the surgeon, walked in front, while the young people brought up the rear, kept in good spirits by Dorothea's indefatigable conversation. Her practical advice to the lovelorn brought a blush to modest Madlen's cheeks: "When two young people are fond of each other and see each other frequently," the blacksmith's daughter remarked, "they mustn't wait too long, for there can easily be a mishap [*unglick*]."[2] That night, when he went to bed, Felix felt strange, "like stone." Was something he had been dreaming about for years soon to come true? Madlen, though still reserved, had shown herself not just cooperative but quite happy. The introduction was one hurdle out of the way. Now he could make an official proposal of marriage. It would be no less complex than the sort of proposal a powerful family might make when negotiating a dynastic marriage. Time was of the essence, because the young couple, their appetites whetted, had agreed to meet, chaperoned only by the ubiquitous Dorothea and Frau Frön, an elderly, blind matchmaker and godmother of Jeckelmann the surgeon. Frau Frön had Madlen's full confidence; indeed, the old woman and the young maiden sometimes shared the same bed. On May 25, the three young people and the old lady went cherry picking just outside the Spalentor. Increasingly amorous, Felix lavished ardent words on his intended, who received them warmly, albeit with her customary modesty. When Felix pressed her, she readily acknowledged that his affection did not displease her. She had nothing against it. Thus she returned tenderness for tenderness, even if the reflection was but a pale copy of the original.

The consent of Madlen's father, Franz Jeckelmann, still had to be obtained, however. Good friends from various segments of Basel society urged the surgeon to award his daughter's hand to Felix. Caspar Krug, one of the city's leading metal dealers, played an important role. The son of a locksmith, well known in town and enormously proud of his prominence, Krug, in his sixties, did not shrink from envisioning a rather grandiose epitaph for himself, inspired by the Latin poet Ennius: "What a small sepulchre for such a great man!" In 1557, Caspar Krug held high positions in various local guilds. The guilds enforced strict professional rules and facilitated social relations among the elite in a sort of freemasonry without the secret rituals and rigamarole. Before long, Krug would be mayor of Basel and would represent the city at international meetings, at the imperial court, at gatherings of the Swiss Confederation, and at royal courts, including that of Henri II. He held Felix in high esteem because his wife, Anna Nussbaum, had recently suffered from exhaustion after giving birth to twins, and the young doctor had treated her. Felix prescribed slices of marzipan concocted of sugar, egg whites, lemon juice, and orange blossom in accordance with a recipe he had brought back from Montpellier. Within a few days, Anna was back on her feet. Felix's "gentle medicine" had worked. What is more, Krug had sounded out the young pharmacist Balthasar Hummel about Felix, and he had passed on the favorable report he had received. Thus the modest shop-keeper (Hummel) and the distinguished merchant (Krug) had joined hands to bestow their blessing on the future doctor of medicine. Felix, they told Jeckelmann, would make a suitable son-in-law.

Equally positive reports reached Jeckelmann via his friends and noble protectors, the Reich zu Reichensteins, a family of Catholic aristocrats. The head of the family, Jacob Reich Jr., known as "the Old Man" (*der Alt*), had one eye askew and sported a well-trimmed beard. He presided over a family of ten children. He was also Dr. Jeckelmann's spiritual kin, because Jeckelmann had been godfather to the old man's son, Jacob Reich III. The surgeon was always visiting the Reichs in their rural for-tress with its deep moats, where great celebrations were often held. A horse from the Reich stables had been placed at Dr. Jeckelmann's dis-posal. At the time, moreover, the Jeckelmanns and the Reichs were in particularly close contact because one of the Old Man's sons, stricken with the pox, was being cared for in a heated room just off the street in Dr. Jeckelmann's surgery. Among the Reichs, Felix found ardent cham-pions of his marriage proposal. What is more, the noble clan enjoyed par-ticular prestige in Basel despite the city's Protestantism, because one of the Reich children had been miraculously healed by the Virgin Mary after a fall in the mountains. Over the next few years, the Reichs of Basel and Alsace would become loyal clients of Dr. Felix Platter.

Krug and Reich, the bourgeoisie and the nobility: all the best people in Basel urged Jeckelmann to consent to his daughter's wedding. The sur-geon still held out. Was Felix's marriage to become an affair of state? The unanimous chorus of burgraves, constituting the upper crust of Basel so-ciety, lacked only the favorable opinion of the high magistrates invested with *auctoritas*—magistrates who, in Basel, tended to be clerics and pas-tors, doctors, politicians, and administrators rather than jurists. The judgment from this quarter would also prove to Felix's advantage, thanks to Professor Dr. Hans Huber, who, with Thomas Platter's consent, was charged with delivering the official proposal of marriage, and also thanks to Franz Jeckelmann himself. Hans Huber, in his fifties, was the son of an innkeeper from Ravensburg.[3] He had gone on to study in a *collège* and then at universities in Sélestat, Paris, Montpellier, and Toulouse. Huber was an extremely active and busy person, much like the man Felix Platter would become. Since 1543 he had been professor of both practical medi-cine and physics at the University of Basel, at times holding both posi-tions simultaneously. He was also the city's *Stadtarzt,* or municipal physician, and rector. A handsome man with a tapered mustache and vel-vety eyes, he had seventeen children by his second wife. Keen for innovation, Huber was for Felix the very embodiment of the good teacher and benign elder, the best and most trustworthy of friends, and a man who could always be counted on to be optimistic and joyful (F 110, 299). Taking it upon himself to convey Felix's proposal of marriage to Jeckelmann, Huber one morning invited the surgeon to the cathedral. With the peremptoriness of the invitation, he stressed his social superiority, as a university professor, to a mere practitioner with lancet and scalpel. When he had heard Huber's requests beneath the sacred arches of the cathedral, did Jeckelmann still need convincing? He raised objections, beginning with Thomas Platter's heavy debts. Huber responded that Platter's land and houses constituted assets at least equal to his liabilities. Jeckelmann then expressed the fear that the din raised by Thomas's boarders on the school playground next to his house might offend his daughter's tender ears. Huber accordingly conveyed Thomas's promise that he would close his boardinghouse, a promise that Thomas had no intention of keeping and in fact did not keep. The final objection was one that the widower Jeckelmann did not voice out loud: he needed his daughter, a good worker, as long as he could have her to keep house for him. This hurdle was easily overcome: for the first years of her married life, Madlen Jeckelmann would manage two households, her husband's and her father's. Hans Huber had an answer for everything, and in any case it was Madlen, not Huber, who would have to bear the exhausting burden.

The time had come to take the fateful step. Jeckelmann gave Professor Huber his tentative agreement. The accord was to remain secret, however, until Felix had obtained his doctorate, the key to all his plans for the future. Over the coming weeks, the young couple were permitted to see a great deal of each other. Felix spent every afternoon and many evenings at the home of his intended. He chatted with her about a thousand and one frivolous things, while she listened in indulgent silence. The couple were never left alone: chaperones were always present, often Jeckelmann himself, who pretended not to notice anything. The indulgent Frau Frön was part of the furniture: though blind, she didn't stuff cotton in her ears. Dorothea, Madlen's good friend and future sister-in-law, could not have been more discreet. And of course, in the next room, we mustn't forget the Junker Mark Reich zu Reichenstein III. The truth is that he heard none of the young lovers' mainly verbal wooing because he was too busy trying to bake or sweat away his pox in front of a fireplace stoked with guaiacum, a harsh treatment that was coupled with strict fasting on bread and water and impressive sweating.

Madlen and Felix were by now on quite good terms at home, but since their engagement was not yet official, "secrecy" still had to be maintained in public, or else people would talk. So once, for example, in early summer, when Felix and Dr. Huber were on their way to Hummel's pharmacy for a friendly chat, they ran into Madlen, who wore ribbons in her hair and a green apron (*griener schuben*). Following Jeckelmann's orders, she did not so much as glance at Felix, who stared at her without embarrassment from the other side of the street (F 301).

There was a similar lack of response when Felix, accompanied by his friend Schoenauer, the post-rider Bempelford, and the jeweler Hagenbach, a weaver's son and professional whistler, staged a nocturnal serenade in furtherance of the marriage plans of Thomas Guérin, a Helvetized Walloon printer, who hoped to marry Elisabeth Isengrien, the daughter of a printer with a shop on Freie Strasse. The concert was held in front of the Isengrien house, Zum Falcken. The players played stringed instruments—two lutes, a viola, and a harp—while Hagenbach accompanied with whistles, his specialty. The Isengriens then regaled the musicians with a *Schlafdrunck*, or nightcap, which was served with a variety of preserves. The party ended quite late, late enough so that the night watch checked the revelers' identity before allowing them to pass. Meanwhile, Felix had persuaded his fellow musicians to repeat their performance beneath Madlen's windows. Killing two birds with one stone, he thus transformed a cordial evening with his friends from Freie Strasse into a concert for his beloved. But the always haughty Jeckelmann kept a watchful eye on the proceedings. No door was opened to welcome the musicians and repay them for their efforts with food and drink. They considered themselves fortunate that no one had poured a bucket of water (or worse) on their heads. The musicians went home disappointed and empty-handed. Every man was king in his own castle, and the surgeon's household was almost puritanical in its ways.

Such amorous premarital secrecy had its share of bizarre consequences. Felix's intended received him warmly in the privacy of her home, but his evening visits eventually came to the attention of the local defenders of public morality, who treated the young man as if he were a criminal and unrepentant seducer. One night, as he was making his discreet exit from the Jeckelmann home, two zealots of virtue spotted him and took out after him with the intention of administering a shellacking (*gesteubt*). He escaped only because he was fleet of foot.

\*   \*   \*

"There is no such thing as love, only proofs of love." When a girl of rather chilly temperament such as Madlen became jealous, was her jealousy, in the absence of more concrete signs of passion, a sign of attachment, of possessiveness toward her beloved? Consider the case of Cleopha Baer, a widow of forty-six and a woman of easy virtue, or so people said—but then people will say anything. She was the daughter of Hans Baer, a man with three claims to fame, for he had been a draper, a court officer, and an ensign at the battle of Marignano, where he had died for Switzerland in 1515. Cleopha was a free woman, that is, a woman not under the tutelage of father or spouse: her husband, a local castellan of noble extraction, had died in 1552. And she had a crush on Felix. During the summer of 1557, she invited him to her house to play the lute at a sort of breakfast or brunch known as *morgen sup* (literally, "morning soup"). And she invited herself to Thomas's house, despite the cool welcome she received from both the master and his son. Madlen, who soon learned of these contacts, gave the man to whom she was now all but officially engaged a hard time about them. Felix was no fool, and certainly not fool enough to try to run down two hares at once. He quickly broke off his dalliance with Cleopha, and Madlen's attitude improved immediately. What Felix omits to tell us is that Cleopha died later that same year, thus putting an end once and for all to any further testing of Felix's affections for his fiancée. Cleopha's son Jonas went on to an administrative career in Innsbruck, where he became a member of the nobility, thus continuing the rise in society that his mother had begun, from textile bourgeoisie to aristocracy.

\* \* \*

Felix's preparations for the doctorate, the last hurdle he had to overcome before he could marry, began with an explicit reconciliation between the Platter family and the faculty of arts of the University of Basel (F 301). The professors of the faculty had long been on bad terms with Thomas, who had balked at granting them even a modicum of control over his Gymnasium. But Felix was a promising young man, and, impressed by his return, the professors threw in the towel. They invited him to come have a drink with them on June 10 at Zur Kronen, the inn kept by Felix's friend Emmanuel Bomhart, where they heaped him with presents (*schankten*), congratulated him, and declared their readiness to help him obtain his doctorate in medicine, which, however, it was not in their power to grant, their province being arts and letters, not the art of Aesculapius. Young Felix was delighted by this stroke of good fortune, not only for himself but also for his father, whose eminent contribution to education in the city had at last been granted a deserved seal of approval by the leading lights of the Basel intelligentsia.

The triumph with the faculty of arts merely whetted Felix's appetite, however. What remained was to win the absolutely indispensable backing of the faculty of medicine, which would grant him his doctorate. He lost no time in proposing his services as a junior lecturer, and his offer was accepted. Between June 10 and July 21, Felix diligently revised his notes. Then, on July 21, he gave his "maiden speech," as it were, an inaugural lesson that was attended by all the professors of medicine—a sort of dress rehearsal for a future thesis defense. Practically no one attended his next lecture, except for two Dutch students whom Felix now took on as private students, meeting with them four times a week starting at eight in the morning. In order to win their loyalty, he invited them to his father's home and authorized them to climb a fruit tree in the yard and eat the fruit. As a further demonstration of his trust, he showed them the curiosities in his personal museum. From his travels Felix had returned with an amateur's collection of stuffed lizards, shells from around Montpellier, fish from Palavas-les-Flots, and similar specimens. During these months of intensive study, Felix rarely lifted his nose from his books. He sold his horse for half what the noble animal had cost him. Worse luck, his father pocketed the money, much to the dismay of Felix, who was perpetually broke. Thomas's behavior seemed at odds with his natural obligations. Nevertheless, Felix consoled himself with music, his faithful companion throughout his life. He played the lute with two friends in one of the cottages on the Rhine that give the old houses of Basel their charm. Joining him were his old friend Thiebold Schönhauer and a new acquaintance, also a music lover, named Johann Jacob Wecker. Born in Basel eight years before Felix, Wecker was a universal man who had studied at universities in Saxony and Italy. Back in his home town, he would soon become a professor of Latin and dialectics and later a professor of medicine and dean of the medical faculty. Ultimately, gripped once again by wanderlust, he would set off for Colmar, where he became *Stadtarzt*. Wecker was interested in ways to make noble women look more beautiful than nature intended. In 1557 his wedding was still recent: he had married the widow Anna Keller, the sister of Professor Isaac Keller of the faculty of medicine. She was the author of a cookbook that attracted some notice in the German-speaking world, culinary backwater that it was. A woman by the name of Platter, also a noted cook, would score a similar success in the seventeenth century, in the time of Louis XIV.

Felix also saw Hans Ruedin occasionaly. Ruedin was still rather unpleasant, much as he had been on the trip from Paris to Montbéliard. Young Platter also saw Ruedin's brother-in-law, Ambrosius Frobenius, a member of the famous dynasty of humanist printers and publishers. At the time Ambrosius was still living in his family's beautiful house at 18, Bäumleingasse, where Erasmus had once stayed. All these young men— Ruedin, Frobenius, and Hummel—were now married, and Felix, for the time being still a lonely hunter and bachelor, burned to follow in their footsteps.

\*   \*   \*

There were five hurdles to overcome in short order before Felix could receive his doctorate: the petition, the *tentamen* (or preliminary examination), the examination, the disputation, and the promotion. The petition began with a petition to make a petition (*sic*), a sort of petition squared, that is, an application to apply for the doctorate in medicine: formalities beget formalities. On Saturday, August 14, 1557, Felix went to the home of Professor Dr. Oswald Baer, dean of the faculty of medicine. Baer, aged seventy-five at the time and originally from the Tyrol, was another Schyron: a preening, pretentious nonentity, a village peacock spreading his feathers at every opportunity, a vain opportunist, the very type of the low academic intriguer and professorial parvenu. He redeemed himself to some extent with a decided passion for music, an ever-smiling good humor, an unshakable affability, and a demonstration of authentic courage in confronting the plague. His remarkable pliability at various junctures had propelled him to the highest posts in Basel medicine, around which he had fluttered for forty years. He was professor, rector, dean, and municipal physician. His very mediocrity had allowed him to replace the extraordinary Paracelsus as *Stadtarzt,* for Paracelsus had, without apparent effort, succeeded in alienating nearly all the city's officials, who were jealous of a genius that often provoked hostility and left no one indifferent. True, Baer, even after he had arrived, sometimes suffered for his lack of scruples, as well as for his practice of splitting fees with his pharmacist first wife, which shocked many people in Basel and many graduates of the university. Still, Oswald Baer was clever enough to escape from more than one bad pass. After his first wife died, he married twice more, each marriage more brilliant than the last. He even managed to survive the religious and cultural upheavals of 1529–32, when Œcolampadian Protestantism captured the city. The revolution somehow spared Baer even as it destroyed the careers of other, less tenacious men. In any case, Professor Baer received Felix in a conciliatory manner because the young man posed no threat to him. Their meeting on August 14 took place in a house near the cathedral, one of several houses placed at the elderly teacher's disposal. Felix easily obtained Baer's approval to petition for the doctorate. The next day, he was summoned again to present his formal petition: once this compulsory ritual was out of the way, he would be officially a candidate for the doctorate.

Accordingly, on Sunday afternoon, Felix once again set out for the Baer house behind the cathedral. In theory this was a private home, but given the professor's position, it also served as a sort of semiofficial dean's office. Felix was well acquainted with the Baer real-estate holdings, since one of the buildings the professor owned was located at the sign of the Great Red Lion on Freie Strasse, not far from the Platters' house.

At Baer's residence Felix was greeted by two other old acquaintances: Professor Huber, who had already lent him a hand in presenting his marriage proposal to Madlen Jeckelmann, and Professor Isaac Keller (Cellarius), a man seven years older than Felix and, since 1552, professor of theoretical medicine. Keller would continue to enjoy a brilliant career in Basel until the day, a quarter of a century later, when he became involved up to his neck in a financial scandal that forced him to start over again as *Stadtarzt* of Sélestat.

Felix showed this magisterial trio his Montpellier degrees, bachelor's and master's. The capital of Languedoc enjoyed the utmost prestige in Basel, a "gallophile" city without a trace of anti-French feeling. With a speech prepared for the occasion, Felix asked for permission to seek the doctorate. Things seemed to be going well when all of a sudden one of the examiners asked his age. Felix, it turned out, would only turn twenty-one that fall. Baer's reaction to this news was hostile: to become a doctor one had to be twenty-four. Dumbfounded, Felix took his leave. He felt as though he was walking on hot coals. That night, Madlen's father unveiled his friendly firepower for the first time, launching this salvo in support of his prospective son-in-law: "If they don't want you here, I'll give you my horse [*gib ich euch mein ross*], and you can go pass your doctorate in Montpellier" (F 305). In addressing Felix, Jeckelmann used the formal form of the second-person pronoun.

The alarm soon proved unwarranted, however. Baer's hostility was actually a sort of initiation ritual: in any thesis defense, objections must be raised, no matter how absurd. The rules of the game demand it. The professors were as upset as Felix because of his brusque departure. By the next day, however, August 16, the whole scene was forgotten, and the candidate was summoned by the university beadle to sit for the *tentamen*, or preliminary examination. His *ad hoc* jury was composed of the same three professors, Minos, Aeacus, and Rhadamanthus, which is to say, Baer, Keller, and Huber, once again gathered in Baer's residence. For several hours they bombarded the young man with questions about their respective specialties. Felix's answers were cordial, respectful, and correct. Then they asked him, in Latin of course, to prepare two presentations for the next day on assigned topics as part of his formal examination, which was scheduled for August 17.

When the *tentamen* was over, Margret Baer, the professor's daughter, served pastry and liqueurs. Felix paid for these refreshments, which put everyone in a good mood, including Margret, who was not particularly happy in her marriage into a family of seigneurial bailiffs. The tradition according to which the doctoral candidate pays for refreshments for the jury has a long history, but in Basel this tradition had a life of its own: Felix, as was customary, would lay out considerable sums throughout the extended doctoral process to entertain not only the members of the jury but also his friends, his friends' friends, his thesis referees, and even, as was only fitting, his enemies.

The examination proper took place on Tuesday, August 17, once again at Baer's residence. The two subjects that Felix had been assigned the day before at the conclusion of the *tentamen* are remarkable for their lack of intellectual interest. One was an aphorism of Hippocrates': "Changes in the weather produce diseases." The other was a saying of Galen's: "Medicine is the science of remedies." It would be difficult to come up with more tired topics than these. When Felix himself became a professor a few years later, he would modernize this age-old exercise. Meanwhile, however, he had to play by the rules, as usual. For more than an hour, therefore, he recited the text he had written and memorized the night before. He pretended, ritually, to be delivering a magisterial lecture, a sort of sermon learned by heart. The three judges who composed his audience then turned the tables on him for the next three hours: it was their turn to shine, echoing the brilliance of the candidate, while Felix listened with bated breath. Oswald Baer, who regarded himself as a philosopher of distinction (*so ein grosser philosophus sein wolt*), took an aggressive attitude and once again succeeded only in making himself look ridiculous. He was definitely a character from a play by Labiche. After enduring the dean's pedantry, the members of the jury asked Felix to withdraw while they deliberated. Then as now, this was a purely formal ritual, because the result was foreordained (although nowadays a candidate may of course succeed in winning an honorable—or dishonorable—mention with his performance on "orals"). Felix was summoned almost immediately and told to prepare for the disputation, the one great moment of public drama in the whole process. So far he had jumped every hurdle and seemed well on his way to finishing the race in style. Once again Felix stood the jury to a round of drinks, served by Margret Baer. Three days later, he paid for a supper at Zur Kronen, which put his three examiners in an excellent mood. Thus Felix was out of pocket for three rounds of refreshment in the space of a week.

During the last ten days of August, Felix girded himself with science for the ultimate test, the disputation. Professor Baer assigned the young candidate two subjects for public debate at the beginning of September. Privately, Felix regarded both subjects as ridiculous. But he was still playing by the accepted rules. He "crammed" for the test he had been assigned. In principle the disputation was open to the public, and in particular to the *doctoribus et professoribus* of the city. Not many medical students would attend this portion of the defense, for their numbers were greatly diminished: there were scarcely more students than professors— a pedagogical ideal. Only in the last third of the century, under the influence of a Felix Platter grown older and more powerful, were the doors of the medical school opened more widely. In 1557 the prevailing attitude was still one of limiting competition for scarce resources—academic Malthusianism, if you will. In August, the candidate paid for the printing of a public notice listing the scientific agenda of the meeting. This notice was to be posted outside the city's four parish churches (the parish, in Basel as in Paris, was still one of the primary geographical units in terms of which communal life was organized).

The Baer-Platter *themata* were thus printed on placards on August 29 and sent to all the *doctoribus et professoribus* of the city in advance of the disputation, scheduled for September 2. In France, this acme or culmination of the doctoral trial later came to be called the *thèse,* or thesis. According to Furetière's seventeenth-century *Dictionnaire universel,* "a *thèse,* in academic parlance, is a placard on which a number of theses, or propositions, are recorded for public display. On the appointed day, these theses in philosophy or medicine are to be defended against all comers. . . . Invitations are issued to attend theses."[4]

\* \* \*

Medicine, or rather disease, reassserted its rights, however, just when it was least expected. The candidate's preparations were briefly interrupted by uncontrollable fits of coughing, the result of a catarrh or perhaps of whooping cough. Some sort of late-summer epidemic seems to have swept a vast stretch of Europe from the scrub around Montpellier to the Swiss plateau in 1557.

On Thursday, September 2, the official disputation for the doctorate was held. For such an occasion the Baer residence was no longer suitable, despite its quasi-official status. The size of the audience and the ceremonial importance of the event required the use of the Medical Hall (*aula medicorum*) of the faculty of medicine, itself located in the *Obere Collegium*, which was none other than a former monastery once occupied by Augustinian monks, who, now that the Reformation had come to Basel, had lost their raison d'être. Felix's *disputatio* began at seven in the morning and continued until the noon meal—three hundred minutes by the clock. In the audience that morning were the handful of students who regularly attended the courses given by Professors Huber and Keller. Baer, trusting to his fifty years of "experience" (half a century of stupidity does not make an intelligent man), brandished the texts of Avicenna to confront Felix on the matter of natural heat. At Montpellier in the middle third of the sixteenth century, Avicenna's star had paled considerably, along with the stars of other Arab physicians once renowned in Languedoc. Felix would not back down, however. Compared with his Basel colleagues, he had the immense advantage of knowing his French (and Greek) medicine like the back of his hand. He crushed Baer with the arguments of Fernel, the illustrious scholar he had recently met in Paris and whose *De naturali parte medicinae* he had read along with other works. On the subject of natural heat, Fernel distinguished, in highly scientific fashion, between plants, which are cold, and animals, especially humans, which stand closer to heat and fire. Bread, meat, wine, pepper, mustard, blood, sperm, spirit, heart, liver, and spleen can be classed with the hot; the brain is cold and moist; some specifics are cool, others warm (in essence), depending on the part of the body to be treated. Fernel, an out-and-out Galenist, described the concepts, causes, and symptoms of diseases in the spirit of ancient medicine. Felix, having no desire to outdo his teacher, simply followed Fernel's lead in his oral thesis defense. Later, however, a time would come when groups of symptoms could at last be correlated with lesions revealed by pathological anatomy; Professor Platter would then base his practice and even his theory on more realistic notions than those imparted to him by Fernel.[5]

By this point in the defense, Baer had sufficiently demonstrated his brilliance, and a new quartet of physicians—Pantaleon, Keller, Huggelin, and Philip Bächi, known as Bechius—proceeded to attack Felix's positions. We are already familiar with Huggelin and the eminent Pantaleon, whose mere presence in the *aula medicorum* shows what an important academic event Felix's disputation was. Bächi is a newcomer to our tale, however. A native of Baden, aged thirty-six, he had studied at Lutheran universities in Saxony and was a Hellenist, Latinist, poet, physician, and, coming from Saxony, an expert on mines; he was also pious, a lover of fine wines, and afflicted with a malady of the lungs. Despite Bächi's many qualities, Felix could not stand him and had an even lower opinion of his wife, a remarried widow whom he accused of inventing stupid practical jokes such as placing a nail-studded board in the bed of a servant by the name of Heidegger whom she happened to fancy, thus running the risk of injuring the man.[6] In the debate, however, Bächi proved to be a worthy adversary for Felix. In this phase of the disputation, he and Huggelin concentrated their criticism on the issue of natural heat previously raised by Baer. The two examiners drew some of their arguments from a work by Pietro d'Albano, a bizarre thirteenth-century Italian philosopher and physician. The son of a notary, Albano was a Hellenist, astrologer, traveler (who had been as far as Byzantium and Scotland), self-styled sorcerer, and possibly atheist; his book was entitled *Conciliator*.[7] Fortunately, Felix knew the work of "Petrus de Abanus" intimately and had no difficulty routing his adversaries. The candidate, no mean student, had acquired considerable book learning in Montpellier, along with his practical study of the anatomy of cadavers.

The *disputatio* (called *Disputatz* in Basel) thus ended well, and Felix's last task was to entertain professors and friends one more time at Zur Kronen, where everyone gathered for a somewhat delayed noon meal. Having depleted the family savings a little further, Felix, now almost a laureate, followed dessert with a brief visit to his fiancée, who worried that a stubborn cold and runny nose might have impaired his oratory. Felix took her by the hands and reassured her. She must have been even more reassured when, four days later, on Monday, September 6, the doctors of the faculty finally informed him that he had been accepted (*zuglossen*) for the doctorate. In the meantime, a second deliberation had taken place, but we know nothing about it other than that its outcome was favorable.

The "promotion," or final, purely ceremonial stage of the doctoral process, was set for Sunday, September 20. This ceremony marked the culmination of Felix's dreams and perhaps the beginning of an even more brilliant future for the recent graduate of the University of Montpellier. In the third week of September, he prepared and memorized the speeches he would deliver a few days later. He also prepared invitations to the event. Small notices were hung on parish bulletin boards. Meanwhile, the university beadle (*pedellus*) took charge of inviting Basel's former and current mayors, high guild officials, professors in various branches of learning, and friends. Guests were invited from as far away as the Black Forest: invitations went out to Peter Gebwiller, the clerk of Rötteln, an old friend who had given Felix a place to stay during the plague epidemic of 1551, and his stepson, Michael Rappenberger, whose wealthy marriages had rapidly transformed him into a castellan living in a newly rebuilt manor. Felix clearly wanted to invite upwardly mobile people. It may come as a surprise that the mayor, aldermen, and other political dignitaries would participate in such a doctoral celebration, which nowadays would be a purely academic affair unless the participation of some elite figure drew in the upper crust. Bear in mind that between 1550 and 1567 only four doctoral theses in medicine were defended in Basel, or roughly one every four to five years. Doctoral candidates preferred to take their degrees elsewhere, in France or Italy,[8] rather like younger scholars today who return to Europe with a master's degree or a Ph.D. from Berkeley or Yale. The presence of the mayor at this scientific gathering was intended to encourage the bold native of the city who had returned home full of learning and knowledge of the world to defend his thesis after a long journey.[9]

Felix's first stop on September 20 was at Professor Baer's house, where he bolstered his courage with several glasses of Greek wine. Then he, along with Professors Baer and Huber, left for the *aula medicorum*. The place could hardly be recognized on account of the huge crowd and the tapestries covering the walls—all for young Platter, who couldn't believe his eyes. Neither could his father. The ceremony lasted four hours. There was a concert of trumpets. Professor Keller gave a speech. Then Felix spoke interminably, in theory on subjects that had come up in the course of the proceedings but in fact known to the candidate in advance. Some additional oratory followed. Then came the procession: the bearded beadle marched in front, wearing a flowing cape, ribbons below his knees and on his shoes, and in his right hand carrying a scepter, a symbol of sovereignty. Behind this representative of order came Felix, smiling vacantly, looking cherubic and almost childish in his red pants, red silk doublet, and wrapped in two feet of velvet over his black doctoral gown. Dean Baer brought up the rear. Everyone climbed onto the podium, where Baer placed the velvet doctor's cap on Felix's head. He also placed a ring on Felix's finger, triggering a reaction of disgust: the new doctor could dissect any cadaver, even one that had begun to stink, but he could not bear to wear a ring, whether of flesh or metal.[10] Finally, Felix gave two speeches, neither of them "spontaneous." Then everyone went back out into the street, with the beadle and a brass band leading the way. Alongside Felix marched Rector Wolfgang Wissenberger, who wore a sword at his side as if he were a noble even though he was the son of a weaver—upward mobility once again. The entourage was no longer strictly medical: Wissenberger was a professor of mathematics and theology, close to Œcolampadius. And Bonifacius Amerbach, who marched beside Felix, was a jurist, humanist, and former rector. Seventy invited guests joined Felix at Zur Kronen, around seven tables, reminiscent of a Brueghel. All this cost the Platters some fifty florins, five of which were provided by Dr. Jeckelmann, Felix's future father-in-law, stingy as usual. The meal lasted until three in the afternoon. The day ended with an *Obendrunck*, a sort of late-afternoon cocktail party, at Michael Rappenberger's house in the suburbs of Basel. Felix's friends were with him through thick and thin: Rappenberger's stepfather had given Felix a place to stay during the plague, and now the stepson conscientiously drank a toast to the new doctor.

Only a short while before, Felix had witnessed a similar doctoral procession and ritual in Montpellier, where the style was much the same. The parade included horses, trumpets, and flutes (T2 69). Everyone wore gloves, there were lots of candles, and candy was distributed. Such parades honored new doctors whom everyone already saw as future professors, whether because of their own genius or thanks to the influence of powerful backers.

*　*　*

The thesis was like the eucharist: if nothing else it effected a transsubstantiation. Dr. Felix Platter was no longer just plain Felix Platter. Young local artisans now looked upon him as someone worthy to be godfather to their newborn children. Within a few weeks of his doctoral triumph, he had held five children over the baptismal font virtually one after another. Among them were the sons of a typographer, a constable, and a hatter, as well as little Margret, the daughter of his friend Hummel the pharmacist.

In 1557 the Platters still moved chiefly within the artisanal milieu. Felix served as godfather to the babies of artisans, while he dealt professionally with physicians, professors, and intellectuals who were themselves upwardly mobile sons of artisans. Sociologists have developed theories of social reproduction that may (or may not) be valid for late-twentieth-century Western societies but that seem much less useful for understanding urban societies in a period of rapid (and not unproblematic) economic and demographic growth like the Renaissance. The ruling strata in these cities had to be replaced periodically owing simply to death from the plague and other causes. They were profoundly shaken, moreover, by the fruitful trauma of the Protestant Reformation, which led to a sweeping renewal of elites in many fields: the religious, of course, but also the political, intellectual, and academic. In the Swiss Confederation in the second third of the sixteenth century, individuals and families apparently had a good chance to improve their status. The Platter family was not the only one to take advantage of this situation.

\* \* \*

Now that Felix had his doctorate in hand, what about the wedding? Dr. Jeckelmann, who held the young couple's future happiness in his hands, continued to stall throughout the month of October. Basically, the widower was still reluctant to give up his incomparable pearl of a daughter, who was also his housekeeper. He kept putting Thomas off, if not indefinitely then at least until early November, when the Basel fairs would be over. There was no choice but to be patient, especially since Jeckelmann was not entirely negative: he opened his house to Felix (the door was never locked, for people may have been afraid of crime but not of robbery—the streets of Basel were not like the thick forests of France and Switzerland). Under Madlen's direction, Felix put up preserves for the surgeon's kitchen (his love of sugar had stayed with him). Sometimes he told his fiancée jokes or played tricks on her. He entertained her by enumerating her charms and the debts he had contracted in Montpellier. He also discussed the loves of Daniel Jeckelmann, his future brother-in-law. He went so far as to offer her a bracelet, which she refused for the time being for fear of what people might say, although she accepted a handsomely bound Bible that Felix had bought for her in Paris. Such a gift was hardly compromising, for it spoke of the engaged couple's deep religious convictions.

\* \* \*

When the fairs were over, a wedding date was finally set. Jeckelmann made all the decisions. The marriage contract would be signed on November 18; the wedding itself would take place on November 22.

On November 18, 1557, the parties gathered at the surgeon's house in a room off the kitchen (*Kuchi*). Madlen's father was flanked by four colleagues drawn from among the city's merchants and distinguished artisans: Caspar Krug, the powerful ironmonger and future bürgermeister; Martin Fickler, an Alsatian draper from a textile family and a naturalized citizen of Basel; Batt Hug, a master fishmonger and the son of a freshwater fisherman, one of those wealthy boatmen of Alsace and Switzerland who went out on the upper Rhine early enough to meet the herons and took several hundred pounds of fish daily using broad-gauge nets for tench, trout, and pike and narrow nets for miraculous draughts of fishes, to say nothing of well-endowed daughters; and, fourth in the group, Gorius Schieli, a butcher, innkeeper, hospital administrator, court clerk, and former police captain. Schieli was a stout fellow and a good organizer; all he lacked was intelligence.

On Thomas's side, the witnesses were comparable to the foregoing in financial status but could boast of more prestigious intellectual credentials or "symbolic capital."[11] Among them was Professor Hans Huber, a leading physician, convinced Protestant, and close friend of Felix's. Huber could be unpredictable: once, while treating the superior of a Catholic abbey near Basel, he had attached his patient's coat of arms to the wall above his private toilet; when the monks learned of the joke, Huber cried copiously and made abject excuses to the abbot. The second Platter witness was Mathis Bomhart, a seventeen-year-old apprentice goldsmith, brother of the owner of Zur Kronen, and ally of the family of Myconius, Thomas Platter's longtime protector. The third and final witness was Henric Petri, an elderly printer whose father had also been a printer and who was a high official in various local guilds and a member of the city council; once married to an ex-nun who had quit her order in 1529 (the year of Basel's religious revolution), he had since remarried, taking the widow of a Frobenius for his second wife.

Both Thomas and Felix would come away from the signing of the marriage contract with bitter memories. Jeckelmann, punctilious as usual, offered a dowry of four hundred gulden, of which one hundred were to be paid in cash, the rest in the form of a trousseau. Did he keep his word (any more than Thomas did)? In any case, Thomas was obliged to acknowledge that he hadn't a penny to put on the table and that all his son could contribute to the new household was the shirt on his back (and of course his thesis), a humiliating confession for both the old teacher and the new doctor. The discussion with Jeckelmann turned bitter, and the parties came close to parting in anger.

In the end, his back to the wall, Thomas promised to contribute four hundred gulden, not a cent of which he could actually lay hands on. He would pay his share gradually by allowing the young couple to share his hearth and table and live at Zum Gejägd at his expense. What a delightful prospect! The schoolmaster further promised, with crossed fingers, to send his boarders elsewhere so as to spare his prospective daughter-in-law the distress of having to put up with their dreadful racket. With this the two fathers more or less patched things up, but there was little joy in the conciliatory supper that followed the negotiations. Felix was dismayed by the absence of any musical accompaniment. Meanwhile, Madlen, who had had her ear glued to the wall during the painful row over finances, was left speechless. To top off this black Thursday, Madlen's brother, Daniel Jeckelmann, got himself completely drunk and, while walking Felix back to Zum Gejägd, said horrible things about his sister. It was a wretched way to end the day, and the future bridegroom went to bed in a foul mood.

*   *   *

On Saturday, November 20, invitations to the wedding were sent out to a total of one hundred fifty people, counting wives and children. Only forty guests were invited to the Norman wedding described in Flaubert's *Madame Bovary*, a minuscule affair compared with the Platter nuptials. Among the guests, of eighty-five family heads whose professions are known, fifty-five were merchants or artisans (including a few artists). In other words, this was a largely middle-class or petit-bourgeois crowd, for this was where the Platters and Jeckelmanns had their roots. Of these fifty-five, the textile trade accounted for eleven; leather for seven; the metal business for eight; and the grocery trade for sixteen. At the top of this commercial group were five goldsmiths and moneychangers; four typographers or printers; and four artists (including a glassblower, a glass painter, and a sculptor). There were also fourteen individuals associated with the medical profession (including four university professors along with various surgeons, physicians, and apothecaries), plus six members of the Protestant clergy and half a dozen minor city officials (clerks, a constable, etc.). Finally, there were four nobles or castellans and of course, as always, a few guests who cannot be assigned to any group.

When we break down the guest list still further, it is clear that the guests invited by Felix and Thomas were, as a group, of higher status than those invited by Madlen's surgeon father. There were many more intellectuals and nobles on the Platters' list than on the Jeckelmanns'. Felix in fact boasts of this superiority, noting that his father invited not only a large number of his Freie Strasse neighbors but also representatives of the guilds, the city council, the university, and the nobility. Of course, since the Platters were relative newcomers to Basel, they had no family in the city. To compensate for this, they honored their neighbors with invitations and made a show of their connections in intellectual circles, connections that would continue to proliferate as Felix pursued his career.

*   *   *

Sunday, November 21, was not a much more cheerful occasion than the preceding Thursday had been. To be sure, the marriage was announced at the cathedral, and tables for the wedding banquet were set up at Thomas's house under the direction of Batt Oesy, the innkeeper and cook at Zum Engel, a suburban inn. An old friend of the Platters, the alchemist Hans Rust, arrived at the house with a giant wheel of Gruyère in honor of the young couple. But nothing went right, and Thomas was in high dudgeon because he felt that all the work of preparing for the wedding had fallen to him. To hear him tell it, his only son was a lazy fellow in thrall to his fiancée, with whom he spent all his time instead of helping his own father. Having to face hostility from three sides—his father-in-law over questions of money, his brother-in-law with his scathing remarks about his bride, and his father, overwhelmed by the preparations for the celebration—Felix felt quite low. Sharing a house and meals with his parents could easily turn into a nightmare. November 21 was a black day indeed. Thomas was rarely in bad humor, but when he was, it was a terrible thing to behold. Perhaps Felix was feeling the onset of a fifth bout of "depression" (having already suffered depressive episodes in Avignon, Montpellier twice, and Narbonne).

By Monday morning, however, things looked brighter. Thomas woke up ready to resume his tirades of the day before, but nothing was amiss. The sideboards groaned with food for the afternoon feast. Before Thomas could spew out a new stream of invective, the kitchen maid Dorothea Schenk lit into him so sharply that he was left speechless. Dorothea, who came from a local family of metallurgists, was a take-charge woman. We have seen several examples of powerful women who knew how to knock an aggressive old man down a peg or two. Frau Platter herself had once put Thomas in his place for being too hard on Felix. And Surgeon Jeckelmann frequently sided with his daughter (whom he adored) against his son.

With calm restored, Felix was able to dress for the wedding: he wore a red silk doublet, flesh-colored breeches, a wedding shirt with short ruff, gold pins, and gilt collar, and a velvet doctoral cap with a braid of pearls and flowers encircling the base where it rested on the groom's head. The bride wore a flesh-colored blouse that matched the groom's breeches. The red in Felix's doublet was matched by Professor Baer's scarlet gown. Despite his seventy-five years, the good professor did not hesitate to wear camlet and a slashed silk doublet. Age differences more or less evaporated when it came time to celebrate. On such occasions no one was afraid of looking ridiculous. Young girls put ribbons in their hair and wore pearls and gold jewelry. The wedding procession, led by the printer Petri, ended at the big church, where a sermon was delivered, rings were exchanged, and bride and groom pledged to have and to hold each other until death did them part. Then it was back to Zum Gejägd for apéritifs and sumptuous gifts for the bride in anticipation of the midday meal.

\*     \*     \*

For this occasion, fifteen well-stocked tables had been set up throughout the house to accommodate the 150 guests. Servants, male and female, kept glasses and plates filled. Jowly, buxom old women with bare arms carried huge wooden trays laden with comestibles. At the end of the meal, the servants were invited to share in the dessert of fruit and cheese. All told, somewhere between 150 and 200 people took part in the dinner. Friends and relatives of the young couple were seated according to a rather "puritanical" notion of segregation by sex. Basel was not like Brueghel's rural Flanders, where men and women rubbed elbows and laughed heartily around the banquet table. Recall that Zum Gejägd, the Platter residence, actually comprised three houses arrayed around a common square. Two large rooms were reserved for male guests: one, off the garden, was kept warm by the stove in the adjacent print shop (the wedding took place on a cool day in late autumn); the other, reserved for the less distinguished male guests, was in the *Mittelhus,* or middle house, and could be reached via a spiral staircase. The more elite women guests were seated in the print shop, where the oppressive heat left them soaked with sweat. Another room was set aside for women of the more "common" sort and still another for unmarried girls. Felix sat with the men of substance, alongside Bürgermeister Theodor Brand, the celebrated surgeon of Ox Street. Felix's new bride, now Frau Platter, presided over the gathering of elite women. Little Madlen Hug, a fishmonger's daughter, aged ten, wore a pearl headpiece that made her one of the ornaments of the younger girls' dining room.

The food was served in four courses (*vier mol uf*): appetizers, fish, roast, and dessert.[12] The same standard order was observed for the evening meal, which followed an interlude of dancing. Indeed, this was the standard order for wedding dinners throughout German Switzerland, where sumptuary excess was frowned upon. On several occasions, and as late as 1628, the city, hoping to encourage frugality, promulgated sumptuary laws governing what could be served at wedding banquets. The Platters offered an impressive variety of dishes: various kinds of fowl, beef, pork, and game, along with several varieties of freshwater fish. Among patricians and aspiring patricians in Basel, marriage was thus an occasion to survey the whole spectrum of social groups (all represented in the guest list), sexes (men, women, and maidens), and comestible fauna (including primarily domestic animals but also wild animals living on land or in the water). (See the chart below)

| | Felix Platter's Wedding, November 1557, Midday Meal | Felix Platter's Wedding, November 1557, Evening Meal | Basel sumptuary regulation of 1628 for weddings |
|---|---|---|---|
| First Course: Appetizer (*voressen*) | Chopped fish Soup Meat Chicken | Chicken Liver Tripe "Meat" soup Chicken | Chopped fish Soup Smoked meat Chicken |
| Second Course: Fish | Boiled pike | Boiled carp | Fish (unspecified) |
| Third Course: Roast | Roast Pigeon, Cock, Goose Boiled Rice Liver slices in aspic | Roast as earlier Black Forest game stew Fish cakes | Roast Pigeon, Chicken, Goose Boiled Rice Pieces of fish in aspic |
| Fourth Course: Dessert | Cheese Fruit | Pastries | Cheese Fruit |

On a comparative note, Flaubert, in his description of Madame Bovary's wedding, favored beef, lamb, and pork (sirloin, veal casserole, leg of lamb, roast suckling pig, and pork sausages with sorrel) over fish and chicken (in contrast to the Platter dinner, the Bovary banquet included no fowl other than a chicken fricassee).[13] But the Norman affair offered greater diversity of drink: the guests at the Bovary wedding drank both red wine and sparkling sweet cider. Felix, on the other hand, was a man of one faith, one woman, and one vintage: he served all his guests a generous quantity of Rang wine from the vineyards of the Thann "mountain" in Alsace, near Engelburg Castle. According to Sebastian Munster's *Cosmographie,* this beverage from the west bank of the Rhine was much appreciated in sixteenth-century Basel. The German saying *"Dass dich der Rang anstoss"* (Let the Rang hit you) referred to the wallop this wine packed. It went down as easily as milk, but a single glass could lay a man out.[14]

This time there was no question of Jeckelmann's vetoing the musical entertainment as he had done to Felix's dismay the Thursday before. The tedium of a lengthy four-course dinner in the middle of the day was relieved by a choral recital, featuring a choir of students from the Platter

Gymnasium accompanied by trumpets and violas under the baton of Roman Winmann, who had recently become the school's assistant headmaster (his predecessor having married and moved to another city to pursue his teaching career [F 325]). Winmann (also known as Oenander) was a native of Basel, an intelligent, moderate man, loyal and unassuming. In 1550 he had been a poor student in Wittenberg, reduced to begging for his dinner. For the past few years he had earned his living as a teacher (*provisor*) in the Platter Gymnasium. After failing in his first appointment as a Protestant minister, he became pastor to a rural community two leagues from Basel, where he remained until 1610. His stint at the Gymnasium served him well in his later career, for it allowed him to perfect not only his Latin but also his skills as choirmaster, both useful in his later church work.[15]

At the wedding banquet the student choir performed, among other things, the "spoon song," a musical setting of a long, tedious poem for which Felix was partly responsible. The poem concerned the classification of spoons, revealing a mania for taxonomy that Felix had already demonstrated in his grouping of guests by sex and social status and in his choice of meat and fish courses.

Between the afternoon and evening meals there was dancing in the presence of a distinguished audience gathered in the large reception hall on the first floor of Professor Baer's residence. Lorentz Richart, a bachelor surgeon whose father was also a surgeon, played the lute. A man named Christellin put down his trumpet and strolled about with a fiddle instead. Felix received the customary applause for his solo performance of a French-style *gaillarde,* but his timid wife refused to accompany him.

These festivities, which had gone on since dawn, might seem lavish and impressive, but they can hardly hold a candle to the absurdly ostentatious displays through which Basel patricians of later generations sought to demonstrate their power and prestige.[16]

When supper was over and the last grateful speeches had been delivered, the family gathered for a discreet and private farewell. Discretion was essential, for there was always a danger that mischievous young men, and especially Thomas's boarders, might attempt some tasteless wedding-night tomfoolery at the newlyweds' expense. Felix and Madlen therefore slipped out to Thomas's bedroom for a private adieu. Astonishingly enough, Jeckelmann was there to shed a tear, even though he lived only a short distance away and could visit his beloved daughter whenever he wished. Madlen also feigned a tear or two. The ever-ready Felix punctuated parting's sweet sorrow by serving sugared claret from his private cask to the godmothers and other matrons who had gathered in certainty that the tearful young bride would crave consolation and a few last words of advice before facing the agitated night ahead.

Finally, the newlyweds once more slipped off to an attic room under the rafters just behind the maid's room and overlooking the garden. It was a lot like the room Felix had occupied as a student in Montpellier. For a short while he and Madlen sat shivering on the edge of the bed—it was November, after all. Finally, unable to hold out any longer, if only because it was so cold, they slipped under the covers. Unlike Thomas, they did not put the moment off for several weeks. A humorous note was struck by Anna Dietschi, Thomas's wife, about whom we have heard little over the past several days even though she had borne much of the burden of the wedding reception. Now that it was all over and her son was safely married, Anna was exultant. With a heavy step she climbed the narrow staircase and entered the privy adjacent to the nuptial chamber, where, venting her joy, she sang at the top of her lungs without regard for the proprieties or her relatively advanced age. At the sound of her voice, Madlen, in bed, recovered her high spirits of the past few weeks and burst out laughing. And so the curtain falls on Felix and Madlen's wedding night. Did the couple start off on the right foot?

# PART FIVE

# Boy or Girl?

CHAPTER TEN

# Gredlin

More than sixteen years had passed since Felix's marriage. The year was 1573 or 1574, and times were hard in northern France and German Switzerland. The harsh winter of 1572–73, "strange and impetuous,"[1] had greatly diminished the grain harvest.[2] During an abbreviated week of the academic year 1573–74, Professor Felix Platter went as usual to the family estate in Gundeldingen, not far from Basel. His career, subsequent to the childhood and youth we have traced in detail, as in a *Bildungsroman*, through 1557, had been brilliant. By 1561, his income from medical and other sources had increased sufficiently to allow him to move out of Zum Gejägd, where he and his wife had lived since their marriage in sometimes stormy proximity to Felix's parents. The two couples parted company without acrimony when Felix bought a house of his own, Zum Rotenfluh (F 17). He also bought a horse, an acquisition comparable to the purchase of an automobile by a young doctor today. He and Madlen could now afford a maid. With substantial honoraria flowing in from a growing number of patients, supplemented perhaps by income from moneylending and usury, Felix could look forward to better days ahead. He liked to travel in neighboring regions, particularly where German was spoken, for pleasure and profit.

By 1559, many people in Basel, professionals and laymen alike, had remarked on the young doctor's skill as an anatomist, a skill enhanced by his collaboration with his father-in-law, Surgeon Jeckelmann. Honors and positions accumulated at an impressive rate: in 1562, Felix, just over twenty-five at the time, was appointed dean of the faculty of medicine (success came early then); in 1570 he was named rector; and in 1571 he succeeded his teacher Hans Huber as *Stadtarzt,* or municipal physician, and professor of practical medicine. For the next four decades, this Montpellier graduate would lord it over the medical profession of Basel. Since his student days he had amassed more than a thousand observations of cases of individual morbidity, and the rector's *Observationes* became a landmark in medical history when published in 1614. To be sure, Dr. Platter was not a medical eminence of the first rank, but he was a top-notch physician. His discoveries concerning retinal vision attracted the attention of one of the leading scientists of the day, Johannes Kepler.[3] And his fellow citizens never forgot the courageous devotion he demonstrated during the regional plague of 1563–64, which killed 4,000 people in Basel, a quarter of the city's population.

As mentioned earlier, the period 1573–74 was also difficult, not because of plague, but because food was in short supply. At Gundeldingen Felix had his father for company: Thomas, of peasant stock, often went to the farm to tend his cattle, hunt fox, fish in the pond, chop wood, and plant trees or make grafts in his orchard. Felix, however, was a city boy, not at all a farmer though drawn at times to gardening. He had no attachment to the countryside, much less to the mountains, which continued to exert a powerful hold on his father. After Thomas died in 1582, Professor Platter's first order of business was to sell off the Gundeldingen estate. (His younger brother Thomas Jr., more faithful to family tradition, would purchase a nearby farm in 1622, however.)

In 1573–74, though, Thomas Sr. was still very much alive, and Felix, as always a dutiful son, visited him on the "country estate" that was the old man's proudest acquisition. It was a period of near famine, and typhus and other diseases raged in the city as well as in the plains and mountains. Basel, ensconced within its walls, shunned outsiders: the city's constables turned away wretched beggars from the surrounding region. With nowhere to go, these unfortunates descended on places like Gundeldingen, which had no high walls to defend it. Felix was rather unhappy about the presence of such vagabonds, or "rabble," on his property; his father's *Meyer,* or steward, a decent fellow, allowed them to sleep in the sheds and stables (F 451). Among the refugees was a married couple: Benedict Simon was French, or at any rate "romanophone," and a native of Pontarlier;[4] his wife, Elsbeth Shärin, was Swiss, from a town near Zurich. Both had worked as agricultural laborers at Bartenheim in Haute-Alsace. Elsbeth was gravely ill, probably with typhus. She was most likely on her way home, hoping to have sufficient strength to make it back to the Zurich region. The pair had a small child with them, a girl not yet one year old. Felix spoke bluntly to the steward: "You shouldn't have allowed people of that sort to stay here. I am greatly displeased [*missfiel mir*]."

\* \* \*

Of course Thomas was still the owner of the property and should have dealt personally with a matter such as whether or not to accommodate paupers. On this particular day, however, he happened to be away. He had gone off for two days of fishing with a professional fisherman, Jacob Jüppen, and another friend, the wife of a Protestant "canon." When the trio returned, still laden with fishnets, they went to look in on Elsbeth Shärin, the dying woman from Zurich, who lay in agony in one of the bedrooms. Her husband, also ill by now, seemed likely to pull through. At the sight of this couple in distress, Thomas was inevitably reminded of his own youth, which had been so hard. A conscientious physician, Felix treated the suffering woman with various potions that had little effect. He peered through a window at the scene inside, glancing also at the child, who lay sleeping outdoors in case her mother was contagious. The child gestured with its little hands (*hendlin*) and bruised its neck on the hard wood of a cradle that was in fact little more than a crate.

Felix and the others who witnessed this affecting scene were moved by it. They felt pity (*bedauren*) for the child, thus casting doubt on the alleged indifference to childhood that Philippe Ariès claimed to find in this period but for which he offered no real proof (F 411).[5] Elsbeth Schärin died. Her body was loaded onto a donkey (a real curiosity in the region) and transported to the St. Margreten cemetery in Gundeldingen. Felix's sister, who died of plague in 1551, was buried in the same cemetery.

Night fell. Felix and Madlen both had dreams (nightmares?) about children. Felix awoke with a start and roused his sleeping wife. His dream had been frightening, but it was also more than that: a child had fallen upon him from heaven.[6] It's raining swaddled babies, ladies, hold out your red aprons! In his dream, Felix stretched out his long professorial gown to break the baby's fall and prevent it from smashing into the ground. Did this dream stem from Felix's having noticed the bruise on the little girl's neck the day before? In any case, one sad fact could not be denied: Felix and his wife were childless. For sixteen years their marriage had remained barren. Felix loved his wife but never really accepted the situation, and Madlen was sorely afflicted by it. She still remembered the futile pilgrimage to the mineral baths of Valais in 1563, to waters that were supposed to have made her fertile.

*   *   *

The next morning was a time for sad farewells: Benedict placed the baby in a basket (*auf einer hurt*) and lifted it onto his back. He returned Felix's jars of medicine and thanked him from the bottom of his heart. Madlen bent down to kiss the child. Everyone was in tears. The two paupers, father and daughter, vanished into the distance, bound who knows where? One wonders if they knew themselves. Benedict took with him a small amount of cash, a gift from the Platters. Death seemed to be the little girl's inevitable fate. How could her father, poor as he was, possibly feed her?

Was this the end of it? The Platters sat down to lunch in a wretched mood. Their consciences would not let them alone. At the table were Felix and Madlen and Thomas and his young wife Hester (Anna Dietschi, Felix's mother, had died in February 1572, and Thomas, a restless widower, had remarried in April). Although Hester was ten years younger than Felix, the good doctor did not hesitate to call her "mother" (*Mutti*). The remaining guests came from various classes of society: they included the fisherman Jüppen and perhaps the seamstress Krössel, although she may have remained standing in order to wait on the others. When the appetizers were served, Felix and Madlen tried to lighten the atmosphere by recounting their dreams. The fisherman, Felix noted, reacted immediately: "Why didn't you keep the baby? You have no child of your own." With characteristic understatement, Madlen said that would have been all right with her, but then she added that she would gladly bring up the child if only she could retrieve her. "If that's what you want, Madlen," Felix replied.[7] The seamstress, putting in her two cents, said that she would knit caps for the baby if the men succeeded in bringing it home. Thomas and his young wife added their voices to the chorus. Everyone was in favor of going after Benedict in the hope of persuading him to give up his daughter, but no one was sure where he had gone. After an interval of silence, Felix wholeheartedly agreed with the idea of searching for the pair, which had now become his wish (*begirt*), as it was also the express wish of Thomas, the family patriarch. A dutiful son is a dutiful son. All that remained now was to find the lost infant.

Thomas took charge. He sent two of his students in hot pursuit, one to the northwest (toward Mulhouse), the other to the southeast. Wherever they went, they were instructed to ask the same question: "Have you seen a man carrying a baby on his back?"

That first night there was no news. The next morning, the scout returned from the southeast empty-handed. Felix had already returned to the university. At midday he went to the student cafeteria, whose hours were strictly regulated.[8] In the middle of his meal, a message arrived: the girl had been found. She and her father were in Bartenheim, almost midway between Basel and Mulhouse, on the same farm where Benedict and Elsbeth had been employed as laborers. Informed of the Platters' offer, Benedict returned to Gundeldingen at once, carrying his child and escorted by the student from Thomas's Gymnasium. The moment they arrived, Madlen began to lavish on the child the treasures of maternal devotion she had been hoarding up for years. She took the infant girl out of her basket and peeled away her swaddling, leaving her entirely naked, without even a cap on her head, then bathed her, wrapped her in fur, and put her to sleep.

Felix, meanwhile, talked things over with Benedict, who cried tears of joy. He would gladly allow the professor to raise, educate, and arrange a marriage for the child. Having obtained what he wanted, Felix dismissed the tramp rather curtly, but not before scheduling a meeting in Basel one week hence for the signing of a contract, which was to be not a formal adoption but rather, if one can put it this way, a long-term loan or lease. A week later, the two men met as planned at Thomas's Gymnasium. Naturally, Thomas kept an eye on the business, which, after all, was being transacted in his house. He had been married to Hester for only a short time, and this adoption was another way of perpetuating his line, even if it involved an external "graft." Present to certify the legality of the arrangement was the notary Ubelin, at thirty soon to become a man of property and already in the early stages of a successful career. It was Felix who drafted the contract, however. Benedict was officially recognized as the child's father and granted visiting rights, but nothing more. Felix, for his part, promised in writing to raise the girl and provide her with trousseau and dowry. He kept his word.

"Thanks to me," the good doctor observed in retrospect, Benedict's daughter "was brought up through childhood and adolescence. She learned to sew, to embroider, [and] to play musical instruments." Did Felix teach the little girl to play the lute? It was common at the time for girls to be given music lessons (F 453). She was also given a name: Margret Simon or Simonin, also known as Margareta Platterin and familiarly called Gredlin. For Thomas, of course, the name evoked memories of the two Margrets he had lost to the plague. Gredlin, a charming child, inspired affection well beyond the narrow circle of the "nuclear family." Hester and old Thomas doted on her. Her relations with Benedict Simon, her natural father, proved to be difficult, however. Simon became a soldier of fortune serving, like other Swiss mercenaries, under foreign princes, a profession in which he no doubt earned a better living than he had commanded as an agricultural laborer. He called on Gredlin from time to time and never forgot her. She found him hard to tolerate, however. He frightened her with his military uniform and swaggering ways.

Gredlin was a happy child, but there was one sad episode in her otherwise sunny existence (the date of this incident is unknown, but it certainly occurred before 1604): certain "nasty people" took it upon themselves to inform her that she was not really the Platters' daughter.[9] She suffered greatly from this revelation, but it did not spoil her good relations with the "parents" who had treated her so well. In the patrician home of the Basel physician, Gredlin was a ray of sunshine. She filled the role of daughter of the house, assuming all or part of the responsibility of running the household, just as Madlen had done for her father, Surgeon Jeckelmann.

Gredlin was getting on in years: she was twenty-seven at the turn of the seventeenth century. To complicate matters still further, she had taken a lover. Her "parents" adored her. They would have liked her to grow old with them, for she had served them faithfully. Perhaps they could have made a better match for her than she made for herself. Felix seems to have reproached himself to a certain extent on this score. In any event, Gredlin settled her own fate: she expressed her desire to marry Michel Ruedin, by whom she was pregnant. Felix and Madlen gave their consent in a joint decision that shows how important a role the doctor's wife had come to play in the family. In short, Gredlin's "mother and father," by this time almost seventy, agreed, in 1604, to a marriage of which they did not disapprove, even if it was not exactly what they would have wished. Michel Ruedin was of rural background and a tailor by trade. He took the Platters back to their peasant and artisan roots. The wedding took place in September 1604: Michel Ruedin married "Margret Simonin" at St. Peter's Church. Ruedin went on to a successful career, rising from tailor to cloth merchant. He was elected a member not only of the tailors' guild but also of the Saffron and the Key, the city's elite organizations. His father-in-law's influence may have had something to do with this, but Felix was already dead by the time the latter two nominations were made, and Ruedin's personal merits certainly played a part.

Michel and Gredlin had six children, all boys, in eight years. The first was of course already conceived at the time of the wedding, proof that the marriage was one of passion and perhaps part of the explanation for Felix's strangely reserved tone in writing about it. The Platters' relations with Gredlin remained warm, even though Hester Gross, who, after Thomas's death, had taken a tile- and brick-maker as her second husband, was apparently shocked by the "misbehavior" of a young woman of whom she had previously been so fond. Felix, however, remained as fond of the girl as ever, so fond, in fact, that he left her more than a thousand gulden in his will, an amount considerably larger than the dowry his wife had brought him in 1557. Even when we allow for the inflation of the intervening years and the considerable increase in the doctor's wealth, this was a substantial gift. What is more, Felix allowed Gredlin's eldest son to be named Felix, despite the fact that he was a love child. In forty years of medical practice, the great doctor had seen more than a few of those. His brother Thomas Jr. would even serve as godfather to another of Gredlin's sons, Michael, who became a surgeon like his "grandfather" Jeckelmann.

## CHAPTER ELEVEN

# Tomilin

T homas Jr. offered the Platters a second solution, another answer to their irrepressible wish to have a child. Thomas Sr., widowed in February 1572, married again in April. His new wife was Hester Gross, aged twenty-five, the daughter of a Protestant pastor (from the Valais, like Thomas himself) and of a schoolteacher from Little Basel by the name of Maria Küeffer. Because her profession was the same as Thomas's, Maria, recently widowed, had been invited to Felix's wedding in November 1557. Thomas, in his seventies, had a number of children by his second wife. Did this upset Felix, who could easily have worried about being deprived of a portion of his father's inheritance? If so, he soon got over it. Thomas, a rumbustious old fellow, fathered six children in eight years: Magdalena Platter (born 1573), Thomas Jr. (1574), who, like his father before him, was known as Tomilin, or "little Thomas," Ursula (1575), Niklaus (1577), Anna (1579), and Elsbeth (1580). Finally, his demographic mission accomplished, Thomas Sr. was free to pass on, which he did on January 26, 1582, at the age of eighty-two. The wedding torch became a funeral torch. Three of his daughters by his second marriage—Ursula, Anna, and Elsbeth—followed him almost immediately into the grave, victims of the plague that raged in Basel between June and October 1582. The eldest daughter, Magdalena, married a judge and lived to the age of seventy-eight. When she died in 1661, she left a cookbook written in her own firm hand. Thomas and Hester's two sons, Thomas Jr. and Niklaus, were respectively eight and five in 1582. The plague threatened them too, of course. The prospect of losing two male Platters horrified Felix: "May it please God to let some of the Platters live" (*Cuperem aliquos Plateros conservari, si Deo placeret*).[1] In fairly blunt language the great doctor therefore wrote to his young stepmother, Hester, whom he called *Mutti,* or "mother," urging her to send the boys to him for safekeeping. She reluctantly complied, sending not only the boys but also their books and clothing. She had good reason to accede, no matter how unwillingly, to Felix's wishes, for she, too, was about to remarry. Shortly after the death of her venerable husband, Hester left the enormous Platter home on Freie Strasse, which henceforth stood empty and forlorn. She found refuge in Little Basel, where she may have cared for her elderly mother, the schoolteacher. After only a few months of widowhood, she married Hans Lützelmann, a manufacturer of tile and bricks. With him she had a first child in the summer of 1583. Having soared for a time among the Basel intelligentsia (her father having being a clergyman and her mother and first husband both teachers), Hester returned to earth with her second marriage to a man who, as a brickmaker with his own business, belonged to a less prestigious but still prosperous group of artisans. As we have seen, she gave up her two sons from her first marriage to her stepson, the illustrious Basel physician, who cited the plague as a convenient pretext for asserting his authority over these scions of the Platter line. Felix gave the two boys rooms in his house and sent them to stay for brief periods at the home of a private tutor. Hester Lützelmann, as she was now called, kept up sporadic contact with her sons through the first decade of the seventeenth century, after which communication dwindled. Trampling on her rights as mother, Felix, who lacked a male heir, thus solved the problem in his own high-handed fashion. Who could resist such a powerful personage, a *pontifex maximus* of the University of Basel? Hester chose to cut her losses.

The good doctor was in fact bound and determined to transfer his double legacy—wealth and professional status—to one of his half-brothers, since he had no son. He had two choices: Thomas, thirty-eight years younger than Felix, and Niklaus, forty-one years younger. Felix's surrogate sons were young enough to have been his grandsons. In the matter of succession, Felix had something in common with the kings of France: after Louis X ("the Headstrong"), the crown went first to his brother Philip V ("the Long") and then to his other brother, Charles IV ("the Fair"); in the sixteenth century, Francis II was followed by Charles IX and Henri III, all three sons of Henri II. Much later, Louis XVI was eventually succeeded by his brothers Louis XVIII and Charles X. Three brothers thus succeeded one another three times in half a millennium of French monarchy: the third occurrence (Louis XVI to Charles X) was not, as it turned out, the lucky one.

Felix knew what he was doing, however. In 1590, he arranged for Thomas Jr., the heir apparent, to enter the University of Basel. Six years later, Thomas followed in his older brother's footsteps: in 1595 he went to study medicine at the University of Montpellier. Meanwhile, young Niklaus, Thomas's last surviving son, was kept in reserve. In 1595, using his influence as rector, Felix easily arranged for Niklaus to enroll at the university, just as he had done for Thomas Jr. His carefully laid plans soon went astray, however: Niklaus died of bloody diarrhea in 1597. Thomas

Jr., genuinely pained by the loss of his little brother, was now the only son still in the running to succeed Felix.

Thus for fifteen years, from 1582 to 1597, there were in effect three children in Dr. Platter's household: Gredlin, Thomas Jr., and Niklaus. Not bad for a couple with no children of their own! And for icing on the cake, yet another child transformed this trio into a quartet. In 1580, Felix lost his brother-in-law Daniel Jeckelmann, Madlen's brother. Like his father before him, Daniel had been a surgeon, as had his brother, Franz Jeckelmann Jr., who had died prematurely in 1565. Felix had always found Daniel a rather disagreeable relative, but he could commiserate when the surgeon lost two small daughters, Madelin and Esterlin, to the plague in 1563 (F 70). When Daniel died at a relatively early age in 1580, he was survived by two other children, one of whom was a daughter named Chrischona, named for her grandmother, Chrischona Jeckelmann, née Harscher, the wife of Franz Jeckelmann Sr.. The elder Chrischona also died young, in 1549. Obviously the Jeckelmanns were a conservative family when it came to the choice of a profession (all those surgeons) or a name (two Chrischonas, two Franzes, etc.).

When his brother-in-law died in 1580, Felix proved both generous and calculating. He took in little Chrischona, who was now practically an orphan, probably with the secret hope of marrying her off one day to Thomas Jr. Felix may not have had his father's surefootedness in the mountains, but he remained a Valaisian in his soul. Arranging marriages in the cradle had long been the custom in the Valais. The calculations of our provident Aesculapius[2] would ultimately turn out to have been quite shrewd. From the outset Chrischona got along famously with Madlen, now her de facto mother. Frau Platter, who took it upon herself to raise Chrischona, was of course actually the girl's aunt (the sister of the child's late father Daniel Jeckelmann). This foster-parenting arrangement also harked back to an old Valaisian custom, a response to the high adult mortality rate: Thomas Sr., whose father died when he was still quite young, had been raised by his aunt. Madlen, moreover, had nothing but praise for her young charge Chrischona, who honored, cherished, and obeyed her foster mother from 1580 to 1600. All that affection earned Chrischona a substantial bequest in Madlen's will. When Thomas Jr., soon to become a doctor of medicine, returned from Montpellier in 1602, he married his former playmate, a superb creature, as pleasant to look at as her husband was not. A portrait of her in the Dutch style has survived: it depicts her as a young Juno of radiant complexion with a ruff around her neck and a gold chain in her hands, the same chain that Felix had given his fiancée Madlen back in 1557, passed on from one couple to the next.

Thus Thomas Jr. followed almost exactly in his brother's footsteps a half century later. In both cases a young physician, soon to become a professor, married the daughter of a surgeon, and the surgeon's daughter in the second instance happened to be the niece (and ward) of the physician in the first. There was a family strategy at work here, to be sure, but also a professional strategy. Both marriages were made partly for love and partly by arrangement, and both joined the two key medical disciplines, the theoretical medicine of Hippocrates and Galen read in the original Greek (Platter) and the resolutely modern surgical anatomy of the great Vesalius (Jeckelmann).

\*   \*   \*

From, broadly speaking, 1580 to 1600, Felix and Madlen thus enjoyed the privilege of four children in the house, two boys and two girls. Thomas Jr. and Gredlin were the oldest, Niklaus and Chrischona the youngest. The Platter children, being relatively close in age—their birth dates ranged from 1573 to 1577—formed a real community. Because of the high mortality rate in the early modern period, many families were broken up as children moved from foster home to foster home. But sometimes whole families were created out of fragments: in the best of cases, such as the one that interests us here, new families arose where death seemed to have left things in a shambles. In the case of Thomas Jr. and Chrischona, it was all the more remarkable that children could be so close yet not have a drop of blood in common, so that they could marry without concern for their future offspring, who proved to be healthy and numerous.

\*   \*   \*

Surrounded by children and sumptuously housed at Zum Samson, the imposing residence that Felix acquired in 1574 and turned into one of the finest natural history museums in Europe, Madlen Platter should have been happy despite her inability to conceive children of her own. She had family, possessions, and wealth to compensate her for her loss. Felix had become one of the richest and most fashionable men in Basel. Her father-in-law, Thomas Sr., loved her as if she were his own daughter. And yet she suffered because she had no child that was physically hers. Her visit to the baths at Leuk in 1563 accomplished nothing, despite the reputed ability of the waters there to work miracles for women who wished to become pregnant.

Felix, though discreet on the subject, blamed his wife's frigidity: she was a sea of ice rather than a volcano. In his mind, the two afflictions were related: his wife could not give birth, and she could not experience pleasure. It was widely believed at the time that the female orgasm was a guarantee of fertility. No one seems even to have entertained the possibility that Felix might have been the cause of the couple's inability to conceive. One wonders if he had any affairs and whether, on one of his medical visits, he impregnated a mistress or fathered an illegitimate child. If we knew, we could say with confidence that he was not the cause of the couple's sterility, but we do not know. Nevertheless, the simple truth is that Madlen blamed herself and suffered for it. She was an avid reader, day and night, of the Lutheran Bible, of which she kept her own personal copy. She identified with Sarah, Abraham's "barren" wife. Over and over again she read the biblical passages describing Sarah's suffering (Genesis 16–23). Abraham blames Sarah for failing to produce children. He lies with his servant Hagar, a Bedouin. Nature reasserts its dominion. Sarah, jealous, drives Hagar into the desert, where she and her son Ishmael (the ancestor of the Arabs) are aided by an angel. Later, Sarah, already old, is visited by an incarnation of Yahweh in the form of three visitors who (in Christian exegesis) prefigure the Holy Trinity. Subsequently, she too gives birth to a son, in the fourth age (of the works of Abraham), a legitimate son, Isaac, whom the Lord uses to test Abraham's faith: the patriarch is about to obey an order to sacrifice his son when an angel stops him. Between 1591 and 1594, Madlen, assisted by her ward and niece Chrischona (both women being skilled embroiderers), created two tapestries illustrating the main themes of this biblical tale: the quarrel between Sarah and Hagar, the expulsion of Hagar, Hagar in the desert, Ishmael saved by the angel, Abraham visited by the three "messengers from God," and, finally, the aborted sacrifice of Isaac.

The reference to Genesis was explicitly indicated at the bottom of these tapestries. The four evangelists appear in the corners of these works, thus establishing a link between the Old and the New Testaments. Two *putti* are depicted playing lutes, Felix's cherished instrument. The two tapestries reflect a whole aspect of Madlen's life, that of the dutiful wife subject to the authority of the patriarch (1 Peter 3:6) and living in intimacy with children not her own. Frau Platter's fears and jealousies were also evoked: might not Felix, like Abraham, have taken a mistress in some nearby town on one of his medical visits? The years during which the tapestries were completed, 1591–94, coincided roughly with the time when Thomas Jr., the "outsider's" child added to the family in the manner of Ishmael, registered at the university (1591), took his baccalaureate (1593), and began work on his master's degree (awarded in July 1595), all leading up to his departure for Montpellier in September 1595. Toward the end of her life,

Madlen, who had been a "vivacious" (F 327) girl in the 1550s, returned, as a bedridden matron, to the same biblical story of Abraham and his wife and servant: she listened as a reader read the Bible and a minister sat by the bedside to comfort her now that she could no longer go to the church where, when her health was better, she had been active in the work of the parish. And Frau Platter's obsession with the Old Testament tale did not end there: at Madlen's express request, the eulogy pronounced over her grave in 1613 compared her to Sarah and Felix to Abraham.

\* \* \*

So Madlen, identified with Sarah, had lived a melancholy life. But what about Felix-Abraham? He was the very embodiment of social success, which for him was not very far from true happiness. The professor's life, like that of his father before him, had placed him at the heart of the Renaissance and Reformation. The origins of the journey went all the way back to the first decade of the sixteenth century, when Thomas, Felix's father, was still an illiterate, "medieval" mountain lad in the Valais. With remarkable zeal, however, he had immersed himself in the renascent cultures of Latin, Greek, and Hebrew. He had simultaneously discovered Protestantism in its more brutal—iconoclastic and Zwinglian and later, in Basel, Œcolampadian—forms. Although the identity crisis had been short-lived, father and son never wavered from the path Luther had blazed, even though both men, and especially Felix, considerably muted the more aggressive aspects of the Swiss Reformation that had marked them in youth. Felix saw a great deal of the humanist Castellion, an excellent conciliator, and he had visited the great "papist" churches of France as if they were so many museums. Later, he paid medical visits to charming abbesses in the Rhineland, gracious women full of good humor. These experiences left him anything but a fierce sectarian. He was, rather, a man open to the varied lessons of an unprejudiced Christianity (and even of Marrano Judaism). Yet at the center of his being he remained a believer, rooted in the certitudes of the Protestant faith and the Lutheran Bible.[3]

Did the Renaissance come to outweigh the Reformation in Felix's life? It is not implausible to think so, if only because of the way he turned his new house into a prodigious museum, filled with animals, minerals, plants, and a whole host of ingredients that went into the medications he prescribed for his patients. A student of Rondelet in Montpellier, himself a disciple of the Italian naturalists, Felix began, as was only proper, with the study of anatomy, which revealed a new inner universe, a prefiguration of the intimate exploration of the body, human as well as animal, that became such a prominent feature of the Renaissance mentality. Felix prepared mouse skeletons for display (which greatly impressed his father-in-law Jeckelmann, by the way), and his exhibits included mammoth bones that he mistook for relics of a monstrous man nearly twenty feet tall. He also displayed the skeleton of a man who had been executed, whose cadaver Felix had personally dissected. The dead man's mother came from time to time to sit in sadness and contemplate her son's bones: it was a merciless century. Felix's museum also contained an herbarium of many volumes, whose pages displayed carefully selected specimens of plants from the Valais, Languedoc, and the Basel region. Thus Felix continued the ancient tradition of the herbalist Dioscorides, which had come down to him through the monks and apothecaries of the Middle Ages. His magnificently rich collections, amassed by an amateur but in many ways worthy of a professional, contained many other things as well: stones, both precious and nonprecious; seeds; insects; antiquities; stuffed crocodiles; guaiacum for "sweating out the pox"; moccasins and ponchos from the New World; Turkish, Chinese, and Japanese objects; antique vases; a large library; a garden of tulips and hyacinths; a lemon orchard, whose fruits were sold at good prices to German princes; American beans and corn; rabbits; pigeons, silkworms; a live elk, that kept the grass mowed and from which Felix derived medicines that amazed scientific Europe.

As a man of the Reformation (prudent despite his anticlericalism) and herald if not hero of the Renaissance, Felix also contributed to the Platter discovery of Europe. His father had explored Germany and Switzerland, the western part of Poland, and perhaps Hungary. Felix was more focused on western Germany and was also an indefatigable explorer of "Welch" territory. He became not only a francophile but also a francophone and even an "occitanophone," which only increased the pleasure he took in visiting France. His choices, freely made, thus ratified the anti-imperial, pro-German, and above all pro-Protestant foreign policy of the Valois monarchs. That policy had been conceived by Francis I, who, after Marignano, had been quick to negotiate a perpetual peace with the Swiss and to ally himself with Lutheran princes against the Hapsburgs. The first "contact" of this sort was in 1528 with Philip of Hesse, who became the French king's friend. Later, Henri II "positioned" himself to follow a similar line of action and thought. Henri, who was well respected in Basel, tried to involve German Protestant principalities in a system of alliances.

From Francis I to Louis XVI, in fact, a very "Platterian," very "Protestantophile" policy snakes its way like a giant sea serpent through the murky history of the Ancien Régime. The objectives of this policy included not only the Germanic world but also the Netherlands and Great Britain. After Henri II, it was carried on by Sully, Henri IV, and the cardinal-ministers Richelieu, Mazarin, Dubois, and Fleury; Louis XIV, of course, stands out as a major and unfortunate exception. This long-standing positive French attitude toward Protestantism, this olive branch held out to heresy, was something of which Thomas Platter Jr. could only approve. His travels in Elizabeth's England and Henri IV's France in 1595 were in part a product of this cultural and diplomatic ecumenicism.

Benevolent spirits emanating from the Renaissance, the Reformation, and an open, tolerant pan-European attitude toward education thus watched over the destiny of the Platter clan. Those spirits rescued the family from the Middle Ages or, at any rate, from what Marx not very charitably called "the idiocy of rural life."[4] Beyond those benevolent spirits, the positive genius of upward social mobility was also at work, tugging at the shoulder of the printer-pedagogue and his son the doctor. Financially speaking, the transformation was palpable: Thomas Sr. was buried in debt, whereas Felix, whose budgets were always in the black, sometimes substantially so, lent far more than he borrowed. In three-quarters of a century, the family went from misery in the Valais to opulence in Basel. Even at the height of his success in northern Switzerland, Thomas the schoolmaster never recruited students beyond the Swiss Alps and Upper Alsace. But Herr Professor Doktor Platter belonged to the medical elite that gathered around the dukes and princes of Renaissance Germany. Such a remarkable ascent in so brief a time was nothing short of miraculous. But it was an ascent with one indispensable prerequisite: each generation had to produce an heir. In continuing the Platter line, the great doctor was thus essentially a surrogate father. He served as parent to a quartet of children: two boys young enough to be his grandsons; Gredlin, almost a foundling; and Chrischona Jeckelmann, his very affectionate homebody of a niece. His wife, Madlen, suffered in the paradoxical role of "barren mother." Felix played the hand he was dealt. He did indeed act as father to this brood, far more of a father than some men whose only claim to the title is chromosomal. Gredlin, in particular, looked upon Felix as her authentic parent, an honor she long refused to bestow on Benedict Simon, the peasant-soldier who was her biological progenitor.

In 1544, in the city of Bourges, which Thomas Sr.'s son would visit a few years later, residents cast themselves in the surrogate father role when they hailed the birth of their future king, Francis II, with a triumphal festival of bonfires, Corpus-Christi-like processions, high masses, chanted prayers, *Te Deums,* farces, morality plays, pastry, drinking, and cannonades. To justify their claim to collective paternity, the citizens of Bourges quoted a verse from Isaiah (9:6) in the Latin of the Vulgate: *Puer natus est nobis et filius datus est nobis.*[5] As an avid reader of the Old Testament, Felix had had many occasions to meditate upon the question of nongenetic filiation. How could he not have thought of this passage from Isaiah when he took Thomas Jr. and Niklaus into his house? Or again in 1595, when Thomas Jr. left for Montpellier, spreading his wings in a way that made his older brother—his "father" if you will—proud?[6] Or yet again, in 1605, when another Felix, the aptly named love child and firstborn of Gredlin, came into the world, soon followed, one after another, by five little brothers born between 1607 and 1613? Or in 1602, 1605, *et cetera,* when the marriage of Thomas Jr. to Chrischona produced Felix Platter Jr., Felix Platter III, Thomas Platter III, and Franz Platter? (Neither the Platters nor the Jeckelmanns had much imagination when it came to first names. Like many other people at the time, they generally drew on the two previous generations' "onomastic stock.")

All these "blessed events" preceded the death of Dr. Felix Platter in 1614. The family's continued presence in the medical profession was now assured for more than a century.[7] Just as the passage from Isaiah had come immediately to the minds of the citizens of Bourges in 1544, it had also occurred to Felix on each of these happy occasions. He found it easily in Luther's translation of the Bible, which he always kept within reach: *Denn uns ist ein Kind geboren, ein Sohn ist uns gegeben . . . Und er heisst wunderbar . . . Ewigvater.* (The King James version is: "For unto us a child is born, unto us a son is given . . . and his name shall be called Wonderful . . . The Everlasting Father.") Now, as the reign of Henri IV, the Swiss cantons' cordial neighbor to the west, drew to a close, the Platter trajectory—now in the seventeenth century no longer astonishing, as it had been in the Renaissance, but simply noteworthy—was firmly mapped out: the baton had been passed, through Felix, from Thomas Sr. to Thomas Jr., from true father to true son. And so, now visible but as through a glass darkly, the long sixteenth century drew to a close: a century of folly and glory, of imbecility and greatness, in love with darkness but even more in love with light.

# NOTES

## CHAPTER ONE

1. Cf. the claim that mineral waters can make women "fertile": Janine Garrisson, *Marguerite de Valois* (Paris: Fayard, 1994), p. 228.

2. The Platters used the term "Welches" to refer to Latins generally, whether Venetians or French, north or south European.

3. In the Valais and in French Switzerland as in east-central and southern France in the fourteenth to sixteenth centuries, a "castellan" was often only an officer of low to high rank charged by local authorities with keeping watch, in a military or nonmilitary sense, on a castle, for the purpose of ensuring the security of the surrounding countryside. Hence the word "castellan" should not necessarily be taken to be imply any sense of aristocratic grandeur.

4. Grächen was a highland hamlet of a few dozen houses on the north slope of the southern chain of Upper Valaisian Alps, more than an hour's walk from Saint-Niclaus, a village also situated above the valley of the Mattervisp (1,121 meters altitude).

5. The German *Stein* (stone) is *lithos* in Greek.

## CHAPTER TWO

1. The use of horns for nursing was common in this "remote" era. See the catalogue of the show "L'enfance au Moyen Age" at the Bibliothèque Nationale (Autumn-Winter 1994).

2. Matthaeüs Schiner (1465–1522) had been bishop of Sitten (Sion) since 1499. He was elevated to cardinal in 1511.

3. Emmanuel Le Roy Ladurie and Orest Ranum, eds., *Pierre Prion, scribe. Mémoires d'un écrivain de campagne au XVIIIe siècle* (Paris: Gallimard, 1985), p. 48.

4. Emmanuel Le Roy Ladurie, "Gavet," *L'Histoire* (March 1979), no. 10.

5. Matthäus Schwarz of Augsburg, though of bourgeois background, also took to the road for several seasons while he was still a small child: see Philippe Braunstein, ed., *Un banquier mis à nu* (Paris: Gallimard, 1992).

6. Norman Davies, *God's Playground: A History of Poland* (New York: Columbia University Press, 1982).

7. A city that would belong to Saxony and later to Prussia.

8. Ernest Lavisse, *Histoire générale* (Paris: Armand Colin, 1894), vol. 4, p. 398.

9. On what follows, see Philippe Dollinger, *Documents sur l'Histoire de l'Alsace* (Toulouse: Privat, 1972), pp. 176ff., and, more generally, the chapters on the Renaissance in Jean-Jacques Hatt, *Histoire de l'Alsace* (Toulouse: Privat, 1970), pp. 190 ff.

10. Jean Châtillon and Pierre Debongnie, "*Devotio moderna*," in M. Viller and

Charles Baumgartner, eds., *Dictionnaire de spiritualité* (Paris: Beauchesne, 1957), vol. 2, pp. 714–747.

11. Hatt, *Histoire de l'Alsace,* pp. 190 ff.

12. François Furet and Jacques Ozouf, *Lire et écrire* (Paris: Editions de Minuit, 1977), vol. 1, pp. 199 ff.

13. Michel Fize, *La Démocratie familiale, évolution des relations parents-adolescents* (Paris: Presses de la Renaissance, 1990). The quoted passage is taken from advertising for the book, in which the author summarizes one of its central themes.

14. On these controversial matters, see J.-V. Pollet, *Huldrych Zwingli* (Paris: Vrin, 1988), pp. 15 ff., 341, and passim.

15. Peter Brown, *The Cult of the Saints* (Chicago: The University of Chicago Press, 1981).

16. On iconoclasm, see Olivier Christin, *Une révolution symbolique, l'iconoclasme huguenot et la reconstruction catholique* (Paris: Editions de Minuit, 1991); Robert Sauzet, in *Revue d'histoire de l'Eglise de France,* vol. 66 (1980), pp. 5–15; and Solange Deyon and Alain Lottin, *Les Casseurs de l'été 1566. L'iconoclasme dans le Nord* (Paris: Hachette, 1981). For a general overview, see the brilliant and profound book of Alain Besançon, *L'Image interdite* (Paris: Fayard, 1994).

17. See the catalogue from the major show at the Louvre, *Sculptures allemandes de la fin du Moyen Age* (Paris: RMN, 1992).

18. This was shortly before the Baden conference (see below), which took place in May 1526 (T 159).

19. Thomas pinpoints the exact moment (T 74, 161) when he emerged from poverty (*armut*) to the point where he was able to count on eating a snack (*zuymbiss*) every day: it coincides with the period described here, when he became the tutor of the two sons of the Zwinglian miller and city councillor Heinrich Werdmüller; the boys later went on to careers in religion and teaching. For some time thereafter, Thomas still occasionally ate "sick meat" with a certain rope-maker, but on the whole his life of poverty was over. This change marks a major psychological and existential turning point in the biography of the boy from the Valais.

20. Alain Belmont, in his recent (unpublished) thesis on "L'Artisanat à Grenoble du XVIe au XVIIIe siècle," gives abundant details concerning such problems of apprenticeship in Alpine and sub-Alpine regions.

21. Stähelin was a native of Swabia (a German province), and Swabians had the reputation of being rather crude.

22. See T 80 and Dollinger, *Histoire d'Alsace,* p. 194.

23. Emile G. Leonard, *Histoire générale du protestantisme* (Paris: Presses Universitaires de France, 1961), vol. 1, p. 140; and *Basler Chronik,* first published 1765, reprinted in 1883, pp. 396–418 (see bibliography).

24. S. Coignard, "Scènes de ménage," *Le Point,* 7 (December 1991).

25. The same "dreamlike or miraculous savior" occurs in the folklore of other mountainous regions in Scotland, the Chartreuse, and the Belledonne.

26. The first was at the time of his initial "schooling," the second when he was staying with the mother of Rudolfus Gwalterus.

27. And not in 1529 as stated in F 50.

28. Andreae Vesalii, *De humani corporis fabrica libri septem* (Basel: [Oporinus],

1543). For a recent edition, see *La Fabrique du corps humain* (Paris: IN-SERM/Actes Sud, 1987); Pierre Huard published a selected iconography with R. Dacosta in 1980.

29. This Cellarius is not to be confused with another Cellarius, Professor Isaac Keller (F 169, and below, chap. 10).

30. Hence she must have been born in the spring of 1530. A recent edition of Felix Platter's memoirs erroneously put her birth in 1529 (F 50). The same edition correctly fixes the time of Thomas and Anna's marriage, however, in the summer of 1529.

31. The epidemic of 1531 is not mentioned in Jean-Noël Biraben, *Les Hommes et la peste* (Paris: Mouton, 1975), vol. 1, p. 411. But Biraben notes that the "disease that sows terror" did afflict Geneva in 1528, 1529, and 1530. The outbreak of the disease in 1531 was probably a vestige of these earlier epidemics, whose germs still lurked on Swiss soil.

32. Yves-Marie Bercé, *Histoire des croquants. Etude des soulèvements populaires en France au XVIIe siècle* (Geneva: Droz, 1974).

33. Biraben, *Les Hommes et la peste,* vol. 1, chronological tables for 1538.

## Chapter Three

1. R. J. Knecht, *Francis the First* (Cambridge, England: Cambridge University Press, 1982), pp. 224–25.

2. Playing with wooden or other "mock" horses had been a major recreation of children since the Middle Ages. Did this interest in horses suggest a fascination with the "equestrian" life of the nobility? See the Bibliothèque Nationale exhibition on childhood in the Middle Ages, cited earlier.

3. Lucien Febvre would have found interesting material here for understanding the irrational outlook of certain sixteenth-century writers: see his *Problème de l'incroyance au XVIe siècle: La religion de Rabelais,* 1942 (reprinted Paris: Albin Michel, 1968), p. 408, translated by Beatrice Gottlieb as *The Problem of Unbelief in the Sixteenth Century: The Religion of Rabelais* (Cambridge, Mass.: Harvard University Press, 1982).

4. Many cities in Western Europe had proud military traditions. This old Swiss tradition of crossbow competitions was later revived in the federal shooting matches.

5. The second Margretlin. Recall that the first died in 1531, before Felix was born.

6. Recall that Felix was also told that snow flakes were really old women. On the question of adoption, see the penultimate chapter of this book.

7. Duc d'Aumale (Henri d'Orléans), *Histoire des princes de Condé* (Paris: Lévy, 1863), vol. 2, p. 112.

8. For more of the same, see F 64, 295, 379.

9. Thomas uses the word *Sod* for well, and Felix (F 69) uses *Sodtbrunnen,* both of which imply that the water was slightly carbonated.

10. Income from interest accounted for 29,296 of the 118,669 pounds of monetary income he received from all sources, including his medical practice, between 1558 and 1612 (F 531–533).

11. Felix's memoirs are more chronologically precise than Thomas's. Felix, educated from early childhood, was in the habit of writing down dates. He also

marked calendars, which have been intelligently studied by the editor of his memoirs, Valentin Lötscher, who has been able to provide important dates concerning his relatives and friends.

12. "La musicologie au CNRS," *CNRS-Info,* June 1991.

13. Anne Chattaway, "La Musique dans le journal intime et les écrits de H. F. Amiel," master's thesis presented to the UER de Lettres Modernes of the Université de Toulouse-Le-Mirail, October 1985.

14. Hartmut Boockmann, Michael Stürmer et al., *Mitten in Europa. Deutsche Geschichte* (Berlin: Siedler, 1984), pp. 132 ff.

15. Ibid., p. 135.

16. Ibid.

17. *Limes:* the northern and eastern border of the Roman Empire, where it came into contact with the territory of the Germanic tribes.

18. F. Mote and Dennis Twitchett, *The Ming Dynasty,* vol. 7 of Dennis Twitchett and John K. Fairbank, eds., *The Cambridge History of China* (Cambridge, England: Cambridge University Press, 1988), chap. 8.

19. Olivier de Serres, *Théâtre d'agriculture* (Grenoble: Dardelet, 1973), book 8, chap. 2.

20. Fernand Braudel, *Civilisation matérielle, économie et capitalisme* (Paris: Armand Colin, 1979), vol. 1, p. 192.

21. When the Platters visited Thomas's native village in June 1563, they were greeted with the same (purely conventional) invocation of the devil, signifying an unwelcome guest (see above, chap. 1).

22. *In partibus* because she actually died in 1549, several years before Felix's marriage to her daughter Madlen in 1557.

23. Madeleine Foisil, *Le Journal de Jean Héroard* (Paris: Fayard, 1989), vol. 1, pp. 75 ff.

24. Olivier de Serres, *Théâtre d'agriculture* (Grenoble: Dardelet, 1973), book 1, chap. 6, p. 47.

25. On this sort of "typological" interpretation, see Catherine Maire, "La trajectoire janséniste au XVIIIe siècle," *Annales ESC* (September–October 1991), pp. 1177–1205; and idem, *Les Convulsionnaires de Saint-Médard* (Paris: Gallimard, 1985).

26. See the catalogue of the Louvre exhibition *Art allemand de la fin du Moyen Age,* November 1991–January 1992 (Paris: RMN, 1992).

27. Felix refers in his memoirs to Covet's heirs, hence he must have written this passage after Covet died in January 1608 (F 86).

28. On this practice, common in both Catholic and Protestant cities at the time, see Ulysse Chevalier, *Mystère des Trois Doms, du chanoine Pra, [joué] en 1509 à Romans* (Lyons, 1887).

29. See Emmanuel Le Roy Ladurie and Jean-François Fitou, "Notes sur la population saint-simonienne," in *Résumé des cours et travaux du Collège de France* (Paris: Collège de France, 1989–1990), pp. 699–728.

30. On the impure and even scatological connotations of money according to certain (Freudian) theories, see Serge Viderman, *De l'argent en psychanalyse et au-delà* (Paris: Presses Universitaires de France, 1992), pp. 7 ff.; and Saint-Simon, *Mémoires,* ed. Boislile (Paris, 1885), vol. 5, pp. 422–23.

31. When a similar fire broke out in Montpellier (see below, chap. 6), Felix

seized the opportunity to compare the corporate solidarity of the citizens of Basel to the extreme individualism of the people of Montpellier.

32. Pierre Chevallier, *Louis XIII* (Paris: Fayard, 1979), p. 98.

33. On the Carnival as an implicit Christian holiday, a "burial of pagan life" in preparation for Lent and a festival marked by dancing, feasting, and satire, see my *Carnavil in Romans,* trans. Mary Feeney (New York: Braziller, 1979), and Michel Feuillet, *Le Carnaval* (Paris: Editions du Cerf, 1991). Feuillet's analyses are quite intelligent despite his minimal bibliography. Evidently the Protestant assault on the Carnival as a pagan festival had not yet begun in this region north of Basel. Indeed, the tenacious festival was thought of as a satirical weapon against the Roman Church, which remained powerful in the region. The Basel Carnival is still an important event to this day.

34. See, for example, the diary of Samuel Pepys, passim.

35. We saw earlier that he once treated a sculptor who had been his enemy.

36. The word *Beruf* in this sense appears for the first time in German in Luther's biblical translation of Ecclesiasticus, chap. 11: *beharre in deinem Beruf, bleib in deinem Beruf.* See also Max Weber, *The Protestant Ethic and the Spirit of Capitalism,* chap. 1, part 3.

## Chapter Four

1. Cratander's Plautus was printed in September 1523, hence Thomas could not have worked in the rope shop before that date.

2. The touchingly possessive words of Ruch's wife upon learning of Thomas's knockout punch are worth quoting: *O we, du hast mier min man zu todt geschlagen!* (Woe is me! You've beaten my husband to death!)

3. Platter (T 122) calls Ruch and his other partner, Winter, by their first names, Balthasar and Ruprecht, but he always respectfully refers to Johannes Herbster using the Greco-Latin honorific "Oporinus."

4. The period 1524–26 is important for an accurate chronology of Thomas Platter's years of apprenticeship. Collinus became an apprentice ropemaker on May 23, 1524 (T 162). Then, after a brief stint of military service in Wurtemberg, he opened a ropemaking shop on February 23, 1526. Hence Thomas's apprenticeship with Collinus must have begun after that date.

5. A copy of the first edition, in Latin and printed by Thomas Platter with a date of 1536, can be found in the Bibliothèque Nationale.

6. *Ring = gering* (T 123).

7. This text should finally convince skeptics reluctant to admit that Mainz was the birthplace of printing.

8. This information is taken from Albert Brückner, *Schweizer Stempelschneider und Schriftgiesser* (Basel, 1943), p. 42 and passim.

9. Much of this is based on Valentin Lötscher, "Felix Platter und seine Familie," *Helbing, Basler Nejahrsblatt* 153(1975):63 ff.

10. The reader may wish to compare Platter's activities with those of his contemporary, the Sire de Gouberville: see Robillard de Beaurepaire, ed., *Le Journal [rural] du sire de Gouberville* (Caen: Delesques, 1892).

11. *Histoire de la France urbaine* (Paris: Seuil, 1980), vol. 1, pp. 15–16.

12. Knecht, *Francis the First,* p. 367.

13. Felix Platter also split his time later on, indeed more so than Thomas and

Oporinus, devoting part of each day to work as a physician, pharmacist, and surgeon.

14. Lötscher, "Felix Platter und seine Familie," p. 26.

15. Ibid., pp. 82–83.

16. Ibid., pp. 46 ff.

17. Thomas's moving letter about his daughter's death was published by Alfred Hartmann in *Basilea latina* (Basel, 1931). See T 139, 179.

18. See also Lötscher, "Felix Platter und seine Familie," pp. 27 ff.

19. Ibid., pp. 81 ff.

20. Ibid., p. 40.

21. At times Anna Dietschi-Platter could also be quite mean-spirited: "After our return home [to the Valais for a brief visit prior to the birth of Margretlin I], Anna was delighted [*fro*]," Thomas tells us, "because the priest had come down with the plague" (T 92). Was the difference of religion the only reason for her jubilation?

## CHAPTER FIVE

1. Danielle Anex-Cabanis et al., *Histoire de Laussane* (Toulouse: Privat, 1982).

2. Paul Guichonnet et al., *Histoire de Genève* (Toulouse: Privat, 1974). See also René Guerdan, *Genève au temps de Calvin* (Geneva: Editions du Mont-Blanc, 1977); idem, *Histoire de Genève* (Paris: Mazarine, 1981); and idem, *La Vie quotidienne à Genève au temps de Calvin* (Paris: Hachette, 1973); Anne-Marie Piuz, *L'Eco-nomie genevoise de la Réforme* (Geneva: Georg, 1990); and above all J.-F. Bergier, *Les Foires de Genève: Genève et l'économie européenne de la Renaissance* (Paris: SEVPEN, 1963).

3. The history of Savoy has been treated in many works, some of them quite remarkable. Among those I have used, let me mention works by Roland Edighoffer (Paris: Presses Universitaires de France, 1992) and especially Paul Guichonnet (Toulouse: Privat, 1973); J.-P. Leguay (Rennes: Ouest-France, 1983); Henri Menabréa (Chambéry: IRC, 1970); V. de Saint-Genis (Marseilles: Lafitte, 1978); A. Perrin (Chambéry, 1900); and of course the important thesis of Jean Nicolas, *La Savoie* (Paris: Maloine, 1978), 2 vols.

4. A Guilbert, *Histoire des villes de France* (Paris: Furne et Perrotin, 1848), vol. 5, p. 122.

5. G. de Bombourg, *Histoire de Nantua et de son abbaye* (Nantua, 1858), p. 156.

6. Olivier de Serres, *Théâtre d'agriculture* (Grenoble: Dardelet, 1973), book 6, chap. 26.

7. I use this word in its modern sense to mean the midday meal.

8. This town is located in the Bourg-en-Bresse district of the canton of Montluel in the department of the Ain.

9. Richard Gascon, *Lyon et ses marchands* (Paris-The Hague: Mouton, 1971), vol. 2, p. 838.

10. In those days *officiers* (or officeholders) were mainly civilian, with a smaller number of military officers.

11. Jules Michelet, *Histoire de France, Renaissance et Réforme*, book 2, chap. 12, and book 3, chap. 2.

12. Frederic J. Baumgartner, *Henri II, King of France* (Duke: Duke University Press, 1988). In French, there is Ivan Cloulas, *Henri II* (Paris: Fayard, 1985).

13. Michelet, *Histoire de France,* book 3: *Guerres de Religion,* chap. 3. The truth of Michelet's assertions, often dubious, is inversely proportional to the remarkable quality of his style, at least so far as Henri II is concerned.

14. See A. Kleinclausz, *Histoire de Lyon* (Marseilles: Laffitte Reprints, 1978); J. Rossiaud, F. Bayard et al., *Histoire de Lyon* (Saint-Etienne: Horvath, 1990); and A. Latreille, ed., *Histoire de Lyon et du Lyonnais* (Toulouse: Privat, 1975). See also Guillaume Paradin, *Histoire de Lyon* (1573), reprinted (Roanne: Horvath, 1973), and the amusing Françoise Bayard, *Histoire de Lyon en bande dessinée* (Roanne: Horvath, 1978). And do not forget the admirable Richard Gascon, *Lyon et ses marchands,* which was cited earlier.

15. Frank Lestringant, the eminent Renaissance historian, sees this march to execution as an allusion to Christ's climb up Calvary Hill.

16. See Heinrich Pantaleon, *Heldenbuch, Prosopographiae heroum* (Basel, 1565–70), vol. 3, pp. 326–29.

17. Gascon, *Lyon,* vol. 1, p. 385.

18. Ibid., vol. 1, p. 186.

19. Ibid. and F 146.

20. Gascon, *Lyon,* vol. 1, p. 170.

21. An enlargement of a later (seventeenth- or eighteenth-century) engraving of these boatwomen is displayed on the main staircase of the École Supérieure des Bibliothèques near Lyons.

22. Michel François, *Le Cardinal François de Tournon* (Paris: Editions De Boccard, 1951), p. 288.

23. Louis Dulieu, "Guillaume Rondelet," *Clio medica* (1966), vol. 1, pp. 89–111.

24. BN, ms. lat. 8647, fol. 15.

25. B. Bligny, *Histoire du Dauphiné* (Toulouse: Privat, 1973), p. 200. See also Jean Boudon, *Histoire du Dauphiné* (Lyons: Horvath, 1992), and Paul Dreyfus, *Histoire du Dauphiné* (Paris: Presses Universitaires de France, 1972).

26. See the map of sixteenth-century Vienne, with various detail views, in Pierre Cavard, *Le Procès de Michel Servet à Vienne* (Vienne: Blanchard, 1953); Thomas Mermet, *Histoire de Vienne* (Paris: Res Universis, 1992); André Pelletier, *Histoire de Vienne* (Roanne: Horvath, 1980).

27. René Favrier, *Les Villes du Dauphiné aux XVIIe et XVIIIe siècles* (Grenoble: Presses Universitaires de Grenoble, 1993).

28. Now the Collège de France.

29. Henri Busson, *Les Sources et le développement du rationalisme dans la littérature française de la Renaissance* (Paris: Letouzey, 1920), pp. 70–94.

30. On Pierre Danès, see Mireille Forget, *Humanisme et Renaissance,* 1936, pp. 365 ff., and 1937, pp. 59 ff. In addition to the works of Danès, who was an apologist for Valois foreign policy, the reader may wish to consult the biography written by his great-grandnephew Pierre-Hilaire Danès, *Abrégé de la vie de Pierre Danès* (Paris: Quillau, 1731).

31. Favier, *Les Villes du Dauphine,* part 1; Albert Caise, "Le registre baptistaire de Saint-Vallier, 1568–1575," *Bulletin de la Société d'archéologie et de statistique de la Drôme* (Valence, 1892), pp. 5 ff.

32. E. Fayard, *Notice historique sur Saint-Vallier* (Lyons: Georg, 1894); see also Albert Caise, *Cartulaire de Saint-Vallier* (Paris-Valence, 1870), pp. 73 (on the influence of Diane de Poitiers, who was born into a family from the region).

33. Caise, "Le registre," pp. 14–15. See also H.-E. Martin, *Paroisses et communes de France. Drôme* (Paris: Centre National de Recherche Scientifique, 1981), p. 494.

34. See T 2–47; see also Catherine Velay-Vallantin, *L'Histoire des contes* (Paris: Fayard, 1992), pp. 30–59.

35. Dominique Julia and Jacques Revel, eds., *Les Universités européennes du XVIe siècle au XVIIIe siècle. Histoire sociale des populations étudiantes* (Paris: Ecole des Hautes Etudes en Sciences Sociales, 1989), vol. 2, p. 486.

36. Abbé Joseph-Cyprien Nadal, *Histoire de l'université de Valence* (Valence: Marc-Aurel, 1861).

37. René Favier, *Les Villes du Dauphiné aux XVIIe et XVIIIe siècles* (Grenoble: Presses Universitaires de Grenoble, 1993); see also Abbé A. Vincent, *Notice historique sur Livron* (Valence: Marc-Aurel, 1853), pp. 24 and passim.

38. Victor Cassien and Alexandre Debelle, *Album du Dauphiné* (Grenoble: Editions des Quatre Seigneurs, 1978), vol. 4, p. 78.

39. Cassien and Debelle, *Album du Dauphiné*, vol. 4, p. 126; Rodolphe Bringer, "Le siège de Pierrelatte," *Le Bassin du Rhône* (Montélimar, 1910), no. 10, pp. 231–35; A. Lacroix, *L'Arrondissement de Montélimar* (Valence: Combier et Nivoche, 1888), vol. 7, pp. 74 ff.; Adolphe Rochas, *L'Abbaye joyeuse de Pierrelatte* (Grenoble: Drevet, 1881), pp. 13 ff.

40. Emmanuel Le Roy Ladurie, *Les Paysans de Languedoc* (Paris: SEVPEN, 1966), pp. 201–3, and *Histoire de Montélimar* (Toulouse: Privat, 1993).

41. Joseph-Antoine Bastet, *Histoire de la ville et de la principauté d'Orange* (Orange: Raphel, 1856), reprinted (Marseilles: Lafitte, 1977), and idem, *Essai historique sur les évêques du diocèse d'Orange* (Orange: Escoffier, 1837), and *Notice historique sur Orange,* 1840; Roland Sicard, *Paroisses et communes de France. Vaucluse* (Paris: Centre National de Recherche Scientifique, 1987), p. 183.

42. Sylvain Ganière et al., *Histoire d'Avignon* (La Calade: Edisud, 1979); Henri Dubled, *Histoire du Comtat Venaissin* (Villelaure: Credel, 1982); and especially the essential work by Marc Venard, *Réforme protestante, Réforme catholique dans la province d'Avignon au XVIe siècle* (Paris: Cerf, 1993).

43. On the general phenomenon of scapegoating as it relates to the particular phenomenon of anti-Semitism, see the important work of Yves Chevalier, *L'Antisémitisme* (Paris: Cerf, 1988), pp. 99–182.

44. See Emmanuel Le Roy Ladurie, *Paris-Montpellier* (Paris: Gallimard, 1982).

45. See C. Devic and J. Vaissette, *Histoire générale de Languedoc* (Toulouse: Privat, 1889), vol. 11, pp. 294 ff., and, in Emmanuel Le Roy Ladurie, *Paysans de Languedoc* (Paris: SEVPEN, 1966), the chapters dealing with the sixteenth century.

46. Hubert Gautier, *Histoire de la ville de Nîmes* (Paris-Nîmes, 1724), p. 59; a modern (1991) reprint is available from C. Lacour in Nîmes.

47. Gautier, *Histoire*, p. 61.

48. T2 106 and Gautier, *Histoire*, p. 61.

49. Raymond Huard, ed., *Histoire de Nîmes* (Aix-en-Provence: Edisud, 1992).

50. Léon Ménard, *Histoire civile, ecclésiastique et littéraire de la ville de Nîmes* (Paris: Ch. Aubert, 1753), vol. 4, pp. 205–23, reprinted in Marseilles in 1975 by Lafitte.

51. There were 5,000 inhabitants in the first half of the fourteenth century; 1370: 725 hearths; 1693: 540 hearths; 1698: 624 hearths; 1709: 664 hearths; 1740: 2,400

residents; 1766: 664 hearths. These figures are taken from Claude Motte et al., *Paroisses et communes de France. Hérault* (Paris: Centre National de Recherche Scientifique, 1989), p. 257; Roger Imbert and Jean Baille, *Lunel et son passé* (Lunel: Peis, 1989): Th. Millerot, *Histoire de la ville de Lunel depuis son origine jusqu'en 1789* (Montpellier, 1881); Abbé A. Rouet, *Notice sur la ville de Lunel au Moyen Age et vie de saint Gérard, seigneur de cette ville au XIIIe siècle* (Montpellier, 1878); E. Rouet, *Essai sur la topographie physique et médicale de Lunel* (Montpellier, 1822) (thesis in medicine).

52. Of course these young people wearing white masks and costumes may have represented or symbolized a procession of ghosts from the Land of the Dead connected with Toussaint or the Day of the Dead. See Carlo Ginzburg, *The Night Battles: Witchcraft and Agrarian Cults in the Sixteenth and Seventeenth Centuries,* trans. John and Anne Tedesch: (Baltimore: Johns Hopkins University Press, 1983). But this would be hard to prove, and in any case this flirtatious, elitist procession shows that what may originally have been a macabre event had been tamed by the forces of social integration, just as the more unbridled aspects of the Carnival were tamed: see Maria Isaura Pereira de Queiroz, *Carnaval brésilien* (Paris: Gallimard, 1992). On all this, see Arnold Van Gennep, *Manuel de folklore français contemporain* (Paris: A. and J. Picard), tome 1, vol. 6, part 4, pp. 2808 ff. Compare D. Fabre, *Carnaval* (Paris: Gallimard, 1992).

53. The bibliography at the end of this volume contains a list of works on Montpellier in the sixteenth century.

## CHAPTER SIX

1. Felix Platter's Montpellier publisher (Coulet, 1892, p. 34) confused Marranos with Moors! The same egregious error can be found in Mark Musa's "bilingual" edition of Machiavelli's *Prince* (New York: St. Martin's Press, 1964), chap. 24, pp. 184–85, where *Marrani* is translated as "Moors."

2. Louis Dulieu, *La Médecine à Montpellier,* vols. 1 and 2 (Lille: Presses Universelles, 1975 and 1979). See also the bibliography concerning Montpellier at the end of this volume.

3. See Le Roy Ladurie, *Paysans de Languedoc,* 1966 edition, vol. 3, graphs on p. 1020.

4. Du Chatel's reputation as a womanizer would follow him, for good reason, all the way to the court of the Valois, where he served, at the height of his career, as royal physician. See Brantôme, *Recueil des Dames* (Paris: Gallimard, 1991), p. 480.

5. Recall that Saint Luke, whose feast day is October 18, is the patron saint of physicians. See Benedictines of Paris, *Vie des saints et des bienheureux* (Paris: Letouzey, 1952), pp. 594–600, for the month of October.

6. See the catalogue of the exhibition at the Bibliothèque Nationale entitled *Des livres et des rois,* edited by M.-P. Laffitte and Ursula Baurmeister (Paris: Editions du Quai Voltaire and Bibliothèque Nationale, 1992), a fundamental work.

7. Dulieu, *La Médecine à Montpellier,* vol. 2; Charles Lichtenthaeler, *Histoire de la médecine* (Paris: Fayard, 1978).

8. Pierre Riché, *Gerbert d'aurillac, pape de l'an mil* (Paris: Fayard, 1987), p. 192.

9. Gilles de Gouberville, *Journal,* ed. Bricquebosz (Pont de Neuville: Les Editions des Champs, 1993), vol. 2, pp. 281 ff., July 16 and July 18–22, 1556.

10. On apocalyptic beliefs among French Catholics in the sixteenth century, see Denis Crouzet, *Les Guerriers de Dieu* (Champ-Vallon: Seyssel, 1990), part 1.

11. This painting was on display at the show "Paysages, paysans" at the Bibliothèque Nationale in the spring of 1994. See the reproduction in the show catalogue, Emmanuel Le Roy Ladurie, ed., *Paysages, paysans* (Paris: Bibliothèque Nationale-RMN, 1994). See also Emmanuel Le Roy Ladurie, *Etat royal* (Paris: Hachette, 1987), pp. 56–57.

12. This adoption was de facto, not necessarily de jure.

13. Lötscher, the editor of Felix Platter's memoirs, misinterprets the words *deigade* and *aiguade,* which for some reason he confuses with the French for "decant."

14. Blaise de Monluc, *Commentaires* (Paris: Renouard, 1872), vol. 1, pp. 440, 466; vol. 2, pp. 66, 67; vol. 4, p. 43. Here the leader of the landsknechts is referred to as Rinckrock.

15. Machiavelli, *The Prince,* chap. 7: execution of Remirro de Orca.

16. The word *ortalisse* or *ourtalis* was commonly used for garden on sixteenth-century Languedocian cadasters. See Frédéric Mistral, *Trésor du félibrige,* art. *ourtalis.*

17. See Didier Gazagnadou, *La Poste à relais* (Paris: Kimé, 1994).

### Chapter Seven

1. G. Saumade, *Fabrègues* (Montpellier: L'Abeille Workers' Cooperative, 1908).

2. Jean Sagnes, *Histoire de Béziers* (Toulouse: Privat, 1986).

3. See Alain Molinier, "De la religion des oeuvres à la réformation dans les Cévennes," *Revue d'histoire de l'Eglise de France,* vol. 72, 1986, pp. 258–59.

4. Sagnes, *Histoire de Béziers,* p. 106.

5. Ibid., pp. 42, 64, 203.

6. Gilles Caster, *Le Commerce du pastel et de l'épicerie à Toulouse de 1450 environ à 1561* (Toulouse: Privat, 1962).

7. The first black slaves destined for sugar and other plantations were exported from Portugal to Brazil in 1559. See Katia M. de Queiros Mattoso, *Etre esclave au Brésil, XVIe-XIXe siècle* (Paris: Hachette, 1979), p. 32, translated by Arthur Goldhammer as *To Be a Slave in Brazil* (New Brunswick: Rutgers University Press, 1985).

8. Germain Mouynes, *Ville de Narbonne. Inventaire des Archives communales antérieures à 1790* (Narbonne: E. Caillard, 1871–79), subseries BB, pp. 1–2 (BB1, February 1557).

9. Anne Blanchard in André Corvisier, ed., *Histoire militaire de la France* (Paris: Presses Universitaires de France, 1992), pp. 263–68.

10. On Narbonne in the sixteenth century, see the admirable thesis on the history of this city from the Middle Ages to the nineteenth century which Gilbert Larguier recently defended at the University of Paris VII. While awaiting publication of this "great work," one can also consult Jacques Michaud, *Histoire de Narbonne* (Privat: Toulouse, 1988), or Paul Carbonel, *Histoire de Narbonne* (Narbonne: Caillard, 1956; reprinted Marseilles: Lafitte, 1988).

11. This is the third depressive episode mentioned in Felix's *Tagebuch,* following two earlier incidents in Avignon and one just after his arrival in Montpellier.

12. Marie-Caroline Roederer, Michel Mollat, and Jean-Pierre Bardet, *Paroisses*

*et communes de France, Aude* (Paris: Centre National de Recherche Scientifique, 1979), p. 357.

13. Fathers Claude Devic and J. Vaissette, *Histoire générale de Languedoc* (Toulouse: Privat, 1879), vol. II, p. 285.

14. See the maps in the appendix to Frank C. Spooner, *L'Economie mondiale et les frappes monétaires en France* (Paris: Armand Colin, 1956).

15. Father Thomas Bouges, *Histoire ecclésiastique et civile de Carcassonne* (Paris: Gandouin, 1741).

16. Devic and Vaissette, *Histoire générale de Languedoc*.

17. For all that follows concerning the location of the presidial, see Jean Guilaine, *Histoire de Carcassonne* (Toulouse: Privat, 1984), p. 116.

18. Claudine Pailhès, *D'or et de sang. Le XVIe siècle ariégeois* (Foix: Editions des Archives Départementales, 1992).

19. Ibid., on Ariège. As for silver from Mexico after 1549, see Henry Bamford Parkes, *A History of Mexico* (Boston: Houghton Mifflin, 1960), pp. 59–79.

20. Gilles Caster, *Le Commerce du pastel et de l'épicerie à Toulouse de 1450 à 1560* (Toulouse: Privat, 1962), pp. 269–372.

21. Philippe Wolff, Bartolomé Bennassar, et al., *Histoire de Toulouse* (Toulouse: Privat, 1974), p. 232.

22. Charles Higounet, *Histoire de Bordeaux,* vol. 4 (Bordeaux: Fédération Historique du Sud-Ouest, 1966), p. 243, n. 171.

23. Wolff, Bennassar et al., *Histoire de Toulouse,* p. 47.

24. Ibid., p. 222.

25. On the cultural climate in Toulouse in the sixteenth century, see the remarkable work of A. London Fell, *Origins of Legislative Sovereignty and the Legislative State* (Westport, Conn.: Greenwood, 1983–1991). This essential work deserves to be rescued from the almost total obscurity in which it is shrouded today, at least in France.

26. Devic and Vaissette, *Histoire générale de Languedoc,* vol. II, p. 317. On the population of Toulouse, see Wolff, Bennassar et al., *Histoire de Toulouse,* p. 294 and passim: in 1335, 35,000; 1398, 24,000; 1405, 22,500; 1550, 30–40,000; 1640, 42,000; 1695, 43,000.

27. Henry Le Bret, *Histoire de Montauban* (Montauban, 1841; reprinted Marseilles: Lafitte, 1976); Daniel Ligou, *Histoire de Montauban* (Toulouse: Privat, 1984), pp. 205–6.

28. Charles Higounet, *Histoire de Bordeaux* (Bordeaux: Fédération historique du Sud-Ouest, 1962), vol. 4 (on the sixteenth century), p. 287. This particular *recette* moved to Bordeaux in 1566.

29. Guilbert, *Histoire des villes de France,* vol. 2, p. 399.

30. Higounet, *Histoire de Bordeaux,* vol. 4, p. 181.

31. Jacques Bernard, *Navires et gens de mer à Bordeaux (vers 1400–vers 1550)* (Paris: SEVPEN, 1968), p. 520 and passim; Higounet, *Histoire de Bordeaux,* p. 277.

32. Higounet, *Histoire de Bordeaux,* p. 153.

33. A similar date in Fécamp: the local liqueur, a stronger ancestor of today's Benedictine, was supposedly produced by a "Normanized" Italian monk in 1510. See Laurence Haloche, *Bénédictine, histoire d'une liqueur* (Lausanne: Conti, 1991), p. 29; see also Hugues et Alfred Le Roux, *La Bénédictine de l'ancienne abbaye de Fécamp* (Rouen: Le Cerf, 1905), pp. 13–14.

34. Higounet, *Histoire de Bordeaux,* pp. 126–28, 163.

35. Ibid.

36. These figures are taken from Jacques Bernard's thesis.

37. Clément Janequin, *Chansons polyphoniques* (Monaco: Lesure, 1965), vol. 1 ("Bordeaux period"), Oiseau Lyre and Les Remparts labels.

38. Robert Etienne, *Histoire de Bordeaux* (Toulouse: Privat, 1990), pp. 40–41.

39. Ibid., pp. 42, 102.

40. R. Doucet, *Les Institutions de la France au XVIe siècle* (Paris: Picard, 1948), vol. 1, pp. 275 ff.

41. Jean-Noël Luc, *La Charente-Maritime, Aunis et Saintonge* (Saint-Jean-d'Angély: Bordessoules, 1981), p. 170. See also G. and J. Musset, *Pons* (La Rochelle: Bergevin, 1926), p. 9 and passim.

42. Alain Michaud, *Histoire de Saintes* (Toulouse: Privat, 1989), p. 120.

43. Ibid., p. 110.

44. Ibid., p. 136.

45. André Baudrit, "Saintes au XVIe siècle," thesis, Faculty of Letters, University of Bordeaux, 1957, vol. 1, pp. 194 ff. I was able to consult a copy of this thesis made available by the Bibliothèque Municipale of Saintes.

46. Higounet, *Histoire de Bordeaux,* vol. 4, p. 131; Eutrope-Louis Dangibeaud, *Etudes historiques: Saintes au XVI siècle* (Evreux: Hérissey, 1863), pp. 53–64.

47. Baron Eschassériaux, *Etudes, documents . . . relatifs à la ville de Saintes* (Saintes: Orliaguet, 1876), p. 33 and passim.

48. Michaud, *Histoire de Saintes,* p. 103.

49. André Chastel, *Le Présent des oeuvres* (Paris: De Fallois, 1993), p. 219.

50. Marcel Delafossse, *Histoire de La Rochelle* (Toulouse: Privat, 1985), pp. 73 ff.

51. On this and what follows, see Louis-Claude Saudau, *Saint-Jean-d'Angély* (Saint-Jean-d'Angély: J.-B. Ollivier, 1886).

52. *Discours des choses les plus remarquables advenues . . . durant le siège de Lusignan en 1574* (Poitiers, 1577), pp. 62 ff., B. N., anonymous, L 634–93.

53. Brantôme, *Oeuvres complètes,* ed. L. Lalanne (Paris: Renouard, 1869), vol. 5, p. 19.

54. Chinon district, canton of Langeais.

55. Jacques Le Goff and Emmanuel Le Roy Ladurie, "Mélusine maternelle et défricheuse," *Annales* (May–October 1971), pp. 587 ff.; Jean Tarrade, *La Vienne, de la Préhistoire à nos jours* (Saint-Jean-d'Angély: Bordessoules, 1986), pp. 108, 377, and passim; Edmond-René Labande, *Histoire du Poitou* (Toulouse: Privat, 1976), pp. 108 ff.

56. Gédéon Tallemant des Réaux, *Historiettes* (Paris: Gallimard, 1967), vol. 1, p. 594.

57. René Crozet, *Histoire du Poitou* (Paris: Presses Universitaires de France, 1970), p. 61.

58. On the history of Poitou in the sixteenth century, see Crozet, *Histoire de Poitou;* Georges Bordonove, *Histoire du Poitou* (Paris: Hachette, 1973); Tarrade, *La Vienne, de la Préhistoire à nos jours;* Labande, *Histoire du Poitou;* Dr. Louis Merle, *La Métairie et l'évolution agraire de la Gâtine poitevine de la fin du Moyen Age à la Révolution* (Paris: SEVPEN, 1958). See also the works of Paul Raveau on Poitou in the sixteenth century for information on agriculture, the peasantry, aristo-

cratic life, and social and economic conditions (Raveau's works were published by Rivière in Paris in 1926 and 1931 and in Poitiers in 1917 and 1935).

59. The vestiges of this amphitheater gradually disappeared in the centuries following the Platters' visits.

60. Labande, *Histoire du Poitou*, pp. 218–21.

61. *Mémoires chronologiques pour servir à l'histoire de Châtellerault,* collected and arranged in 1788 by Roffay des Pallus and published by Camille Page (Châtellerault: Rivière, 1909), p. 71; and Alfred Hérault, *Histoire de Châtellerault* (Châtellerault: Videau, 1926), pp. 11 ff.

62. Karl Baedeker, *Le Centre de la France* (Leipzig-Paris: Ollendorf, 1889), p. 22.

63. Bernard Chevalier, *Tours, ville royale* (Louvain-Paris, 1975), pp. 258, 347; and idem, *Histoire de Tours* (Toulouse: Privat, 1985), p. 136.

64. Georges Duby, *L'Economie rurale et la vie des campagnes dans l'Occident médiéval* (Paris: Aubier, 1962), pp. 171–76; and F. L. Gansho, *Qu'est-ce que la féodalité?* (Paris: Tallandier, 1982).

65. Chevalier, *Tours*, pp. 122–52.

66. Ibid., pp. 130–52.

67. Ibid., pp. 528 ff.

68. Sabine Baring Gould, *Cliff Castles and Cave Dwellings in Europe* (London: Seeley, 1911; reprinted Detroit: Singing Tree Press, 1968), chap. 2.

69. Patrick Saletta, *Voyage dans la France des troglodytes* (Antony: Sides, 1991), pp. 145, 153, 161, 167, 185, 201.

70. C. Croubois, *Le Loir-et-Cher* (Saint-Jean-d'Angély: Bordessoules, 1985), p. 191.

71. Roger Dion, *Val de Loire* (Tours: Arrault, 1934), vol. 1, p. 418, reprinted Marseilles: Lafitte, 1978.

72. Ibid., pp. 357–58, for all that follows.

73. Madeleine Chabrolin et al., *Histoire de Nevers* (Saint-Etienne: Le Coteau, Horvath, 1984), p. 171.

74. François Lebrun et al., *Histoire des pays de la Loire* (Toulouse: Privat, 1972), pp. 219 ff.; Claude Croubois, ed., *Le Loir-et-Cher de la préhistoire à nos jours* (Saint-Jean-d'Angély: Bordessoules, 1985), pp. 193 ff.; Philippe Mantellier, *Histoire de la communauté des marchands fréquentant la rivière de Loire et fleuves descendant en icelle,* vol. 2 (Orléans: Jacob, 1864).

75. In the département of the Moselle, Sarrebourg district, Phalsbourg canton.

76. Yvonne Labande-Mailfert, *Charles VIII et son milieu (1477–1498)* (Paris: Klincksiec, 1975), p. 580 (with many references).

77. On Amboise: Léon-Auguste Bosseboeuf, *Amboise, le château, la ville et le canton* (Tours: Pericat, 1897); Abbé Casimir Chevalier, *Inventaire analytique des archives communales d'Amboise, 1421–1789* (Tours: Georges-Joubert, 1874); Jacqueline Melet, *Le Développement historique de la ville d'Amboise des origines jusqu'au XVIIIe siècle,* reviewed in *Positions des thèses soutenues par les élèves de la promotion de 1972* (Paris: Ecole des chartes, 1972), pp. 107–13; Jacqueline Melet-Samson, "La ville d'Amboise aux XVe et XVIe siècles," *Bulletin de la Société archéologique de Touraine* (1973), pp. 263–68; idem, "Provenance des matériaux utilisés pour la construction des édifices publics de la ville d'Amboise aux XVe et XVIe siècles," *Congrès national des sociétés savantes* (Saint-Etienne, 1973), pp. 225–34.

78. Exhaustive searches of thousands of death certificates over a period of two centuries have turned up only one or two cases of suicide: see Alain Croix, *La Bretagne aux XVIe siècles* (Paris: Maloinc, 1980), 2 vols.; and Alain Molinier, *Stagnation et croissance. Le Vivarais aux XVIIe et XVIIIe siècles* (Paris: EHESS/Touzot, 1985).

79. Yves Denis, *Histoire de Blois et de sa région* (Toulouse: Privat, 1988), pp. 65–67, 95.

80. Ibid., p. 95.

81. Michel Melot, article in *Gazette des Beaux-Arts* (December 1967), p. 326 (fundamental).

82. Machiavelli, *The Prince,* chap. 20.

83. See also Jean Bernier, *Histoire de Blois* (Paris: Muguet, 1682), pp. 21–22.

84. On Blois, see Ursula Baurmeister and M.-P. Lafitte, *Des livres et des rois* (Paris: Bibliothèque Nationale, 1992); Dr. Frédéric Lesueur, *Le Château de Blois, tel qu'il fut* (Paris: A. et J. Picard, 1970); Louis Bergevin and Alexandre Dupré, *Histoire de Blois* (Marseilles: Laffitte, 1977, reproduced from an earlier edition: Blois: E. Dezairs, 1846–1847); Jean Caplat, *Histoire de Blois depuis les origines jusqu'à nos jours* (Blois: Caplat, 1968).

85. These figures do not include a small number of houses reserved for clerics.

86. On the great church at Cléry, see Canon Lucien Millet, *Notre Dame de Cléry* (Paris: Lethielleux, 1961); Jean Mercier, *Notre-Dame de Cléry* (Cléry: Paroisse Notre-Dame, 1988); Michel Caffin de Mérouville, *Notre-Dame de Cléry* (Paris: Plon, 1963); Louis Jarry, *Histoire de Cléry et de l'église collégiale et chapelle royale de Notre-Dame de Cléry* (Cléry: Editions de l'Association des Amis de Cléry, 1984), facsimile of the Orléans edition of 1899.

87. See Saint-Simon, *Mémoires,* ed. Boislisle (Paris: Hachette), vol. 8, p. 239.

88. On Orléans, see Louis d'Illiers, *Histoire d'Orléans* (Marseille: Laffitte, 1977; reprinted from the second edition, Orléans: Ruddé, 1954); Jacques Debal, *Histoire d'Orléans et de son terroir,* vol. 1 (Roanne: Horvath, 1983); Jean de Viguerie, ed., *Histoire religieuse de l'Orléannais* (Chambray: CLD, 1983); J. de La Martinière, "Le monument de la Pucelle sur le pont d'Orléans," *Mémoires de la Société archéologique et historique de l'Orléannais,* vol. 37 (1936), pp. 109 ff.; François Lebrun, ed., *Histoire des Pays de la Loire, Orléannais, Touraine* (Toulouse: Privat, 1972).

89. Jean-Marc Moriceau, *Les Fermiers de l'Ile-de-France* (Paris: Fayard, 1994).

90. See Michel Billard, *Voyages à travers l'histoire d'Etampes* (Etampes: Editions du Soleil 1985); idem, *A la découverte d'Etampes. Sur les pas des pèlerins de Saint-Jacques* (Etampes: Editions du Soleil, 1987); idem, *Eglises et chapelles d'Etampes, autour de Notre-dame* (Etrechy: Editions du Soleil, 1988); Maxime Legrand, *Histoire d'Etampes* (Res Universis; a facsimile of the 1902 edition was published under the title *Etampes pittoresque* in Paris in 1991); Justin Bourgeois, *Quelques recherches sur le port d'Etampes* (Etampes: A. Allier, 1860); Basile Fleureau, *Les Antiquités de la ville et du duché d'Etampes* (Marseilles: Laffitte reprints, 1977; reproduction of the 1683 Paris edition published by J.-B. Coignard); Léon Guibourgé, *Etampes, ville royale* (Etampes, 1958); Liliana Klein, *Etampes d'hier et d'aujourd'hui* (Etampes: Editions du Soleil, 1988); Maxime de Montrond, *Essais historiques sur la ville d'Etampes* (Etampes: Fortin, 1836); *Les Très Riches Heures du duc de Berry,* with an introduction by Jean Longnon (Paris: Vilo, 1969); Charles Forteau,

"Comptes de recettes et de dépenses de la maladrerie d'Etampes," *Annales de la Société historique et archéologique du Gâtinais,* vol. 21, pp. 100 ff.; Joseph Délivré, "L'immigration dans le doyenné d'Etampes après la guerre de Cent Ans," *Mémoires et documents de la Société historique et archéologique de Corbeil, de l'Essonne et du Hurepoix,* vol. 14, 1988, and, in the same volume, the article by Joseph Crocy on "L'Hôtel-Dieu d'Etampes."

91. Abel Cornaton, Jean Burtin, et al., *Arpajon, les grandes étapes de son histoire* (Arpajon, 1968); Abbé J.-M. Alliot, *Les Curés d'Arpajon* (Arpajon: Lamouche, 1889); *Histoire de pays de Châtres. Chronologie des principaux événements de l'histoire d'Arpajon et de sa région* (Etampes: Editions Soleil, 1988); Jean-Joseph Beaugrand, *Notes historiques sur Arpajon* (Paris, 1833); Jacques Dupâquier et al., *Paroisses et communes de France. Dictionnaire d'histoire administrative et démographique. Région parisienne* (Paris: Centre National de Recherche Scientifique, 1974), article "Arpajon."

92. Jean Jacquart, *La Crise rurale en Ile-de-France* (Paris: Armand Colin, 1974).

93. André Jouanen, *Montlhéry, douze siècles d'histoire* (Etampes: Editions du Soleil, 1989), and idem, *Montlhéry et son histoire* (Ballainvilliers: Association Renaissance et Culture, 1983).

## CHAPTER EIGHT

1. Jean-Pierre Babelon, *Nouvelle histoire de Paris au XVIe siècle* (Paris: Hachette, 1986), pp. 247–259 and passim.

2. Jean-Marc Moriceau, *Les Fermiers de l'Ile-de-France* (Paris: Fayard, 1994), part 1, as well as p. 645 and passim. Moriceau's remarkable book helps us to understand the countryside of the Ile-de-France at the time of Felix's visit.

3. Babelon, *Nouvelle histoire,* pp. 247–53.

4. This is according to Jean-François Pernot, who is currently writing a book on the Chambre des Comptes of Paris under the Ancien Régime.

5. K.-P. Poussou, "Les métropoles, parasites ou stimulants?" in Jacqueline Beaujeu-Garnier, ed., *La Grande Ville, enjeu du XXIe siècle,* texts in honor of Jean Bastié (Paris: Presses Universitaires de France, 1991), pp. 17–29.

6. It is not always easy to accept the characterization of the Valois kings, and especially Francis I, as "absolute monarchs": see Philippe Hamon, *L'Histoire,* no. 183, December 1994. The American historian Russell Major has given a much less absolutist picture of "Renaissance monarchy." See his *Representative Institutions in Renaissance France* (Madison: University of Wisconsin Press, 1960), a work of fundamental importance.

7. A member of Utenhove's family was a boarder in Erasmus's house in 1528–29 according to Alfred Hartmann, ed., *Die Amerbach-Korrespondenz* (Basel: Editions de la Bibliothèque Universitaire de Bâle, 1942), vol. 4, p. 418, note 1.

8. August Hirsch, *Biographisches Lexicon aller hervorragenden Ärzten aller Zeiten,* new edition (Munich-Berlin: Urban, 1962), vol. 4, art. "Rufus."

9. J. Karcher, *Felix Platter, Lebensbild des Basler Stadtarztes* (Basel: Helbing, 1949), p. 23; Hirsh, *Biographisches Lexicon,* vol. 2, art. "Duret."

10. Karcher, *Felix Platter,* p. 23. On Fernel, see also Jean Goulin, *Mémoires littéraires, critiques . . . pour servir à l'histoire ancienne et moderne de la médecine* (Paris: Bastien, 1777), pp. 286–408.

11. J. Maritain, *Trois réformateurs* (Paris: Plon, 1925), p. 44.

12. In the period 1531–35 alone, Wechel published 148 different works, mostly in Latin and Greek. For the titles of these works, see Brigitte Moreau, *Inventaire chronologique des éditions parisiennes du XVIe siècle,* based on the manuscripts of Philippe Renouard, vol. 4, 1531–1535 (Abbeville: Imprimerie Paillar, 1992).

13. *Amerbach-Korrespondenz,* vol. 6, p. 312.

14. Christiane Riboulleau, *Villers-Cotterêts, un château royal en forêt de Retz* (Amiens: Association pour la généralisation de l'Inventaire général en Picardie, 1991).

15. Ferdinand Lot, *Recherches sur les effectifs des armées françaises, 1494–1562* (Paris: SEVPEN, 1982), chap. 10.

16. Ivan Cloulas, *Henri II* (Paris: Fayard, 1985), p. 460.

17. Jean-Marie Pérouse de Montclos, *Le Guide du Patrimoine* (Paris: Hachette, 1987), p. 291.

18. Babelon, *Nouvelle histoire,* p. 192.

19. T2 599; see also Babelon, *Nouvelle histoire,* pp. 223–24 and passim, for all that follows.

20. Babelon, *Nouvelle histoire,* pp. 226–282.

21. Ibid., pp. 148–49.

22. On bookbinding in France under Henri II, "the greatest French bibliophile of his time," see L.-M. Michon, *La Reliure française* (Paris: Larousse, 1951), chap. 5.

23. Babelon, *Nouvelle histoire,* p. 232.

24. Ibid., pp. 390–442.

25. *La Ligue* was the confederation of French Catholics that played an essential role in the Wars of Religion after 1576.—Trans.

26. Michel Félibien, *Histoire de l'abbaye royale de Saint-Denis en France* (Paris, 1973), pp. 105 ff.

27. J. B. M. Jaillot, *Recherches critiques sur la ville de Paris* (Paris: Lottin, 1774), XVIe quartier, place Maubert, p. 6. Lötscher (in F 281, note 141) confuses the rue d'Arras with the rue d'Assas.

28. *Amerbach-Korrespondenz,* vol. 6, p. 422; and Emile Châtelain, *Les Etudiants suisses de Paris, aux Xve et XVIe siècles* (Paris: Emile Bouillon, 1891), p. xlviii.

29. Félibien, *Histoire de l'abbaye royale de Saint-Denis en France,* for the year 1556.

30. R. Giesey, "Cérémonial et puissance souveraine," *Cahiers des Annales* (Paris: Armand Colin, 1987), p. 26, and idem, *Le roi ne meurt jamais* (Paris: Flammarion, 1987), pp. 102–10.

31. D. Gaborit and M.-P. Laffitte, *Le Trésor de Saint-Denis* (Dijon: Faton, 1992), p. 99.

32. Ibid., pp. 20, 74.

33. Alain Erlande-Brandenburg, *L'Eglise abbatiale de Saint-Denis* (Paris, 1976).

34. The Convention ordered the violation of the royal tombs in the summer of 1793, but its decision was scarcely legal, for although it was in theory a body chosen in free elections to represent the Nation, it had in fact been purged several months earlier by a very Parisian, anti-Girondin "putsch" on May 31, 1793. On the event itself in Saint-Denis, see Alain Boureau, *Le Simple Corps du roi* (Paris: Editions de Paris, 1988), *in fine.*

35. And not a horn, as Felix's editor erroneously transcribes [F 282].

36. Monin, *Histoire de la ville de Saint-Denis* (Saint-Denis, 1928; reprinted Marseilles: Laffitte, 1977), p. 239.

37. Gaborit and Laffitte, *Le Trésor de Saint-Denis,* p. 204; see also Monin, *Histoire,* p. 237.

38. Ibid., pp. 272 ff.

39. Ibid., p. 198.

40. Ibid., p. 80.

41. Sylvie Chaber d'Hières, *Que lire sur l'histoire de la Seine-Saint-Denis* (Seine-Saint-Denis: Archives Départementales, 1986); Roger Bourderon and Pierre de Perreti, *Histoire de Saint-Denis* (Toulouse: Privat, 1988); Alain Erlande-Brandeburg and Georges Chassé, *L'Eglise abbatiale de Saint-Denis* (Paris: Librairie de la Nouvelle Faculté, 1976), especially "Historique et visite. Les tombeaux royaux"; Michel Félibien, *Histoire de l'abbaye royale de Saint-Denis en France* (Paris: Editions du Palais-Royal, 1973); Henry Monin, *Histoire de la ville de Saint-Denis et de la basilique* (Marseilles: Lafitte, 1977); Ralph E. Giesey, *Le roi ne meurt jamais* (Paris: Flammarion, 1987), pp. 102–10, and idem, *Cérémonial et puissance souveraine* (Paris: Armand Colin, 1987); Fernand Bournon, *Histoire de la ville et du canton de Saint-Denis* (Paris, 1892); and the fundamental work of D. Gaborit and M.-T. Laffitte, *Le Trésor de Saint-Denis* (Dijon, Faton, 1992), as well as B. de Montesquiou-Fezensac and D. Gaborit, *Trésor de Saint-Denis* (Paris: Picard, 1973).

42. Louis-Sébastien Mercier, *Tableau de Paris* (Paris: Mercure de France, 1994), vol. 1, chap. 178, pp. 429, 1618.

43. Chalres II, who is usually (and mistakenly) referred to as Charles III, duc de Lorraine (1543–1608), had been duke of Lorraine since 1545. On him and his family, see Saint-Simon, *Mémoires,* ed. Boislisle (Paris: Hachette, 1901), vol. 15, pp. 24–25 and notes.

44. Babelon, *Nouvelle histoire,* p. 40.

45. The area traditionally known as "Berry" corresponds to what is today included in the *départements* of Indre and Cher.

46. On all of this, see G. Devailly, *Histoire du Berry* (Toulouse: Privat, 1987), p. 168.

47. Emile Meslé, *Histoire de Bourges* (Roanne: Horvath, 1988), p. 6. Can the difference between the two figures be explained by efforts between 1567 and 1599 to bolster the city's security in the face of the interminable Wars of Religion?

48. This is taken from Father Jean Glaumeau, *Journal* (Bourges and Paris: Editions Hiver, 1867), p. 86.

49. Ibid., p. 7.

50. Meslé, *Histoire de Bourges,* p. 113.

51 Ibid., p. 65.

52. Buhot de Kersers, *Statistique départementale du Cher* (Bourges: Tripault, 1883, vol. 2, p. 94; reprinted Marseilles: Laffitte, 1977).

53. We encountered his vagueness about Joan of Arc earlier, at the time of his visit to Orléans.

54. Bernard Quilliet, *Louis XII «père du peuple»* (Paris: Fayard, 1986), p. 258.

55. Glaumeau, *Journal,* notes for 1555–58.

56. On Bourges, see Meslé, *Histoire de Bourges;* Jean Chaumeau, seigneur de

Lassay, *Histoire du Berry* (Lyons: Gryphe, 1566; reprinted 1985 by the Cercle d'histoire d'Argenton); A. Buhot de Kersers, *Histoire et statistique monumentale du département du Cher,* vol. 2 (canton of Bourges) (Bourges, 1883); Pierre Pradel, *La Cathédrale de Bourges* (Paris: Tel, 1939); *Journal de Jehan Glaumeau de Bourges, 1541–1562* (Bourges: Just-Bernard, 1867); Guy Devailly, ed., *Histoire du Berry* (Toulouse: Privat, 1987).

57. Gérald Jack Gilbank, *Les Vignobles de qualité du sud-est du bassin de Paris* (Paris: by the author, 1981), p. 380.

58. On Sancerre, see Gérald Nakam, *Au lendemain de la Saint-Barthélemy: l'Histoire mémorable du siège de Sancerre (1573) de Jean de Léry* (Paris: Anthropos, 1972), p. 100 and passim; Abbé Camille-Marie Charpentier, *Le Beffroi de Sancerre dans l'Histoire des beffrois* (Sancerre: Société de Presse Berrichonne, 1956); idem, *Sancerrre et Saint-Satur dans l'histoire de France* (Sancerre: Société Coopérative Ouvrière d'Imprimerie, 1951); *Histoire de la ville de Sancerre* (BN, anonymous) (Cosne: Gourdet, 1826); Vincent Poupard, *Histoire de Sancerre* (Bourges: J. Bernard, 1858; reprinted Marseilles: Laffitte, 1975); A. Buhot de Kersers, *Statistique monumentale du département du cher,* vol. 7 (Bourges, 1895); Gilbank, *Les Vignobles de qualité.*

59. Alfred Faivre, *Cosne à travers les âges. Essai historique et archéologique* (Horvath: Le Coteau, 1986), a reprint of the 1895 edition with important maps and engravings; the same work has also been published under a different title: *Histoire de Cosne* (Paris: Res Universis, 1990).

60. Guilbert, *Histoire des villes de France,* vol. 4, p. 252.

61. G. Gauthier, "La peste à Clamecy au XVIe siècle," *L'Echo de Clamecy,* April 30, 1905.

62. Guibert, *Histoire des villes,* vol. 4, p. 268; Paul Cornu, *Les Forêts du Nivernais* (Nevers: Editions de la Société Académique du Nivernais, 1981), pp. 99ff. For our purposes there is little of interest in Charles P. Milandre, *Vieilleries clamecycoises* (Clamecy: Editions de la Société Scientifique et Artistique de Clamecy, 1938).

63. M. Gally, *Voyage dans l'Avallonnais. Vézelay monastique* (Tonnerre: Bailly, 1887), pp. 87–110; and the review *Zodiaque,* nos. 12–13, 1953, especially the appendix with map; Claude Jean-Nesmy, *Le Pèlerinage et la Cité. Inventaire de Vézelay* (Zodiaque, 1970), esp. pp. 8–16; Nicolas-Léonard Martin, *Précis historique sur la ville et l'ancienne abbaye de Vézelay* (Auxerre: Gallot-Fournier, 1832), pp. 192–213; Joseph Calmette, *Les Grandes Heures de Vézelay* (Paris: Sfelt, 1951), pp. 184–87; Pierre Meunier, *Iconographie de l'église de Vézelay* (Avallon: Odobé, 1862) (a very detailed work). On the verdigris of Montpellier, see F 178.

64. Gaston Roupnel, *La Ville et la campagne au XVIIe siècle. Etude sur les populations du pays dijonnais* (Paris: Armand Colin, 1955), pp. 354ff.

65. On Dijon and the Carthusian monastery of Champmol, see BN-Estampes, *Topographie de la France* (Côte-d'Or, Dijon, la chartreuse de Champmol), H. 117.442 to H.117.577; Pierre Gras, ed., *Histoire de Dijon* (Toulouse: Privat, 1987); Jean Richard, *Histoire de la Bourgogne* (Toulouse: Privat, 1978), reprinted 1988; Cyprien Monget, *La Chartreuse de Dijon* (Montreuil-sur-Mer: Imprimerie Notre-Dame-des-Prés, 1898); Kathleen Morand, *Claus Sluter, Artist at the Court of Burgundy,* with photographs by D. Finn (London: Harvey Miller, 1991); Pierre Quarré, *La Chartreuse de Champmol, foyer d'art au temps des ducs Valois* (Musée de Dijon, Palais des Ducs de Bourgogne, 1960); idem., *La Chartreuse de Champmol,*

*centre d'art européen* (Dijon: Publication du Centre Européen d'Etudes Bur-
gondes), no. 3, 1961 (Rencontres d'Utrecht, 4 and 5 November 1960); Laurence
Blondaux, "Le puits des prophètes de la chartreuse de Champmol: conservation
et restaurations depuis le Moyen Age," *Gothiques,* no. 27, 1991, pp. 17–29; Chris-
tian de Mérindol, "Nouvelles observations sur la symbolique royale à la fin du
Moyen Age. La chartreuse de Champmol," *Bulletin de la Société nationale des an-
tiquaires de France,* 1988, pp. 288ff.; Georges Lengherand, *Voyages de Georges
Lengherand, 1485–1486,* with an introduction by the marquis de Godefroy-
Menilglaise (Mons: Imprimer de Masquillier et Dequesne, 1861) (Société des
Bibliographes de Mons); also cited by J. Chipps Smith in "The Chartreuse de
Champmol in 1486: The Earliest Visitor's Account," *Gazette des Beaux-Arts,* vol.
106, July-August 1985.

66. J. Theurot, p. 71.

67. Jacky Theurot, Daniel Bienmiller, et al., *Histoire de Dole* (Roanne: Horvath, 1982); Jacky Theurot, *Dole, évolution d'un espace urbain: du Moyen Age à nos
jours,* 1981; Annie Gay and Jacky Theurot, *Dole pas à pas* (Roanne: Horvath, 1985);
idem, *Essor et apogée d'une capitale provinciale, 1274–1674* idem, *Dole au comté de
Bourgogne;* Jules Gauthier, *Les Fortifications de Dole* (Caen, 1894), excerpt from a
paper read to the Fifty Eighth French Archeological Congress at Besançon in
1891; Elie Puffeney, *Histoire de Dole* (Besançon, 1882; reprinted Marseilles:
Laffitte, 1975).

68. Claude Fohlen, *Histoire de Besançon, des origines à la fin du XVIe siècle* (Paris:
Nouvelle Librairie de France, 1964), reprinted 1981; José Gentil Da Silva, *Banque
et crédit en Italie au XVIIe siècle* (Paris: Klincksieck, 1969).

69. Rev. John Viénot, who rightly championed tolerance toward his coreligionists, does not appear to have expressed much outrage in his great works (see
below) on Protestantism in the Montbéliard region about this intolerant decree
of the Lutheran authorities against local Catholics.

70. After Servetus, Socinius became one of the leading opponents of the
dogma of the Trinity in the second half of the sixteenth century.

71. On Montbéliard and Franche-Comté in general, see Johen Viénot, *Histoire
de la Réforme dans le pays de Montbéliard, depuis les origines jusqu'à la mort de P.
Toussain, 1524–1573* (Montbéliard: Imprimerie Montéliardaise, 1900), and idem,
*Histoire du pays de Montbéliard à l'usage de la jeunesse et des familles* (Audincourt:
Villard, 1904); Charles Duvernoy, *Ephémérides de l'ancien comté de Montbéliard*
(Besançon: Deis, 1832), reprinted by Blaise Mériot, 2 vols. (Montbéliard: Société
d'Emulation de Montbéliard, 1953–1959); R.-E. Tuefferd, "Histoire des comtes
souverains de Montbéliard," *Mémoires de la Socété d'émulation de Montbéliard,*
1877, pp. 380ff.; Michel Billerey, "La principauté de Montbéliard et l'évêché de
Bâle, introduction à leur histoire comparée," *Mémoires de la Société pour l'histoire
du droit,* 21st fascicule (Dijon, 1960), pp. 103–9; *Le Pays de Montbéliard et l'ancien
évêché de Bâle dans l'histoire* (Société d'émulation de Montbéliard and the Société
jurassienne d'émulation, 1984); Guy J. Michel, *La Franche-Comté sous les Habs-
bourg, 1413–1678* (Wettolsheim-Colmar: Editions Mars et Mercure, 1978); Roland
Fiétier, ed., *Histoire de la Franche-Comté* (Toulouse: Privat, 1977); Jean-Etienne
Caire and Christian Deloche, *Histoire des Franc-Comtois* (Paris: Nathan, 1981);
Lucien Febvre, *Histoire de Franche-Comté* (Paris, 1922; reprinted Marseilles:
Laffitte, 1983); Lucien Febvre, *Philippe II et la Franche-Comté* (Paris: Champion,

1912), reprinted, unfortunately without notes (Paris: Flammarion, 1970 and 1984); Jean-Marc Debard, *Le Pays de Montbéliard, du Wurtemberg à la France, 1793. Bicentenaire du rattachement de la principauté de Montbéliard à la France* (Montbéliard: Société d'émulation de Montbéliard, 1992).

72. Carl Roth, *Basler Jahrbuch,* 1936, pp. 1–30.

## CHAPTER NINE

1. See Alain Boureau, *Le Simple Corps du roi* (Paris: Editions de Paris, 1988), on revolutionary exhumations at the end of the eighteenth century.

2. Such a mishap did indeed happen to Felix's "adopted" daughter Gredlin at the beginning of the seventeenth century. We can understand why he would have been struck by Dorothea's remark, made in 1557, when he began working on the fair copy of his *Tagebuch* in 1609 and especially after 1612 (when Louis XIII was king of France).

3. In Baden-Wurtemberg today. Upward social mobility in sixteenth-century Basel seems to have been considerable, owing largely to repeated plague epidemics and to the effects of the Protestant Reformation. From tavern or inn to the professions was often but one step, or, more precisely, one generation.

4. Furetière, *Dictionnaire universel,* 1690, art. "thèse," reprinted in facsimile edition (Paris: Robert, 1978).

5. On Jean Fernel, see L. Figard, *Un médecin philosophe au XVIe siècle* (Paris: Alcan, 1903); Dr. Alexandre Herpin, *Jean Fernel, médecin et philosophe* (Paris: Vrin, 1949); Jacques Roger, *Jean Fernel et les problèmes de la médecine de la Renaissance* (Paris: Editions du Palais de la Découverte, 1960); and above all Jean Goulin, *Mémoires pour servir à l'histoire de la médecine* (Paris: Bastien, 1777), a remarkable monograph on Fernel.

6. F 363ff. and *Amerbach-Korrespondenz,* vol. 7, pp. 273–79.

7. *Conciliator, Petri Aponensis . . . liber* (Venice, 1521), fol. 83 and passim (on heat). Pietro d'Albano figures in the printed catalogue of the BNF, at letter P, under the name Petrus de Abanus. There were at least four editions of his *Conciliator* between 1472 and 1548. Felix Platter had certainly studied one of them. The reference given by Valentin Lötscher (F 308, n. 18) on this point is, for once, completely off the mark, because he uses the dictionary of medicine published by B. Mayrhofer, *Wörterbuch* (Jena, 1937), whose article on *conciliator* is inept and only adds to the stockpile of human ignorance. It is astonishing that Lötscher sought the advice of two of Basel's greatest physicians only to reproduce Mayrhofer's absurd article, whose publication in 1937, at the height of the Nazi period, cannot excuse its imbecility. Lötscher, usually so competent, would have done better to use Goulin, *Mémoires littéraires, critiques . . . pour servir à l'histoire . . . de la médecine* (Paris: Bastien, 1777), pp. 30ff. (translation by Goulin of an Italian note on Albano by G. M. Mazzuchelli).

8. Edgar Bonjour, *Die Universität Basel* (Basel: Helbing, 1960), p. 172.

9. Joachim Du Bellay, *Regrets,* sonnet 31, "Heureux qui comme Ulysse" (Paris: Gallimard, 1975).

10. See above, chap. 3, for the origin of this phobia.

11. The term "symbolic capital" was first proposed by Pierre Bourdieu.

12. The corresponding French (royal) order during the Ancien Régime would

have been: hors-d'oeuvres and soups, entrées, roast meat or game, entremets and desserts.

13. Gustave Flaubert, *Madame Bovary* (Paris: Gallimard/Pléiade, 1983), vol. 1, p. 350.

14. Abbé Adolphe Mosschenross, *Thann à travers son passé* (Rixheim: Sutter, 1947), pp. 7–8, n. 2; and Max Rieple, *Maierisches Elsass* (Bern: Hallweg, 1964), p. 25.

15. F 325 and *Amerbach-Korrespondenz,* vol. 8, p. 10, no. 2.

16. Still, the wedding expenses were considerable. Besides the usual reasons for ostentatious consumption, it was basically a matter of making marriage indissoluble on account of the considerable financial investment that its staging required. A couple would have to think twice before separating. Wedding celebrations also brought unmarried young people together and thus paved the way for future marriages. As for other major expenditures alluded to previously, such as the expenses that Felix incurred in obtaining his doctorate, the investment required obviously tended to exclude clever sons of the poorer classes. Felix no longer belonged to this category, since his father, though born poor, now enjoyed a certain wealth and a "decent" social status. Thus upward mobility from the artisan or peasant class to the status of physician theoretically took at least two generations.

## Chapter Ten

1. On this subject, see my *Paysans de Languedoc* (Paris: SEVPEN, 1966), vol. 1, p. 48.

2. Lötscher is inclined to place the Gredlin story in 1572. Since Felix does not give a precise date, there is room for disagreement on this point.

3. See H. M. Koelbing, "L'apport suisse à la renaissance de l'ophthalmologie," *Médecine et hygiène* (Geneva), vol. 22, no. 637, 1964, p. 5.

4. The period from December 1572 to December 1573 was a time of serious famine in Franche-Comté: see Lucien Febvre, *Philippe II et la Franche-Comté* (Paris: Champion, 1911), p. 766. The fact that the baby's father was from Franche-Comté tends to confirm the chronology I proposed at the beginning of this chapter.

5. An exposition on childhood in the Middle Ages at the Bibliothèque Nationale in November 1994 under the direction of Pierre Riché cast a judicious eye on Ariès's celebrated thesis, which, though ingenious and correct in some respects, can also be highly misleading.

6. Was there, in this new dream, a remembrance of earlier childhood dreams? See chap. 2 above.

7. This is the actual dialogue as recorded in Felix Platter's text (F 452).

8. Edgar Bonjour, *Die Universität Basel* (Basel: Helbing, 1960), pp. 75 ff.

9. When Gredlin married in 1604 at the age of thirty, she freely recorded her name in the parish register as Margret *Simonin* (daughter of Benedict Simon) (F 453). Hence the painful revelation of her birth had to have occurred before this date. She had already survived the psychological shock.

## Chapter Eleven

1. Valentin Lötscher, "Felix Platter und seine Familie," *Basler Neujahrsblatt,* no. 153, 1975, p. 155.

2. "Felix Platter, Aesculapius of his city and of the entire world," was Thomas Jr.'s epitaph for Felix Platter, quoted in Lötscher, "Felix Platter und seine Familie," p. 176.

3. A few words on Biblicism and Hellenism in Basel generally and more particularly in the Platters: at the time of the Swiss cultural revolution in the third and fourth decades of the sixteenth century, Thomas Sr. knew Latin and Greek, but he was also a Hebrew scholar steeped in Joshua-style Old Testament iconoclasm and fanaticism. Later, however, Hebrew seems to have played a much smaller role in the Platters' cultural milieu, where it was supplanted by Greek, a language that many of Felix's friends taught and that he himself knew well. This change reflects a transition to Erasmian and, by definition, Hellenizing New-Testament style evangelism. It also reflects a shift to a more tolerant and scholarly humanism as exemplified by a "man of letters" like Castellion. At the same time, medical scholars also became humanists as they turned back to the classical medical works of Antiquity in the manner of the late-sixteenth-century and increasingly "Platterized" University of Basel.

4. See two articles with incredible titles, "Rural Idiocy" and "Peasant Idiocy," in Josef Wilczynsky, *An Encyclopedic Dictionary of Marxism* (Berlin-New York: De Gruyter, 1981), pp. 424 and 501. Marx's uncharitable remarks on rural life, the "barbaric countryside," and troglodyte peasants can be found primarily in *The German Ideology, Capital,* and *The Eighteenth Brumaire of Louis Napoleon.* Fernand Braudel, in private conversations on this subject, told me that these Marxian texts had greatly impressed him. See also Robert C. Tucker, *The Marx-Engels Reader* (New York: Norton, 1978), pp. 176, 608–9.

5. Glaumeau, *Journal,* p. 13 and passim.

6. When Felix died in 1614, Thomas Jr. referred to him as my "brother or, rather, father." See Lötscher, "Felix Platter und seine Familie," p. 176.

7. Ibid., p. 172.

# BIBLIOGRAPHY

*Manuscripts*
(from the catalogue of the University of Basel)

Platter, Thomas Sr. *Lebensbeschreibung*, 1572, A λ II 1a, 1b, 1c, 2a, 31a, 31a *bis*.

Platter, Felix. *Der Stadt Basel Beschreibung*, 1610, A λ III 3 Nr 6b.

———. *Brief an Heinrich Strübin*, Januar 1609, A A II 2a, Beilage hinten.

———. *Historie vom Gredli*, A λ III 3 Nr 9b.

———. *Kaiser Ferdinand kommt gen Basel*, 1562, A λ III 3 Nr 8.

———. *Gedichte*, A GV 30.

———. *Lebensbeschreibung und Biographisches*, A λ III 3 Nr 1–3.

. *Sieben regierende Pestilenzen*, 1539–1611, A λ III 5a.

———. *Rechnung über seine Einnahmen*, 1558–1612, A λ III 3 Nr 5.

———. *Reis Markgrafen Georg Friedrich zu Baden und Hochberg etc. nach Hochingen [ . . . ] auf die Hochzeit, so zwischen Graf Johann Georg von Zollern mit Fraülein Franziska Wild- und Rheingräfin gehalten worden*, 1598, A λ III 3 Nr 7c.

———. *Reis Markgrafen Georg Friedrichen zu Baden und Hochburg gon Stuttgarten [ . . . ] zu der Kindstaufen des Herzogen v. Würtemburg Suns Augustigennunt [ . . .]*, 1596, A λ III Nr 7b.

———. *Reis gen Simringen auf Graf Christoph von Zollern Hochzeit*, 1577, A λ III 3 Nr 7a

———. *Verzeichnis der Personen, so in dem Königreich auf der Kindtaufen gewesen*, 1600, A λ III 3 Nr 7cc.

———. *Autographischer Eintrag*, 1609, A λ II 2a, Beilage vorn.

———. *Ex libris* (von Hans Heinrich Glaser), 1618, A λ II 31a, B1. IVr.

———. *Beschreibung von Basel, aus den Pestschriften*, V. B. mscr P 15 no 14.

———. *Selbstbiographie*, V. B. mscr P 42 e Nr 1

Platter, Thomas Jr. *Beschreibung der Reisen durch Frankreich, Spanien, England und die Niederlande, 1595–1600*, A λ V 7.8.

———. *Brief an Heinrich Strübin*, 1609, A λ II 2a, Beilage hinten.

———. *Hauptbuch, mit Testamenten und Inventaren*, 1615, A λ V 9.

———. *Inventarium und Register über [ . . . ] liegende and fahrende Hab und Güter*, 1622, A 6 V9, 491.

———. *Autographischer Eintrag*, 1609, A λ II 2a, Beilage vorn.

———. *Schreiber*, A λ III 3, *passim*.


## ON THE PLATTER FAMILY

*Epitaphia Basiliensia Platterorum*, A λ II 1b Anhang.

*Epitaphia Basiliensia Platterorum*, A λ II 1c Anhang.

*Genealogia Platteriana*, A λ II 1a Beilage.

*Genealogia Platteriana*, A λ II 31a Beilage VII.

The Library of the University of Basel has preserved approximately five hundred letters of Thomas Platter Sr., Felix Platter, and Thomas Platter Jr., the vast majority of which are written in Latin and for the most part unpublished.

*Platteriana*
Bibliography of printed texts, in chronological order

THOMAS PLATTER SR.

*Historiae vitae Thomae Platteri.* Zurich, 1724.

*Lebensbeschreibung,* ed. M. Lutz. Basel, 1790.

*Thomas Platters Leben,* ed. E. G. Baldinger. Marburg, 1793.

*Lebensbeschreibung,* ed. J. F. Franz, in *Leben berühmter Gelehrter.* Saint- Gall, 1812.

*Thomas Platter and Felix Platter, zwei Autobiographien, ein Beitrag zur Sittengeschichte des XVI Jahrhunderts,* ed. D. A. Fechter. Basel, Seul und Mast, 1840.

*The Autobiography of Thomas Platter, a Schoolmaster of the Sixteenth Century,* trans. E. A. MacCaul, 3rd ed. London, 1847.

"Ein fahrender Schüler," in *Bilder aus der deutschen Vergangenheit,* ed. G. Freytag. Leipzig, 1852.

*La Vie de Thomas Platter, écrite par lui-même,* trans. E. Fick. Geneva, Impr. J. G. Frick, 1862.

*Zur Sittengeschichte des 16 Jahrhunderts,* ed. H. Boos. Leipzig, 1878.

*Thomas Platters Selbstbiographie.* Gütersloh, 1882.

*Thomas Platters Leben,* ed. H. Düntzer. Stuttgart, Spemann, 1882.

*Thomas Platters Briefe an seinen Sohn Felix,* ed. A. Burckhardt. Basel, Detloff, 1890.

*Thomas Platters Lebensgeschichte.* Zurich, 1891.

*Vie de Thomas Platter (1499–1582). Suivie d'extraits des Mémoires de Felix Platter (1536–1614),* trans. E. Fick. Lausanne, Bridel, 1895.

*Avtobiografija Fomi Plattera,* trans. N. V. Speranskij. Ocerki po narodnoj skoly, Moscow, 1896.

*Thomas Platters Selbstbiographie,* Frankfurt, 1910.

*Lebensbeschreibung.* Munich, 1911.

*Thomas Platter. Geisshirt, Seiler, Professor, Buchdrucker. Rektor.* Leipzig, 1912.

*Lebensbeschreibung.* ed. A. Hartmann, preface by W. Muschig. Basel, Schwabe, 1944 (fundamental).

*Lebenserinnerungen.* Zurich, 1955.

*Autobiographie,* ed. and trans. Marie Helmer, *Cahier des Annales,* no. 22. Paris, A. Colin, 1964.

*Lebenserinnerungen.* Basel, 1969.

*Ma vie,* trans. E. Fick. Lausanne, L'Age d'Homme, 1982

*Autobiographia,* F Cichi e L. de Venuto, eds. Rome and Salerno, E. Campi, 1988.

*La mia vita (1505–1585),* ed. G. O. Bravi. Bergamo, P. Lubrina, 1988.

There are many editions of the writings of the three Platters in modern German for a broad audience and sometimes fictionalized. See the bibliography given by Valentin Lötscher in his edition of Felix Platter's Beschreibung der Stadt Basel (see below). There is also a Japanese edition, translated by K. Abe (Tokyo, 1984). The works of the Platters are therefore known to an extensive readership in Germany, Switzerland, and indeed throughout Europe. The more recent editions are available to interested readers in libraries and bookstores.

### FELIX PLATTER (SEE ALSO THOMAS PLATTER SR.)

*De corporis humani structura et usu.* Basileae, 1583; reprinted in 1603 (with illustrations by Vesalius).

*De mulierum partibus generationi dicatis.* Basileae. 1586 ; reprinted Argentinae, 1597.

*De feribus liber.* Francofurti, 1595.

*Praxeos seu de cognescendis. praedicendis.* Basileae, Waldkirch, 1603 ; reprinted twice in 1609.

*Observationes in hominis affectibus plerisque corpori et animo functionum laesione, dolore aliave molestia et vitio incommodantibus,* libri tres. Basileae, 1614; reprinted in 1641 et 1688.

*Praxis medica.* Basileae, 1602–1608; reprinted in 1625, 1656, 1666, 1680 and 1736.

*Quaestionum medicarum paradoxarum et eudoxarum centuria,* posthuma. Basileae, 1625.

*Thomas Platter und Felix Platter. Zwei Autabiographien,* ed. D. A Fechter. Basel, 1840.

"Eines jungen Gelehrten Hochzeit und Haushalt," in *Bilder aus der deutschen Vergangenheit,* ed. G. Freytag. Leipzig, 1852.

*Mémoires de Felix Platter,* trans. E. Fick, Geneva, J. G. Fick, 1866; 2nd edition, Lausanne, 1895.

*Felix und Thomas Platter, ein Beitrag zur Sittengeschichte des 16. Jahrhunderts.* Leipzig, 1878.

*Aus Felix Platters Bericht über die Pest zu Basel in den Jahren 1609 1611.* Basel, 1880.

*Briefe.* Basel, 1880.

*Felix Platters Erinnerungsblätter.* Gütersloh. 1882.

*Felix Platters Reisen an die Höfe der Grafen van Hohenzollern-Sigmaringen und Hechingen, 1575 und 1598.* Basel, 1890.

"Die Historie vom Gredlin," ed. H. A. Gessler. *Basler Jahrbuch,* 1893.

*Felix et Thomas Platter à Montpellier (1552–1557 et 1595–1599),* travel notes of two students from Basel based on original manuscripts belonging to the Library of the University of Basel, trans. M. Kieffer. Montpellier, Coulet, 1892 ; reprinted Marseilles, Laffitte, 1979.

"Extraits, relatifs à la Provence, des Mémoires de Felix et Thomas Platter," in Ludovic Legré, *La Botanique en Provence au XVIe siècle.* Marseilles, 1900.

*Aufzeichnungen.* Munich, 1911.

*Tagebuchblätter aus dem Jugendleben eines deutschen Arztes.* Leipzig, 1913.

*Felix Platters Ungdoms-Erindringer,* trans. T. Gertz. Copenhagen, 1915.

*Felix Platters Reisen an die Höfe der Grafen von Hohenzollern-Sigmaringen und Hechingen, 1575 und 1598.* Hechingen, 1927.

*Thomas und Felix Platter.* Zurich, 1935.

*Tagebuchblätter.* Zurich, 1955.

*Beloved Son Felix. The Journal of Felix Platter, a Medical Student in Montpellier in the 16th Century,* trans. S. Jennett. London, 1961.

"Little-known English versions of the *Praxis and Observationes* of Felix Platter (1662 and 1664) ," *Journal of the History of Medicine,* no. 17, 1962.

*Observationes I,* trans. G. Goldschmidt, ed. H. Buess. Bern, Huber, 1963. (*Obser-*

*vationes II* and *III* were not published, but the manuscript of the translation is preserved at Basel's Library for the History of Medicine.)

*Funktionnelle Störungen des Sinnes und der Bewegung.* Bern, 1963.

*Tagebuchblätter.* Basel, 1969.

*Tagebuch,* ed. V Lötscher. Basel, Schwabe. 1976 (the text and footnotes are of fundamental importance).

*Lebenserinnerungen und Tagebuchblätter,* ed. Rosa Schudel-Benz. Basel, GS-Verlag, 1977.

*Beschreibung der Stadt Basel 1610 und Pestbericht 1610/1611,* ed. V. Lötscher. Basel, Schwabe, 1987.


THOMAS PLATTER JR. (SEE ALSO FELIX PLATTER)

*Huit jours à Genève en 1595,* trans. C. Le Fort, *Mémoires et documents de la Société d'histoire de Genève,* no. 20, 1934.

*Un étudiant bâlois à Orléans en 1599,* trans. P. de Félice. Orléans, H. Herluison, 1879.

*Visite de Thomas Platter à Nîmes et au pont du Gard (février 1596),* trans. A. Alioth. Nîmes, Peyrot-Tinel, 1880.

*Voyage à Rouen (1599),* trans. M. Keittinger. Montpellier, Impr. J. Martel aîné, 1890.

*Thomas Platter et les Juifs d'Avignon,* trans. S. Kahn. Paris, Société des études juives, 1892.

*Description de Paris (1599),* trans. L. Sieber and M. Weibel, *Mémoires de la Société de l'histoire de Paris et de l'Ile-de-France,* vol. 23. Paris, 1896.

*Une description de Bruges.* trans. M. Letts. Bruges, 1924.

*Thomas Platter des Jüngeren Englandfahrt in Jahre 1599,* ed. U. Hecht, Halle, 1929.

*Visite à Bourges de deux étudtants bâlois,* trans. R. Gandilhon. Bourges, 1934.

*Travels in England, 1599,* trans. C. Williams. London, 1937.

*Journal of a Younger Brother, The Life of Thomas Platter, a Medical Student in Montpellier,* trans. S. Jennet. London, 1963.

*Beschreibung der Reisen durch Frankreich, Spanien, England und den Niederlanden,* ed. Rut Keiser. Basel, Schwabe, 1968 (fundamental).

"Hausbuch oder Hauptbuch, enthaltend Testamente und Inventare der Familie, geschrieben 1615 von Thomas Platter," ed. V. Lötscher. *Basler Neujahrsblatt.* no. 153, 1975.


CONTEMPORARY TEXTS

Ramus, Petrus. *La Basilea ad senatum populumque basiliensem,* n.p., 1571.

Zwinger, Theodor. *Theatrum vitae humanae,* preface by Felix Platter. Basileae, Froben, 1565.

———. *Methodus apodemica in eorum gratiam qui cum fructu in quocumque tandem vitae genere peregrinari cupiunt.* Basileae, Hervag, 1577.

Wurstisen, Christian. *Baszler Chronicken.* Basel, Henric Petri, 1580 (reprinted in 1765, 1883).

Burckhardt, Jacob. *Oratio funebris de vita et obitti celeberrimi Felicis Plateri.* Basileae, 1614.

Gast, Johannes. *Tagebuch (1531–1552),* ed. P. Burckhardt, Basler Chroniken, vol. 8, Basel, l945.

Montaigne, Michel de. *Journal de voyage en Italie*. in *Oeuvres complètes*. Paris, Gallimard. 1980.

Amerbach, Bonifacius, *Amerbach-Korrespondenz*, ed. A Hartmann et B. R. Jenny. Basel, Verlag der Universitätsbibliothek, 1991. 10 vols.

### Secondary Works on the Platters
(in alphabetical order)

"Vom Anfang neuer Zeit. Drei Selbstbiographien aus dem Jahrhundert der Glaubenskämpfe. Thomas und Felix Platter und Théodore Agrippa d'Aubigné," in *Erlebnis und Bekenntnis*, ed. O. Fischer, vol. 1. Munich, 1911.

Bruckner, Albert. "Drei Briefe von Anna Platter-Dietschi an ihren Sohn Felix," Basler Nachrichten, no. 32, 7 August 1932.

Buess, Heinrich. "Gynäkologie und Geburtshilfe bei Felix Platter," in *Festschrift für A. Labhardt*. Basel, 1941.

———. "Schweizer Arzte als Forscher," *Entdecker und Erfinder*. Basel, 1945.

———. "Ein Basler Gedenktag," *National-Zeitung*, no. 405, 3 septembre 1964.

———. "Der Einfluss Vesals auf die praktische Anatomie am Beispiel Felix Platters," *Med. Monatsschrift*. no. 18, 1964.

Burckhardt, Albrecht. *Die medizinische Fakultät zu Basel*. Basel, 1917.

Buxtorf-Falkeisen, Karl. "Blicke in das Privatleben Dr. Felix Platters," *Basler Taschenbuch*, 1850, pp. 88–105.

———. *Baslerische Stadt- und Landgeschichten aus dam 16. Jahrhundert*. Basel, 1868.

Carlen, Louis. "Rechtsgeschichtliches aus Frankreich, Spanien, England und den Niederlanden in einem Reisebericht von 1595–1600," Brig, in *Schriften des Stockalperarchivs*, Heft 22, 1971.

Christoffel, Hans. "Psychiatrie und Psychologie bei Felix Platter," *Monatsschrift für Psychiatrie und Neurochirurgie*, no. 127, Basel, 1954.

———. "Eine systematische Psychiatrie des Barock, Felix Platters *Laesiones mentis*," *Schw. Archiv für Neurologie und Psychiatrie*, vol. 77, 1956.

Ernst, Felix. "Die beiden Platter," *Neue Schweizer Rundschau*, no. 20, Zurich, 1927.

Fehlmann, Hans-Rudolf. *Der Einfluss der Pharmazie in Montpellier auf den Basler Arzt Felix Platter*. Stuttgatt, 1975.

*Felix Platter (1536–1614) in seiner Zeit*. Proceedings of the Basel Colloquium, 8 November 1986, ed. H- Buess and U. Trohler. Basel, Schwabe, 1991.

Gorsse, Pierre de. *Toulouse au XVIe siècle vue par deux étudiants bâlois*. Toulouse. 1940.

Häfliger, Joseph. *Felix Platters sogenannte Hausapotheke*. Zurich, 1936.

Hunziger, Rose. *Felix Platter als Arzt und Stadtrat in Basel*. Zurich, 1938.

———. (Under the name Reiman). "Felix Platters Abhandlungen über die Zustände und Krankheiten des Geistes," *Schweizer Archiv für Neurologie und Psychiatrie*, no. 62, 1948.

Jenny, Ernst. "Goethe und Thomas Platter," *Basler Jahrbuch*, 1902.

Karcher, Felix. *Felix Platter, Professor, praxeos und Stadtarzt von Basel*. Basel, 1943.

———. *Felix Platter. Lebensbild des basler Stadtarztes*. Basel, 1949.

———. *Theodor Zwinger und seine Zeitgenossen*. Basel, 1956.

Koelbing, Huldrych M. "Felix Platter als Ophtalmologe," *Ophtalamolgica*, no. 133, 1957.

———. "Felix Platters Stellung in der Medizin seiner Zeit," *Gesnerus*, no. 22, Aarau, 1965.

———. *Renaissance der Augenheilkunde, 1540–1630*. Berne, Stuttgart, 1967.

———. "Diagnose und Aetiologie bei Felix Platter," in *Festschrift für H. Goerke*. Munich, 1978.

———. "Felix Platter als Augenarzt," *Gesnerus*, no. 47, 1990.

Kölner, Paul. "Das Gelehrtengeschlecht Platter ," *Basler Nachrichten*, no. 33, 19 August 1956.

Landolt, Elisabeth. "Materialien zu Felix Platter als Sammler und Kunstfreund," *Basler Zeitschrift*, no. 72, 1972.

Liebenau, Theodor von. "Felix Platter von Basel und Rennward Cysat von Luzern," *Basler Jahrbuch*, 1900.

Liechtenhan, Francine-Dominique. "Theodor Zwinger, théoricien du voyage," *Littérales*, no. 7, 1990

Lötscher, Valentin. "Felix Platter und seine Familie ," *Basler Neujahrsblatt*, no. 153, 1975.

———. *Gedächtnisausstellung zum 400. Todestag von Thomas Platter*. Gemeindehaus zu Grächen, 1982.

———. "Thomas Platter, Bürger zu Basel, zum 400. Todestag," *Basler Zeitung*, 30 January 1982.

Merlan, Peter. "Nachrichten über Felix Platters Naturaliensammlung," *Berichte der Verhandlungen der Naturforschenden Gesellschaft*, 1833–1840, vol. 4. Basel, 1840.

Merian, Wilhelm, "Felix Platter als Musiker," *Sammelbände der Internat. Musikgesellschaft*, XIII, Jg. 2. Leipzig, 1912.

Miescher, Friedrich. *Die medizinische Fakultät*. Basel, 1860.

Rytz, Walter. *Geschichte eines Herbars*. Bern, 1931.

———. "Das Herbarium Felix Platters," *Berichte der Verhandlungen der Naturforschenden Gesellschaft*, vol. 44. Basel, 1932.

Schnidrig, Aloys. *Die Platterfamilie rehabilitiert*. Pratteln, 1972.

———. "Rehabilitation der Platterfamilie," *Basellandschaftliche Zeitung*, 1966, no. 294.

Schiewek, Ingrid. "Zur Autobiographie des Stadtarztes Felix Platter," *Forschungen und Fortschritte*, no. 39, 1964.

Skerlak, Vladimir. *Felix Platter und seine Zeit. Eine Ausstellung zu seinem 450. Geburtstag, Diss. Med.* Basel, 1989.

Stähelin, Margrit. "Felix Platter, der Basler Stadtarzt," *Basler Jahrbuch*, 1909.

Steiner, Gustav. "Arzte and Wundärzte, Chirurgenzunft und medizinische Fakultlät in Basel," *Basler Jahrbuch*, 1954.

Stoll, Clemens "Zum Basler Apothekerwesen im 16. Jahrhundert, der Briefwechsel von Balthasar Hummel and Felix Platter zwischen 1555 und 1557," in *Zur Geschichte des schweizer Apothekerwesens*. Zurich, Juris-Verlag, 1988.

*Das Thomas Platter Haus*. Basel, 1966.

Vortisch, Christian Martin. "Felix Platter als Pestarzt," in *Das Marrkgräflerland*. Schopfheim, 1989.

*Voyager à la Renaissance*. Proceedings of the Tours Colloquium of 1983, H. Céard and J.-C. Margolin, eds. Maisonneuve et Larose, 1987.

Despite their many similarities, the memoirs of the three Platters (the best modern editions of which are the 1944 for Thomas Sr., the 1976 for Felix, and the
1968 for Thomas Jr.) represent three distinct intellectual generations (not the
same as biological generations). In describing a virtuous hero (himself) and his
struggles against adverse fortune, Thomas Sr. was working in the Renaissance
tradition of Petrarch's *Epistolae familiares*, a work that as a teacher and publisher
he knew fairly well and more or less at first hand. Thomas Jr., though the youngest of the three Platters, was the second to write his memoirs, at the turn of the
seventeenth century, and his writing reflects the ideal of the humanist travel
diary—scholarly, objective, and at times pedantic, à la Theodore Zwinger. Felix was the last of the three to write, shortly after either 1608 or 1611. Though
much older than Thomas Jr, Felix is also the most modern of the three, writing
in a tradition that was still new in 1610 but destined to become dominant: the
modern travel account. The modern travel writer is at once extroverted and, to
an even greater degree, introverted. The modern tradition was begun by Montaigne and continued, after Felix Platter, by Jean-Jacques Rousseau, Frédéric
Amiel, and many others. (See Francine-Dominique Liechtenhan, "Autobiographie et voyage entre la Renaissance et le Baroque: l'exemple de la famille
Platter," *Revue de Synthèse*, nos. 3 4, July-December 1993, pp 455–71.)

## OTHER SECONDARY WORKS

Most but not all of the works listed below concern the history of Montpellier in
the sixteenth century.

Archives municipales de Montpellier (Tour des Pins). BB 393. Manuscript record
of the deliberations of the city council in the 1550s.

Archives de la ville de Montpellier. *Inventaires et documents*, vol. 6: Inventaire de
Joffre, Archives du greffe de 1a maison consulaire, Armoires A et B (compoix),
ed. M. Oudot de Dainville. Montpellier, L'Abeille, 1934.

Archives de la ville de Montpellier. *Inventaires et documents*, vol. 7: Inventaire de
Joffre, Archives du greffe de la maison consulaire, Armoire C (sous-série BB),
municipal deliberations, ed. M. Oudot de Dainville. Montpellier, L'Abeille,
1939.

Archives communales de Nîmes, registre LL8 (manuscript), municipal deliberations for the 1550s (subsequent to 21 August 1552).

Barral, Marcel. *Les Noms de rues à Montpellier du Moyen Age à nos jours.* Montpellier, P. Clerc, Espace Sud, 1989.

Baumel, Jean. *Vie, moeurs et traditions populaires à Montpellier et dans ses environs
au cours de la deuxième moitié du XVe siècle, d'après les frères Platter.* Montpellier,
Dehan, 1974.

———. *Montpellier au cours des XVIe et XVIIe , siècles. Les guerres de religion (1510–
1685).* Montpellier, Causse, 1970.

*Beloved Son Felix. The Journal of Felix Platter,* trans. Seán Jennett. London, Muller,
1961. (Contains important maps of Montpellier and the Platters' world in the
sixteenth century.)

Benedict, Philip, ed. *Cities and Social Change in Early Modern France.* London,
Unwin Hyman, 1989. (Especially the chapters on Montpellier, Paris, Dijon,
Aix-en-Provence, and Toulouse in the sixteenth century.).

Benedict, Philip. *Rouen during the Wars of Religion*. Cambridge, Cambridge University Press, 1981. (For comparative purposes.).

Bosc, Henri. *Les Grandes Heures du protestantisme à Montpellier*. Montpellier, Reschly, 1957.

Braudel, Fernand, *La Méditerrannée et le monde méditerranéen au temps de Philippe II*. Paris, Armand Colin, 1966 (2 volumes).

Cholvy, Gerard. *Histoire de Montpellier*. Toulouse, Privat, 1984.

Darmon, Pierre. *Les Cellules folles*. Paris, Plon, 1993 (especially chap. 2.).

Darnton, Robert. "A Bourgeois Puts His World in Order: The City as Text," in *The Great Cat Massacre*. New York, Basic Books, 1984, pp. 107–44.

Delormeau, Charles. "Les circonscriptions ecclésiastiques protestantes du Languedoc méditerranéen aux XVIe et XVIIe siècles," in *Actes du XXXVIIe Congrès de la Fédération historique du Languedoc méditerranéen et du Roussillon*. Limoux, 1964, p. 63 ff.

[Delormeau, Charles]. Catalogue of exhibition "Coligny et la Réforme à Montpellier au XVIe siècle" at the Salle Pétrarque in Montpellier, 16–30 November 1974. Documents and information by Charles Delormeau. Montpellier, 1974.

———. "Les débuts de la Réforme à Montpellier," in *Hommage à Jacques Fabre de Morlhon. Mélanges historiques et généalogiques, Rouergue-Bas-Languedoc,* ed. Jean-Denis Bergasse. Albi, Ateliers professionnels de l'OSJ, 1978, pp. 239–48.

Dulieu, Louis. "Les locaux médicaux de l'enseignement à Montpellier à travers les âges," *Monspeliensis Hippocrates,* no. 4 (1959).

———. "Une famille médicale à la Renaissance: les Saporta," *Languedoc médical,* no. 2, 1963.

———. "Quelques aspects des relations médicales entre Bâle et Montpellier à l'époque de la Renaissance," in *XIXe Congrès international d'histoire de la médecine*. Basel, 1964.

———. "Les Étudiants en médecine de Montpellier à l'époque de la Renaissance," *Monspeliensis Hippocrates,* no. 38 (1967).

———. "La chirurgie à Montpellier au XVIe siècle," in *Medizingeschichte in unserer Zeit,* Festgabe für Edith Heischkel-Artelt und Walter Artelt zum 65. Geburtstag, ed. Hans-Heinz Lamer. Stuttgart, Ferdinand Enke Verlag, 1971, pp. 145–59.

———. *La Médecine à Montpellier,* vol. 2: *La Renaissance*. Avignon, Les Presses Universelles, 1979 (important).

———. *La Médecine à Montpellier du XIIe siècle au XXe siècle*. Paris, Hervas, 1990.

Fabre, Jean-Henri. *Souvenirs entomologiques*. Paris, Robert Laffont, 1989, II, pp. 890–91. (A remarkable work on the diet of peasants in Mediterranean France in times past.)

Freedman, Joseph S. "Aristotle and the Content of Philosophy Instruction at Central European Schools and Universities during the Reformation Era (1500–1650)," *Proceedings of the American Philosophical Society,* vol. 137, no. 2, June 1993, pp. 213–53. (Interesting on the use of taxonomic categories for the refinement of knowledge, a technique used by the Platters.)

Gariel, Pierre. *Idée de la ville de Montpellier*. Montpellier, P. Pech, 1665 (facsimile by Editions de la Tour Gile, Péronnas, 1993).

Germain, Alexandre C. "La Renaissance à Montpellier," *Publications de la Société archéologique de Montpellier,* ire série, section des lettres, vol. 6. Montpellier, Martel, 1870–71, pp. 9–64 (important).

————. "Les étudiants de l'école de médecine de Montpellier au XVIe siècle. Etude historique sur le *liber procuratoris studiosorum,*" *Revue historique,* 1877.

Grasset-Morel, Louis. Montpellier. ses sixains, ses îles . . ." Montpellier, L Valat, 1908 (facsimile by C. Lacour, Nîmes, 1989).

Grmek, Mirko D. *Les Maladies à l'aube de la civilisation occidentale.* Paris, Payot, 1944, pp. 199–225. (On venereal discases in the sixteenth century.)

Guiraud, Louise, *Histoire du culte at des miracles de Notre-Dame des Tables.* Montpellier, 1885. (All of Louise Guiraud's work is essential for understanding Montpellier in the Renaissance.)

————. *La Paroisse Saint-Denis de Montpellier.* Montpellier, Martel, 1887.

————. *Les Fondations d'Urbain V à Montpellier,* vol. 1: *Le collège des Douze Médecins ou collège de Mende.* Montpellier. J. Martel aîné, 1889; vol. 2: *Le collège Saint-Benoît, le collège Saint-Pierre, le collège du Pape.* Montpellier, J. Martel aîné, 1890; vol. 3: *Le monastère Saint-Benoît et ses diverses transformations depuis son érection en cathédrale en 1536.* Montpellier, J. Martel, 1891.

————. *Recherches topographiques sur Montpellier au Moyen Age.* Montpellier, Coulet, 1895.

————. *Le Procès de Guillaume Pellicier, évêque de Maguelone-Montpellier (1527-1567).* Paris, Picard fils, 1907.

————. *Etudes sur la Réforme à Montpellier.* Mémoires de la société archéologique de Montpellier, vols. 6 and 7. Montpellier, 1918 (fundamental).

————. "Un registre inconnu de l'université de droit de Montpellier (1536–1570)," *Bulletin philologique et historique (jusqu'à 1715),* year 1913, nos. 1 and 2. Paris, Imprimerie nationale, 1913.

————. "Plans successifs de la cathédrale Saint-Pierre de Montpellier," Société archéologique de Montpellier (after 1905).

Hauser, Henri. *La Modernité du XVIe siècle.* Paris, PUF, Alcan, 1930.

Hébert, Brigitte. "Le lansquenet dans les contes drolatiques Allemands au XVe siècle," in *L'Homme de guerre au XVIe siècle.* Publications de l'Université de Saint-Etienne, 1992, pp. 244–56.

Hyrvoix, Albert, "François Ier et la première guerre de religion en Suisse," *Revue des questions historiques,* 1902, pp. 465–537 (on the limited pro-Helvetic philo-Protestantism of the French monarchy, chiefly after 1530).

Imbert, Jean. *Le Droit hospitalier de l'Ancien Régime.* Paris, Presses Universitaires de France, 1993.

Irvine, Fred. "Social Structure, Social Mobility and Social Change In Sixteenth-Century Montpellier: From Renaissance City-State to Ancien-Régime Capital," Ph. D. thesis, University of Toronto (Department of History), 1979.

Jouanna, Arlette. "La première domination des Réformés à Montpellier (1561–1563)," in *Les Réformés, enracinement socio-culturel,* XXVe Colloque international des humanistes, Tours, 1–13 July 1982, Etudes réunies par Bernard Chevalier et Robert Sauzet. Paris, Editions de La Maisnie, 1985.

Koelbing, Huldrych. "Montpellier,vu par Felix Platter, étudiant en médecine (1552–1557)," in *110e Congrès national des sociétés savantes,* Montpellier, 1985.

Le Roy Ladurie, Emmanuel. "Sur Montpellier et sa campagne aux XVI et XVIIe siècles," *Annales ESC,* 1957, pp. 223–30. I also deal with the Platters in my *Paysans de Languedoc* (Paris: SEVPEN, 1966); in Philippe Wolff, ed., *L'Histoire du Languedoc* (Toulouse: Privat, 1988), chap. 8; and in my *Histoire du Languedoc* (Paris: Presses Universitaires de France, 1962), where I coined the phrase *le beau XVIe siècle* that has since been taken up by many other French historians.

Leboutte, René. "Offense against family order: infanticide . . . from the fifteenth through the early twentieth centuries," *Journal of the History of Sexuality,* 1991, vol. 2, no. 2.

Léry, Jean de. *Indiens de la Renaissance. Histoire d'un voyage fait en la terre du Brésil, 1557,* with an introduction by Anne-Marie Chartier. Paris, Ed. Epi, 1972. (Léry made his ocean voyage in the same year that Felix Platter traveled in France, 1557.)

Lichtenthaeler, Charles. *Histoire de la médecine.* Paris, Fayard, 1978.

*Mademoiselle* [sic] *Louise Guiraud* (Bio-bibliography of). Montpellier, Roumégous et Dehan, 1920 (important).

Mallary Masters, G. "L'humanisme montpelliérain au service des sciences naturelles: quelques préfaces Iittéraires de textes médicaux de la Renaissance," *Bulletin de l'Académie des sciences et lettres de Montpellier,* vol. 22, 1991, pp. 323–37.

Marques, Corinne. "Les Guidons da taille montpelliérains de 1549, 1565, 1576, 1581, 1591 et 1599. Démographie historique et géographie sociale (aspects statistiques)." Master's thesis directed by Mme Arlene Jouanna. Université PauI-Valéry de Montpellier, June 1990.

Michau, Françoise. "Montpellier, son consulat, ses consuls, 1550–1558." Master's thesis directed by Mme Arlene Jouanna. Université PauI-Valéry de Montpellier, June 1985.

Michon, Louis M. *La Reliure française.* Paris, Larousse, 1951 (especially the sections concerning the reign of Henri II).

Muchembled, Robert. "Les jeunes, les jeux et la violence . . . au XVIe siècle," in *Les Jeux à la Renaissance.* Paris, Vrin, 1982 (for comparative purposes).

Otis, Leah Lydia. *Prostitution in Medieval Society. The History of an Urban Institution in Languedoc.* Chicago, University of Chicago Press, 1985.

Pomian, Krzysztof. *Collectionneurs, amateurs et curieux. Paris, Venise: XVIe-XVIIIe siècle.* Paris, Gallimard, 1987 (important for understanding Felix Platter's outlook as a collector).

*Rabelais et son temps.* Exhibition at the Cour de Cassation, Paris, June–July 1994, Catalogue edited by Annick Tillier. Paris, Cour de cassation, 1994 (especially pp. 25ff. on medicine in Montpellier in the sixteenth century).

Revillout, Charles. "Les promoteurs de la Renaissance à Montpellier," *Mémoires de la Société archéologique de Montpellier,* 2e série, vol. 2, 1re fascicule. Montpellier, Martel, 1900, pp. 14–383 (fundamental).

Rey, Roseline. *Histoire de la douleur.* Paris, La Découverte, 1993, pp. 70ff. (on "Vesalian" anatomy).

Schneider, Robert A. *Public Life in Toulouse, 1463–1789: From Municipal Republic to Cosmopolitan City.* Ithaca, Cornell University Press, 1989 (important).

Serres. Pierre. *Abrégé de l'histoire du calvinisme dans la ville de Montpellier,* ed. Marcel Banal and Michel Péronnet. Montpellier, Editions de l'Entente bibliophile, Tour de la Babote, 1977.

Sournia, Bernard et al. *Montpellier, la demeure médiévale. Inventaire général des Monuments.* Paris, Imprimerie nationale, 1991.

Spooner, F. *Economie mondiale et frappes monétaires en France (1493–1680).* Paris, SEVPEN, 1956.

Teissier, M.-F. "Documents sur Montpellier au XVIe siècle d'après les [premiers] registres d'état civil huguenot," Société de l'histoire du protestantisme français, *Bulletin historique et littéraire*, 48e année, 8e année de la 4e série, no. 1, 15 January 1899.

Thomas, Louis J. *Montpellier, ville marchande*. Montpellier, Valat, Coulet, 1936.

Villa, Robert. "Montpellier à l'heure de l'«Union», 1574–1577." Master's thesis, directed by Mme Arlette Jouanna, Université Paul-Valéry de Montpellier, June 1983.

Wolfe, Martin. *The Fiscal System of Renaissance France*. New Haven, Yale University Press, 1972.

Further bibliographic information can be found in the notes, in particular concerning Felix Platter's travels in France. Finally, I wish to express my gratitude to the authors of the various unpublished master's theses cited above, as well as to Professor Arlette Jouanna, who directed their work; their scholarship was most valuable.

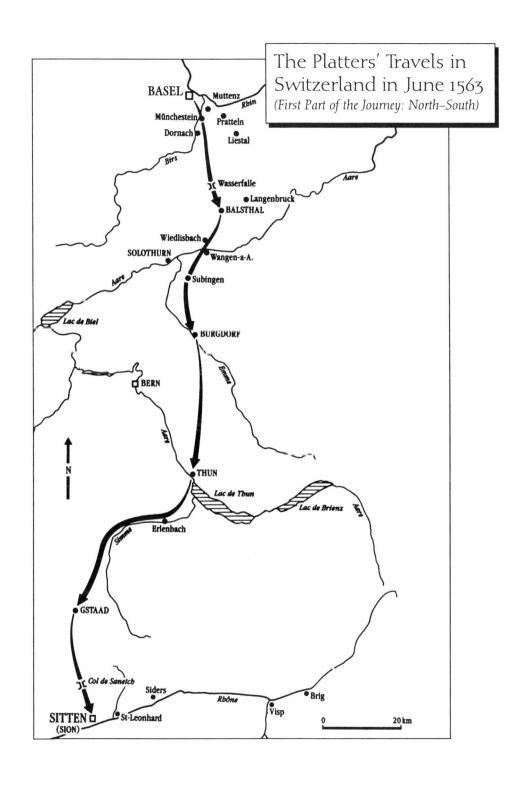

The Platters' Travels in
Switzerland in June 1563
(First Part of the Journey: North–South)

BASEL
Muttenz
Rhin
Münchestein
Pratteln
Dornach
Liestal
Birs
Aare
Wasserfalle
Langenbruck
BALSTHAL
Wiedlisbach
SOLOTHURN
Wangen-a-A.
Aare
Subingen
Lac de Biel
BURGDORF
Emme
BERN
Aare
N
THUN
Lac de Thun
Lac de Brienz
Aare
Erlenbach
Simme
GSTAAD
Col de Sanetch
Siders
Brig
Rhône
Visp
SITTEN
(SION)
St-Leonhard
0          20 km

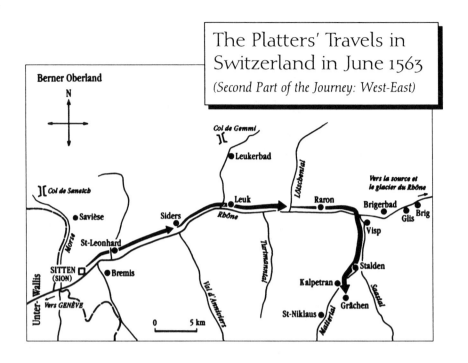

The Platters' Travels in
Switzerland in June 1563

(Second Part of the Journey: West-East)

Berner Oberland

N

Col de Gemmi

][

●Leukerbad

][ Col de Sanetch

Vers la source et
le glacier du Rhône

●Savièse

Siders

Leuk
●

Raron
●

Brigerbad
●

Rhône

Lötschental

Glis ● Brig

Visp

St-Leonhard

Stalden
●

SITTEN
(SION) □

●Bremis

Turtmanntal

Kalpetran ●

Unter-Wallis

Morge

Vers GENÈVE

Val d'Anniviers

Saastal

Grächen
●

St-Niklaus ●

Mattertal

0        5 km

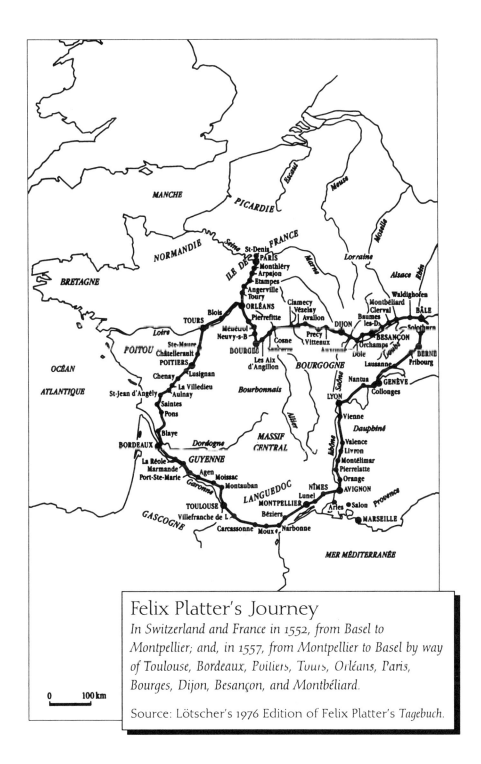

## Felix Platter's Journey

In *Switzerland and France in 1552, from Basel to Montpellier; and, in 1557, from Montpellier to Basel by way of Toulouse, Bordeaux, Poitiers, Tours, Orléans, Paris, Bourges, Dijon, Besançon, and Montbéliard*.

Source: Lötscher's 1976 Edition of Felix Platter's *Tagebuch*.

0    100 km

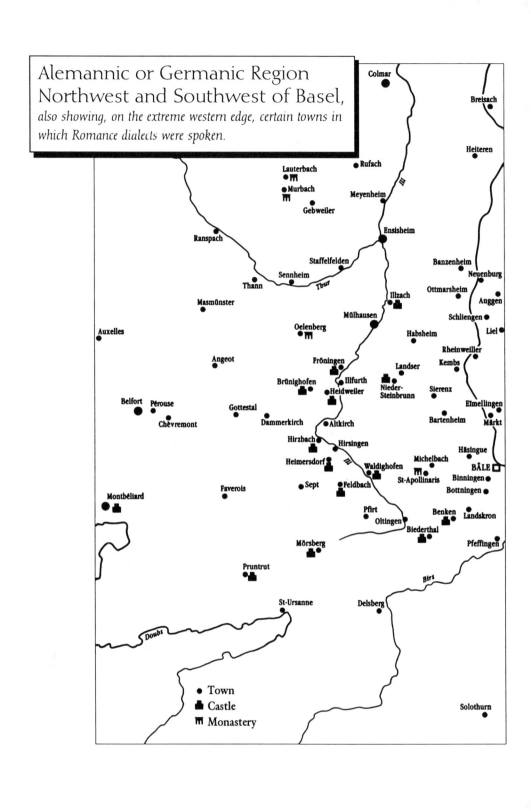

Alemannic or Germanic Region Northwest and Southwest of Basel,

*also showing, on the extreme western edge, certain towns in which Romance dialects were spoken.*

Colmar

Breisach

Heiteren

Rufach

Lauterbach
ᛗ
Murbach
ᛗ
Meyenheim
Gebweiler

Ensisheim

Banzenheim

Ranspach

Staffelfelden

Neuenburg
Sennheim
Ottmarsheim
Thann
Tbur
Auggen
Illzach
Masmünster
Schliengen
Mülhausen
Liel
Auxelles
Oelenberg
Habsheim
ᛗ
Rheinweiler
Fröningen
Kembs
Angeot
Landser
Brünighofen
Illfurth
Sierenz
Heidweiler
Nieder-
Steinbrunn
Elmellingen
Belfort
Pérouse
Gottestal
Bartenheim
Märkt
Chèvremont
Dammerkirch
Altkirch
Hirzbach
Häsingue
Hirsingen
Heimersdorf
Michelbach
BÂLE ☐
Waldighofen
ᛗ
Montbéliard
Faverois
Sept
St-Apollinaris
Binningen
Feldbach
Bottningen
Pfirt
Benken
Landskron
Oltingen
Biederthal
Pfeffingen
Mörsberg
Birs
Pruntrut
St-Ursanne
Delsberg
Doubs

● Town
🪨 Castle
ᛗ Monastery

Solothurn

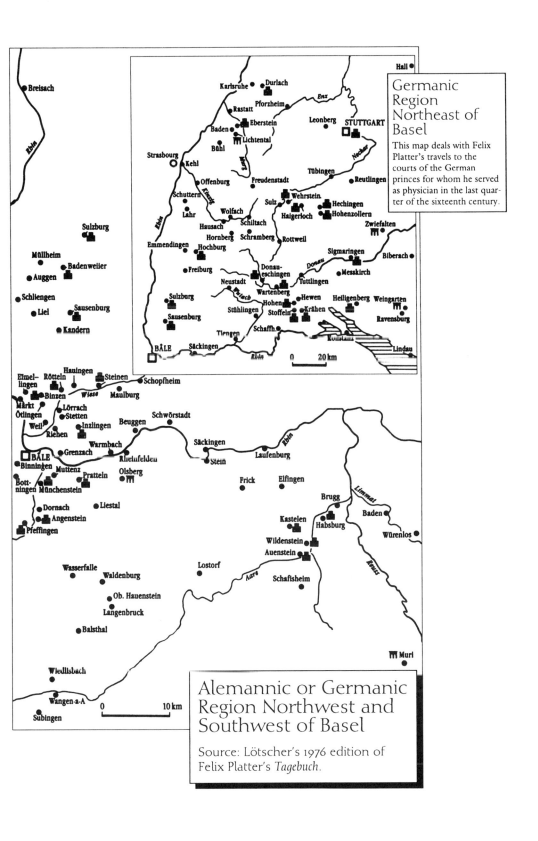

**Germanic Region Northeast of Basel**

This map deals with Felix Platter's travels to the courts of the German princes for whom he served as physician in the last quarter of the sixteenth century.

Breisach

Karlsruhe · Durlach
Rastatt
Pforzheim
Leonberg · STUTTGART
Eberstein
Baden
Lichtental
Bühl
Strasbourg
Kehl
Offenburg
Freudenstadt
Tübingen · Reutlingen
Schuttern
Sulz · Wehrstein
Lahr
Wolfach
Haigerloch · Hohenzollern
Hausach
Schiltach
Zwiefalten
Hornberg
Schramberg
Rottweil
Emmendingen
Hochburg
Sigmaringen
Freiburg
Donau-
eschingen
Messkirch
Biberach
Neustadt
Wartenberg
Tuttlingen
Sulzburg
Hewen
Heiligenberg · Weingarten
Stühlingen
Hohen
Stoffeln · Krähen
Ravensburg
Sausenburg
Schaffh.
Tiengen
BÂLE
Säckingen
Konstanz
Lindau

0    20 km

Hall

Sulzburg

Müllheim
Badenweiler
Auggen
Schliengen
Sausenburg
Liel
Kandern

Elmel-
lingen
Hauingen
Röttein · Steinen
Schopfheim
Binzen
Wiese
Maulburg
Markt
Ötlingen
Lörrach
Stetten
Schwörstadt
Weil
Inzlingen
Beuggen
Riehen
Säckingen
Warmbach
BÂLE
Grenzach
Rheinfelden
Stein
Laufenburg
Binningen
Muttenz
Prattein
Olsberg
Bott-
ningen
Münchenstein
Frick
Elfingen
Dornach
Liestal
Brugg
Angenstein
Kastelen
Baden
Pfeffingen
Habsburg
Wildenstein
Würenlos
Auenstein
Wasserfalle
Lostorf
Waldenburg
Schafisheim
Ob. Hauenstein
Langenbruck
Balsthal
Muri
Wiedlisbach
Wangen-a-A
0    10 km
Subingen

**Alemannic or Germanic Region Northwest and Southwest of Basel**

Source: Lötscher's 1976 edition of Felix Platter's *Tagebuch*.

# INDEX